Baedeker, Karl

Handbook for Travellers

Inktank publishing

Baedeker, Karl

Handbook for Travellers

Inktank publishing, 2018

www.inktank-publishing.com

ISBN/EAN: 9783747726891

BELGIUM AND HOLLAND.

HANDBOOK FOR TRAVELLERS

BY

K. BÆDEKER.

With three Maps and thirteen Plans.

COBLENZ,
KARL BÆDEKER.
1869.

LONDON,
WILLIAMS & NORGATE.
14 Henrietta Street, Covent-Garden.

PARIS,
HAAR & STEINERT.
9 Rue Jacob.

"Go, little book, God send thee good passage,
And specially let this be thy prayere
Unto them all that thee will read or hear,
Where thou art wrong, after their help to call,
Thee to correct in any part or all."

Chaucer.

PREFACE.

The chief object of the Handbook for Belgium and Holland is to render the traveller as independent as possible of the embarrassing and expensive services of commissionaires, guides, and other members of the same fraternity, to enable him to derive the greatest possible amount of pleasure and instruction from a tour in these interesting countries, and to place him in a position to employ his time, his energies and his finances to the best advantage.

The Handbook has been compiled entirely from the Editor's personal experience, and he has used every endeavour to furnish information acceptable to enlightened travellers of every class. The present edition, which corresponds to the 11th in the German language and the 5th in the French, has been carefully revised and altered in accordance with the most recent time-tables, catalogues, government statistics etc.; and the Editor has frequently availed himself of much valuable information afforded by travellers, which he here gratefully acknowledges. It need, however, hardly be remarked that bonâ fide statements by travellers founded on their personal observation, are alone acceptable. The Editor especially craves the indulgence of his readers if the enumeration of pictures, curiosities in museums etc. should in any instance be found inaccurate. Whilst it is confidently hoped that this is not at present the case, it must be observed that in some of the public galleries in Belgium the arrangement of the pictures etc. is very frequently changed, with the express object of rendering all but the authorised catalogues useless. As a general rule, the data afforded by the Handbook will enable the traveller to eschew these expensive and often bewildering compilations.

The Maps and Plans, on which the utmost care has been bestowed, will prove of material service to the traveller when steering his course through the intricacies of the curious mediaeval cities of Belgium, or when entangled in the network of railways, rivers and canals by which the whole of the Netherlands is overspread.

The hotels indicated by asterisks are those which the Editor or some of his numerous friends and correspondents have found comfortable and worthy of commendation. The self-laudations of inn-keepers and others of the same class are of course entirely disregarded. The average charges, fees etc., although liable to constant fluctuation, are given in order that the traveller may be enabled to form some idea of his probable expenditure.

CONTENTS.

Belgium.

Holland.

Maps.

Plans of Towns.

Abbreviations used in the Handbook.

R. = Room.
L. = Light.
B. = Breakfast.
D. = Dinner.
A. = Attendance.
M. = English mile.
N. = North.
S. = South.
E. = East.
W. = West.
r. = right.
l. = left.
hr. = hour.
min. = minute.

NB. Everything particularly worthy of note is indicated by an asterisk.

BELGIUM.

I. Plan of Tour.

Those who desire to derive intellectual profit as well as pleasure from their tour should not only frame some definite plan before starting, but should endeavour to turn every hour of their time to the best possible account. To assist such travellers in their object is the aim of the following work, which, it need hardly be observed, will render little service to that happily decreasing class who though prodigal of money and time are too often indifferent to those objects which afford instruction and elevate the taste.

Churches are generally open to the public from 6 to 12 o'clock in the morning. When the architecture or the pulpit is the chief object of interest the traveller may dispense with the services of the sacristan. None of the most celebrated pictures, however, can be seen without the aid of that functionary, as they are either covered with curtains, or preserved in the closed chapels. The churches which contain objects worthy of careful and minute inspection should be visited between 12 and 3 or 4 p. m., when there is no divine service. Application for admission must then be made to the sacristan.

Picture Galleries and other public Collections are generally accessible daily from 10 or 11 till 3 or 4 o'clock. The traveller will find the most celebrated paintings and objects of interest enumerated in the Handbook, and may therefore dispense with catalogues.

Gratuities, see p. XVI.

Belgium is now so completely intersected by a network of railways, that the traveller will rarely have occasion to travel by any other conveyance. A steamboat-trip on the Meuse, the drive to Waterloo, and a few excursions on horseback or on foot in the neighbourhood of Liège, Namur, Dinant, Spa etc. should by no means be forgotten, as Belgium boasts of many beautiful districts, and is rich in historical reminiscences. On the whole, however, painting and architecture are the great attractions; and as a large proportion of the traveller's time will probably be spent in the cities and larger towns, he is recommended to select the spring or autumn in preference to the summer for his tour. Those who are already acquainted with the towns and their treasures of art, or whose object is retirement and repose, will find many delightful spots for spending the summer on the banks of the Meuse, or in the environs of Spa.

The following tour, commencing at Ostende and terminating at Antwerp, will serve to convey an idea of the time requisite for a glimpse at the chief attractions of Belgium. Travellers entering Belgium from France, Holland or Germany will find no difficulty in framing 'skeleton tours' with the aid of the map.

Ostende and Bruges	1½	day
Ghent	1	„
Courtrai, Tournai, Mons	2	„
Charleroi, Namur	1	„
Valley of Meuse, Dinant	1½	„
Liège and Seraing	1	„
Mastricht and Petersberg	1	„
Louvain and Brussels	2	„
Waterloo	1	„
Malines	1	„
Antwerp	2	„
	15	days.

The linguist, the ethnologist, and indeed every observant traveller will not fail to be interested in the marked differences between the various races of which the Belgian nation is composed. The *Walloons* (of Namur, Liège, Verviers etc.) are believed to be partially of Celtic extraction; they are remarkable for their enterprising and industrious, and at the same time passionate and excitable character, and their language is a very corrupt patois of French, with traces of Teutonic and Celtic influences. The *Flemings*, who constitute two-thirds of the population, are a somewhat phlegmatic race of Teutonic origin; they are pre-eminently successful in agriculture and those pursuits in which energetic action is less requisite than patient perseverance, and their language is of the Teutonic stock and closely akin to the Dutch. A third element may perhaps appropriately be termed the *French.* Political refugees and obnoxious journalists frequently transfer the sphere of their labours from Paris to Brussels, whilst a considerable proportion of the Belgian population in the principal towns now affect French manners and customs, are frequently educated in France, and often entirely ignore their Flemish origin and language. A valuable and interesting work, to which reference is frequently made in the Handbook, is the '*Descriptio totius Belgii*' by the learned Florentine *Guicciardini* (d. 1589), who in his capacity of ambassador resided for several years in the Netherlands. '*Leodicum* (Liège)', he says, '*utitur lingua Gallica, Aquisgranum* (Aix-la-Chapelle) *Germanica: viri Leodicenses alacres, festivi, tractabiles; Aquisgranenses melancholici, severi, difficiles. In summa, tantum alteri et natura et moribus, totaque adeo vitae ratione ab alteris differunt, quantum Galli discrepant a Germanis*'.

II. Money and Travelling Expenses.

Francs and centimes are the Belgian, as well as the French currency: 1 franc, 100 centimes, 8 silbergroschen, 28 S. German kreuzer, 40 Austrian kreuzer, 47 Dutch cents, 20 Amer. cents and $9^{3}/_{4}$ pence are all nearly equivalent (comp. money-table at the beginning of the book). The coins in common circulation are French Napoleons (20 fr.) in gold; 5, $2^{1}/_{2}$, 1, $^{1}/_{2}$ and $^{1}/_{5}$ fr. pieces in silver; 10, 5, 2, 1 c. in copper; 20, 10, 5 c. in nickel. English and French banknotes and English gold are received in all the principal towns, hotels, railway-stations etc. at their full value (1 *l.* = 25 fr.). Belgian notes from 20 to 1000 fr. realise their full value in all parts of Belgium, but not in France or elsewhere.

Hotels of the highest class are somewhat expensive at Brussels and some of the Belgian watering-places, but in most other parts of the country they will be found considerably cheaper than in England. The average charges may be stated as follows: bed 2—3 fr., breakfast (plain) 1—$1^{1}/_{2}$ fr., dinner 3—4 fr., $^{1}/_{2}$ bottle Bordeaux $1^{1}/_{2}$ fr., attendance 1 fr. — The charges at hotels of the second class are about one-third lower, and a further saving of time and money may be effected if the traveller avoid the public tables d'hôte and dine at a restaurant or café. — The fees payable at public galleries, churches etc. amount to 3—4 fr. per day, travelling expenses to 8—10 fr., and hotel expenses to 10—15 fr., so that the traveller should be prepared for a daily expenditure of 25—30 fr. unless he is disposed to practise that frugality which not unfrequently interferes with enjoyment. On the other hand the 'voyageur en garçon', the artist, the student, the pedestrian etc. may easily reduce their expenditure to half that sum without any great diminution of comfort.

III. Passports.

These documents are now dispensed with in Belgium, but they are occasionally useful in proving the traveller's identity, procuring admission to private collections etc., especially in the case of a prolonged sojourn.

IV. Language.

Whilst nearly two-thirds of the population speak Flemish as their mother-tongue, and one-third Walloon, the French language is universally employed by the educated and wealthier classes in their intercourse with strangers and one another. Guicciardini speaks of the dialect of the Walloons as '*sermo communiter Gallicus; sed quia Galliam inter atque Germaniam positi, corruptus valde et perabsurdus*'. The linguist who desires to form some acquaintance with the Walloon language is referred to two excellent works published at Liège in 1845: *Poésies en patois de Liège, précédées d'une dissertation grammaticale sur ce patois et suivies d'un glossaire par Simonon*', and the '*Dictionnaire étymologique de la langue Wallonne par Ch. Grandgagnage*', the latter unfortunately uncompleted. The following popular rhymes from the '*Almanach par maître Matthieu Laensbergh*' will serve as a specimen of the language:

January:

Il gna pu d'broûli ki d'poussîr.	Il a plus de brouillard que de poussière.

February:

Li chôd' sop' so on vi stoumak,	La chaude soupe sur un vieil estomac,
So n'freut pai, on bon spet cazak,	Dans un pays froid une bonne épaisse casaque
Ni fri nin pu d'bin ki l'solo,	Ne ferait pas plus de bien que le soleil
Si volêf lûr on po sor no.	S'il voulait luire un peu sur nous.

April:

…st l'useg dis't-on d' s'attrapé	C'est l'usage, dit-on, de s'attraper
…'l'ak et l'auf', li prumî d'avri;	L'un et l'autre le premier d'avril;
…Sc'n'esteu ko qu'po s'diverti,	Si ce n'était que pour se divertir,
…ils'on koirah' in' gol' â s'dupé!	Qu'on cherchât un peu à se duper!
…ais c'n'est pu po rir' qu'on s'surprin,	Mais on n'est plus pour rire qu'on se surprend,
Dèmon si on se reie, ci n'est k'de gros des din.	Du moins si l'on en rit ce n'est que du gros des dents.
On s'tromp', on s'dispoie al tournaie:	On se trompe, on se dépouille tour à tour:
C'est l'prumî d'avri tot l'annaie!	C'est le prem. d'avril toute l'année.

The **Flemish** language differs but slightly from the Dutch, its roots, like those of the latter, being generally identical with those of the German, Swedish and Danish languages. Flemish, however, although a rich and expressive language, is far less highly cultivated than its four sister tongues, being spoken by the uneducated classes only, and possessing but little original literature. Notwithstanding the efforts, therefore, which have frequently been made to elevate it to the rank of a national language, it is probable that it will never be regarded otherwise than as a provincial patois, especially as upwards of one-third of the population of Belgium is entirely ignorant of it, whilst in all official and scientific matters, as well as in the best society, it is totally ignored. French has long been, and will doubtless continue to be the language employed by the government in all its departments, by the universities, newspapers etc., and to the Belgian who is unacquainted with that language no career is open except that of a small farmer or an artizan.

The following peculiarities of pronunciation are common to Flemish and Dutch: *y* (in Dutch *ij*) is pronounced like the English i (but in West Flanders like e), *u* like the French u, *eu* like the French eu, *eeu* like the English a (in *fate*), *oe* like oo, *ae* like ah, *ou* as in English, *ui* like oi, *oei* like we, *sch* like s and the guttural ch in the Scotch *loch*, *sch* at the end of a word like s. — As already remarked, Verviers, Liège and Namur are the chief towns of the Walloons, while Flemish is spoken by all the uneducated Belgians to the N. of a line drawn nearly in a straight direction from Liège to Tournai. It may here be stated approximately that of every 1000 inhabitants of Belgium 569 are Flemish, 421 Walloon, 8 German and 2 English. After what has been said, it need hardly be added that a slight knowledge of French alone will enable the traveller to make himself understood by every one with whom he is likely to come in contact, and that an acquaintance with the Flemish and Walloon dialects will probably prove of little service except to the philologist. Those who are unfortunately ignorant of French will doubtless derive consolation from the fact that English is spoken at all the best hotels in the most frequented places.

V. Fees.

A single visitor usually pays 1/2 fr. to the sacristan of a church or the custodian of a public gallery, a party 1 fr. or more. Where higher fees are exacted, the circumstance will be noted in its proper place in the Handbook.

The traveller who is provided with this volume will be enabled to dispense with the congenial and costly services of a '*commissionnaire*'. Members of this fraternity charge 2—3 fr. for half-a-day, 4—5 fr. for a whole day, and 1/2 fr. for a single commission or errand. The traveller whose time is limited will (in all the larger towns) escape most effectually from the importunities of guides, and arrive most rapidly at his destination by hiring a '*vigilante*', or cab (generally 1 fr. per drive).

VI. Railways.

The most trustworthy time-tables are contained in the '*Guide officiel des voyageurs sur tous les chemins de fer de Belgique*', published monthly, and sold at all the principal railway-stations for 30 c.

The fares on most of the lines are extremely moderate, and probably the lowest in the railway world. Thus the express fares from Brussels to Verviers (77 1/2 M.) are 6, 4 and 3 fr.; ordinary fares 5 fr., 3 fr. 35 c. and 2 fr. 50 c. — i. e. less than one-third of the English, and less than one half of the German rates. It should, however, be observed that these low rates are available exclusively for the passenger-traffic within the limits of Belgium. Through-tickets are charged for at a much higher rate, and the traveller about to cross the frontier who does not object to a trifling increase of trouble may often effect a considerable saving by booking himself and his luggage to the last Belgian station only (e. g. Verviers, Quiévrain, Tournai, Mouscron etc.), and there purchasing a fresh ticket, for which sufficient time is generally allowed, provided he be not overburdened with 'impedimenta'.

Luggage must be booked and paid for separately, and the cost of its transport not unfrequently amounts to as much as a second or third class fare. The traveller is, therefore, strongly recommended to restrict his 'requirements' to the limits of a travelling-bag or moderate valise, which he can wield without assistance and carry with him in the railway-carriage without the formality or expense of booking it for the luggage-van.

VII. History of Art.

Painting. Three distinct periods are to be observed in the development of art in the Netherlands, the schools of which are usually regarded as offshoots of the Old German, or Teutonic school. The term 'Flemish', although often understood to embrace these three periods, is more strictly applied to the first only, during which art in Holland was still in its infancy. The 'Brabant school' is that of the second and third periods, during which the Dutch gradually elaborated the style for which they are so justly celebrated.

I. Flemish School. This period extends from about 1420 to the close of the century. Whilst art was hastening towards its culminating point in Italy, the Flemings were plodding soberly on in their unsophisticated style, producing their tame, quaint, Gothic forms, and aspiring to little more than great accuracy and delicacy of execution. At the same time it must be admitted that their works possess a peculiarly vigorous and original character, the result of the wholly independent and unassisted exertions of the masters. The greatest painters of this period were the

Van Eycks (p. 32), whose works, although not entirely free from the hardness of outline and unscientific treatment of atmosphere which characterise the pictures of their age, are far in advance of those of their contemporaries and even of their followers. Their paintings will be best appreciated if the details, which are often most elaborate and almost perfect studies from nature, be examined separately. The uniform and consistent care with which they are executed forms one of their chief merits. — The principal pupils and followers of the Van Eycks were: *Gerard van der Meire* (d. 1512), whose master-piece is in the church of St. Bavon at Ghent; *Peter Christophsen* (1499); *Hugo van der Goes* (1470); *Rogier van der Weyden*, or *Roger of Bruges* (b. at Tournai in 1400, d. 1464), the most talented pupil of the Van Eycks; *Hans Memling* (1495), the most laborious and successful master of this school, whose style is remarkable for its minuteness and accuracy, combined with delicacy and freedom of touch, and refined sentiment. *Antoine Claeyssens*, the last adherent of the Van Eyck School, flourished as late as the middle of the 16th century. Several of his works are preserved in the church of St. Sauveur at Bruges.

II. Earlier Brabant School. This period embraces the greater part of the 16th century, during which 'genre-painting' was gradually approaching its consummation in Holland. This style of painting, for which the Dutch are especially famous, is the representation of scenes 'du genre bas', i. e. of a low kind as compared with the religious, heroic and poetic compositions which had hitherto been almost exclusively in vogue. 'Genre', therefore, in its technical sense, is most appropriately rendered by 'every-day life'. The Flemish masters, and more especially those of the province of Brabant, now gradually became aware of the higher attainments of their brethren of the South, and began to employ all their energies in imitating the more showy and attractive style of the Italian masters. The great objects now sought to be attained were richness of colouring, effectiveness of arrangement, and vigour of action. The most celebrated representative of this school was

Quentin Massys (1455—1531), whose principal work is in the Antwerp Museum (p. 123). The Italian influence is observable in his works, which are far more showy and effective than those of his predecessors, whilst his execution was hardly less elaborate and faithful to nature. His subjects were chiefly religious; but he occasionally painted genre. Two misers counting their money is a scene which he has several times represented. The following masters also endeavoured, although with indifferent success, to graft the Italian upon their native style: *Bernard van Orley* (1471—1541), by whom there are several good pictures in the gallery at Brussels, in St. Jacques at Antwerp, and St. Sauveur at Bruges. He was a pupil of Raphael, and is even said to have assisted that great master in the execution of some of his principal works. *Jean Mabuse*, or *de Maubeuge* (1470—1532), several small pictures by whom are preserved in the Antwerp Museum.

Jean Schoreel (1495—1562), a pupil of the latter, is celebrated for the beauty and delicacy of his heads. *Antoine Moor*, a pupil of Schoreel, was a skilful portrait-painter. *Michael Coxcie* (1497—1592), a pupil of Van Orley, afterwards became a close imitator of Raphael. His most celebrated work is an admirable copy of the Van Eyck altar-piece (p. 37). *Martin Heemskerk* and *Lancelot Blondeel* also belong to this period. — The earliest Flemish landscape-painters, to whose efforts the Van Eycks had given the first impetus, were *Joachim Patenier* of Dinant (1490—1548) and *Henrymet de Bles*, surnamed *Civetta* (d. 1550).

The following masters adhered still more exclusively to the Italian style: *Frans Floris*, or *de Vriendt* (1520—1570), sometimes styled the 'Flemish Raphael', a title which his works hardly justify. His best work is the 'Descent of the Fallen Angels' in the Antwerp Museum. *Martin de Vos* (1531—1603), a pupil of Floris, afterwards studied in Venice, where he formed his style after that of Tintoretto, and surpassed his Flemish master in warmth of colouring and fidelity to nature. Eleven of his pictures are preserved in the Antwerp Museum. *Ambrose* and *Frans Franken* are remarkable for the richness and vigour of their colouring. *Pourbus* the Elder (d. 1580) and *Pourbus* the Younger (d. 1622) were both skilful and accurate portrait-painters. *Otto van Veen*, or *Vaenius* (1558—1629), many of whose works may be seen in the galleries of Brussels, Antwerp etc., was the first master of Rubens. Harmony of arrangement is one of the chief merits of his works.

III. Later Brabant School. The culminating point of art, both in Flanders and Holland, was attained during this period, the golden era of Teutonic art, extending from about 1600 to 1690. The Flemish and Dutch schools now became more widely divergent. This is chiefly attributable to the difference of religion which had now sprung up between the Netherlanders of the north and those of the south. Holland now professed the Reformed faith, whilst the whole of Flanders had continued to adhere to Rome. Painting in Holland had ceased to be the handmaid of Religion, and the loss of ecclesiastical patronage effected a complete revolution in the objects and aspirations of Dutch artists. Their newly awakened sense of independence appears to have developed to its highest perfection an entirely new and original sphere of art. Philosophy and history were abandoned for

b*

scenes of everyday life, landscapes and portraits. Religion was not entirely banished, but occasionally found expression through a homely, realistic medium, in which however scriptural significance and true piety are often by no means wanting. During this period the Dutch excelled in genre-painting, a sphere which their brethren of Brabant by no means neglected, although chiefly celebrated as painters of historical and devotional subjects. The following are the most celebrated of the Flemish genre-painters:

'Old Peter Breughel' (1510—1570), whose favourite theme was boorish festivities. He also occasionally represented religious subjects, such as the 'Slaughter of the Innocents', a Flemish village in the snow, with ponderous boors killing children. He was the father of *'Hell Breughel'*, thus named on account of his fantastic predilection for the representation of imps, goblins and infernal monsters. *'Velvet Breughel'*, a brother of the latter, derived his sobriquet from his partiality to that material. *David Teniers the Elder* (1582—1649), an imitator of Hell Breughel, has several times represented the 'Temptation of St. Antony' with considerable success. *David Teniers the Younger* (1610—1690), the son of the latter, unquestionably holds the highest rank among the genre-painters of Belgium (comp. p. 113). His favourite subjects are derived from rustic festivities, the farm-steading, the then prevalent mania for alchymy, and the guard-house. His works are remarkable for ease and delicacy of manipulation, combined with great fidelity to nature and harmony of arrangement. The character of his colouring varied at different periods of his long career, culminating in a luminous golden tone, and afterwards subsiding into a cold, grey hue. The charm of his humour and appreciation of nature is occasionally marred by a want of sentiment and a degree of monotony, especially in his larger works. Teniers was one of the most versatile and prolific of painters, and fine specimens of his workmanship are preserved in almost all the public, and many of the private galleries in Europe.

Of the historical and devotional school of this celebrated period, by far the most illustrious master was unquestionably

Rubens (p. 112), the 'Prince of Flemish Painters', in whom the Brabant School attained its highest consummation. He excelled in power and versatility of imagination, by means of which he was enabled to transfer to his canvas scenes replete with life and action. In gorgeousness of colouring he is unsurpassed, although his taste may sometimes be questioned. His great defects are an almost entire want of poetic or refined sentiment, and inaccuracy of drawing, and but for the transcendant merits of his works in other respects, they would frequently be pronounced coarse and unpleasing. A conspicuous element in all his works has been aptly termed 'ponderosity of flesh', an expression very characteristic of the full and sensual outlines of his figures. Many of the very numerous works attributed to Rubens were designed by him and executed by his pupils. Although chiefly celebrated as a painter of devotional and historical subjects, Rubens was a skilful painter of portraits, landscapes, and even genre-pieces.

Van Dyck (p. 113), Rubens' most celebrated pupil, displays talent of the very highest order in his historical and religious compositions. His taste is much more refined and elevated than that of Rubens, his treatment quite as admirable; but in power and imagination he is inferior to his great master, and his colouring is sometimes deficient in depth and warmth. He was an inimitable painter of portraits, rivalled, but hardly surpassed by Titian alone.

Although the transcendant genius of Rubens and the refined sentiment of Van Dyck were vouchsafed to none of their successors, yet many of the latter enjoy a high and well-merited reputation, and their labours tended greatly to consolidate and perpetuate the memory of the celebrated school to which they belong. *Jacques Jordaens* (1593—1678) of Antwerp is remarkable for his admirable drawing and vigorous distinctness of conception. *Gerard Seghers*, or *Zegers* (1589—1651) of Antwerp was an historical painter of considerable merit, and his brother *Daniel* (1590—1660) is well known for his admirable flower-pieces. *Caspar de Crayer* (1582—1669) has produced a number of excellent works, which although somewhat cold and formal, and destitute of bold originality and warmth of colouring, are dignified, impressive and well drawn. Even Rubens, with his gorgeous taste, is said to have pronounced De Crayer unrivalled in these last respects. *Nicholas Roose*, surnamed *Liemakere* (1575—1636), is also worthy of mention. Several admirable pictures by these two last masters are preserved at Ghent.

The following masters, who do not belong to the school of Rubens, must also be mentioned here. *Abraham Janssens* (1569—1650), a virulent rival of Rubens, resembled the latter solely in the sensuality of his taste. *Peter Neefs* (1570—1651), a skilful painter of architectural pieces, has frequently represented the interior of a Gothic church with great success. *Frans Snyders* (1579—1657) of Antwerp is perhaps unrivalled in the grandeur and fidelity of his celebrated hunting-scenes. *Paul Brill* (1554—1626), a landscape-painter of considerable repute, is noted for the character of calm repose which he has generally imparted to his works.

Erasmus Quellin, the last eminent painter of the School of Rubens, died in 1678. A degenerate age, characterised by the fashion of pigtails and hoops, and by the prevalence of the baroque and rococo styles, now set in, and Belgium became a servile imitator of the city of the 'Grand Monarque'. Throughout the 18th, and during the early part of the present century, the Flemings, like most of their European neighbours, were totally unable to rise above the meaningless mannerism of their age. David, the well-known Parisian artist (d. at Brussels in 1825), whose style combines cold formalism with sumptuous externals, was closely imitated by his pupil *Joseph Paelinck* of Ghent (1781—1839). *Andreas Lens* (1740—1822), however, succeeded to some extent in shaking off the fetters of bad taste, and is even termed by his epitaph '*le régénérateur de la peinture en Belgique*'; his 'Annunciation' in St. Michael's at Ghent (p. 40) is remarkable for delicacy of treatment. *Ignace van Bree* (1773—1839) also succeeded in rising above French influences.

Three great epochs may accordingly be observed in the history of Belgian art, inaugurated, with intervals of two centuries, by John van Eyck about 1430, Rubens about 1630, and the Revolution in 1830, respectively. The first indication of the revival of good taste and independent exertion during the present century was afforded by several works by *Navez* (d. 1863), and more especially by the 'Siege of Leyden' by *Wappers*, painted in 1830. The latter master, who was afterwards director of the Antwerp Academy, contributed greatly to improve the taste of his countrymen and direct their attention to the illustrious masters of the 17th century, instead of to their immediate predecessors. The annual exhibitions, which take place at Brussels, Antwerp and Ghent alternately, generally contain several admirable modern works, and bear testimony to the re-awakened national enthusiasm for art. The historical works of *Wappers*, *De Keyzer*, *De Bièfve*, *Maes*, *Gallait* and *Braeckeleer*, the animal-pieces of *Verboeckhoven*, the forest scenes of *Hellemans*, *Fourmois* etc., and the genre-paintings of *Madou* are unsurpassed in any country of modern Europe, and the activity of the present period almost resembles that of the glorious days of Rubens and Van Dyck. *Dyckmanns*, *Leys*, *De Block* and *Pauwels* also deserve mention as among the most talented artists of the present day.

Architecture. As the political prosperity of Belgium did not begin before the middle of the 14th cent., Byzantine and Romanesque edifices are far rarer here than in France and Germany. The few fragments in these styles which are still extant are cumbrous in form and poor in detail; the ruins of the Abbey of St. Bavon as Ghent, and the older portions of St. Jacques at Liège and the Cathedral at Tournai alone deserve mention.

The early Gothic structures of the 13th cent. will not bear comparison with those of France and Germany. The walls are generally too massive; the flying buttresses, which at once impart strength and elegance to the edifice, are either entirely wanting, or replaced by unwieldy piers; the windows are destitute of mullions and mouldings, and the columns of articulation, whilst the towers often appear more appropriate to fortresses than to churches. These characteristics are presented by most of the churches at Ghent, Bruges, Valenciennes, Lille, Malines and Louvain.

A far higher degree of development is exhibited by the churches of the 15th and 16th centuries, but the style soon again degenerates, displaying a too florid and decorative character. The most admirable structure of this epoch is the Cathedral at Antwerp, which in the interior especially produces a most imposing and harmonious effect, although it is obvious that the architect has aimed at picturesqueness of form rather than the beauty peculiar to the purest Gothic style. This aim is most manifest in the exquisite and highly decorated open-work of the magnificent tower. Other fine examples of the same style are St. Gudule at Brussels, St. Pierre at Louvain, St. Martin at Hal, St. Wautrude at Mons, St. Sauveur at Bruges etc.

The Flamboyant edifices of the 16th century, such as the Palais de Justice at Liège, the Hôtel de Ville at Ghent, the staircase of the Chapelle du Saint Sang at Bruges etc., appear to exhibit a fantastic desire to conceal the true function of stone as a building material beneath a superabundance of foliage and other ornamentation. The transition from the moderately pointed arch to the unnaturally elongated form of a 'flame' has given rise to the name by which this style is generally known.

The enthusiasm for art, the commercial intercourse with Italy, and the great wealth of the Netherlands in the 15th century gave rise at an early period to the erection of edifices in the Renaissance, or 'cinquecento' style, based on classical models, such as the sumptuous church of the Jesuits at Antwerp.

The *Secular Edifices* of Belgium, such as town-halls, markets, belfries, city-gates etc., exhibit far more strikingly than the ecclesiastical the national spirit of independence, and the power and affluence of the cities. They present a remarkably bold and tasteful embodiment of the Gothic style of the 15th century, and are unrivalled of their kind. The most beautiful example of this secular Gothic architecture is the Hôtel de Ville at Louvain, whilst the town-halls of Brussels and Ypern are more imposing. Those of Ghent, Bruges, Oudenaerde, Arras and Mons are also peculiar and interesting structures of the same character.

The finest guild-halls are those at Brussels, Antwerp and Ghent, the most interesting old gateways are to be seen at Brussels, Bruges and Namur, and belfries, or clock-towers, are met with in almost every town in Belgium. The Netherlanders of the 15th and 16th centuries also exhibited considerable practical sense combined with taste in their domestic architecture, of which most of the towns of Belgium, especially Bruges and Antwerp, still contain examples.

VIII. History and Statistics.

The Belgium of the present day, which was originally peopled with a race of Celtic origin, and was subsequently overrun by Teutonic invaders, was conquered by *Caesar*, and remained subject to the Roman supremacy until the beginning of the 5th century, when the Salic Franks established themselves in the district between the Schelde, the Meuse and the Lower Rhine.

In the 9th century the country formed a portion of the Empire of Charlemagne, by whose successors it was granted as a feudal holding to certain of their vassals. The latter, however, soon contrived to release themselves from their dependent condition, and continued to pay a nominal homage to the Empires of France and Germany.

Thus the independent states of *Flanders*, *Artois*, *Hainault*,

Namur, the duchies of *Brabant* and *Limburg*, the principality of *Liège*, the country of *Antwerp* and the lordship of *Malines* took their rise. These were eventually united, by means of marriage and other contracts, inheritance etc., under the supremacy of the Dukes of Burgundy, who were indebted for their great power to the wealth and commercial enterprise of their Flemish subjects.

In 1477 the Netherlands came into the possession of the House of Hapsburg by the marriage of Mary of Burgundy, the daughter of Charles the Bold. the last Duke of Burgundy, with *Maximilian*, afterwards Emperor of Germany. *Charles V.*, grandson of Maximilian, who was born at Ghent in 1500, and subsequently became Emperor of Germany and King of Spain, succeeded to the whole of these provinces. Thenceforward the Netherlands were subject to the Spanish Supremacy, which during the reign of *Philip II.* became so intolerable that the whole country took up arms towards the close of the 16th century with a view to shake off the Spanish yoke. Success was achieved by the northern provinces only, those which now constitute the Kingdom of Holland, whilst the southern districts, the present Kingdom of Belgium, after protracted and fierce struggles still remained subject to the Spaniards. Belgium, however, succeeded under the regime of the Spanish governor *Alexander Farnese*, duke of Parma, in regaining the civic liberties in behalf of which the war had originally broken out.

In 1598 the 'Spanish Netherlands' were ceded by Philip II. as a fief to his daughter *Clara Isabella Eugenia* on the occasion of her marriage with *Albert*, Archduke of Austria, the Spanish governor. After the death of the archduke and his wife the Netherlands reverted to Spain, by which they were governed till 1714, when they were adjudged to the House of Austria by the Peace of Rastadt.

The 'Austrian Netherlands' were wisely and beneficently governed by the archdukes of Austria, who held the office of Stadtholder, and for a brief period the glorious days of the Burgundian regime appeared to have returned. The governors of that period, especially under the Empress Maria Theresa, are still gratefully remembered by the Belgians. The opposition which the reforms of the Emp. *Joseph II.* encountered at length gave rise to the 'Brabant Revolution' in 1789, but the independence thus achieved lasted for a single year only. Under Emp. *Leopold II.* Austria again obtained possession of the country.

This revolution, however, paved the way for the interference of the French, whose aid had been invoked by the ecclesiastical and the liberal parties. In 1794 the entire country was occupied by French Republicans, and Belgium was now divided into nine departments. In 1814 the French supremacy was finally shaken off.

The Treaty of London, of June 28th, 1814, and the provisions of the Congress of Vienna, of June 7th, 1815, united Belgium and Holland under the name of the Kingdom of the Netherlands, and elevated *William of Orange*, son of the former stadtholder of the Seven Provinces, to the newly constituted throne. Belgium was again severed from her *constrained* union with Holland by the Revolution of 1830. On Nov. 10th the provisional government summoned a national congress, by which the Duc de Nemours, son of Louis Philippe, was invited to become the sovereign of Belgium. The French monarch having declined the dignity in behalf of his son, *Leopold of Saxe-Cobourg* was next selected by the congress, and that prince accordingly ascended the throne on July 21st, 1831.

The treaty of the intervening powers, signed at London on Nov. 15th, 1831, by the representatives of the five great powers and of Belgium, although not finally recognised by the exasperated King of Holland till 1839, constituted the Kingdom of Belgium one of the independent European states, and determined the boundaries and the international relations between the two disunited kingdoms.

King Leopold II., born in 1835, the son of Leopold I. (b. 1790, d. 1865) and his second queen Louise, daughter of Louis Philippe, ascended the throne on Dec. 10th, 1865. *His Queen* is Marie Henriette, daughter of the late Archduke Joseph. *Crown Prince* Leopold, Duke of Brabant, born in 1858 (d. 1869), and two daughters. Charlotte, the widow of Maximilian, Emp. of Mexico (d. 1867) and brother of the Emp. of Austria, is a sister of Leopold II.

Extent. The extreme length of the kingdom of Belgium, from N. W. to S. E., is 179½ Engl. M., breadth from N. to S. 110½ Engl. M., area 11,363 sq. M.

Population (in 1864) 4,894,071 (in 1831, 3,785,864 only), of whom about 2½ millions are Flemings, and about 2 millions Walloons. About 10,000 only of the population do not profess the Rom. Catholic faith, and among these 1400 only are Jews. The principal Protestant communities are at Brussels, Antwerp, Ghent, Liège and Verviers. In East Flanders, the most densely populated district, there are 695 inhab. to each sq. M., in the Province of Luxembourg, the most thinly populated, 119 only. With the exception of some of the manufacturing districts of England, E. Flanders, and next to it the Provinces of Brabant and Hainault, are among the most densely peopled districts in the world. In W. Flanders one person in 8 is a pauper, E. Flanders one in 16, Hainault one in 20, Limburg one in 24, Liège one in 28, Brabant one in 36. Antwerp one in 41, Namur one in 91, and in the wooded Province of Luxembourg one in 660 only. On the other hand there are 3 persons only in the entire Province of Luxembourg who are qualified to become senators, i. e. who pay taxes to the amount of 2116 fr. and upwards and are above 40 years of age, whilst in Brabant the number of such persons amounts to 119.

Clergy. The number of the Roman. Catholic secular clergy is 5150, that of the regular 2600. There are also upwards of 13,000 nuns and sisters of charity, who as well as the monks, are chiefly engaged in tuition and attendance on the sick and indigent. The annual donations and subscriptions to the funds of the Church amount to 803,132 fr. annually. The Archbishop of Malines is the primate of Belgium, and there are five episcopal dioceses, viz. those of Liège, Namur, Tournai, Ghent and Bruges.

Army. The Belgian land-armament, in time of war, consists of 96,977 men, of whom 3373 are officers; during peace, of about 40,000 men (8754 cavalry). The army is composed of the following regiments: 1 carabineers, 2 riflemen (infantry), 12 infantry of the line, 1 grenadiers (consisting of 5 battalions, of 5 companies each), 2 cuirassiers, 2 lancers, 2 riflemen (cavalry), the regiment of Guides (whose celebrated band is one of the best in Europe), 4 artillery, and 1 sappers and miners. The army is divided into four 'corps d'armée', the staffs of which are under the command of lieutenant-generals at Ghent, Brussels, Liège and Mons. Of 1000 recruits about 340 can neither read nor write, whilst many more are imperfectly educated. Those of Luxembourg and E. Flanders are the most enlightened. The men are generally of short stature, but vigorous and active. The principal military depôt is at Antwerp.

The national colours, which were adopted in 1831, are red, yellow and black, placed in three perpendicular stripes. These were the colours of the ancient Duchy of Brabant, and under them the successful revolution of 1789 was organised by *Van der Noot* and *Vonk* (see above). The armorial bearings of Belgium consist of the Lion of Brabant, with the motto *'L'union fait la force'*. The only national order is that of 'Leopold', founded in 1832, and comprising five different grades.

Revenue. The national income averages 157 million francs (6,280,000 *l.*, i. e. less than one-eleventh of that of Great Britain and Ireland, the population of which is about six times that of Belgium). The national debt amounts to 632 million francs, the civil list of the king 2,751,322, and that of the crown-prince $^1/_2$ million francs.

Local Characteristics. Those indicated by the following monkish lines are said to exist to some extent even at the present day:

> *"Nobilibus Bruxella viris, Antwerpia nummis,*
> *Gandavum laqueis, formosis Bruga puellis,*
> *Lovanium doctis, gaudet Mechlinia stultis."*

(Brussels rejoices in noble men, Antwerp in money, Ghent in halters, Bruges in pretty girls, Louvain in learned men, and Malines in fools.) Halters are mentioned in connection with Ghent in allusion to the frequent humiliations to which its turbulent citizens were subjected by their sovereigns. The unenviable reputation of the citizens of Malines was originated by the story that they once mistook the moon shining through their tower for a conflagration, and endeavoured to extinguish it by means of the fire-engines.

Maps. The best maps of Belgium are executed at the *Etablissement Géographique de Ph. Vandermaelen* at Brussels (p. 83). The admirable *Carte de la Belgique* (price 500 fr.), consisting of 250 sheets, is in the scale of 1:20,000; each sheet is also sold separately at $2^1/_2$ fr. Another map of Belgium in 25 sheets, scale 1:80,000, costs 150 fr., or 7 fr. per sheet. The *Carte Géologique de la Belgique par André Dumont*, and another termed *'Sous Sol'*, each comprising 9 large sheets, scale 1:160,000, price 80 fr., are admirably executed, and strongly recommended to the notice of the scientific.

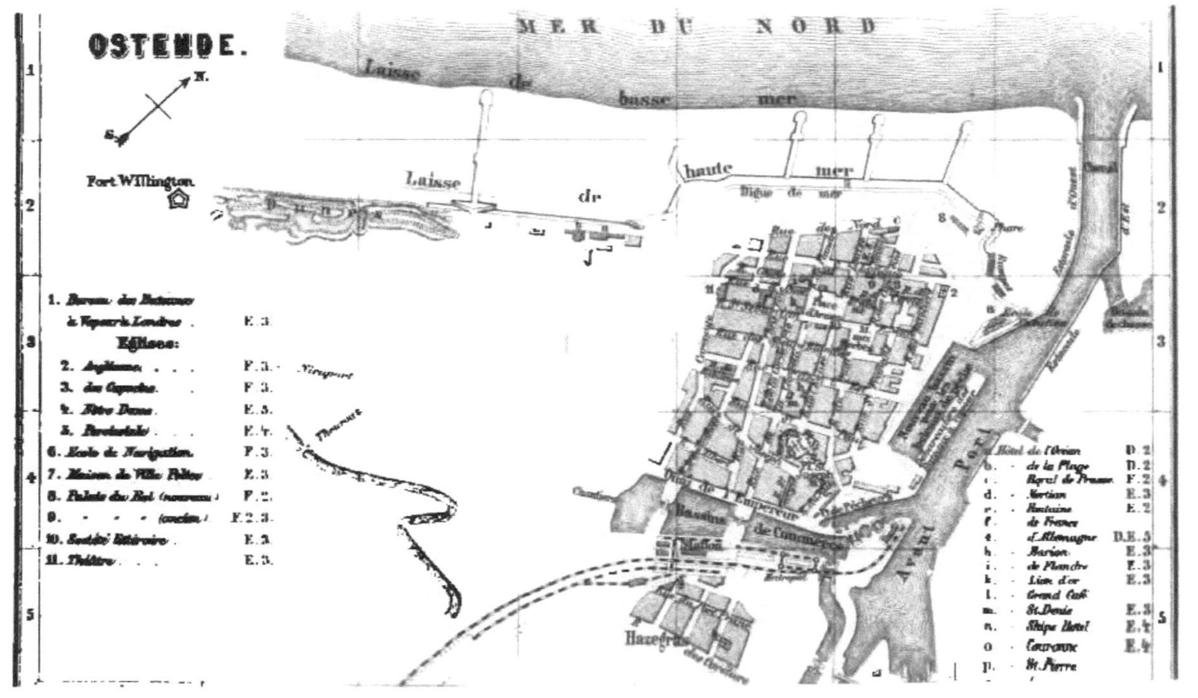
OSTENDE.
MER DU NORD
Laisse de basse mer
Laisse de haute mer
Fort Willington
Port
Avant Port
Bassins de Commerce
Hazegras

1. From London to Ostend.

There are two direct routes from London to Ostend: 1. Viâ Dover twice daily in $8^1/_2$—10 hrs.; 2. By Gen. Steam Nav. Co.'s steamers, twice weekly, in 10—14 hrs. — The former route is recommended to those whose time is limited; the latter is pleasant in favourable weather, and considerably less expensive. — Comp. R. 8.

Hotels at Ostend. *On the Beach:* Hôtel de l'Océan, connected with the Cercle des Bains (see below); Hôtel de La Plage, both large establishments of the first class, situated S. W. of the town. Rooms may also be procured at the 'Pavillons' *du Phare*, *Royal*, *des Dunes*, *du Rhin* etc. (see below).

In the Town: *Hôtel Royal de Prusse, comfortably fitted up, view of the sea from the upper stories, D. 4 fr.; *Hôtel Mertian, R. from $2^1/_2$, L. and A. $1^3/_4$, D. 3 fr.; *Hôtel Fontaine, near the Digue, spacious dining-room containing several old Dutch pictures of some merit. *Hôtel de France, Rue St. Nicolas, and *Hôtel d'Allemagne (near the railway stat., at a considerable distance from the sea, to which omnibuses run), both less expensive than the above. — Hôtel Marion, Rue de l'Eglise, D. $2^1/_2$ fr.; Hôtel de Flandre; *Lion d'Or, an old fashioned Belgian inn, R. $2^1/_2$, D. $2^1/_2$, B. 1, pension 7 fr.; Hôtel du Grand Café, good cuisine; the two latter on the Parade. *Hôtel St. Denis, Rue de la Chapelle, moderate, pension $5^1/_2$ fr. — Ship Hotel, on the quay; Couronne, on the harbour, opposite the station; St. Pierre, Rue du Lait Battu; Hôtel de l'Agneau; these four are tolerably comfortable and inexpensive. — Apartments may also be obtained at the restaurants in the town and on the Digue. High rents are demanded for the latter during the season.

Restaurants *in the Town:* *Frères Provençaux, Rue de Flandre, and *Rocher de Cancale, Rue Louise, D. in both at 5 p. m., 4 fr.; Cour Impériale; Grand Restaurant de Paris, good cuisine, D. 3 fr., good *vin ordinaire* 3 fr. per bottle; Cadran Bleu. — *Médoc*, the cheapest table wine, costs $1^1/_2$—2 fr. per bottle.

The Cursaal on the Digue, a fanciful structure in the Moorish style, open to subscribers only (per week 18, month 36 fr.; 2 pers. 50, 3 pers. 60 fr. per month), is the principal resort of the fashionable world during the bathing season. Balls and concerts alternately every evening at 8. 30. The establishment comprises a good café-restaurant, with Belgian, French and other newspapers. — The Cercle des Bains, another favourite rendezvous, is elegantly fitted up, and contains a few sleeping apartments at high charges. 'Soirées Dansantes' daily. — Farther along the beach, the Pavillon des Dunes (or *Hôtel Baerblock*), with a good restaurant. Still more distant, the *Pavillon du Rhin, near the 'Paradis' (p. 4), with extensive oyster and lobster 'park'; D. at 2 and 5 p. m. 3 fr., R. 5—6 fr. per day, A. 1 fr. per day extra, unless expressly included in the charge for rooms. — At the opposite (N.) end of the Digue, the *Pavillon Royal, an excellent, but expensive restaurant, with a few rooms at 5—20 fr. per day. Adjoining it, the Pavillon du Phare, D. $2^1/_2$, R. 2—5 fr. — It is customary at all these establishments to give a few sous to the waiter at each repast.

Cafés etc. *in the Town.* The *Société Littéraire (Pl. 5), to which strangers are introduced by a member (first 10 days gratis, afterwards 3 fr. per month), contains an excellent restaurant, reading-room etc. Ball-room on the upper floor, where several balls take place weekly during the summer (3 fr. for non-subscribers). Café du Nord, Rue de Flandre, where rooms may also be engaged. — Jardin Léopold, a public garden near the W. gate of the town, where concerts and other entertainments may be enjoyed.

Private Apartments are let at the beginning or towards the close of the season (June 1st to Oct. 15th) for 10 fr. and upwards per week, but in August rents are everywhere nearly doubled. The contract should be committed to writing if the hirer purpose making a prolonged stay. The usual charge for a plain breakfast is 75 c., for attendance 25 c. per day. French is often imperfectly understood by the Flemish servants. — Filtered rain-water is at present used at Ostend for domestic purposes, but an Artesian well has been commenced. Seltzer water will be found more wholesome and agreeable for drinking. — Wine at 1 fr. and upwards per bottle may be purchased of *Van der Mersch*, in the Parade, or *Van der Heyden*, Rue St. Sébastien.

Baths (p. 4). Machine and towels 75 c. — Invalids and persons unaccustomed to sea-bathing may procure the services of a '*baigneur*' or '*baigneuse*' for 50 c. more.

Warm Salt-water Baths at *Tratsaert's*, Rue St. Sébastien 26, with 'douche de force' 2, per doz. 12 fr.; shower-bath 5, per doz. 50 fr.

Cabs (*Vigilantes*) 1 fr. per drive in the town, $1^1/_2$ fr. in the suburbs.

Donkeys for hire at the S. end of the Digue, 1 fr. per hour.

Sailing Boats with 2 men for 1—2 hrs. 6 fr., larger boats with 4 men 12 fr. — There is no fixed charge for crossing the harbour to visit the new lighthouse. For the trip there and back 1 fr. is an ample remuneration, but an agreement must be made beforehand. — Guns may be hired for shooting sea-fowl, which sometimes afford tolerable sport. — The *Courier des Bains*, which is published once weekly (3 fr. for the whole season) is furnished gratis to the subscribers to the Cursaal. A *Liste des Etrangers* is also published.

Physicians. *Dr. Verhaeghe, Dr. Janssens, Dr. de Ceunynck* etc.; fees 5 fr. or upwards per consultation.

English Church at the E. extremity of the Rue Longue.

Ostend (17,159 inhab.), since the separation (in 1830) of Belgium from Holland, has been the second seaport of Belgium, and owes much of its importance to the great passenger traffic between London and the continent, of which this otherwise insignificant place may be termed one of the principal keys. A number of sandbanks in front of the harbour present a serious impediment to the entrance of large vessels; but this defect has been remedied to some extent by the construction of a large dock *(Bassin de Chasse)*, closed by gates, whence the water, confined at the level of high tide, is suffered to escape suddenly at low tide, thus tending to deepen the channel. The present harbour, the basin and the docks of Slykens (p. 6) were constructed during the reign of Joseph II.

The town successfully resisted one of the most remarkable sieges on record, which lasted from 1601 to 1604, and it was only surrendered to the Spanish general Spinola in consequence of orders received from the States General. In the Spanish War of Succession, after the Battle of Höchstädt, Ostend was occupied by the Allies under Marlborough. An East India commercial company was established here in 1718, and confirmed in its privileges by Charles VI., but was soon dissolved in consequence of differences with England and Holland. In 1745 Louis XV. took the fortress after a siege of 18 days, but was compelled to restore it to Austria by the Peace of Aix-la-Chapelle. In 1794 it was again taken by the French to whom it belonged until 1814. It next belonged to the kingdom of the Netherlands till 1830, when it finally became Belgian in consequence of the revolution. The fortifications have been demolished and converted into promenades since 1865.

None of the public buildings are worthy of note. The **New Church** contains a monument to Queen Louise (p. 84), who died here in 1850. (Sacristan's address: No. 18, Place St. Joseph: fee $1/2$—1 fr. for 1 pers., 1—2 fr. for a party.) On the N. side of the church rises a 'Mt. of Olives' (p. 120) of considerable height: at the summit is the crucified Saviour with the holy women; beneath are the tormented souls in purgatory behind a grating, with the inscription: *"Helpt ons door uwe gebeden en goede werken"* (i. e. help us through your prayers and good works).

Ostend is a very favourite Watering Place, patronised principally by Germans, of whom 15,000 visit it annually. The only promenade worthy of mention is the ***Digue,** a stone dyke or bulwark $^3/_4$ M. in length, 6—8 yds. wide and 30 ft. in height, separating the town from the sea on the N.W. side. It forms a prolongation of the Rue de la Chapelle, with which it is connected by a new bridge. The scene presented by this promenade and its environs during the height of the season will not fail to strike the English traveller who witnesses it for the first time as novel and amusing. The fact that a very large proportion of the visitors have now for the first time in their lives beheld the open sea, and are rejoicing in its health-restoring breezes and its ever-varying aspect, sufficiently accounts for the popularity of a place which affords few other attractions. The traveller therefore, by spending an hour or so on the Digue on a warm summer evening, will be enabled at a glance to see the most characteristic phase of Ostend life.

The Bathing Places adjoin the Digue, both on the N.E. and the S.W. side. Most of the visitors bathe in the morning; the bathing machines are 600 in number. Tickets are purchased at one of the offices, and the bathers furnished with towels and a bathing costume. (Those who make a prolonged stay for the purpose of bathing should purchase the indispensable articles for their private use.) There is here, as at French watering-places, no separation of the sexes; but the strictest propriety is observed. Ladies avoid much publicity by bathing at a very early hour, whilst gentlemen who prefer bathing '*sans costume*' should go to the '*Paradis*', where, as its name is intended to indicate, they are permitted to dispense with a 'costume'. This privileged spot is at the end of the Digue, towards the S.W., and is farthest removed from the impurities of the harbour.

The ***Lighthouse,** 180 ft. in height, is an object of interest to visitors, and should be inspected by those who have never seen the interior of such a structure. The lantern (fee $^1/_2$ fr.)

contains a series of prisms, resembling beehives in shape, and reflectors of copper plated with platina, by which arrangement the light is said to be rendered one thousand times more intense, and to be visible at a distance of 45 M. The top commands an extensive view in clear weather. Nieuport, Furnes and even Dunkirk are seen towards the S.W., the Cursaal of Blankenberge to the N.E., and the towers of Bruges to the S. The gates of the Bassin de Chasse are passed on the way to the lighthouse.

The **Oyster Parks** *(Huitrières)* are extensive reservoirs on the N.E. and S.W. sides of the Digue (e. g. one at, another outside the Bruges Gate), where vast quantities of oysters are stored throughout the greater part of the year. They are imported from the English coast, and here kept in a sound and healthy condition by daily supplies of clarified sea-water. Their price varies from 5 to 8 fr. per hundred. Abundant and fresh supplies may therefore always be procured, except in the summer-months, when they are out of season. Lobsters, brought chiefly from Norway, are kept in separate receptacles in the huitrières. They realise a price of 2—6 fr. according to circumstances. — Fish is generally plentiful, especially in summer when transport is difficult. A turbot of large size may often be purchased for 10—15 fr.; soles, cod, haddocks, mackarel and skate are of course less expensive.

Most of these fish are caught near Blankenberge (p. 8), and sold by public auction between 7 and 9 a. m. in the fish-market of Ostend, under the supervision of the municipal authorities. The principal sales take place on fast-days (Wed. and Frid.). The official fixes a high price in sous for each lot, and then gradually descends until a bidder calls out *"myn"* and thus becomes the purchaser. The great advantage of this 'Dutch auction' is that a single bid settles the matter, and much confusion is thus avoided. Most of the purchasers are women, who afterwards proceed to retail the fish in the market. The Flemish language alone is employed on these occasions, and the spectator has an excellent opportunity of witnessing a characteristic scene of Belgian life.

The luminous appearance of the sea, especially on sultry summer nights, is a never-failing source of interest to many of the visitors. It is best observed when the lock-gates of the Bassin de Chasse (p. 3) are opened at low tide, provided of course the hour be suitable. This spectacle is one which really merits the traveller's attention.

Various ecclesiastical and popular **Festivals** are celebrated at Ostend during the months of July and August. In these the Belgian archers, of whom there are numerous societies, always act a prominent part. The Ostend archery-ground is at the Bruges Gate. Those who are interested in this graceful exercise will often be struck by the strength and skill displayed by some of the amateurs of Ostend.

The **Piers** ('estacades', or stoccades, so called from the '*estaches*' or piles), of which the western is $1/2$ M. in length, the other about 100 yds. longer, afford an entertaining promenade, especially on the departure or arrival of the steamers.

Slykens, $1^1/2$ M. E. of Ostend, a village on the road to Bruges, formerly contained a valuable *Natural Hist. Collection*, the property of M. *Paret*, whose heirs are now gradually disposing of it to private purchasers.

A pleasant walk along the beach may be taken to **Mariakerk,** a village about 3 M. to the S.W., separated from the sea by lofty sandbanks. Halfway to it is situated *Fort Wellington*, which formerly protected the entrance to the harbour on this side, whilst the N.E. side is commanded by *Fort Napoléon*. About 3 M. beyond Mariakerk lies *Middelkerk*, the starting-point of the submarine telegraph-cable to the English coast. There is nothing to mark the spot except the watchman's hut on the sand-hill.

Near *Plasschendael*, the first railway-station on the line to Bruges, is situated **Oudenburg,** an oasis of productive gardens in the midst of a sandy and sterile district, and the chief source from which Ostend is supplied with fruit and vegetables. Oudenburg is said once to have been a flourishing commercial town, and to have been destroyed by Attila about the middle of the 5th cent.

Nieuport, a small seaport, 12 M. S. of Ostend, is occasionally visited as a sea-bathing place. A bath-house for the reception of guests was opened in 1865.

2. Blankenberge.

Railway to Bruges in 25 min., thence to Blankenberge in ½ hr.; fares by ordinary trains 3 fr., 2 fr. 20, 1 fr. 50 c. — Outside seats pleasant in fine weather. Small station at *Lisseweghe*, see p. 9.

Hotels. *On the Beach:* Grand Hôtel des Familles, near the old lighthouse, a spacious new establishment built by a company, containing upwards of 200 apartments, and surrounded by its own grounds, where a band occasionally plays; R. towards the sea 2–8 fr., towards the land less expensive, pension from 5 fr., A. ½ fr. — Hôtel du Cursaal (see below), with 120 rooms. — Hôtel Godderis, table d'hôte at 1 and 5 o'clock 2½ fr., pension 7–15 fr. — Hôtel Victoria Pavillon du Phare, farther W., on the quay. — *In the Town:* *Hôtel d'Hondt, moderate, pension 5½ fr.; *Dr. Verhaegen, comfortable, pension 7 fr.; Marchand's *Maison des Bains, moderate, pension 7 fr.; Hôtel de France, pension 7½ fr. — Hôtel du Chemin de Fer, Neyrinck, Van Muller (with warm baths), Lion d'Or, all in the Rue de l'Eglise. Hôtel de Bruges.

Restaurants. *On the Beach:* Hôtel Godderis (see above); Cursaal, R. 5–20 fr., an elegant and comfortable establishment, but noisy; it comprises a café and a concert-room; D. at 1. 30 and 5, 2½–3 fr. — Pavillon des Bains, café, with table d'hôte. — *In the Town:* Hôtel du Rhin, where apartments may also be obtained at very moderate charges.

Private Apartments. *On the Beach:* Maison Segaert, with a large balcony; Maison Gobart, near the old lighthouse, rooms towards the sea with balconies 4–15 fr., A. ½ fr.; *Maison de Schryver de Meester, pension with room towards the sea 10½ fr., comfortable; subscribers may dine at the table d'hôte without living in the house. There are also three other houses of the same description at the W. end of the beach. — *In the Town:* Private apartments abound in almost every street, average charge 2–4 fr. per day, A. 25 c.; in the height of the season, however, they are sometimes all engaged. Those who have not previously written for rooms should arrive at Blankenberge early in the day, in order that they may be able to return to Bruges the same evening in case of disappointment.

Physicians: *Dr. Verhaegen* and *Dr. van Muller*.

Bathing Machines 60 c.; the attendants expect a trifling fee from regular bathers. — *Tents*, for protection against sun and wind (not against rain) may be hired on the beach for 50–75 c. per day. — *Bathing Dresses* may be purchased in the town for 5–8 fr.

Boats. For a row of 1–2 hrs. 5 fr. are demanded; for a party 1 fr. each. — *Donkey* to Heyst (p. 8) 2–3 fr., or for other excursions along the beach.

Omnibus to Heyst and back 3 fr. (railway in course of construction), starting from the Hôtel des Familles at 10 a. m., and returning from Heyst at 4 p. m.

'*La Plage*', published on Thursd. and Sund., and '*La Vigie de la Côte*', published on Sund. only, are two journals containing a list of the visitors, notices of the tide etc.

Warm Baths in the *Grand Hôtel des Familles* (see above), at *Dr. Muller's*, Rue de l'Eglise, and at *P. van Wulpen de Langhe's*, Bakkerstraat 8, $1^1/_2$ fr. each; arrangements everywhere still defective.

Blankenberge, 12 M. N.E. of Ostende, and 9 M. N. of Bruges, is a fishing-village with 2000 inhab., consisting of small, one-storied houses, and greatly resembling Scheveningen (p. 238). The place still retains many of its primitive features, combined with all the pretensions of a modern bath, and is therefore in a state of transition. The 'dunes' (downs, or sand-hills) have recently been paved, and a promenade upwards of 1 M. in length has thus been formed, skirted by a number of hotels and new buildings, the principal of which is the Curhaus in the centre. The construction of a harbour was commenced in 1862 on the S.W. side, and the lighthouse transferred thither. A number of "estaminets" have sprung up in this neighbourhood, which is reached by traversing the levelled dune ($^1/_2$ M.). It is expected that, on the completion of the harbour, this gap will gradually be occupied by new houses, and that Blankenberge will then become a still more formidable rival of Ostende. Blankenberge was first resorted to as a sea-bathing place about 1840, and for nearly twenty years was a primitive and quiet retreat. But within the last ten years it has become a place of more fashionable repute, the accommodation has greatly improved, and charges have risen in proportion. The average number of visitors is now 5000—6000 annually. Those who prefer country to town will find the environs quieter and the air purer here than at Ostende. The place is particularly recommended for ladies and children.

Fish abounds, but the best is generally sent to Ostende, where it realises a higher price. It may, however, easily be obtained in perfection by personal application to the fishermen or their wives. The landing of their cargoes, the mending of their nets, the preparations for departure, and the various other scenes usually witnessed in fishing-villages afford (as at Scheveningen) admirable subjects for the pencil of the artist.

Heyst, a small village $4^1/_2$ M. N.E. of Blankenberge, is also visited as a sea-bathing place, and possesses tolerable hotel-accommodation, bathing machines etc.

Hôtel de la Plage and **Hôtel du Phare**, both on the beach, pension $5^1/_2$ fr. — In the village, $^1/_4$ M. from the beach, **Maison des Bains** and **Hôtel Ste. Anne**, both comfortable. The **Hôtel de Bruxelles**, near the sluice-gates, $^1/_2$ M. from Heyst, is much frequented, but is not recommended for a prolonged stay on account of the unwholesome effluvia which occasionally rise from the canal.

Those to whom the modern pretension and expense of Blankenberge are distasteful frequently retire to Heyst; which is now annually visited by 600 guests. The canals which here empty themselves into the sea drain an extensive plain at two different levels, and are closed by huge sluice-gates.

Lissewege, $4^1/_2$ M. S.E. of Blankenberge, has a small station on the railway to Bruges, from which however it is $1^1/_2$ M. distant. Those who are interested in architecture should visit its * *Church*, a handsome structure of the 13th cent. The tower, although two-thirds of it only are completed, is a very conspicuous object in the landscape.

From Blankenberge to Ostende by the coast is a pleasant, but somewhat monotonous walk of 12 M. The finest point of view is the hut of a douanier on the highest hill near *Wenduyne*.

3. Bruges.

Flemish *Brügge*.

Hotels. ***Hôtel de Flandre**, Rue Nord du Sablon (Pl. a), R. $2^1/_2$, D. at 1 and 4 o'clock 3, half-bottle of wine $1^1/_2$ fr.; excellent fish-dinners on Fridays. **Hôtel de Londres** (Pl. b) at the station, with café; **Hôtel du Commerce** (Pl. c), Rue St. Jacques; **Fleur de Blé** (Pl. d). — ***Panier d'Or** (Pl. e), opposite the covered market, on the W. side of the extensive market-place, a good second-class inn.

Cafés. **Aigle Noir** and **Vache Hollandaise**, elegant establishments which attract numerous visitors. **Café de Foy**, Grande Place.

Vigilantes 1 fr. per drive; first hour $1^1/_2$, each follg. hr. 1 fr.

Railways to Blankenberge (R. 2), Courtrai (R. 4), Ghent (R. 6).

English Church in the Rue d' Ostende.

Principal Attractions: Hospital of St. John (p. 14), Notre Dame (p. 13), Church of St. Sauveur (p. 11), Chapelle du Saint Sang and Palais de Justice (p. 19), Academy (p. 21). Commissionaires and beggars are numerous and importunate at Bruges. — The pictures at Notre Dame, the Hospital of St. John, the Chapelle du Saint Sang, the Palais de Justice and the Academy are shown for a fixed charge of $^1/_2$ fr. in each case. Tickets obtained on the spot. No other gratuity therefore need be given.

The railway traveller alights at the former Marché de Vendredi. Here on March 30th, 1128, the townspeople, after having elected Count Theodoric of the Alsace to be Count of Flanders, returned the following spirited answer to the deputies of the king of France, who had sent to object to their choice: "Go, tell your master that he is perjured; that his creature William of Normandy (usurper of the sovereignty of Flanders) has rendered himself unworthy of the crown by his infamous extortions; that we have elected a new sovereign, and that it becomes not the king of France to oppose us. That it is our sole privilege, as burghers and nobles of Flanders, to choose our own master".

In the 14th cent. Bruges (which in Flemish means *bridges*, so called from the numerous bridges across the canals) was the great commercial centre of Europe. Factories, or privileged trading companies from seventeen different kingdoms had settled here; twenty foreign ministers resided within the walls, and inhabitants of remote districts encountered unheard of difficulties in order to visit the renowned city. Early in the 13th cent. Bruges became one of the great marts of the Hanseatic League and of the English wool trade. Lombards and Venetians conveyed hither the products of India and Italy, and returned home with the manufactures of England and Germany. Richly laden vessels from Venice, Genoa and Constantinople might be seen discharging their cargoes here simultaneously, and the magazines of Bruges groaned beneath the weight of English wool, Flemish linen and Persian silk. In 1301, when Johanna of Navarre, with her husband Philippe le Bel of France, visited Bruges and beheld the sumptuous costumes of the inhabitants, she is said to have exclaimed: "I imagined myself alone to be queen, but here I see hundreds of persons whose attire vies with my own". Bruges was long the residence of the Counts of Flanders. It attained the culminating point of its magnificence during the first half of the 15th cent., when the Dukes of Burgundy held their court here. It owes its reputation as a cradle of the fine arts to John and Hubert van Eyck (p. 32), who flourished at that period. The celebrated order of knighthood of the Golden Fleece was founded by Philip le Bon, Duke of Burgundy and the Netherlands, at Bruges on Jan. 10th, 1429, on the occasion of his marriage with Isabella, daughter of John I. of Portugal. It was instituted for the protection of the church, and the fleece was probably selected as its badge rather in allusion to one of the staple commodities of Flanders, than to the Golden Fleece of mythology. Knights of the order still exist in Austria and Spain.

The broad streets and richly decorated mediæval houses still indicate its ancient glory. Of all the cities of Belgium Bruges has most faithfully preserved the external characteristics of the middle ages. The town now presents a melancholy and deserted appearance, its commerce is insignificant and its prosperity gone. Nearly one-third of the 43,819 inhab. are said to be paupers. The town is, however, a favourite retreat for retired and wealthy merchants, many of whom settle here to spend the evening of a busy and fatiguing life in undisturbed repose.

To the r. in the street leading from the railway-station into the town is situated the ***Cathedral** (*St. Sauveur*, Pl. 11), an early Gothic structure of the 13th and 14th cent. (choir of the 13th, vaulting of choir and its five chapels 1482—1527). Externally it is a cumbrous brick building, destitute of a portal, disfigured by later additions, and surmounted by a tower, which somewhat resembles a castle and has a Moorish aspect. The interior is adorned with numerous paintings, all furnished with the names of the artists and the dates. West side: *Van Oost*, Descent of the Holy Ghost, l. the portrait of the master, r. that of his son; **Van Hoeck*, Crucifixion; *Backereel*, St. Carlo Borromeo administering the Eucharist to persons sick of the plague; **Van Oost*, Triumph of Christ over Time and Death; **Zegers*, Adoration of the Magi. — S. Aisle: *Schoreel*, Death of Mary, a copy of the picture in the Academy; **Memling* (ascribed by many to Thierry Stuerbout), Martyrdom of St. Hippolytus (covered).

The four saints in 'grisaille' on the outside of the shutters are St. Charles, St. Hippolytus, St. Elisabeth and St. Margaret. The principal picture represents the saint about to be torn to pieces by horses. The rider on the grey horse and the man by the side of the chestnut are remarkably easy and life-like. The three functionaries in the background are stiff and destitute of expression. On the whole the picture is less pleasing than most of the other works of the master. — The picture on the r. represents a king distributing alms; that on the l. the donor and his wife, admirable portraits. The grouping and the landscape of the former exhibit all the charms of Memling's best style.

Van der Meire, Crucifixion (covered); *Maes*, St. Rosalia and St. Dorothea; *Van Oost*, Portiuncula, St. Francis receiving absolution from the Virgin. In the Transepts six large pictures by *Jan van Orley* (1725), representing the history of the Saviour. Beneath these, to the S., *M. de Vos*, Consecration of St. Eligius; N., *Van Oost*, Conversion of St. Hubert; opposite *Deyster*, Sufferings of Christ. The choir is separated from the nave by a screen of black and white marble. — The Choir contains two large marble *monuments of the bishops Castillion (d. 1753) and Susteren (d. 1742), both by *Pulinx*. High altar-piece, Resurrection by *Janssens*; beneath it, *Van Thulden*, Christ and Mary, * *Van Oost*, Peter and John. The choir-stalls are adorned with the armorial bearings of the Order of the Golden Fleece (*Toison d'Or*). Gobelins tapestry copied from Van Orley's pictures is exhibited here annually during the month of May. — Chapels of the Choir. 1st: *Memling*, Presentation in the Temple, with the donors, a small winged picture l. of the altar. Opposite to it, on the posterior wall of the choir, two pictures by *Erasmus Quellin*, representing St. Augustine. 2nd Chapel: *Van Oost*, Flight into Egypt. 3rd: *J. v. Eyck*, Mater Dolorosa (covered); also a tombstone richly gilded and enamelled; *J. v. Oost*, The Saviour predicting his passion; His appearance after the Resurrection. At the side, Portrait of Philippe le Bel (son of Maximilian V. and father of the Emperor Charles V.) on a gold ground (covered), master unknown. The inscription beneath terms him "*Philippus Stok*", a sobriquet applied to him by the citizens of Bruges in allusion to his habit of carrying a stick, and mentions him as the founder of the '*Broedersсap der Wee'en*' (i. e. brotherhood of suffering), a fraternity which still exists. 4th Chapel, at the back of the high altar: * *Pourbus*, Last supper, with two lateral pictures. The four small pictures, by *Coninxloo*, painted in 1570, also merit inspection. The stained glass is by *Jean Béthune* (1861). 5th Chapel: Tomb of Bishop Jean Carondelet. 6th Chapel: *Van Oost*, St. Joseph watching the Infant Saviour playing with shavings; *Frickx*, Crucifixion, after Van Dyck (1780). 7th Chapel contains nothing worthy of note.

On the wall of the choir: *Roose*, Virgin and St. Dominicus; *Janssens*, Adoration of the Shepherds. On the pillar to the r.: * *Claeyssens*, Descent from the Cross, a winged picture (covered).

Baptistery: *Claeyssens*, Christ scourged; **Maes*, Baptism of Constantine, after Van Dyck; at the entrance two large monumental *brasses, that on the r. executed in 1423, that on the l. in 1515, the latter particularly fine, resembling those in St. Jacques (p. 22). This chapel also contains a Crucifixion painted 'a tempera' in 1315, before the invention of oil-painting. **N. Aisle.** In one of the Chapels, Job, by *Deyster*. Over the N. and S. **Doors**, fine wood-carving, gilded, dating from the 15th cent. The Sacristy contains a few antiquities.

***Notre Dame** (Flem. *Onze Vrouw*, Pl. 17), in the immediate vicinity, is less remarkable for its architecture (12th cent.) than for the sculptures and pictures which it contains. The tower, surmounted by a new spire, the old having got out of the perpendicular, is 442 ft. in height. Lovers of art should not omit to examine the bronze doors. — In the **S. Transept**, over the *altar*, stands a small *Statue of the Virgin and Child, attributed to *Michael Angelo*, either an early work of that great master, or an admirable specimen of Italian workmanship of his age. Horace Walpole, who was a great admirer of art, is said to have offered 30,000 fl. for it. The French carried it off to Paris during the Revolution. One of the chapels in the choir contains the ***Tombs** of Charles the Bold (d. 1477), Duke of Burgundy, and his daughter Mary (d. 1482), wife of the Emp. Maximilian, the last scions of the House of Burgundy and of the princes of the S. Netherlands. The latter tomb, the more valuable as a work of art, was executed by *Jan de Beckere* of Brussels in 1495; the former was erected in 1558 by Philip II., a descendant of Charles the Bold, who is said to have paid the sculptor Jongelincx (d. 1606) of Antwerp the then enormous sum of 24,000 fl. The Emp. Charles V. caused the remains of the duke, his great-grandfather, to be conveyed hither from Nancy. These tombs were visited by Napoleon and the Empress Marie Louise in 1810, on which occasion the emperor presented a sum of 10,000 fr. for their restoration. The life-size, recumbent figures of the duke and his daughter, in bronze richly gilded, repose on marble sarcophagi; at the sides are the enamelled armorial bearings of the duchies, counties and estates which the princess, the richest heiress of that age, brought to the House of Austria on her marriage with Maximilian. The sumptuousness of these tombs, the historical associations attaching to the illustrious father and daughter, and the touching story of the early death of the latter in consequence of a fall from her horse whilst hunting with her husband near Bruges, all tend to arrest the attention of the most indifferent spectator.

Pictures, the larger of which are furnished with the names of the painters. W. wall: **De Crayer*, Adoration of the Shepherds (1667), St. Dominicus and St. Helena in front; S., *Zegers*, Adoration of the Magi; *Pourbus*, Christ's Passion and Crucifixion, a large winged picture. On the 2nd pillar in the S. transept, *Pourbus*, Transfiguration, a winged picture (closed); *Maas*, The Angel appearing to Joseph and Mary (altar-piece); farther to the r., near the confessional, **de Bles*, Annunciation and Adoration ot the Magi; *Pourbus*, Last Supper; on the altar Michael Angelo's statue of Mary (see above). In the choir: Esther and Ahasuerus; *Maes*, St. Margaret kneeling before the Infant Jesus; *Horebout*, St. Dionysius; opposite to it, * *Van Dyck*, Christ expiring on the Cross; above it, *Van Oost*, St. Margaret, contending with the dragon; then to the r. the chapel with the tombs (see above). The chapel behind the high-altar contains some good stained glass. In the N. aisle a Madonna and Child as altar-piece; beside it, to the l., *Mostaert*, The mourning Mary (covered); **Pourbus*, Adoration of the Shepherds, a winged picture with the donors (covered); *Jac. van Oost*, Triumph of the Church; *Crayer*, St. Thomas with two angels; under it (covered), *Claeyssens*, Foundation of the church of S. Maria Maggiore at Rome, r. St. Peter's; opposite to it, *Van Oost*, Jesus and the Pharisees; *Mich. Angelo da Caravaggio*, Christ at Emmaus; r. the Assumption. In the N. aisle, *Van Laer*, Flight into Egypt; Temptation of St. Antony. On the pillar to the r., The Dead Christ, after *Van Eyck; Erasmus Quellin*, Betrothal of St. Catharine.

The *Pulpit*, a beautiful specimen of carving in oak, was executed at the close of the 16th cent. by *Klaussaert*.

A gateway (at which visitors ring) adjoining the entrance to the church leads to the ***Hospital of St. John** (Pl. 24), where the sick are attended by Sisters of Charity. Strangers are admitted 9—12 a. m. and 1—6 p. m. The hospital contains a collection of **Pictures by *Memling*, which alone would amply repay a visit to Bruges.

Hans Memling†, according to the story popularly current, was born about the year 1430, either in Flanders or in Germany, and died at the beginning of the 16th cent. at Burgos in Spain. In 1477, after the Battle of Nancy, in which he had fought under Charles the Bold and been wounded, he arrived at Bruges in a state of sickness and abject poverty, and was hospitably received and entertained by the Sisters of Charity in the Hospital. After his recovery he endeavoured to show his gratitude to his benefactresses by employing his art in the decoration of their poor church and the house where their kindness had rescued him from death. This romantic story is, however, without foundation, and documents recently discovered appear to prove that Memling was a Frank from Mümling, near Aschaffenburg in Germany, that he was living at Bruges in the position of a wealthy citizen at the time when the above calamities are said to have befallen him, and that he died there about the year 1495. He is considered to surpass his great predecessor John van Eyck in depth of sentiment, but not in execution. As an illuminator he is unsurpassed. The celebrated Grimani Breviary contains beautiful specimens of his work.

The finest of these works (No. 2) are the paintings on the Châsse of St. Ursula, a reliquary of Gothic design, each of the sides of which are divided into three sections. These six fields, each about 8 in. wide, are filled with beautifully executed, almost miniature paintings in oil, representing scenes from the legend of St. Ursula and the 11,000 virgins. The chronicles of the hospital are said to record that Adrian Reims, the governor of the establishment at that period, ordered the reliquary in 1480, that Memling undertook two journeys to Cologne during the prosecution of his task, and that the work was completed in 1486. 1st Scene: Landing at Cologne; the Cathedral, Gross St. Martin and the Bayenthurm are distinctly recognisable; St. Cunibert and St. Severin less faithful. 2nd Scene: Landing at Bâle, the Alps in the background. 3rd Scene: Reception of the Virgins at Rome by the Pope (St. Cyriacus); a number of pious British youths have joined the party; baptism and confession of the converts. 4th Scene: Embarcation of the Virgins at Bâle on their return.

† This master is frequently called *Hemling*, a spelling which has been thought justified by the inscription on the frame of the Betrothal of St. Catharine (p. 16). The name there is MEMLING, the first letter of which however is not an H, but a not uncommon mediæval form of M, which occurs (e. g.) on the seal of Maximilian I., the centre M of which has precisely this form. The Netherlanders, moreover, have always called him *Memling*, the Italians *Memelino*. The admirable historical catalogue of the Antwerp Gallery adduces good authorities to prove the name to have been *Hans van Memmelinghe*.

5th and 6th Scenes: Landing at Cologne and Massacre of the virgin saints by the heathen soldiers of the Emp. Maximin. On one end of the reliquary the Virgin and Child are represented, with two kneeling nuns at the sides; on the other end St. Ursula with a javelin, protecting her companions beneath her outspread robe. The six medallions on the lid represent St. Ursula with her companions, the Coronation of the Virgin, and angels with musical instruments. The pedestal being moveable, each picture in turn can be viewed in the most favourable light.

A second picture by *Memling*, painted in 1497, restored in 1826, the largest of his works extant, is a winged picture (No. 1), the 'Betrothal of St. Catharine', formerly in the Julius Hospital at Bruges; the figures and the grouping have the stiffness of the Byzantine style, but the details are executed with the richness and ease which characterise the talented master. The Virgin is represented with the Child, who holds an apple in his left hand, and with the right places a ring on the finger of the kneeling St. Catharine; beside her an angel playing on the organ; farther back John the Baptist; r. St. Barbara reading; beside her an angel holding a book, in which Mary reads; in the background St. John the Evangelist, blessing the cup, a figure of great dignity and beauty. On the wings: interior, Beheading of John the Baptist, Vision of the Evangelist St. John in the island of Patmos. Exterior: Donors of the picture, two brothers of the hospital; behind them St. James, St. Antony and two sisters; farther back St. Agnes and St. Clara (inscription see note, p. 15).

The third picture by *Memling*, a smaller work, also with wings, is (No. 3) an *Adoration of the Magi, painted in 1479 (under glass). The thin, bearded man, looking in at the window, with the cap still worn by the convalescents of the hospital, is said to be a portrait of the master himself; but it bears little resemblance to two other portraits of Memling which are still extant. To the r. Brother Florin, the donor, kneeling. On the inside of the shutters, the Nativity and Presentation in the Temple; outside, John the Baptist and St. Veronica. The Presentation is perhaps the most charming of Memling's works.

A fourth small picture (No. 4), consisting of two wings, painted in 1487, represents the Virgin with a red mantle, offering an apple to the Child; on the other wing the donor, Martin van Newenhowe (under glass).

Another picture by *Memling* (No. 5) represents a female Bust, with high cap and white veil, termed by the modern inscription "Sibylla Zambetha", but probably a portrait of the daughter of Wilhelm Moreel, Memling's patron.

A Descent from the Cross (No. 6), also sometimes attributed to *Memling*, but probably by an inferior contemporary, possesses little or nothing of the life and richness of colouring which characterise Memling. There are also several good pictures by the two *Oosts* (a Philosopher, No. 1, is the masterpiece of one of them), a Madonna by *Van Dyck* (No. 29), portraits by *Pourbus* etc. in the same room (hall of the chapter, in the court of the hospital).

The hospital itself (containing 240 beds) is well worthy of a visit. The large, open hall, divided by partitions into bedrooms, kitchen and other apartments, and remarkable for its cleanliness and order, is interesting from having retained its mediæval aspect unchanged. A new and more commodious building, fitted up in the modern style, has been erected adjacent to the original hospital.

The street from the station to the town passes a small open space planted with trees, and adorned with a poor **Statue of Simon Stevin** (Pl. 29), the supposed inventor of the decimal system (d. 1635), and leads to the *Grand' Place*, or market-place. One side of the square is occupied by the **Halles**, a large building erected in 1364. One wing was originally destined to be a cloth-hall, the other is now the flesh-market. The **Belfry** *(Grande Tour*, Pl. 23), erected at the end of the 14th cent., 320 ft. in height, leans slightly towards the S.E.; very extensive view from the summit. The chimes (comp. p. 35), which date from 1743, and are said to be the best in Europe, play every quarter of an hour (doorkeeper 1/2 fr., custodian at the top 1/2 fr.).

On the W. side of the market-place, at the corner of the Rue St. Amand, is the house termed '*Au Lion de Flandre*', now a shop, a handsome old building in the mediæval style. According to a popular, but probably erroneous tradition, it was occupied for a time by Charles II. of England, whilst living here in exile about the middle of the 17th cent. The citizens of Bruges accorded to him a title of royalty by creating him "King of the Guild of Archers".

In the opposite house, termed the **Craenenburg** (Pl. 10), now a tavern, the citizens of Bruges kept the German King Maximilian, the 'last of the knights', prisoner during twelve days in the year 1488, on account of his refusal to concede the guardianship of his son Philip, heir to the crown of the Netherlands, to the king of France. The Pope threatened them with excommunication, and the Imperial army was directed to march against the city, notwithstanding which Maximilian was not liberated until in the presence of the guilds and the townspeople he had solemnly sworn to renounce his claim to the guardianship of his son, to respect the liberties of Bruges, and to forget the affront he had received. A few weeks later, however, he was released from his oath by a congress of princes held at Mechlin, at the instance of his father, the Emp. Frederick III.

The long building on the E. side of the market, surmounted by a dome and occupied by shops and cafés, was erected in 1789 on the site of the so-called Water Hall, an extensive covered harbour in which vessels could be loaded and unloaded under shelter of a roof.

The **Hôtel de Ville** (Pl. 25), an elegant Gothic structure with six towers, three in front and three in the rear, was commenced about 1370. The 48 niches in the façade are filled with statues of the Counts of Flanders and others. On the arrival of the French sansculottes (in 1792) these 'statues of tyrants' were torn down and demolished in the market-place, but they have since been replaced by others. The Counts of Flanders, on their accession to the throne, were in the habit of showing themselves to the people from one of the windows or balconies in front of this building, and swearing to maintain the laws and privileges of the city (p. 10). The restoration of the façade, commenced in 1854, is now nearly completed. A battle-piece in the hall below (Finding of the body of Charles the Bold after the Battle of Nancy, in 1477), by *H. Dobbelaare*, was purchased for Bruges by the citizens with the aid of the government. Up stairs, in the vestibule of the library, is a representation of the principal squares of the town; also a large picture by *Dobbelaare*, representing the Works of Charity. The municipal Library (open from 10 to 1 o'clock), in the great hall which occupies almost the entire length of the building, is worthy of a visit on account of its fine Gothic roof of pendent wood-work. It also contains some remarkable old MSS., many of them with miniatures, missals of the 13th and 14th cent., the first books printed by Colard Mansion, the printer of Bruges (1475—84). (The Archives, preserved in the *Maison de l'Ancien Greffe*, adjacent to the Hôtel de Ville, open in summer from 2 to 6 p. m., contain the list of prizes of a lottery drawn at Bruges in 1445. This proves that lotteries are an institution of earlier origin than is commonly supposed, and that they were probably invented in Flanders, and not in Italy.) The statue of Pourbus, executed by *Van Weydefeldt* in 1859, is, with several others which are now in progress, destined to adorn the front of the Academy.

To the r. in the corner adjoining it, is the *** Chapelle du Saint Sang** (Pl. 5), a small and elegant church of two stories, the lower of which dates from the 12th, the upper probably from the 15th cent.; the portal and staircase were constructed in 1533 in the richest Flamboyant style. The chapel derives its appellation from some drops of the blood of the Saviour, which Count Theodoric of Flanders (p. 10) is said to have brought from the Holy Land in 1150, and to have presented to the city. The building was pillaged and partially demolished by the sansculottes during the Revolution, but was judiciously and magnificently restored in 1829—39, and adorned with beautiful stained glass windows. The latter comprise portraits of the Burgundian princes down to Maria Theresa and Francis I.; and the history of the Passion, and the arrival of the Holy Blood at Bruges, in four compartments. The *altar, a beautiful specimen of modern sculpture in the Gothic style, was executed by *Michael Abbeloos* in 1858. The pulpit consists of a semi-globe, resting on clouds, with the equator, meridian and a few geographical names. On one of the pillars: *Memling* (?), Conveyance of the Holy Blood to Bruges. The confessional is modern. The valuable silver reliquary was presented by the monastic fraternities in 1617. The 'Holy Blood' is exhibited every Friday, 6—11. 30, a. m. The miniature crown was presented by the Princess Mary of Burgundy (p. 13).

On the N. side of the Hôtel de Ville is the **Palais de Justice** (Pl. 28), formerly the town-hall of the *Franc de Bruges*, i. e. the district of the "*Buitenpoorters*", or inhabitants of the neighbouring district who were not subject to the jurisdiction of the city. It occupies a portion of the site of a former palace of the Counts of Flanders, which was presented by Philippe le Bel to the 'Liberty of Bruges'. The council-chamber is mediæval, although the greater part of the structure is not earlier than 1722. The *Chimney-Piece, occupying almost the entire side of the room, is a superb and unique specimen of carving in oak, probably executed in 1529 to commemorate the Battle of Pavia, restored in 1850 by the sculptor *Geerts*. The statues, finely carved and nearly the size of life, represent Charles V. (in the centre), his maternal ancestors, Mary of Burgundy and Maximilian of Austria, on the left, and his paternal ancestors on the right of the spectator; in the small medallions his parents Philippe le Bel and Johanna of Castille, with the armorial bearings of Burgundy, Spain etc.; the whole decorated with genii and foliage. Beneath the wood-work are four reliefs in marble, dating from the same period, representing the history of Susannah. The tapestry on the walls was manufactured at Ingelmünster (p. 24) in 1859, in imitation of the original, portions of which were found in the cellar. The open space here, the *Place du Vieux Bourg*, was adorned in 1858 by a small *Statue of Memling*, designed by *Pickery*.

The ***Academy** (Pl. 1) of Art, founded in 1719, possesses a somewhat meagre collection of pictures, several of which, however, are by Van Eyck and Memling, and should by no means be overlooked. The small Place de Van Eyck in front of the Academy is embellished with a marble statue (Pl. 31) of that master by *Calloigne* (1820). It is surrounded by numerous mediæval houses, most of which belong to the 15th and 16th cent. The academy-building, a Gothic edifice of the 14th cent., termed *De Poorters Loodse* (i. e. Citizens' Lodge; *poorters*, those who live within the *port* or gate), was formerly an assembly hall for the townspeople. It was entirely remodelled in 1755. The façade is in course of being decorated with statues by sculptors of Bruges. The entrance is in the Rue de l'Académie at the side (admission on Sundays gratis, 10—1 o'clock). A few of the more interesting pictures are here enumerated. In the first Passage modern works: 95. *Mersseman*, Old women with children; in the circular space, 42. *Suvée*, Invention of the art of drawing; 43. *Odevaire*, Portraits of former directors of the Academy; 44. *V. d. Donckt*, Vicomte de Croeser, a former burgomaster of Bruges. I. Room, beginning on the r.: 51. *Odevaire*, Death of the Athenian general Phocion; 56. *Claeys*, Coast of Portugal; below it: *De Vos*, Society of artists; 58. *Van Hollebeke* (1817), Last moments of a condemned criminal; below it, *Gendre*, Festival of St. Sebastian at Bruges; 62. *Kinsoen* (d. 1839), Belisarius at the death-bed of his wife; below it: *Putte*, Landscape with cranes; *Walloys*, Mary of Burgundy visits Memling in the hospital; 17. *P. Pourbus*, Last Judgment (1551); 77. Jacob and Esau, master unknown; 26. *J. v. Oost the Elder*, Portrait of a man; 28., 29. same master, St. Antony in his trance, St. Antony resuscitating a dead man. — II. Room: on the r. 7., and l. 8., *Claeyssens* (?), Condemnation of Cambyses, and execution of the sentence, a scene painfully true to nature, both painted in 1498; *4. *Memling*, St. Christopher carrying the Infant Jesus across the Jordan, r. St. Benedict, l. St. Egidius with the donors, painted in 1484; 15., 16. *Pourbus*, Portraits; 19. *J. v. Eyck* (?), St. Barbara, the cathedral of Cologne in the background (a drawing); 6 Death of the Virgin, master unknown; *1. *J. v. Eyck*, Virgin and Child, with St. George, St. Donatus, and an admirable portrait of the donor. A copy of this picture, probably by Horebout, is preserved in the Antwerp Museum (p. 128). 2. *J. v. Eyck*, Portrait of his wife, half life-size, painted in 1439; 3. *J. v. Eyck*, Head of Christ, with the date 1440, and the inscription *Johes de Eyck Inventor*. The second figure 4 in the date, being partially obliterated and resembling a 2, has led to the erroneous conclusion that this was the first picture painted in oils by the master. The genuineness of the picture is moreover questioned, and it is supposed by some to be a faithful copy of a Head of Christ in the Museum of Berlin, painted by Van Eyck in 1438. *5. *Memling* (?), Baptism of Christ, on the inner wings the donors, on the outer the Virgin and Child, adored by a woman with a child, in the background St. Clara. — None of the sculptures are worthy of note.

The **Eglise de Jérusalem** (Pl. 14) is remarkable only on account of its being an imitation of the church of the Holy Sepulchre at Jerusalem. The founder 'Messire Peter Adornes', a burgomaster of Bruges in the 15th cent., undertook two journeys to Jerusalem, for the purpose of perfecting the resemblance, which however is doubtful. The church is moreover in a somewhat remote part of the town, so that on the whole it hardly repays a visit. Near it, at the W. end of the town, is an English Nunnery (*Couvent des Dames Anglaises*, Pl. 8), with which an excellent school is connected. The church of the convent contains an altar, executed at Rome, and composed of 22 pieces of the rarest Persian and Egyptian marbles.

St. Jacques (Pl. 15), erected in 1240, situated near the Hôtel de Commerce, contains, besides several pictures by *Van Oost*, *Honthorst* and *Pourbus*, the mediæval monumental Brasses of several Spanish families, in a chapel to the l. of the high altar. One of these, with date 1577, to the memory of Don Francesco di Lapuebla and his wife, is very elaborately executed; another, date 1615, is to the memory of Don Pedro de Valencia and his wife. The traveller should not omit to examine these brasses, as they are almost the only Spanish monuments still to be seen in Belgium. The chapel on the S. side contains a fine Mary and Child in terracotta.

The Cour des Princes (Pl. 4), the ancient palace of the Counts of Flanders, where the nuptials of Charles the Bold with Margaret of York were celebrated in 1468, and where Philippe le Bel, father of Charles V., was born, has entirely disappeared, with the exception of a few fragments within the precincts of a private house.

The **Béguinage** (Pl. 3), at the S.W. end of the town, founded in the 13th cent., is inferior to that of Ghent (p. 45); but the traveller should not fail to visit one of these interesting and extensive nunneries.

The Convent of the Soeurs de Charité (Pl. 8), opposite the Béguinage, contains a school for the destitute, where 150 poor children are taught lace-making, besides the other branches of education.

Bruges still maintains the reputation for handsome women which it enjoyed at an early period ("*formosis Bruga puellis*", as the monkish lines record).

Six canals converge at Bruges, viz. from Ghent, Sluis (the seaport of Bruges), Nieuport and Veurne (Furnes), Ypern and Ostende. The last is navigable for vessels of considerable tonnage.

Dante (*Inferno* XV., 4—6) compares the barrier which separates the river of tears from the desert, with the embankments which the Flemings have thrown up between Sluis (or rather the island of Cadzand) and Bruges, to protect the city against the encroachments of the sea:

"Quale i Fiamminghi tra Gazzante e Bruggia,
Temendo il fiotto che inver lor s'avventa,
Fanno lo schermo, perchè 'l mar si fuggia".

Damme, a village N.E. of Bruges, on the canal leading to Sluis, was once a considerable and fortified seaport. It was the birthplace of the Flemish poet **Jacob Maerlandt** (13th cent.), to whom a statue was here erected in 1860, executed by Pickery of Bruges.

4. From Bruges to Courtrai and Tournai.

Railway from Bruges to Courtrai in $1^1/_2$–2 hrs.; fares 4, 3, 2 fr. — From Courtrai to Tournai in 1 hr.; fares 2 fr. 60, 1 fr. 70, 1 fr. 15 c. — From Tournai to Brussels see p. 54.

This railway, which, unlike most of the lines in Belgium, belongs to a private company, connects a number of small and insignificant towns and villages of West Flanders with the more important arteries of traffic. The stations are numerous, and the speed slow, so that the longer route by the government line viâ Ghent occupies little more time. The flat, agricultural district traversed presents all the usual Flemish characteristics, somewhat resembling many parts of England.

Thourout, the first important station, the second town of the Arrondissement of Bruges, derives its name from the Germanic god Thor (*Thorhout* = grove of Thor), to whose worship a grove was once consecrated here. The abbey is said to have been originally founded by Dagobert I., presented in 830 by Louis le Debonnaire to the Bishop of Hamburg, and afterwards destroyed by the Normans. It contains a population of 7891, a seminary for teachers in connection with the diocese of Bruges, and a handsome new church. In the neighbourhood, $1^1/_2$ M. to the W., are the ruins of *Wynendaele*, a castle once appertaining to the Counts of Flanders. Next stat. *Lichtervelde*.

The Branch Railway from Lichtervelde to Furnes passes by the small town of **Dixmuiden**, the church of which possesses a fine screen, erected at the beginning of the 16th cent. in the richest Flamboyant style, and a picture by *Jordaens*, the Adoration of the Magi.

Next stat. *Gits*, then **Rosselaere**, French *Roulers*, a town with 12,433 inhab., high above which rises the handsome Gothic tower of the church of St. Michael. Here, on July 13th, 1794, a fierce contest took took place between the Austrians under Clerfait, and the French under Pichegru and Macdonald, in which the latter were victorious. This defeat was the prelude to that of Fleurus (p. 151), 13 days later, which sufficiently demonstrated to the Austrians the hopelessness of carrying on war successfully at a distance of 600 M. from their own country. The linen-market of Rosselaere is one of the most important in the province.

The following stat. *Rumbeke* possesses a fine Gothic church and a château of Count de Thiennes. Stat. *Iseghem*, with 7753 inhab., contains numerous linen-factories. Tobacco is extensively cultivated in the environs. Between Iseghem and the next stat. *Ingelmünster* the handsome château of Baron Gillés is situated. (Branch-line from Ingelmünster to *Deynze*, by *Thielt*, a town with 11,497 inhab.). Then stat. *Lendelede*, and *Heule*, with a clumsy Gothic church. Near Courtrai the train crosses the *Ley* (or *Lys*). The lofty tower of St. Martin's church (see below) becomes visible.

Courtrai, Flem. *Kortryk* (*Damier*, *Lion d'Or*, both in the Grand' Place; **Hôtel du Midi*, opposite the station, moderate; opp. to it, *Hôtel du Nord*; *Hôtel des Armes de France*, Rue de Lille; *Restaurant* at the station), a manufacturing town with 23,382 inhab., situated on the *Ley* (*Lys*), is celebrated for its table-linen and its lace, in the manufacture of which 5—6000 women are employed. The flax of Courtrai enjoys a high reputation, and is manufactured in various districts of Belgium, as well as in the town itself. It is prepared with great care and skill. After it is cut, it is carefully sunned and dried, stored for a year, then steeped in the water of the Lys and sent to the factory. About one-twentieth of the soil in the environs produces flax. There are also extensive bleaching-grounds in the vicinity.

The *Town Hall, re-erected in 1526, was subsequently so disfigured by alterations that the original character of the façade was entirely destroyed. Its restoration, commenced in 1846, was lately completed, with the exception of some of the statues. Two richly decorated *Chimney-pieces in the interior are worthy of notice. The more interesting is that in the Council-Chamber upstairs, in the rich Flamboyant style, and completed before 1527. A series of half-reliefs below appear to refer to events in the earlier history of the town; above them, women on horseback, holding banners in one hand and daggers in the other; then a third row of symbolical figures, representing Patience, Moderation, Chastity etc. Statues of Charles V., to the r. the Infanta Isabella, and to the l. Justice, are placed on consoles. The walls are covered with large plans of the town and its jurisdiction ('*castelany*'), painted in oil. The lower hall, where the police-court is held, contains the other chimney-piece, the principal figures of which represent the standard-bearers of the Knights of Courtrai; the statues are those of the Archduke Albert and his consort. The Exchange is on the ground-floor of the Town Hall, r. of the entrance. (The porter admits visitors to the council-chamber for a trifling fee.)

Nearly opposite the Town Hall rises the *Belfry* (comp. p. 34), and farther N. the lofty tower of St. Martin's Church, erected in the 15th cent. The choir contains a beautiful sacrament-house in stone, of the year 1585. The church was struck by lightning in 1862, and entirely destroyed by fire, with the exception of the bare walls. The pulpit and the sacrament-house alone were saved. The adjacent church of Notre Dame is said to have been founded in 1238 by Count Baldwin of Flanders, afterwards Latin Emperor, in honour of a hair of Christ, brought from Palestine by his uncle Philip of Alsace, and to this day an object of superstitious veneration. The chapel behind the choir contains the Raising of the Cross, one of *Van Dyck's* best pictures, resembling a Rubens in the boldness of the design; it is inferior in freshness of colour, but the profound expression of tenderness and pain in the countenance of the Crucified are unsurpassed. The altars to the r. and l. are adorned with good reliefs in marble of the 18th cent., by *Lecreux*, representing St. Rochus among those sick of the plague, and Mary Magdalene with angels. The canopy is also executed in marble. Many other decorations of a similar description were liberally bestowed on the church during the last century. The Chapel of the Counts on the r. was added to the church in 1373.

In the Rue de la Chaussée, near the Belfry, is the Museum of the Courtrai *Academy of Art* (always accessible, fee 25 c.), containing several good modern pictures. The following are the best, beginning on the l.: **De Keyser*, Battle of the Spurs (see below); *Verboeckhoven*, Sea-piece; *Robbe*, Cattle; *Van Dewin*,

Grey horse; *Steinicke*, Tyrolese landscape; **Dobbelaere*, Memling painting the reliquary of St. Ursula in St. John's Hospital at Bruges (see p. 15).

Beneath the walls of Courtrai, on July 11th, 1302, was fought the famous Battle of the Spurs, in which the Flemish army, consisting chiefly of weavers from Ghent and Bruges, under Count John of Namur and Duke William of Jülich, defeated the French under the Count of Artois. Upwards of 1200 knights and several thousand soldiers fell. The victors afterwards collected 700 golden spurs, an ornament worn by the French knights alone, and hung them up as trophies in a monastery-church which has since been destroyed. A small Chapel outside the Ghent Gate, erected in 1831, marks the centre of the battle-field.

Branch Railway to Ypern and Poperinghe in $1^{3}/_{4}$ hr. First Stat. **Menin**, Flem. *Meenen*, a small town with 9752 inhab., where the Prussian General Scharnhorst (d. 1813) first distinguished himself against the French. Stat. *Wervicq*, with 6802 inhab., possesses a number of tobacco-manufactories; the Church of St. Medardus dates from the middle of the 14th cent. Stat. *Comines* (3501 inhab.), formerly a fortified town, was the birthplace of the historian Philip of Comines (d. 1509). The l. bank only of the Lys here belongs to Belgium.

Ypern (**Tête d'Or; Chatellenie*), an old and strongly fortified town on the *Yperlée*, with 17,095 inhab., possessing broad and clean streets and situated in a fertile district, was formerly the capital of West Flanders. The environs were once so marshy and unhealthy that sickly persons were proverbially said throughout Belgium to resemble the "Death of Ypern". Most of the marshes have now been drained and rendered arable. In the 14th cent. Ypern had a population of 200,000 souls, and upwards of 4000 looms were in constant activity.

The prosperity of the town is now a mere matter of history. A most interesting memorial of that period, however, has been preserved in the handsome **Cloth Hall*, the most considerable of the civic edifices of Belgium. It is a rich specimen of the Gothic style, commenced in 1200, completed in 1304, less uncommon than the Halles at Bruges, but far superior in lightness and elegance. The E. portion, supported by columns, is of later date. The square *Belfry*, which rises from the centre, is unquestionably the oldest part. The edifice, being now no longer required for its original purpose, is employed as a Town Hall. It is said to have served as a model to the eminent architect Mr. Gilbert Scott in his successful design for the Town Hall of Hamburg. The statues which originally adorned the façade, 44 in number, were restored in 1860, executed by *P. Puyenbroeck* of Brussels. They represent 31 sovereigns who bore the title of 'Count of Flanders', from Baldwin of the Iron Arm to Charles V., with their consorts.

The **Cathedral of St. Martin*, of the 15th cent. (choir earlier), constructed externally in the purest Gothic style, contains a picture representing the history of the Fall in different sections, erroneously attributed to *J. van Eyck*; it bears the date 1525, and is probably a work of *Peter Pourbus*, or a master of similar character. A flat stone in the choir marks the grave of *Jansenius* (d. 1638), Bishop of Ypern, the founder of a sect named after him and still existing in Holland (p. 293). — Lace is largely manufactured here.

Stat. **Poperinghe**, a town with 10,690 inhab.

At Courtrai the Tournai line quits the flat land and enters an undulating and picturesque district. After 1/2 hr. the train stops at *Mouscron*, the Belgian Douane, a large village with 7308 inhab., of which the railway traveller however sees little. (From Mouscron to Lille and Calais see p. 54).

Beyond Mouscron, between stat. *Nieschheim* (Fr. *Néchin*) and *Templeuve*, the Belgian line quits the province of West Flanders and enters that of *Hainault* (or Hennegau). Flemish is the language of the former, French of the latter. To the l. rises *Mont St. Aubert* (p. 30), 300 ft. in height, also called *Ste. Trinité* from the small church on its summit. It is 4 M. distant from Tournai, and is much visited on account of the fine view which it commands. Near *Tournai* the train crosses the *Schelde*, and finally stops on the handsome quay constructed by Louis XIV.

5. Tournai.

Hotels. Hôtel de l'Impératrice, *Singe d'Or (R. 1, B. 1, A. 1/2 fr.), both in the town. Hôtel de Bellevue, to the l. near the station.

Tournai (31,172 inhab.), Flem. *Doornik*, the most important and prosperous town of Hainault and one of the most ancient in Belgium, was the *Civitas Nerviorum* of Cæsar and the earliest seat of the Merovingian kings. It was, however, entirely modernised under Louis XIV., so that no trace of its venerable age now remains. The extensive new fortifications, constructed by Vauban by order of that monarch, fell to decay at the close of last century, but were extended after the second Treaty of Paris. During a siege in 1581 by Alexander of Parma the defence of the town was conducted by the Princess d'Espinoy, of the noble house of Lalaing, who is said to have combined the most undaunted bravery with all the circumspection of an experienced general. Although wounded in the arm, she refused to quit the ramparts, and did not surrender the fortress until the greater part of the garrison had fallen. A monument in bronze to the memory of this heroic woman, designed by Dutrieux, was erected in the Grand' Place in 1863. She is represented in a complete suit of armour, with a battle-axe in her hand, leading her troops against the enemy.

The *Schelde (Escaut)* divides the town into two nearly equal parts; that on the l. bank, however, is by far the more important and animated. The handsome, broad **Quays**, planted with trees, contribute greatly to render Tournai one of the most pleasing and picturesque towns in Belgium. The river is generally crowded with barges, most of which are laden with coal from the mines of Mons, and are bound for Ghent and other important places on the river.

Above the houses of the l. bank rises the imposing ***Cathedral** *(Notre Dame)*, with its five towers, one of the grandest existing examples of the Romanesque style. The nave dates from the middle of the 11th, the transept from the 12th, and the choir from the 13th cent. The latter is a noble specimen of the pointed style, resembling the choir of the cathedral of Cologne. The W. Portal is in the later Gothic style. Each aisle consists of two vaulted passages, one above the other. The interior was purged in 1852 of all the unsuitable additions by which it was disfigured in the course of centuries, and is now peculiarly striking and impressive. The church contains but few pictures. In the first chapel of the S. aisle, on the posterior wall, a Crucifixion by *Jordaens*; in the transept a Holy Family with a glory of angels, painted by *M. de Negre* in 1650; on the S. wall of the choir, Christ restoring the blind to sight, by *Gallait*, 1833, this master's first important work; on a pillar on the N. side of the choir, opposite the l. side of the high altar, a picture by *Rubens*, Rescue of souls from Purgatory, a bold composition, a female figure in the lower part of the picture particularly beautiful.

Most of the stained glass windows are believed to be by *Stuerbout*. To the l. of the high altar is the Gothic reliquary of St. Eleutherius, the first Bishop of Tournai (6th cent.), elaborately executed in silver about the year 1200, and adorned with the figures of the 12 Apostles. Opposite to it, r. of the high altar, there is a similar reliquary of the 8th or 9th cent., containing the relics of St. Peter the Martyr. The screen which separates the choir from the nave was erected in 1566; it is surmounted by a large group in bronze by *Lecreux*, representing St. Michael overcoming Satan. The stained glass of the choir by *Capronnier* is modern. One of the windows was presented by the Duke of Brabant.

At the back of the high altar a monument by *Duquesnoy* has been erected to the memory of all the bishops and canons of Tournai. The Sacristy contains a very valuable crucifix in ivory by the same master. The treasury is also worthy of inspection (sacristan $^1/_2$ fr.).

***St. Quentin,** near the cathedral, in the spacious Grand' Place, is a remarkably elegant structure, justly termed '*la petite cathédrale*' by the townspeople. It is especially interesting to architects as a perfect example of the transition style. The stained glass is by *Béthune* (1858).

St. Jacques is another similar structure. The pulpit represents a huge trunk of oak, around which vines are clinging, with a grotto opening at the side. The lateral altar on the l. is adorned with a copy of Rubens' picture of Souls rescued from Purgatory in the cathedral.

The handsome **Belfry** (comp. p. 34), adjoining the cathedral, erected in 1190, was restored in 1852.

Pursuing his route and ascending to the r., the traveller passes a *Concert Hall* supported by columns, and reaches the gate of the former *Monastery of St. Martin.* The buildings of the priory above serve as an **Hôtel de Ville,** the tympanum of which contains the arms of the town, a tower with three lilies, surmounted by the Belgian lion. The small picture-gallery contains a few good works, e. g. The dead bodies of the Counts Egmont and Horn (p. 77) by *Gallait* (a native of Tournai).

St. Brice, a church of the 12th cent., on the r. bank of the Schelde, contains the remains of Childeric (d. 480), king of the Franks. A number of interesting curiosities, now preserved in the Imperial Library at Paris, were found in a coffin here in 1655; among them were upwards of 300 small figures in gold, resembling bees, with which the royal robes are said to have been decorated. Napoleon, on the occasion of his coronation, preferred them to the fleurs de lys as insignia of the imperial dignity. These relics were the property of Archduke Leopold William (d. 1662), stadtholder of the Netherlands. After his death they were presented by Emp. Leopold I. to the Elector of Mayence, who in 1664 sent them as a gift to Louis XIV.

Stockings and carpets are the staple commodities manufactured at Tournai. The latter are generally known as Brussels carpets. The art of weaving carpets is said to have been brought to Europe by Flemings, who learned it from the Saracens at the time of the Crusades. The *Manufacture Royale*, the principal manufactory at Tournai, although it has lost much of its original importance, still employs about 2400 hands. Most of the carpets are made by the work-people in their own dwellings. There are but few large factories in the town, in consequence of which it presents a much cleaner and pleasanter appearance than the other large industrial towns of Belgium.

Mont St. Aubert (p. 27), although only 300 ft. in height, commands a very extensive panorama, being the only eminence in the entire district, and is well worthy of a visit. The summit is about 4 M. distant. Carriage in $^3/_4$ h. (3—4 fr.). A voiturier lives near the Belfry.

6. From Bruges to Ghent.

There are two railways between Bruges and Ghent, the *Chemin de Fer de l'Etat*, and the *Waesland Line*, the property of a private company. The trains of the former run between the two cities in $^3/_4$—1 hr. (fares 3 fr. 50, 2 fr. 70, 1 fr. 80 c.), those of the latter in 65—95 min. (fares 3 fr. 5, 2 fr. 35, 1 fr. 45 c.). The district traversed by both lines is equally uninteresting.

Ghent, Fr. *Gand*.

Hotels. *Hôtel de Vienne, in the Marché aux Grains, R. 2, L. $^3/_4$, F. $1^1/_4$, D. $2^1/_2$, A. $^3/_4$ fr.; *Hôtel Royal, in the Place d'Armes; Armes de Zélande, R. 1, B. 1 fr.; Comte Egmont; Hôtel de Courtrai and Duc de Wellington, both in the Rue aux Draps.

Café des Arcades, an elegant establishment in the Place d'Armes; Café du Théâtre, by the theatre; Café Royal, E. side of the Palais de Justice; Café des Etrangers, Rue du Marché aux Oiseaux; Cour Royale, Rue de la Station 3.

Vigilantes per drive 1 fr.; first hour $1^1/_2$, each following hour 1 fr. It should be observed that the station of the Waesland Railway (p. 50) is nearly 1 M. from that of the Government Line.

Theatre, adjoining the Place d'Armes, handsomely fitted up. Boxes and stalls (comp. p. 57) 4, parquet $2^1/_2$, pit 1 fr. Performances in winter only, 4 times weekly. Opera generally good. Flemish pieces are performed in the new Theatre Minard, Rue St. Pierre.

Station d'Ecloo
Boulevard
Grand Bassin
Promenade du Dok
Canal de Bruges
Canal de la Coupure
Boulevard de la Biloke
Boulevard
Maison
Ecole de Natation
Hôtels:
a H. de Vienne C.3.
b H. Royal D.4.
c H. aux Armes de Zélande
d H. Comte Egmont D.3.
e H. de Courtrai C.4.
f H. de Willington C.4.
Cafés:
g des Arcades D.3.
h Royal D.4.
A
B
C
D
1
2
3
4
5
6
stadt. Ed. Wagner

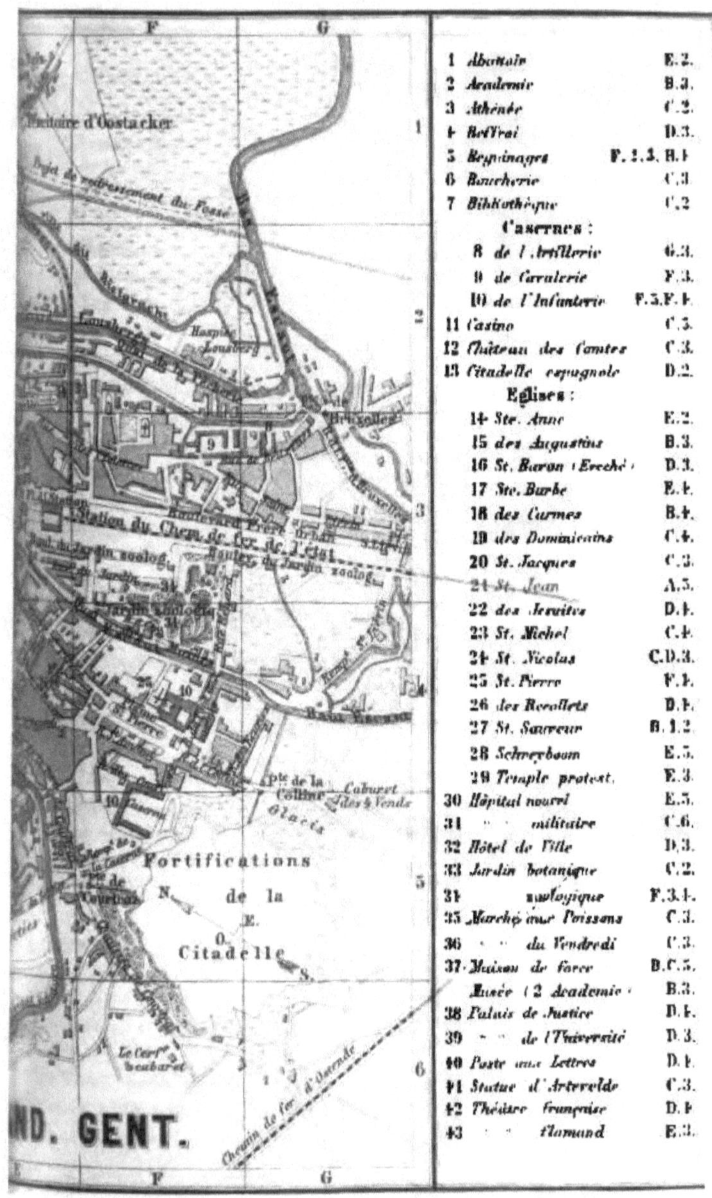

F
G
Cimetière d'Oostacker
Projet de redressement du Fossé
Station du Chemin de fer de l'État
Jardin zoolog.
Fortifications
de la
Citadelle
Pl. de la Colline
Glacis
Chemin de fer d'Ostende
ND. GENT.
1 Abattoir E.2.
2 Academie B.3.
3 Athénée C.2.
4 Beffroi D.3.
5 Béguinages F.2.3. B.4
6 Boucherie C.3
7 Bibliothèque C.2
Casernes :
8 de l'Artillerie G.3.
9 de Cavalerie F.3.
10 de l'Infanterie F.5.F.4.
11 Casino C.5.
12 Château des Comtes C.3.
13 Citadelle espagnole D.2.
Églises :
14 Ste. Anne E.2.
15 des Augustins B.3.
16 St. Baron (Evêché) D.3.
17 Ste. Barbe E.4.
18 des Carmes B.4.
19 des Dominicains C.4.
20 St. Jacques C.3.
21 St. Jean A.5.
22 des Jésuites D.4.
23 St. Michel C.4.
24 St. Nicolas C.D.3.
25 St. Pierre F.4.
26 des Recollets D.4.
27 St. Sauveur B.1.2.
28 Schreyboom E.5.
29 Temple protest. E.3.
30 Hôpital nouvel E.5.
31 " " militaire C.6.
32 Hôtel de Ville D.3.
33 Jardin botanique C.2.
34 zoologique F.3.4.
35 Marché aux Poissons C.3.
36 " " du Vendredi C.3.
37 Maison de force B.C.5.
Musée (2 Academie) B.3.
38 Palais de Justice D.4.
39 " " de l'Université D.3.
40 Poste aux Lettres D.4.
41 Statue d'Artevelde C.3.
42 Théâtre française D.4
43 " " flamand E.3.

Flowers and *exotics* of great beauty at the nursery-garden of Vanhoutte, at Gentbrügge, outside the town (adm. 1 fr.); also at that of Verschaffelt, Rue du Chaume.

English Church in the Rue Digue de Brabant.

Principal attractions: Cathedral (p. 36), St. Michael (p. 40), Hôtel de Ville, exterior only (p. 35), Béguinage (p. 45), view from the Belfry (p. 34) or from the tower of the cathedral (p. 36).

Ghent, the principal manufacturing town of Belgium, with 16,960 houses and 121,255 inhab., is situated on the *Schelde* and the *Ley (Lys)*, the numerous ramifications of which intersect the city in all directions. At the beginning of the 13th cent., when the County of Artois was united to France, Ghent became the capital of Flanders and the usual residence of the Counts. At a very early period a spirit of independence developed itself among the inhabitants, more especially the weavers; and they succeeded in obtaining from their sovereigns those concessions which form the foundation of constitutional liberty. At one period the citizens had become so powerful and warlike that they succeeded in repulsing an English army of 24,000 men, under Edward I. (1297), and a few years later they were the principal combatants in the 'Battle of Spurs' (p. 26), to the issue of which their bravery mainly contributed. Their subjection to the Counts of Flanders and the Dukes of Burgundy appears to have been little more than nominal; for, whenever these princes attempted to levy a tax which was unpopular with the citizens, the latter sounded their alarm-bell, flew to arms, and expelled the obnoxious officials who were ordered to exact payment. On these occasions the citizens, who were always provided with arms, wore white bandages on their arms, or white caps, as a species of revolutionary badge. During the 13th, 14th and 15th cent. revolutions seem almost to have been the order of the day at Ghent. Matters, however, sometimes reached such a climax, that their princes collected their armies and marched against the city. The burghers, brave, but undisciplined, were soon compelled to succumb, and the day of retribution and humiliation had arrived. Enormous contributions were then extorted, the most valuable privileges of the city suspended or cancelled, and the corporation and principal citizens compelled to walk out at the gate with halters round their necks, and to kiss the dust before the feet of their master and conqueror. The turbulent spirit of the Ghenters ultimately proved their ruin. Their wealth and liberty had rendered them so presumptuous that they at last openly declared war against their sovereign, Philip the Good of Burgundy; and the best proof of the vastness of their resources is that they succeeded in carrying on the war for a period of five years (1448—53). They were at length compelled to yield; and heavy fines, a thorough humiliation, and a complete stagnation of all commerce were the disastrous consequences of the war.

In the year 1400 Ghent is said to have boasted of 80,000 men capable of bearing arms; the weavers alone, 40,000 in number, could furnish 18,000 fighting men from their guild. A bell was rung several times daily to summon the weavers to their work and their meals; and, as long as it continued to ring, no vessels were permitted to pass the drawbridges, and no one ventured into the streets lest they should encounter the vast living stream which was hurrying in every direction. The same peal is rung to this day, but the times have changed in all other respects.

Ghent was the principal sphere of the labours of the illustrious masters Hubert and John van Eyck, who inaugurated a new epoch in the history of painting. Their native place was probably Eyck (now Alden-Eyck), near Maas-Eyck, where Hubert was born about the year 1366. John, the younger brother by many years, was born about 1390, probably of a different mother. The brothers became members of the corporation of painters at Ghent in 1421. Hubert, about whose private history little is known, died in 1426. John held the offices of court-painter and chamberlain to Jean Sans-Pitié, Duke of Burgundy, and to his successor Philip le Bon. The latter even employed him on diplomatic missions. In 1428 the painter accompanied the Duke's embassy to Portugal, to solicit the hand of the Princess Isabella, daughter of John I., for his master. Whilst at Lisbon he painted a portrait of the princess, and afterwards made a short tour in Spain. In 1429 he returned home, and received the sum of 80 francs for the portrait and 'sundry secret services' rendered to the Duke. When Hubert died at Ghent, his brother John was a resident at Bruges, where he purchased a house in 1431. The date of his marriage is unknown, but it is recorded that a daughter was born to him in 1434, to whom Philip le Bon stood godfather. John died at his house in Bruges on July 9th, 1440, and was buried in the ancient Church of St. Donatianus. Of Lambert and Margaret van Eyck, a younger brother and sister of Hubert and John, nothing certain is known. Margaret, who died in 1430, is said to have displayed great talent as a painter, and to have been enthusiastically devoted to her art.

The works of the Van Eyck's, although not entirely free from the Gothic rigidity of outline and unscientific treatment of atmosphere which characterise the pictures of their age, are far in advance of those of their contemporaries, and even of the most distinguished of their followers. Their pictures will be most justly appreciated if the parts, which are generally elaborate and almost perfect studies from nature, be examined separately. The uniform and consistent care with which they are executed forms one of their chief merits.

The Van Eyck's are commonly termed the "inventors of oil-painting", but this is not strictly an accurate expression. They were rather the discoverers of a new colouring-medium, which was in fact "varnish-painting". Long before the period of the Van Eyck's, painting in oils was practised in Germany and Italy; but, as most of the works prior to that time were painted in distemper, the term "oil-painting" was thought sufficiently accurate to mark the introduction of an epoch, when, in consequence of the advantages presented by the new method, painting in oils became more universal. Vasari, the great Italian historian of art, who explains this matter very minutely, distinctly states that the secret consisted in the discovery that linseed and nut-oils were the most siccative, and that, when boiled with other mixtures, they produced an excellent *varnish*, that grand desideratum of all painters. Vasari also relates how the new method was carried to Italy by Antonello da Messina, who travelled to Bruges on purpose to learn the secret. Having thoroughly mastered the process, he returned to Italy, and communicated the method to Domenico Veneziano at Venice. The latter is said to have been afterwards murdered at Florence by Andrea del Castagno, one of the initiated few, in order to prevent him from communicating his knowledge to others.

At Ghent the nuptials of the Archduke Maximilian with Mary of Burgundy, the heiress of Charles the Bold, who by her marriage brought the wealthy Netherlands into the power of Austria, were celebrated in 1477. Here, too, on Feb. 24th, 1500, the Emp. Charles V. was born in the Cour des Princes, a palace of the Counts of Flanders long since destroyed, but the name of which survives in a street near the Bruges Gate. During his reign Ghent was one of the largest and wealthiest cities in Europe, and consisted of 35,000 houses with a population of 175,000. Charles V. is said to have boasted jestingly to Francis I. of France: *"Je mettrai votre Paris dans mon Gand"*. The turbulent spirit of the citizens having again manifested itself in various ebullitions, the emperor caused a Citadel *(Het Spanjaerds Kasteel)* to be erected near the Antwerp Gate in 1540, for the purpose of keeping them in check. No trace of the structure now remains. Counts Egmont and Horn were imprisoned in this castle in 1568 for several months before their execution. Within its precincts lay the ancient Abbey of St. Bavon, of which Eginhard, the secretary and son-in-law of Charlemagne, is said once to have been abbot. The ruins of the Chapel of St. Macaire, which was connected with the abbey, and dates from the 12th cent., are interesting to architects. The moats of the old citadel have recently been filled up, and the remains of the ramparts removed in order to make room for new streets.

The city now presents a striking combination of commercial bustle and modern comfort, with many quaint mediæval peculiarities. In the Place d'Artevelde, near the station, rises the *Church of Ste. Anne*, erected by M. Roeland in the Byzantine style. The frescoes with which the interior is in process of being adorned, are by *Canned*.

The ***Belfry** (*Belfrood*, or *Beffroi*, Pl. 4), a lofty square tower, two thirds only of the projected height, rises nearly in the centre of the city. It commands a fine panorama of Ghent, the great extent of which (8 M. in circumference) the spectator here completely surveys. According to a note written upon the original design, which is preserved in the city archives, the construction was commenced in 1183, but archæologists believe the foundation not to have been laid till a century later. In 1339 the works were suspended. Etymologists differ as to the origin of the word "belfrood" or belfry, but the most probable derivation is from *bell* (Dutch *bellan*, to sound, to ring) and *frood* or *fried* (jurisdiction). One of the first privileges usually obtained by burghers from their feudal lords was permission to erect one of these watch or bell-towers, peals from which were rung on all important occasions, to summon the people to council or to arms. According to the modern inscription, the belfry is the "*gedenkteeken der gemeente vryheden van Gent*" (token of the common liberties of Ghent).

The concierge, who demands 2 fr. for accompanying visitors to the top of the tower, lives in the vicinity, but is not always to be found. The total height of the tower is 396 ft. The cast iron spire is surmounted by a vane, consisting of a gilded dragon, 10 ft. in length, which was taken by Count Baldwin IX. from the church of St. Sophia at Constantinople in 1204, and presented to the Ghenters. The view embraces a great portion of Flanders, as well as an admirable survey of the city. When the Duke of Alva proposed to the Emp. Charles V. that he should destroy the city which had occasioned him so much annoyance, the monarch is said to have taken him to the top of the belfry, and there to have replied: "*Combien fallait-il de peaux d'Espagne pour faire un Gant de cette grandeur?*" thus repudiating the cruel suggestion of his minister.

The mechanism of the **Chimes** may be examined at the top of the tower. They are played by means of a cylinder, like that in a barrel-organ, the spikes on which set the tongues and hammers of the bells in motion. They may also be played by a musician, who uses an apparatus resembling the keyboard and pedal of an organ. The tower contains 44 bells. A hole in one of them was made by a cannon-ball fired at the belfry by the Austrians from the old citadel in 1789, in order to prevent the citizens from ringing the alarm. The ball did not miss its aim, but failed to effect its purpose; for the tone of the bell continued unimpaired. One of the oldest and heaviest bells, which was recast in 1659, bears the inscription: "*Myn naem is Roeland; als ick klippe dan is't brandt; als ick luyde, is't victorie in Vlaenderland*" (My name is Roland; when I am rung hastily, then there is a fire; when I resound in peals, there is victory in Flanders).

The lower portion of the Belfry serves as a town-prison, termed "**Mammelokker**", a Flemish word applied to the colossal statue over the entrance to the Place of the Hôtel de Ville (representing a woman giving sustenance from her own breast to an old man in chains at her feet), and expressive of the filial act she is performing ("*Charité Romaine*"). The portal and figures belong probably to the 17th cent. A Gothic building adjoining the Belfry, erected in 1325, was formerly the cloth-hall.

The adjacent ***Hotel de Ville** (Pl. 32) possesses two entirely different façades. That to the N., constructed in 1481 in the later florid Gothic (Flamboyant) style, restored in 1829, is perhaps the most richly decorated in Belgium. The E. façade, dating from 1595—1628, is in the Italian Renaissance style, consisting of three different tiers of half-columns, the lowest of which are of the massive Doric order, the next Ionic, and the highest Corinthian. The "Pacification of Ghent", a treaty drawn up by a congress of the Confederates who assembled here in 1576 with a view to expel the Spaniards from the Netherlands, was signed in the throne-room here. There is a tolerable picture in the interior, by *Van Bree*, representing the Prince of Orange inter-

3*

ceding for the oppressed Rom. Catholics, but nothing else worthy of mention.

The **University** (Pl. 39), on the other side of the Belfry (entrance at the back, Rue Longue des Marais), is a very handsome edifice, erected in 1826 by William I., King of Holland. The façade does not show to advantage, the street being too narrow; but the interior is imposing. The Aula is a remarkably fine hall, supported by massive columns of marble, and capable of containing 1700 persons. The entrance-hall is decorated with new frescoes. The *Natural Hist. Museum* is a collection of considerable merit; there are also cabinets of coins, medals and Roman antiquities. Ghent and Liège possess the only universities in Belgium which are supported by government; those of Brussels and Louvain are dependent on their own resources *(universités libres)*. — An *Ecole du Génie Civil* and an *Ecole des Arts et Manufactures* are connected with the university. The annual number of students is about 420.

The ***Cathedral** of *St. Bavon*, or *Sint Baefs* (Pl. 16), is a cumbrous and unattractive Gothic structure externally, but the interior is one of the most richly decorated in Belgium. The crypt was founded in 951, the choir and chapels were re-constructed in 1228, and the whole completed about the middle of the 16th cent., soon after which, however, it suffered severely from puritanical outrages. The walls of the choir are partially covered with black marble, the balustrades are of white or variegated marble, and the chapel-gates of bronze. High up in the nave are the names and armorial bearings of Knights of the Golden Fleece. The last (23rd) meeting of the Order was held in this church by Philip II. in 1559.

The Statue of St. Bavon, in his ducal robes, resting on clouds, by *Verbrüggen*, adorns the high altar. The walls of the choir are decorated with scenes from the New and Old Testament, in grisaille, by *Van Yeschoot*. The four massive copper Candlesticks, bearing the English arms, are believed once to have adorned St. Paul's in London, and to have been sold during the Protectorate of Cromwell. On each side of the choir, near the altar, are four handsome Monuments to bishops, large sculptured groups of the two last centuries. The best is that of Bishop *Triest*, by *Duquesnoy* (d. 1654), the first to the l. The

Pulpit, by *Delvaux* (d. 1778), half in oak, half in marble, represents the Tree of Life, with an allegory of Time and Truth.

The 24 Chapels of the aisles and choir contain pictures which are here enumerated in order from the W. entrance. Nos. 1, 6, 7, 9 and 10 of the choir-chapels contain admirable works, worthy of the most careful examination; that in the 6th is of European celebrity. Most of them being covered, the visitor should at once secure the services of the sacristan (fee 1 fr.; for each additional pers. $^1/_2$ fr.).

S. Aisle. 1st Chapel: **De Crayer*, Beheading of John the Baptist. 2nd: *Paelink*, St. Coletta receiving permission from the magistrates to found a convent. 3rd, behind the pulpit: **De Cauwer*, Baptism of Christ.

*Choir. 1st Chapel: **Pourbus*, Christ among the doctors, most of the heads are portraits, l. near the frame Alva, Chales V., Philip II. and the master himself; on the inner wings the Baptism and Circumcision, on the outer the Saviour and the donor of the picture. 2nd: *De Crayer*, Martyrdom of St. Barbara. (Opposite to it, a fine modern monument in marble, to the brothers Goethals, by *Parmentier*.) 3rd: * *Van der Meire* (a pupil of Van Eyck), Christ between the malefactors, a winged picture, opposite the altar. 4th: *Van den Heuvel*, The Adulteress. 5th: Nothing worthy of note. 6th: ** *John* and *Hubert van Eyck*, Adoration of the Immaculate Lamb, painted for Philip the Good in 1420—32.

This magnificent work originally consisted of 12 sections; i. e., the portions still preserved in this cathedral were each capable of being covered by two pairs of wings, or folding shutters, as shown by the following plan.

Wings Open.

1 Br.	2 B.	Mary G.	God the Father G.	John the Bapt. G.	3 B.	4 Br.
5 B.	6 B.		Adoration of the Lamb Ghent		7 B.	8 B.

Wings Closed.

9	10	11	12
13 B.	14 Br.	15 Br.	16 B.
17 B.	18 B.	19 B.	20 B.

1. Adam (now at Brussels); 2. Singing Angels (at Berlin); 3. St. Cecilia; 4. Eve; 5. The Just Judges; 6. The Champions of Christ; 7. Hermit Saints; 8. Pilgrim Saints; 9. Micah; 10., 11. Sibyls; 12. Zachariah; 13.–16. The Annunciation: 17. Jodocus Vyts, the donor; 18. John the Baptist; 19. St. John the Evangelist; 20. Lisbeth Vyts, wife of the donor.)

The picture was carried off by the French to Paris, where six of the wings (marked B.) fell into the hands of a dealer, who sold them to an Englishman for 100,000 fr. They were subsequently purchased for 410,000 fr. for the of Museum of Berlin, of which they still constitute one of the greatest treasures. Nos. 1. and 4., being deemed unsuitable for the public eye, were sold by the Ghenters for 50,000 fr., and are now at Brussels. Four only, therefore, now remain at Ghent: God the Father, the Virgin Mary and John the Baptist above, and below them the Adoration of the Lamb, whence the whole work derives its name. The three upper figures on gold ground are somewhat stiff, but this defect is compensated for by the great beauty and richness of the colouring. Whilst these figures present the hard and monumental characteristics of mediæval painting, the picture below possesses all the ease and life peculiar to the School of Van Eyck. The Lamb on the altar forms the centre of the picture, in front of which is the mystic fountain of the Apocalypse. Four great multitudes approach to worship the Lamb; above, in the background, are the holy martyrs, in front the spiritual and temporal orders. There is a considerable degree of sameness in the dense throng of heads, but the eye occasionally rests with pleasure on figures which possess more marked characteristics. The landscape will of course bear no comparison with more modern works, but the colouring is fresh and clear. The towers of the heavenly Jerusalem are discerned between the mountains which bound the horizon. — This celebrated picture, which unites so much of the ease and charm of real life with the most profound earnestness, has not inappropriately been compared to the great work of Dante.

Copies of the six wings at Berlin, by M. Coxcie, were presented to the church by the government, at whose instance Nos. 1. and 4. (Adam and Eve) were purchased in 1861 for the Brussels Museum.

7th Chapel: **Honthorst*, Descent from the Cross; at the side, **De Crayer*, Crucifixion. 8th: On the l. the monument of Bishop *Van der Noot* (d. 1730), who is represented as mourning for the scourging of Christ. On the r. the monument of another bishop of the same name (d. 1770), represented kneeling before the Virgin. The altar-piece, representing the so-called Betrothal of St. Catherine with the Infant Jesus, and the Virgin with the holy women are both by *Roose*, surnamed *Liemackere*. 9th: **Rubens*, St. Bavo renounces his military career, in order to become a monk. The figure of the saint is said to represent the master himself in the upper part of the picture, where he is received on the steps of the church by a priest, after having distributed all his property among the poor. To the l. are the two wives of Rubens, both in the costume of that period; one of them appears to be disengaging a chain from her neck, as if she would follow the example of the saint. Opposite to this picture: * *Venius*, Raising of Lazarus, near which is the monument of Bishop *Damant* (d. 1609). 11th: *Zegers*, Martyrdom of St. Livinus, the tutelary saint of Ghent. *Paqué*, Death of St. Rochus, modern. 12th: Martyrdom of St. Catherine, after a *Rubens* in the Church of St. Catherine at Lille. Opposite to this chapel is the monument of Bishop *Van Eersel* (d. 1778). 13th: Nothing worthy of notice. 14th: *M. Coxcie*, The seven Works of Mercy.

The N. Transept contains the font in which Charles V. was baptized in 1500.

N. Aisle. 4th Chapel: *De Crayer*, Assumption. A marble slab opposite records the names of the priests who refused to acknowledge Bishop Lebrun, appointed by Napoleon in 1813. 3rd: **De Crayer*, St. Macharius praying for those attacked by the plague. 2nd: *Van Huffel*, St. Lambertus bringing charcoal in his chorister's robe in order to ignite the incense. 1st: **Rombouts*, Descent from the Cross; *Janssens*, Pietà.

The Crypt beneath the choir also contains 15 chapels, an arrangement very prevalent in large churches down to the 13th cent., and intended as a reminiscence of the early period of Christianity, when the faithful assembled in the catacombs at the tombs of the martyrs. On certain days mass was celebrated here at night, or at a very early hour in the morning, but the custom has long been abandoned. This crypt is said to have been consecrated as early as 941, but many of the stunted pillars certainly do not appear older than the upper part of the building which they support. Hubert van Eyck and his sister Margaret are said to be buried here.

The *Tower* (446 steps) affords a fine prospect similar to that from the Belfry (fee 2 fr. for 1—4 pers.).

The **Episcopal Palace** is a modern building on the E. side of the church.

The ***Church of St. Nicholas** (Pl. 24), although added to and altered in 1582 and 1623, is still a fine and interesting example of the earliest Gothic style. It is situated in the *Marché aux Grains*, or corn-market, the busiest part of Ghent. The ten turrets on the lower tower have given rise to the bon mot: "*L'église a onze tours et dix sans* (same pronunciation as *cents*) *cloches*". Many old treasures of art disappeared from the church during the religious wars and the barbarous excesses of the iconoclasts, but have been partially replaced by modern works, the best of which are here enumerated: *De Cauwer*, Descent from the Cross, high up to the r. of the principal portal; 2nd Chapel on the S.: **Maes*, Madonna and Child with St. John; 4th: *Quellin*, Crucifixion. Choir, 2nd Chapel: *Roose*, The good Samaritan; 4th: *Janssens*, St. Jerome. High altar-piece by **Roose*, Call of St. Nicholas to the episcopal office, this master's best work. N. Aisle, 3rd Chapel: *Steyaert*, Preaching of St. Antony. An inscription under a small picture on an opposite pillar in the nave records that *Olivier Minjau* and his wife are buried here, "*ende hadden tesamen een en dertich kinderen*" (i. e., they had together one and thirty children). When Emp. Charles V. entered Ghent, the father with twenty-one sons who had joined the procession, attracted his attention. Shortly afterwards, however, the whole family was carried off by the plague. The stained glass in the windows of the choir are by *Capronnier* and *Laroche*, 1851.

On the quay *(Graslei)* behind the W. side of the Corn Market there are several interesting old buildings. The handsome *Skipper House* (No. 29) was erected in 1531 by the Guild of the Skippers.

***St. Michael's Church** (Pl. 23), a handsome Gothic edifice begun in 1445 (nave completed 1480, tower unfinished), was employed in 1791 as a "Temple of Reason", and lost most of its treasures of art at that period. These have been replaced by a number of large modern pictures which should not be overlooked.

S. Aisle. 3rd Chapel: Model of the tower as originally designed. *Van Bockhorst*, Conversion of St. Hubert. 4th: *Van den Heuvel*, Mary bewails the Death of Christ. 5th: *V. d. Heuvel*, Flight into Egypt. — S. Transept. **François*, Ascension; **Lens*, Annunciation, both covered. *Van Oost*, Cure of a sick man by the invocation of the Virgin. — Choir. 1st Chapel: **De Cauwer*, Soul released from Purgatory. 2nd: *Van der Plaetsen*, The Pope exhorting Louis XI. to submit to the will of

God, painted in 1838; **Spagnoletto*, St. Francis. 3rd: **De Crayer*, Assumption of St. Catharine, one of the master's best works. 4th: *Ph. de Champaigne*, Pope Gregory teaching choristers to sing; *Honthorst*, Conversion of St. Hubert. 5th: *Van Mander*, St. Sebastian and S. Carlo Borromeo. 6th, at the back of the high altar: *Van Boekhorst*, Allegory, Moses and Aaron typical of the Old Testament, St. John, St. Sebastian and the Pope of the New. 7th: **Maes* (d. 1856), Holy Family. 8th: *Van Bockhorst*, David's Repentance; *Van den Heuvel*, Martyrdom of St. Barbara. 9th: **Zegers*, Scourging of Christ. 10th: *Th. v. Thulden*, Martyrdom of St. Adrian. 11th: *De Crayer*, Descent of the Holy Ghost. — N. Transept: **Van Dyck's* celebrated Crucifixion, the only picture in Ghent by this master, said to have been painted for the church in 6 weeks for 800 fl. A horseman extends the sponge to the Saviour with his spear; John and the Maries below, weeping angels above. **Paelink*, Finding of the Cross by the Empress Helena; painted at Rome in 1822. — N. Aisle. 4th Chapel: *Venius*, Raising of Lazarus. 2nd: *De Crayer*, St. Bernard, St. Joseph and St. George worshipping the Trinity. 1st: *Van Balen*, Assumption. — *Pulpit by *Frank*, 1846, a master-piece of taste and careful execution. It rests on the trunk of a fig-tree of marble; Christ healing a blind man forms the principal group below.

***St. Pierre** (Pl. 25), which looks down upon the railway-station from the height to the left, is architecturally an edifice of little interest, but possesses a number of valuable pictures. The building was destroyed by the iconoclasts in 1578, but restored in 1720. It was employed as a picture-gallery from 1797 to 1809. The pictures, none of which are covered, are enumerated in order, beginning on the r.; the sacristan's services are therefore unnecessary. 1. **Janssens*, The miraculous Draught of Fishes, a scene which is little more than an accessory to the extensive and pleasing landscape in which it is placed. 2. **Roose*, Nativity of Christ, an effective picture; the shepherds, figures of the old Flemish type, particularly good. 3. *Erasm. Quellin*, Triumph of the Church. 4. **Roose*, St. Francis Xavier, the apostle of the Indians. Above the entrance to the choir on the r., a Scene from the history of St. Livinus, master unknown. On the pillar: Christ crowned with thorns, after *Van Dyck* (original in the Museum at Antwerp). — Choir: *Van den Avond*, Holy Family, with dancing angels; a large landscape with two hermits as accessories, similar to No. 1. At the back of the high altar: * *Zegers*, Christ healing a blind man. The chapel contains five small pictures by *Van Duerselaer*, of the period of the Spanish supremacy, illustrative of the virtues of the miraculous image of the Virgin on the altar. Above the Sacristy: * *Zegers*, Raising of Lazarus. Altar-piece to the l. in the choir: * *De Crayer*, St. Benedict recognising the equerry of the Gothic King Totilas. Crucifixion, after *Rubens* (p. 125). *Van den Heuvel*, Distribution of the rosary. * *Janssens*, Liberation of Peter. — N. Aisle: *Th. van Thulden*, Triumph of the Cath. Church; *Van Thulden*, Time raises up Truth; Luther, Calvin, Wickliffe and Huss lie in the dust. *Erasm. Quellin*, St. Francis Xavier preaching. * *Ryschot*, Landscape, the healing of a blind man as accessory. — Isabella, sister of Charles V., and consort of Christian II. of Denmark, reposes in this church, but no monument marks the spot.

The open space in front of the church has been formed by the demolition of part of the old abbey-buildings. Another part serves as a barrack.

The **New Citadel**, which adjoins the church, commenced in 1822, completed in 1830, and surrendered to the Belgian insurgents the same year, belongs to a chain of fortresses constructed during the Dutch regime to protect the Belgian frontier. It commands the course of the Schelde and the Ley, and together with the church is situated on the Blandinusberg, the only eminence in the entire district.

To the l. at the extremity of the Rue Basse, and bounded on two sides by the Ley, is situated the **Palais de Justice** (Pl. 38), an imposing edifice by *Roelandt*, completed in 1844, with a peristyle of the Corinthian order. A broad staircase leads from the E. entrance to the "*Salle des Pas Perdus*" (240 ft. long, 72 ft. high), a hall from which the different courts and offices are entered. Opposite to the Palais is the **Theatre** (Pl. 42), by the same architect. The effect of the fine façade is unfortunately impaired by the narrowness of the street. It also contains a handsome ball-room.

The Rue des Champs (*Veldstraet*) forms a prolongation of the Rue Basse. At No. 53, the property of Count d'Hane de Steehuyse, Louis XVIII. spent the greater part of the "Hundred Days" (March, April, May) in 1815. The following are the chief objects of interest in the streets leading by the corn and vegetable markets to the Academy:

To the l. in the Marché aux Herbes *(Groenselmarkt)* rises the extensive **Grande Boucherie** (Flem. *Groot Vleeschhuis*, Pl. 10), erected at the end of the 14th cent. The lion with the flag-staff on the gable was placed there by the Guild of Butchers, the descendants of Charles V. and the pretty daughter of a butcher, who secured for her son and his descendants the sole right of slaughtering and selling meat in the city. The son of the emperor had four sons, who were the ancestors of all the members of the guild down to 1794. An interesting mural painting in oil, of the 15th cent., was discovered in 1855 in the old chapel of the building.

Crossing the Place de Pharailde, the traveller reaches a gateway in the corner to the l., erected in 1689 in the Rococo style by the sculptor *Arthus Quellyn*, and leading to the **Marché aux Poissons** (Pl. 35). The gateway is surmounted by a statue of Neptune ("*Neptuno Ganda tropaeum*"); r. and l. are the river-gods of the Schelde and the Ley, with the inscriptions:

"Hannoniae servit Scaldis, Gandamque secando,
In mare festinans volvere pergit aquas."
"Lysa vehit merces quas nunc Artesia mittit
Et placido gaudens flumine pisce scatet."

The **Oudeburg** (*Gravenkasteel, Gravensteen, Château des Comtes;* Pl. 12), a massive old castellated-looking gateway, with loop-holes, rises among modern houses in the same place, at the corner of the street. It is a remnant of the ancient palace of the Counts of Flanders, where Edward III. with his Queen Philippa were sumptuously entertained by Jacques van Artevelde in 1339, and where their son John of Gaunt (i. e. Gand or Ghent) was born in 1340. Here, too, the beautiful Jacqueline, Countess of Holland (see below) was kept a prisoner for three months by Philip the Good of Burgundy in 1424. The palace was built in 868, but the gateway not before 1180. The latter, now the entrance to a cotton-factory, is one of the oldest structures in Belgium. A subterranean passage, $2^1/_2$ M. in length, leading to a point outside the city, and probably employed for admitting soldiers to the palace in case of an emergency, has recently been discovered here.

Jacqueline of Bavaria, Countess of Holland, born in 1400, was the only daughter of William VI., Duke of Bavaria and Count of Holland. In 1415 she married Jean, Duke of Touraine, became a widow in 1417, and succeeded to the estates of her father the same year. She then married John, Duke of Brabant, who was persuaded by her ambitious uncle Jean sans Pitié, Bishop of Liège, to cede here states to him for 12 years. This occasioned a revolt in Holland, and Jacqueline now urged her husband to avail himself of the opportunity to recover the estates. The Duke declining, Jacqueline resolved to desert him, and fled to England, applying at the same time to the Pope for a divorce. Without waiting for an answer from the court of Rome, she married the Duke of Gloucester, who was captivated by her beauty and touched by her distress. She now persuaded him to accompany her with an army into the Low Countries in order to recover possession of her estates. Philip le Bon, Jacqueline's cousin and heir to her estates, vigorously opposed the invaders, and Gloucester was compelled to fly, but Jacqueline was captured and imprisoned at Ghent. She now vainly endeavoured to effect a reconciliation with her former husband, the Duke of Brabant. Soon after this failure, however, she succeeded in escaping from prison by bribing the guards, and repaired to the Hague. Her ambitious uncle being now dead, she again became mistress of Holland. Her severity, however, occasioned a revolt, of which Philip took advantage, and compelled her to recognise him as governor of her dominions. Meanwhile the Duke of Brabant had also died, and Jacqueline's marriage with the Duke of Gloucester had been declared null. She was therefore again free, and resolved to marry François de Borselen, a simple chevalier and one of her subjects. The Duke of Burgundy, being apprised of this, caused Borselen to be arrested and condemned to death. Jacqueline, however, saved his life by entirely ceding her estates to Philip. She then married Borselen in 1433, and retired to the castle of Teilingen on the banks of the Rhine, where she died in 1436, after a brief and romantic, but not altogether unblemished career.

The **Academy** of Art (Pl. 2), with 700 students, established in the old monastery of the Augustines, adjoining the insignificant Augustine Church, contains a collection (**Musée**) of about 140 pictures, most of the older of which are from the monasteries of Ghent which were dissolved in 1795. Visitors are admitted at any hour (fee ½ fr.). There are no works of pre-eminent merit, but the collection should on no account be overlooked. To the r. and l. of the entrance: 10. *De Crayer*, Francis I. of France presenting his sword to the Chevalier Lannoy after the Battle of Pavia (1525); 11. Emp. Charles V. landing in Africa on his expedition against Tunis. These large pictures, of which boldness of outline is almost the sole merit, afford a good insight into the luxury of festivities of the 16th cent. To the l., farther on: 12. *Van Volxum*, Processions in the Marché de Vendredi on Oct.

18th, 1717, on the occasion of the reception of Emp. Charles VI. as Count of Flanders. *3. *Adrian of Utrecht*, Fish-dealer. 9. *Jordaens*, Portrait of St. Ambrose. *5. *Rubens*, St. Francis receiving the Stigmata, similar to the picture in the Cathedral of Cologne. *16. *De Crayer*, Coronation of St. Rosalia. 4. *De Crayer*, Tobias with the Archangel Raphael. 8. *Van Helmont*, Christ on the Cross. On the posterior wall: 24. *Jordaens*, Christ and the Adulteress. 74. *Rombouts*, Themis sitting in judgment, a picture with numerous figures. *25. *Jordaens*, Reconciliation (Matth. V., 23, 24). On the r. side of the saloon: 21. *M. Coxcie*, Last Judgment. 17. *Duchastel*, Processions in the Marché de Vendredi, at the reception of Charles II. of Spain as Count of Flanders (1666). 6. *De Crayer*, Solomon's Judgment. 18. *Verhagen*, Presentation in the Temple. 73. *Hanselaer*, Copy of Rubens' picture at Alost (p. 51). — In the central apartment: *31. *Pourbus*, Isaiah announcing to Hezekiah his recovery, with the miracle of the sun going ten degrees backward. On the wings a Crucifixion, and the donor, the Abbot del Rio. — The last saloon contains modern pictures, many of them mediocre, the greater number painted about the beginning of the present century. The following are perhaps most deserving of notice: 1., 133. *Paelink*, Saul; 92. *Paelink*, Anthea and her companions in the Temple of Diana at Ephesus; 98. *Piqué*, Hebe; 138. *Geirnaert*, Giving a pledge; *150. *De Vigne*, Forest scene; 89. *Hanselaer*, Abel's Offering; **De Keyser*, Slaughter of the Innocents; 145. *Funck*, Tyrolese Landscape; *153. *Wittcamp*, Jailer; 149. *Vennemann*, Children playing; 109. *Gallait*, Jesus and the Pharisees; 146. *Verweer*, Katwyk aan Zee, near Leyden (mouth of the Rhine); 83. *Paelink*, Judgment of Paris; *144. *Verboeckhoven*, Landscape with herd and cattle; 137. *Hanselaer*, St. Sebastian; 118. *Van Maldeghem*, Emp. Charles V. meditating on his lot; 139. *De Noter*, Winter-scene in Ghent.

The extensive ***Béguinage** (Pl. 5) (*Beggynhof*, from *beggen*, to beg; or from *St. Begga;* or from *Le Bègue*, a priest of Liège. The first derivation is believed to be the correct one, although the sisterhood cannot now be classed among the mendicant orders), at the Porte de Bruges, founded in 1234, was one of the few nunneries which the Emp. Joseph II. suffered to escape dissolution. It remained unmolested also during the French Revolution. The objects of this excellent female society are a religious life, works of charity, and self-support. They are subject to certain conventual regulations, and bound to obey their superior *(Groot Jufrouw)*, but are unfettered by any monastic vow. It is, however, a boast of the order that very few of their number avail themselves of their liberty to return to the world. There are at present twenty béguinages in Belgium, with about 1600 members.

The Béguinage of Ghent, the most important in Belgium, forms a little town of itself, with streets, squares and gates, and is enclosed by walls and moats, which are crossed by six bridges. It contains 103 small houses, 18 convents, a large and a small church. The Sisters, about 700 in number, many of them persons of rank and property, attend Vespers daily in the church. The traveller should not omit to be present at one of these services. The scene is very impressive. The Sisters all wear black robes (failles), and a white linen covering on their heads. Novices have a different dress, whilst those who have recently been admitted to the order wear a wreath round their heads. The doors of the houses, in which the Sisters reside, sometimes alone, sometimes several together, are inscribed with the names of their tutelary saints. Lace-making is the principal occupation of the Béguines, beautiful specimens of whose work may be purchased at the magazine, or of the portress, at more reasonable prices than in the town.

The **Maison de Force** (Pl. 37), or *"House of Detention"*, near the Bruges Gate, is a penitentiary of European celebrity. It is in the form of an octagon, with nine courts in the interior, communicating with each other by strong gates. The prison (1200 convicts) constitutes an extensive factory, where the inmates are chiefly employed in manufacturing linen for the use of the army. The lower chambers are destined for prisoners condemned to penal servitude for life. Part of the building is fitted up as a hospital, with a laboratory, bath-room etc. Order and cleanliness are everywhere scrupulously observed, and discipline is rigorously maintained. A portion of the profits of the prisoners' work is set apart for them. If industrious, they may earn 20—30 fr. in a year. In order to prevent the possibility of bribery, zinc tokens are used instead of money within the precincts of the prison. The building, which can accommodate 2600 convicts, was begun under Maria Theresia in 1772, but not completed until 1825.

It was visited by Howard, the English philanthropist, and strongly recommended by him as a model for imitation. In consequence of the trouble formerly occasioned by crowds of visitors, access cannot now be obtained without permission from the Minister of Justice at Brussels. Professional men, however (physicians, judges, professors etc.), are admitted by applying at the Hôtel du Gouvernement at Ghent. — The new *Prison* for solitary confinement, on the new promenade outside the Bruges Gate, containing 368 cells, is also worthy of inspection.

On the r. bank of the Coupure, a canal completed in 1758, connecting the Ley with the great Bruges Canal, is situated the **Casino** (Pl. 11), nearly opposite to the Penitentiary. This handsome building, erected in 1836, is employed for the biennial flower-shows of the Botanical Society (*Maetschappy van Kruidkunde*). Ghent, not without reason surnamed "*La Reine des Fleurs*", has a specialty for horticulture, and annually exports whole cargoes of camellias, azalias, orange-trees and other hothouse plants to Holland, Germany, France, Italy and even Russia. There are 62 nursery-gardeners and upwards of 400 hothouses in the environs of the city.

The visitor should now return into the city and proceed to the **Marché de Vendredi** (*Vrydagmarkt*) (Pl. 36), an extensive square surrounded by antiquated buildings. The most important events in the history of Ghent have taken place here. Homage was here done to the Counts of Flanders on their accession, in a style of magnificence unknown at the present day, after they had sworn: "*all de bestaende wetten, voorregten, vryheden en gewooten van't graefschap en van de stad Gent te onderhouden en te doen onderhouden*" (to maintain and cause to be maintained all the existing laws, privileges, freedoms and customs of the County and of the city of Ghent). Here the members of the mediæval guilds, "*ces têtes dures de Flandre*", as Charles V. termed his countrymen, frequently assembled to avenge some real or imaginary infringement of their rights, and here the standard of revolt was invariably erected. One of the most disastrous civic broils took place here in 1341, when Gerhard Denys at the head of his party, which consisted chiefly of weavers, attacked his opponents the fullers with such fury that even the elevation of the host failed to separate the combatants, of whom upwards of 500 were slain.

Jacques van Artevelde, the celebrated "Brewer of Ghent" (see below), then in power, was afterwards assassinated by Denys. This fatal day was subsequently entered in the civic calendar as "*Kwaede Maendag*" (Wicked Monday). In this square, too, Philip van Artevelde, son of Jacques, received the oath of fidelity from his fellow-citizens (1381), when urged by them to lead them against their sovereign, Count Louis "van Maele".

Jacques van Artevelde, the celebrated "Brewer of Ghent", was a clever and ambitious demagogue, who is said to have caused himself to be enrolled as a member of the Guild of Brewers in order to ingratiate himself with the lower classes, although himself of noble family; but of the latter nothing is known, and it is probable that he was really of humble origin. He was a powerful ally of Edward III. in the war between England and France (1335—45), in which the democratic party of Ghent supported the former, and the Counts of Flanders the latter. It is recorded that Edward condescended to flatter him by the familiar title of "dear gossip". For seven years Artevelde reigned supreme at Ghent, putting to death all who had the misfortune to displease him, banishing all the nobles and those who betrayed any symptom of attachment to their sovereign, and appointing magistrates who were the mere slaves of his will. Artevelde at length proposed that the son of Edward should be elected Count of Flanders, a scheme so distasteful to the Ghenters, that an insurrection broke out, in which Jacques was slain, Aug. 19th, 1345. During this period, in consequence of the alliance with Ghent, the manufacture of wool became more extensively known and practised in England. Ghent also realised vast profits from its trade with England, a circumstance which induced the citizens to submit so long to the despotic rule of Jacques, to whom they were indebted for their advantageous alliance with Edward.

Philip van Artevelde, son of Jacques, and godson of Queen Philippa of England, possessed all the ambition, but little of the talent of his father. When he was appointed dictator by the democratic party in 1381, during the civil war against Count Louis, he accepted the office with a show of the utmost reluctance and diffidence. His administration was at first salutary and judicious, but he soon began to act with all the caprice of a despot. In 1381, when Ghent was reduced to extremities by famine, and the citizens had resolved to surrender, Philip counselled them to make a final venture, rather than submit to the humiliating conditions offered by the Count. He accordingly marched at the head of 5000 men to Bruges, where Louis, who sallied forth to meet them, was signally defeated and himself narrowly escaped capture. Elated beyond measure by this success, Philip now assumed the title of Regent of Flanders, and established himself at Ghent in a style of great pomp and magnificence. His career, however, was brief. In 1383 war again broke out, chiefly owing to the impolitic and arrogant conduct of Philip himself, and Charles VI. of France marched against Flanders. Philip was soon afterwards defeated and slain at the disastrous Battle of Rosselaere or Rumbeke (p. 24), where 20,000 of the bravest Flemings are said to have perished.

During the supremacy of the cruel Duke of Alva, the Marché de Vendredi was the scene of the Auto-da-Fés of the Inquisition, the horrors of which the citizens had in a great measure brought upon themselves by their turbulent and revolutionary dispositions. Thousands of them emigrated at that period, and nearly one-half of the city was left untenanted. A statue of Charles V. stood here till 1796, when it was destroyed by the French sansculottes. In 1863 it was replaced by a **Statue of Jacques van Artevelde*, by Devigne-Quyo. A survey of the principal towers of the city is obtained from the N. side of the market.

In the corner of a street on the W. side of the Marché de Vendredi is placed a huge **Cannon**, termed the "*Dulle Griete*" (Mad Meg), one of the largest in the world, 18 ft. long, and nearly 3 ft. wide at the mouth (resembling "Mons Meg" in the Castle of Edinburgh). Above the touch-hole is the Burgundian Cross of St. Andrew, with the arms of Philip the Good; the piece must therefore have been cast between 1419 and 1467. It is said to have been employed at the siege of Oudenærde in 1452. The arsenals of Bâle and Soleure contain cannons of similar shape, which formed part of the Burgundian booty taken by the Swiss.

At the back of the E. side of the Marché de Vendredi rises the **Church of St. Jacques** (Pl. 20), said to have been founded in 1100. The present edifice dates from the end of the 15th, or beginning of the 16th cent., but the towers are perhaps older. It contains nothing worthy of note except an excellent picture by *Jan Maes*, representing the Departure of the youthful Tobias (probably the best work of the master, who was a native of Ghent), and two pictures of Apostles by *Van Huffel*.

The **Botanical Garden** (*Plantentuin*, Pl. 33), in the immediate vicinity, is reputed one of the finest in Europe. It was first established in 1797, and is commonly known as the *Baudeloohof*. The Victoria Regia is a fine example. The former Baudeloo Monastery contains the *University* and *Town Library* (100,000 vols.; 700 MSS., some of them very rare). The handsome reading-room is open to the public.

The **Kauter** (Flem. *field*), or *Place d'Armes*, is the military esplanade of Ghent, where a band plays on Sunday mornings, when the choicest produce of the numerous hothouses of Ghent and tastefully arranged bouquets may be seen in perfection.

The house occupied by the brothers *John* and *Hubert van Eyck* was on the E. side of the Kauter. They painted their celebrated picture here, and here Hubert died in 1426. The site is now occupied by the Café des Arcades, on which the names of the proprietor and the architect are faithfully recorded; but every reminiscence of these illustrious masters is now obliterated. Kalenderberg, No. 16, immediately to the l., was once the residence of *Jacques van Artevelde*, the great *"Ruwaerd van Vlaendern"* (Dictator of Flanders), whose bust, with a French inscription, was placed here in 1845.

Ghent, like Antwerp and Brussels, also boasts of a **Zoological Garden** (Pl. 34), near the railway-station (admission 1 fr.).

Ghent is connected with the sea by a broad **Canal**, 18 ft. in depth, by means of which vessels of considerable tonnage are enabled to reach the city and unload in the harbour beneath its walls. The canal, which secures to the city all the advantages of a seaport, unites with the Schelde at *Terneuzen*. At *Sas van Ghent* (i. e. "Sluice of Ghent"), about 12 M. to the N., there are sluices by means of which the whole district can be laid under water. — A second canal connects the Ley with the canal between Bruges and Ostende.

Ghent possesses a very beneficial kind of trades-union in the *Conseil des Prud' hommes*, formed of employers and employed elected annually, who adjust all questions between master and workman, prevent infringement of the rights of manufacturers, and grant certificates to artisans at the close of their apprenticeship, without which documents they are not eligible for any situation.

7. From Ghent to Brussels, to Malines, or to Antwerp.

From Ghent to Brussels viâ Alost in $1^1/_4$—2 hrs.; fares 3 fr. 40, 2 fr. 35, 1 fr. 70 c. — This is the direct route; that by Malines (which diverges at stat. Schellebelle, where carriages must sometimes be changed) occupies $^1/_2$ hr. more.

From Ghent to Malines in $1^3/_4$—$2^1/_2$ hrs.; fares 3 fr. 25, 2 fr. 25, 1 fr. 65 c.; no express trains on this part of the line.

From Ghent to Antwerp *(Waesland Railway)* in $1^1/_4$—2 hrs.; fares 4 fr. 50, 3 fr., 2 fr. — This is the direct route. Travellers from Ostende or Bruges should book to Ghent only, where they take a fresh ticket at the Station of the Waesland line, 1 M. from that of the government-railway. The latter line carries passengers round by Malines, $^3/_4$ hr. longer, and fares higher.

The direct Railway to Brussels passes stations *Melle*, *Wetteren* (a large village with 9039 inhab.) and *Schellebelle*, where the line to Malines diverges. Stat. *Lede*, then

Alost, Flem. *Aelst (Maison d'Autriche; Pays Bas; Trois Rois)*, a town with 19,383 inhab., on the *Dendre*, formerly the capital of the Province of Imperial Flanders, and the frontier town of the County in this direction. The *Church of St. Martin*, commenced in a very imposing style, is little more than a mere fragment; two-thirds of the nave, as well as the tower and portal, are entirely wanting. It contains an admirable picture by *Rubens*, said to have been painted in 1631 in one week: The Prayer of St. Rochus for the cessation of the plague. The arrangement of the picture is the same as that of Rubens' work in St. Bavon at Ghent; above, Christ and St. Rochus; below, the effects of the plague. Copy of this picture in the museum at Ghent, see p. 45. Alost carries on a considerable hop-trade. Chimes were invented here, and printing was practised at Alost earlier than in any other town in Belgium. A statue was erected to *Thierry Maertens*, the first Belgian printer, in 1856.

At stat. *Denderleeuw* the train crosses the Dendre. Stat. *Termuth* is a small town in a district of a very Dutch aspect. Hops are extensively cultivated in the neighbourhood. As the train approaches Brussels, it skirts the park and grounds of the royal château of *Laeken* (p. 84). Farther on, immediately to the l. of the line, is the *Mausoleum* of the late Queen of the Belgians (d. 1850), in the form of a small Gothic church. The train crosses the *Senne*, and a few minutes later enters the station of

Brussels, see p. 55.

Ghent to Malines. To stat. *Schellebelle*, see above. Beyond stat. *Audeghem* the train crosses the Dendre. The next important place is stat. **Dendermonde,** Fr. *Termonde (Plat d'Etain; Aigle; Demi-Lune)*, a small fortified town (8160 inhab.) at the confluence of the *Dendre* and *Schelde*. Louis XIV. besieged this place with a considerable army in 1667, but was compelled to retreat, as the besieged by opening certain sluices laid the whole district under water. The Emp. Joseph II. caused the fortifications to be dismantled in 1784, but they were reconstructed in 1822. The old church of *Notre Dame* possesses two good pictures by *Van Dyck*, a Crucifixion, and Adoration of the Shep-

4*

herds; also a work by *De Crayer*, and several ancient fonts. The train stops at several unimportant stations, beyond which the *Senne* and the *Louvain Canal* are crossed.

Malines, see p. 105.

From Ghent to Antwerp. This line traverses the Waesland *(Pays de Waes)*, one of the most populous districts in Europe, and in proportion to its extent one of the most highly cultivated and productive. At the time of the civil wars in Flanders it was a sterile moor, but at the present day every square yard of ground is utilised. The train passes through arable land, pastures, gardens, woods and plantations in rapid succession, whilst comfortable farm-houses and thriving villages are seen at intervals. It is said that the attention usually devoted to a garden or a flower-bed is here given to every field; for the natural soil, being little better than sand, requires to be artificially covered with garden-soil. The agriculture of this tract enjoys a European celebrity, and is worthy of the notice of farmers.

In other respects the country is uninteresting. Stat. **Lokeren** *(Miroir)*, with 17,000 inhab., possesses a church (St. Lawrence) which contains numerous old and modern works of art; extensive bleaching-grounds in the vicinity. Stat. **St. Nicholas** *(Quatre Sceaux)*, with 23,900 inhab., is the busiest and most industrial town in the Waesland. One of the churches contains well executed mural paintings by the eminent Antwerp artists Güffens and Swerts, representing the Seven Sorrows of the Virgin. Stat. *Beveren*, a wealthy village with 6999 inhab., is noted for the lace it produces. *Flamsch-Hoofd*, or *Tête de Flandre*, the tête-de-pont of Antwerp, lies on the l. bank of the Schelde, where a steam ferry-boat awaits the arrival of the train. Napoleon I. considered this a more favourable site than that of Antwerp on the r. bank, and contemplated founding a town here.

During the siege of Antwerp (1832) the Dutch succeeded in cutting the embankment above Tête-de-Flandre, in consequence of which the entire surrounding district, lying considerably below high-water mark, was laid under water to a depth of 4 ft., and remained so for three years. Twelve Dutch gunboats cruised over the fields and canals, cutting off all communication with the city in this direction. The rise and fall of tide covered a vast area with sand; and the once productive soil, becoming saturated with salt-water, was converted into a dreary waste. Those parts from which the water was not thoroughly drained became unhealthy swamps, a disastrous result of the war felt most keenly in the environs of the city, where land was of great value. Enormous sums were expended on the work of restoration; the repair of the embankment alone cost 2 mill. francs. Almost every trace of the calamity is now happily obliterated.

Antwerp, see p. 109.

8. From London to Brussels viâ Calais.

Viâ Dover and Calais Brussels is reached in $10^1/_2$—11 hrs. from London. Sea-passage $1^1/_2$—2 hrs. — Fares: 2 *l.* 10 *s.* 11 *d.* and 1 *l.* 17 *s.* 8 *d.* — Luggage registered at London is not examined till the traveller reaches Brussels.

London to Calais by Gen. Steam Nav. Co.'s steamer 6 times monthly in 10—12 hrs.; actual sea-passage 4—5 hrs. — Fares to Calais: 11 *s.* and 8 *s.* — Passengers' luggage is examined on arriving at Calais. From Calais to Brussels in 5—7 hrs.; fares 23 fr., 17 fr. 25, 11 fr. 40 c. — (From London to Brussels viâ Dover and Ostende 2 *l.* 7 *s.* 10 *d.* and 1 *l.* 14 *s.* 1 *d.*; by Gen. Steam. Nav. Co. 1 *l.* 3 *s.* 8 *d.* and 18 *s.* 10 *d.* — Comp. RR. 1, 6, 7.)

Calais (*Hôtel du Buffet*, at the station, conveniently situated; *Hôtel Dessein* and *Hôtel Meurice* in the town, both of the first class. Hôtels *de Paris*, *de Londres*, *de Flandre* etc., of the second class. Two *English Churches*, one at Calais itself, the other in the Basse Ville), a fortified town with 15,475 inhab., is an unattractive place, where few travellers will make a voluntary stay. The N. side is bounded by the *Bassin à Flot*, the *Fort de l'Echouage* and the *Bassin du Paradis*. To the r. of the latter is situated the suburb of *Courgain*, inhabited exclusively by a fishing and sea-faring community. The *Quai de Marée* affords a pleasant walk. The white cliffs of the English coast are visible in clear weather. The English community of Calais numbers nearly 2000, although comparatively deserted since the days of railways. Many of these residents are manufacturers of lace and merchants.

St. Omer, the first important station, is an uninteresting fortified town with 25,000 inhab.; environs flat and marshy, but not considered unhealthy. The *Cathedral* is a fine structure in the transition style. The English Rom. Catholic Seminary here, at which O'Connell was educated, is now almost deserted. A considerable number of English families reside at St. Omer for purposes of economising and education. English Church and resident chaplain. — Stat. *Hazebrouck* is the junction of this line with the railways N. to Dunkirk, and S. to Amiens and Paris.

Lille, Flem. *Ryssel (Hôtel de l'Europe; Paris; Bellevue; Commerce; Chemin de Fer* etc. — *English Church)*, an important manufacturing town with 131,827 inhab., and surrounded by fortifications, contains little to interest travellers. The staple commodities of the place are thread, calico, lace, beetroot sugar and oil. The *Hôtel de Ville*, formerly a palace of the Dukes of Burgundy, erected 1430, contains a small collection of pictures. The fortifications were planned by the celebrated Vauban, but portions of them have been demolished to make room for the extension of the city, and replaced by more modern works.

Travellers from Lille to Brussels were formerly conveyed either by Douai, Valenciennes and Mons, or by Courtrai and Ghent. The direct route is now by Tournai and Ath (in 2¾ hrs.).

The country between Lille and **Tournai** (p. 27), which is the first Belgian town on the line, presents no attractions. Beyond Tournai the undulating and well-cultivated province of Hainault is traversed. *Mont St. Aubert* (p. 30) long remains conspicuous to the l. Stat. *Leuze*, a small town on the *Dendre*, possesses a large silk-factory. Stat. *Ligne*, a small place whence the princely family of that name derives its title.

Stat. **Ath** *(Cygne; Paon d'Or; Hôtel de Bruxelles; Hôtel de l'Univers)*, on the *Dendre*, formerly a fortress, with 8206 inhab., contains nothing to detain the traveller. The *Hôtel de Ville* was erected in 1600. The church of St. Julian, founded in 1393, was re-erected in 1817 after a conflagration. The *Tour du Burbant*, the most ancient structure in the town, dates from 1150.

Belœil, the celebrated château and estate of the Prince de Ligne, which has been in possession of the family upwards of 500 years, lies about 6 M. to the S. of Ath. The grandfather of the present proprietor, the well-known talented general and statesman, gives a long account in his letters of this estate with its park and gardens. Delille, in his poem "Les Jardins", describes Belœil as "*tout à la fois magnifique et champêtre*". The château contains numerous curiosities of artistic, as well as historical interest; a considerable library, with many rare MSS.; admirable pictures by *Dürer*, *Holbein*, *Van Dyck*, *Velasquez*, *Leonardo da Vinci*, *Michael Angelo*, *Salvator Rosa* and a number of modern artists; relics (fragments of the "True Cross" and the "Crown of Thorns") and numerous gifts presented to members of the family by emperors and kings, from Charles V. to Napoleon I. Access to the château is rarely denied by the noble proprietor.

Stat. *Enghien*, the next important place on the line, a small town with 3000 inhab., possesses a château of the Duc d'Aremberg, with pleasant park and gardens. Stat. *Hal* (Hôtel des Pays Bas), a town situated on the Senne and the canal of Charleroi, with 7813 inhab., is celebrated throughout Belgium as a place of pious resort, on account of the miracle-working image of the Virgin which it possesses in the church of *Notre Dame*, an edifice in the purest Gothic style. The church possesses numerous costly treasures presented by Emp. Maximilian I., Charles V., Pope Julius II., Henry VIII. of England, the Burgundian Dukes and the Spanish governors. The altar is a fine work in alabaster, of the Renaissance style, date 1533. The font, in bronze, was cast in 1446. A monument in black marble with the figure of a sleeping child is sacred to the memory of the son of Louis XI., who died in 1460. Another chapel contains 33 cannon-balls, caught and rendered harmless by the robes of the wonder-working image during a siege of the town. — Several small stations, then *Brussels*.

9. Brussels.

French *Bruxelles*.

Hotels in the *upper* part of the town, near the park; Bellevue, *de Flandre, de l'Europe, de la Grande Bretagne, all in the Place Royale; Hôtel de France, Rue Royale, opposite the middle entrance to the Park. De la Régence and Windsor, both in the Rue de la Régence near the Place Royale. All these hotels are well situated, handsomely fitted up, and somewhat expensive: R. 3—10 fr., D. 4—5, L. 1, A. 1 fr.

In the *lower* part of the town: *Hôtel de Suède, Rue de l'Evêque; *de l'Univers; de l'Empereur; *de Saxe, starting-point of the Waterloo coaches (p. 85), the two latter hotels in the Rue Neuve, leading from the Station du Nord into the town. Hôtel des Etrangers, Rue des Fripiers; de Hollande, an old-fashioned house, Rue de la Putterie; de Brabant, Marché aux Charbons. Charges: R. 2—4, D. 3—4, L. and A. $1^1/_2$—2 fr. — Of the *Second Class:* Hôtel de la Poste, Rue Fossé aux Loups 48; Grand Monarque, Rue des Fripiers 17; Pays-Bas, Rue de l'Hôpital 16; Grand Miroir, Rue de la Montagne 28; Groenendael, Rue de la Putterie; *Hôtel Callo, Rue des Bouchers 27, unpretending; *Hôtel de Vienne, Rue de la Fourche. — In the Quartier Léopold, near the Luxembourg station, Hôtel du Pélican and St. Michel, both of the second class.

Restaurants. *Allard, Rue Fossé aux Loups, near the theatre; Rocher de Cancale in the same street; *Dubost, Rue de la Putterie 23;

Prince of Wales, Rue Villa Hermosa 8; Globe Tavern, Place Royale; London Tavern and Café Riche, Rue de l'Ecuyer; Oxford, Rue Royale; Victoria, Rue des Fripiers; Aigle d'Or, Rue de la Fourche; Café des Boulevards, Place des Nations; *Puth, Rue du Tir 20, Faubourg de Namur; *Liégeois, opposite the Station du Nord: Hôtel de la Monnaie, opposite the theatre.

Cafés. Mille Colonnes, Suisse and Trois Suisses, all in the Place de la Monnaie, and resembling the great Parisian cafés. Café des Arts, Galerie St. Hubert. Marugg, Rue Treurenberg, good ices; also at Marchal's ("*Vauxhall*") in the Park, N. E. corner, where a band plays every evening in summer. English beer may be obtained at all these establishments, Bavarian at Puth's (see above). — Belgian beer (*Faro*, *Louvain* and *Lambicq)* is largely consumed by the natives, but will probably be found very unpalatable by the traveller. The *Estaminets*, or beer-houses, are very numerous.

Baths. Bains St. Sauveur, Montagne aux Herbes Potagères 33, with good swimming-basin. Bains Léopold, Rue des Trois Têtes 8.

Shops. The best in the Rue de la Madeleine and Montagne de la Cour, the principal streets leading from the upper to the lower part of the city; also in the Rue Neuve and the Passage (p. 79). Fixed prices at the most respectable establishments. Bronzes, *Corman et Co.*, Rue d'Assaut 22. Toys, *Schueremans*, Passage St. Hubert; *Foire de Leipzig*, a well stocked bazaar, Montagne aux Herbes Potagères. Lace, *Van der Kelen-Bresson*, Rue du Marquis 1 (p. 84). Money Changers, several in the Montagne de la Cour, Marché aux Herbes and Rue des Fripiers. Horticulturists: *Van Riet*, Rue Camusel; *Linden*, in the Zoolog. Garden; also in the *Marché Couvert* (p. 79).

Booksellers. Kiessling et Co., Montagne de la Cour 26; Muquardt, Place Royale; Agence de Publicité, Montagne de la Cour. *Engravings:* Goupil et Co., Montagne de la Cour; Geruzet, Rue de l'Ecuyer.

Post-Office (Pl. 35), Rue de la Montagne 83, near the Cathedral. Other offices in the Chaussée de Wavre and at the railway-station, all with telegraph office, and open from 5 a. m. to 9 p. m. — Letter-boxes in all the principal streets.

Carriages. Fiacres (2-horse) per drive $1^1/_2$, first hour 2, each succeeding hour $1^1/_2$ fr. — Vigilantes (1-horse) per drive (6 a. m. to 11 p. m., at night double fares) 1, first hour $1^1/_2$, each succeeding $^1/_2$ hr. $^1/_4$ fr.; drive to the suburbs $1^1/_2$ fr.; a trifling fee is usually given to the driver. The charges *à l'heure* are not observed in the suburbs, unless by previous agreement. The Voitures de Remise (2-horse) are recommended for excursions into the country, 25 fr. per day; tolls are paid by the hirer. Office, Fossé aux Loups 16, near the Place de la Monnaie.

Omnibuses. 1. Grande Place to the Chaussée de Hæcht (20 c., brown vehicles): Grande Place, Rue de la Montagne, Banque Nationale, Rue de Ligne, Rue Royale, Place de la Reine, Chaussée de Hæcht. — 2. Saint Gilles to the Place Liedts (20 c., yellow vehicles): St. Gilles, Chaussée de Waterloo, Porte de Hal, Rue Haute, Rue de l'Escalier, Rue des Eperonniers, Marché-aux-Fromages, Grande Place, Rue des Fripiers, Rue Neuve, Place des Nations, Rue de Brabant, Place Liedts. — 3. Rue

Rogier to Ixelles (20 c., red vehicles): Rue Rogier, Rue du Progrès, Station du Nord, Rue Neuve, Place de la Monnaie, Rue des Fripiers, Grande Place, Rue des Chapeliers, Rue de l'Hôpital, Rue de Ruysbroeck, Rue de la Paille, Grand Sablon, Petit Sablon, Rue des Petits Carmes, Rue de Namur, Chaussée d'Ixelles, Place Communale. — 4. Molenbeek to the Station du Luxembourg (20 c., orange vehicles): Quatre Vents, Chaussée de Gand, Rue de Flandre, Marché-aux-Poulets, Grande Place, Rue des Chapeliers, Rue de l'Hôpital, de Ruysbroeck, de la Paille, Grand Sablon, Rue de la Régence, Place Royale, Place des Palais, Rue du Luxembourg, Station du Luxembourg. — 5. Place de la Duchesse to St. Josseten-Noode (20 c., blue vehicles): Place de la Duchesse, Chaussée de Ninove, Rue des Fabriques, des Chartreux, Marché-aux-Poulets, Grande Place, Rue de la Montagne, Banque Nationale, Rue de Ligne, Rue Royale, Rue de Louvain, Chaussée de Louvain. — 6. Anderlecht to Brussels (20 c., violet vehicles): Place Communale, Chaussée de Mons, Rue d'Anderlecht, Rue du Marché-aux-Charbons, Grande Place. — 7. Brussels to Laeken (20 c., crimson vehicles): Rue des Fripiers, Rue de l'Evêque, Rue de Laeken, Chaussée d'Anvers, Pont de Laeken, Avenue de la Reine. — 8. Station du Midi to Station du Nord (20 c., green vehicles): Place Rouppe, Rue du Midi, Rue des Lombards, Rue de l'Étuve, Grande Place, Rue des Fripiers, Place de la Monnaie, Rue Neuve, Place de la Nation.

Theatres. Théâtre Royal, Place de la Monnaie, performances (opera etc.) daily, except Saturdays, during the autumn, winter and spring. Interior well fitted up and richly decorated. This theatre is supported by the town. Boxes and stalls 5 fr., 2nd boxes and parquet (reserved seats between the stalls and pit) 4 fr., pit $1^1/_2$ fr. — Théâtre des Galeries St. Hubert (comedies, vaudevilles etc.) in the Passage of that name (p. 79), boxes 4 fr. — Théâtre du Parc (operettas, vaudevilles, dramas), stalls 3 fr. — Théâtre du Cirque, Rue du Cirque (Flemish plays), fauteuil d'orchestre 3 fr. 60 c. — There are also several inferior theatres, frequented by the humbler classes, and cafés chantants: *Molière*, Rue de Cologne; *Théâtre Lyrique* (Flemish), Rue du Casino; *Théâtre des Delassements*, near the Ancienne Porte de Namur; *Casino des Galeries*, in the Passage; '*Alcazar Royal*, Rue d'Aremberg. — Concerts in the open air: in the park every evening in summer (June 1st to Aug. 31st) at 8 p. m.; in the *Vauxhall* (50 c.), at the *Jardin Zoologique* (1 fr.) etc.

Popular Festivals. Church festivals about the end of July; anniversary of the Revolution Sept. 23rd—26th. Flemish merriment becomes somewhat boisterous on these occasions.

English Church Service in the Chapelle Royale, adjoining the Museum, in the Protest. Church in the Boulevard de l'Observatoire, and in a third church in the Rue Belliard.

Principal Attractions: Park (p. 59); Cathedral, sacristan's services unnecessary (p. 68); Notre Dame de la Chapelle (p. 78), with its modern pictures by Van Eycken; Museum (p. 68); historical pictures in the Palais de Justice and the Church of the Augustines (pp. 73, 79); Hôtel de Ville, exterior only (p. 75); Martyrs' Monument (p. 80); Colonne du Congrès (p. 65); Passage St. Hubert (p. 79), in the evening by gaslight; Marché Couvert (p. 79), early in the morning.

Brussels, the capital of Belgium, residence of the royal family and seat of government, situated on the small river *Senne*, has a population of 185,982 (6000 Protest.), or including the suburbs 300,341. There are upwards of 12,000 German and 6000 English residents. The majority of the latter reside in or near the *Quartier Léopold* (p. 82), the handsomest and best situated part of the town.

At the end of the 6th cent. there was a hermitage of the Christian Apostle *St. Géry* on an island in the Senne, and on a small marshy piece of ground adjacent a few huts sprang up (*broek*, marsh; *broeksele*, dwelling on the marsh, whence the present name of the city). In the 10th cent. the village had assumed the dimensions of a town. In 1044 it was considerably extended and surrounded by walls, and soon became an important station on the great commercial route between Bruges and Cologne. The princes and nobility erected their mansions on the heights rising gradually from the Senne, and after the 12th cent. Brussels became the residence of the Dukes of Brabant. The Burgundian princes, who subsequently resided here, were generally surrounded by a large retinue of French knights, in consequence of which French even at that period became the most fashionable language among the nobility of the Netherlands. Thus the character of the city and its inhabitants gradually developed itself: in the upper part the court, the nobility, French language and manners, — in the lower quarters the citizens, commerce, and the Flemish language and customs.

These characteristics of the upper and lower parts of the city are distinctly recognisable at the present day. The former, which was rebuilt after a great conflagration in 1731, contains the palaces of the king, the Chambers, the aristocratic *Rue Royale*, nearly 1 M. in length, the *Rue de la Loi* and *Rue Ducale* with the ministerial offices, the *Place Royale* with the largest hotels, the *Quartier Léopold* etc. The well-known ball of the Duchess of Richmond on the eve of the Battle of Waterloo was given in one of the houses of the Rue Royale nearest to the former Porte de Schaerbeck. The lower parts of the town, especially the streets descending from the Rue Royale, present a busy commercial appearance. The extensive market-place with the magnificent Hôtel de Ville forms one of the finest pictures of civil Gothic architecture in existence, embodying almost every period of later mediæval history, and presenting an interesting contrast to the otherwise almost entirely modern city.

French is always the language of the upper classes, whilst Flemish is spoken by the lower. The majority of the citizens, especially those engaged in commerce, know both languages. Persons of the lowest rank are sometimes met with who do not understand French, whilst many members of the educated classes are entirely ignorant of Flemish. The French spoken, and more particularly that written, by the higher ranks at Brussels is generally considered unexceptionable. The accent, however, differs slightly from that of Paris, and provincialisms are occasionally heard. Uneducated Flemings have a difficulty in pronouncing *ch* and *j*; thus, *Sarles* instead of *Charles*, *suse* instead of *juge*. Their French, too, is usually interlarded with Flemish expletives, such as the often recurring "Godverdom".

Brussels, which has many points of resemblance with the French capital, can now lay claim with more justice than formerly to the title of "Paris in miniature". Great improvements have taken place of late years, the obnoxious *Octroi* formerly levied at the gates has been abolished, new streets and promenades have been constructed, and the population has become doubled. The Park, the Allée Verte, and the Bois de Cambre may be regarded as modest imitations of the garden of the Tuileries, the Champs Elysées and the Bois de Boulogne; whilst in the boulevards, the cafés, the shops and the public amusements the resemblance is more apparent. A "Pré-Catelan" was even instituted at Brussels, but did not survive above a year. Brussels possesses many educational advantages, living is considerably cheaper here than at Paris, and all the objects of attraction, promenades etc. are within comparatively a narrow compass. The Belgians, too, are a very musical race, scarcely less so than the Germans, whilst their wealth enables them to cultivate their taste in the most advantageous manner. The opera and concerts are generally excellent. The military band of the "Guides" is one of the most celebrated in the world.

The ***Park**, situated between the Rue Royale, Rue Ducale, Rue de la Loi and Place des Palais, is an attractive spot, although of very limited extent (500 yds. in length, 300 yds. in width). Of the statues which adorn the fountains two only are worthy of notice as works of art, viz. the Diana and Narcissus of the fountain opposite the Palais de la Nation, both by *Grupello*. A small basin in one of the hollows is dedicated to the memory of Peter the Great, near which is Magdalene by the sculptor *Duquesnoy*. The bust of the czar was presented to the city by Prince Demidoff. The park in its present form was laid out by Maria Theresa. It is a fashionable resort on Sundays from 1 to 2. 30 p. m. (chairs 5 c.), when a military band plays. There is also military music here on most summer evenings after 6 o'clock (also in the Vauxhall, p. 57). The park, or rather the streets descending from it, afford a fine survey of the lower part of the town. The Park and the Allée Verte are closed in Jan., Dec. and the latter half of Nov. at 5 p. m.; in Feb., Oct. and the first half of Nov. at 6; in May and August at 9, and in June and July at 10 o'clock. A bell is rung to apprise visitors of the approaching hour. During the eventful days of Sept. (23rd—26th), 1830, the park was one of the principal scenes of the conflict, and was occupied by the Dutch. Traces of the injury occasioned to the trees by the shot and cannon-balls are still observable. The Bellevue Hôtel, situated between the Park and the Place Royale, which was the position occupied by the Belgians, was the central point of the action, and was completely riddled with shot. — The sculptures over the entrance opposite the palace, representing Summer and Spring, are by *Poelaert* and *Melot*.

To the l. in a small *Place*, near the Place Royale and one of the entrances to the Park, rises the marble **Statue** (Pl. 36), by *Geefs*, of Count Belliard, a French general (d. 1832) who held the appointment of ambassador at the newly-constituted court of Belgium. The inscription records the gratitude of the nation to the ambassador for the able manner in which he performed the difficult functions of his office.

Of the buildings which surround the Park the most important are the Royal Palace on the S., the former Palace of the Prince of Orange on the N.W., and the Parliament House or Palais de la Nation on the N. side, opposite to the Palais du Roi. The fourth side is bounded by the Rue Royale.

The **Palais du Roi** (Pl. 33) presents few attractions to the traveller, either externally or internally. It is now in process of being considerably extended on the l. side, towards the garden.

The r. wing was the residence of the prefect during the French régime. Napoleon and Josephine also resided here in 1803. The apartments are luxuriously fitted up, and contain a considerable number of works of art, but few of great merit. The finest pictures are several by *Verboeckhoven;* Crusaders at Jerusalem, by *Ccomans;* Citadel of Antwerp immediately after its capture, by *De Braekeleer;* Temptation of St. Antony, by *Gallait;* same subject by *Wappers*, and a Crucifixion and some portraits by *Van Dyck*. Permission to visit the interior of the palace must be obtained from the minister of the household, or from the intendant. A flag hoisted above the palace announces that the King is either here or at Laeken.

Adjoining the Royal Palace, at the corner of the Rue Ducale, is situated the former **Palace of the Prince of Orange** (Pl. 32), commonly known as the *Palais Ducal*. It was erected at the national expense and presented to the Prince, afterwards King William II. (d. 1849), in 1829. Since the Revolution it has been the property of the government. The basement-floor of the Palais Ducal is now converted into a **Musée des Sculptures**. The first floor contains a spacious concert-room with an organ, and the ***Musée Moderne**, a gallery of works of art by modern Belgian masters.

The garden on the side towards the park, adorned with a statue of the Victor by *Geefs*, is always accessible. The Palace is open daily from 10 to 4 o'clock (gratuities prohibited). The pictures are not numbered, and there is no catalogue.

Entrance Hall (1st Floor): *Jos. Lies*, Baldwin, Count of Flanders, punishing robbers. *Stallaert*, Destruction of Pompeii; in front of it, Vengeance and Death, sculptures by *Vanhoof* (now a painter). *Left*, 1st Room: Statuettes. Over the chimney-piece the pediments of the Palais de la Nation and the Château of Laeken. — 2nd R.: r. **Kindermans*, Amblève Valley in the Ardennes; *Clays*, Roads of Yarmouth; *J. Jacobs*, Wood-cutting in Norway; *Vendrée*, Festival of Corpus Christi in St. Peter's at Rome; *Van Moer*, Interior of the Cathedral of Lisbon; *Willems*, Adornment of a bride. — 3rd R.: *Steffens*, Lady in a dress of rich lace; *De Jonghe*, Landscape in the Ardennes; *Van Eycken*, The painter Parmeggianino at the plundering of Rome by the Connétable de Bourbon (1527); *Roeloffs*, Group of trees; *Navez* (former director of the Académie des Beaux Arts), Hagar in the wilderness; *Kuytenbrouwer*, Return from the chase; *Verlat*, Shepherd-dog defending his flock against an eagle; *Vendrée*, Fountain in Italy; Fisherman's expectant wife, sculpture by *De Braekeleer*. — 4th R.: *F. de Vigne*, Going to Church in winter; *Noordecker*, Doves. — 5th R.: **A. Thomas*, Judas flying on the night after the Crucifixion of Christ; *Kindermans*, View from the Ardennes; *Leys*, Opening of the Cathedral at Antwerp after the devastations of the iconoclasts (1566); *Degroux*, Fr. Junius preaching the Reformation at Antwerp. Autumn, sculpture by *Jaquel*. — 6th R.: *Stevens*, Dog-dealer; *Noordecker*, View of Waterloo; *Ferd. de Braekeleer*, Distribution of fruit in a school ("le comte de mi-carême"); *Braekeleer*, Golden Wedding-day; above the former of these two, the Schelde at Mœrdijk, by *C. L. Verboeckhoven; Verlat*, Conquest of Jerusalem by Godfrey de Bouillon. — 7th R. (formerly the dining room): Copies from ancient sculptures. *Begas*, Girl bathing. — 8th R.: *Navez*, Christ and the rich man; **E. Verboeckhoven*, Herdsman with oxen, sheep and goats in the Campagna of Rome; *Navez*, Judgment of Solomon; *Navez*, Athalia. Love-sick lion, a sculpture by *Geefs*. — 9th R.: *Hamman*, Adr. Vessel in a monastery at Bruges, playing on the organ; *Stroobant*, Hôtel de Ville of Brussels; *De Knyff*, Landscape in rainy weather; *Bossuet*, Cathedral of Seville; *Hunin*, Distribution of alms; *Lamorinière*, Park. Neapolitan Boy, a sculpture by *A. Sopers*. — 10th R.: Works by French masters. *Eugene Delacroix*, Ceiling of the Apollo saloon in the Louvre (a sketch); *Madou*, Village ball interrupted. A door leads from this saloon into the concert-room, which contains nothing worthy of mention. — 11th R.: *Clays*, Harbour of Ostende; **Verboeckhoven*, Flock of sheep in a storm; *Tschaggeny*, Diligence; *Gourmois*, Landscape with a mill. Marble statue by *Fréson*. — 12th (small) R.: Two water-colours, and sculpture by *Simonis*. — 13th R.: *Robbe*, Landscape with cattle; *Gentisson*, Archduke Albert and Isabella in the Cathedral of Tournai in 1600; *Robert*, Invasion of a convent. Captive Cupid, a sculpture by *Fraikin*. — 14th R.: *Robbe*, Large cattle-piece. Sleeping Cupid, a sculpture by *Geefs*.

The Gallery of Sculpture chiefly contains copies and casts; e. g. monuments of Andr. Vessel at Brussels, Prince Charles (unfinished) and Rubens. Also a cast of Ghiberti's celebrated bronze doors of the Baptistery at Florence.

The **Palais de la Nation** (Pl. 31), on the N. side of the Park, opposite to the Palais du Roi, erected by Maria Theresa for the assemblies of the old Council of Brabant, was the *Palais des Etats Généraux* from 1817 to 1830. The half relief representations in the pediment, by *Godecharles* (1782), are illustrative of the administration of justice. The vestibule, which is open to the public, is adorned with modern *statues in stone. Left: Pepin of Héristal (d. 714), major-domo of the Austrasian Empire (p. 177), by *Simonis;* Theodoric of Alsace, Count of Flanders (d. 1168, see p. 10), by *Jehotte;* Count Baldwin of Flanders (d. 1206), the Greek emperor, by *J. Geefs*. Right: Duke John of Brabant (d. 1294, see p. 80), by *Geerts;* Philip the Good (d. 1467), Duke of Burgundy, by *De Cuyper;* Emp. Charles V.

(d. 1558), by *De Boy*. In the centre are four allegorical figures in plaster: Freedom of the Press, of Religious Rites, of Associations and of Instruction. — The upper floor contains a large picture, painted by *Odevaere* in 1817, representing the Battle of Waterloo at the moment when the Prince of Orange was wounded, a work of no great artistic merit, which attracts the eye of the traveller who visits the assembly-halls of the Senate and the Chambers. The statue of King Leopold I. over the seat of the president is by *Geefs*. The hall of the Senate is embellished with 15 pictures by *Gallait*, portraits of celebrated Belgians. The public are admitted to the sessions of the Chambers; entrance at the back of the building, in the Rue de l'Orangerie. They usually commence at noon, and last till 5 p. m. (daily, except Sund. and Mond., from Nov. to May).

The ***Cathedral** (*St. Michel et Ste. Gudule*, Pl. 10), in the vicinity of the Palais de la Nation, is closed from 12 to 4 p. m.; access between these hours is obtained by paying 1 fr. to the funds of the church, and 1 fr. to the Suisse. — This imposing Gothic church, the finest in Brussels, stands on a somewhat abrupt slope overlooking the lower part of the town, and below the level of the Rue Royale. The grand façade was restored in 1848. The interior with its massive columns has a somewhat heavy aspect. The choir and transept are of the 13th, the unfinished towers and the nave of the 14th, the aisles of the 15th, the large (N.) chapel of the Sacrament of the 16th, the (S.) chapel of Notre Dame de Délivrance of the 17th century. In 1435 Philip the Good of Burgundy, and in 1516 Emp. Charles V. held chapters of the Order of the Golden Fleece here.

Most of the pictures formerly here disappeared at the time of the first French Revolution. The *Stained Glass, which happily escaped the ravages of that period, presents an admirable and progressive view of specimens of the art from an early date down to the present day. The finest are those of the *Chapel of the Sacrament (N.), erected *"Deo et Sacrae memoriae Caroli V."*: 1st window, behind the altar, Charles V. and his queen Eleonora Isabella Louisa; 2nd, his brother Emp. Ferdinand I. and his queen Anna; 3rd, Francis I. of France and his queen Leonora; 4th, Louis of Hungary and his queen Maria; 5th, John of Portugal and his queen Catharine. The last three queens were sisters of Charles V. — Then in the N. transept Charles V. again, and in the S. transept Louis of Hungary. All these figures, easy and life-like, although of a monumental character, and finely coloured, were designed by *M. Coxcie* and *B. van Orley*, and presented to the church by the above illustrious princes themselves in 1546—47. The same chapel contains a 6th stained-glass window, put up in 1848, representing the Last Supper, designed by *Capronnier* and *Navez*. The colouring will bear favourable comparison with the best works of an earlier, as well as of a later date. The altar in carved wood (by *Goyers*, 1849) is beautifully executed.

The windows of the Chapel of Notre Dame (S.), of the 17th cent., designed by *Theod. van Thulden*, show the manifest decline of the art, both in the drawing and the colouring. They represent episodes from the life of the Virgin, with portraits of Archduke Leopold (d. 1662), Archduke Albert (d. 1621), and the Archduchess Isabella Clara Eugenia (d. 1633); then Emp. Ferdinand II. (d. 1658) and Leopold I. (d. 1705).

The same chapel contains a *Monument in marble, by *Geefs*, to the memory of Count Merode, who fell in a skirmish with the Dutch at Berchem in 1830. The figure of the expiring count, who wears a blouse and grasps a pistol in his right hand, is in an easy, half-recumbent posture. The armorial bearings of the Merode family have the excellent motto: "*Plus d'honneur que d'honneurs.*" — Over the monument, the Assumption, a large modern picture by *Navez*. — This chapel also contains the monument of the Spanish general Count *Isenburg-Grenzau* (d. 1664), the last of a noble Rhenish family.

The upper windows of the lofty choir contain portraits of Maximilian of Austria and his queen Mary of Burgundy, their son Philip le Bel and his queen Johanna of Castile, their sons the Emp. Charles V. and Ferdinand, and Philip II., son of Charles V., with his queen Mary of England. The modern stained glass (1842) by *Capronnier* and *Navez* wants depth of colouring. The windows in the chapel behind the choir were presented by a Count Merode in the 18th cent. — In the choir is the monument of Duke John II. of Brabant (d. 1312) and his duchess Margaret of York, in black marble, with a recumbent lion in gilded copper, cast in 1610; opposite to it, the monument with recumbent figure of Archduke Ernest (d. 1595), brother of Emp. Rudolph II. and stadtholder of the Netherlands. Both monuments were erected by Archduke Albert (brother of Ernest) in 1610.

The window of the W. Portal, a Last Judgment by *F. Floris*, is remarkable for the crowd of figures it contains, a peculiarity rarely met with, and hardly appropriate in this branch of art.

Of the Statues of the 12 Apostles on the pillars of the nave, four (Paul, Bartholomew, Thomas, Matthew) are by *Duquesnoy*. The *Pulpit, originally in the church of the Jesuits at Louvain, was executed in 1699 by the celebrated *Verbrüggen*. It is a representation in carved wood of the Expulsion from Paradise. In the foliage are all kinds of animals — a bear, dog, cat, eagle, vulture, peacock, owl, dove, squirrel, ape eating an apple etc. Above is the Virgin with the Child, who crushes the head of the serpent with the Cross. In the S. part of the nave, near the pulpit, is the monument of Canon *Triest* (d. 1846), noted at Brussels for his benevolence, by *Simonis*. The government and the city itself have for many years expended considerable sums annually on the embellishment of the sacred edifice.

The massive flight of steps by which the W. Portal is approached was completed in 1861. — The handsome new edifice on the r. is the *Banque Nationale*, completed in 1864. Over the pediments are placed statues representing Industry, Commerce and Navigation. The symbolical decorations are also tastefully executed.

In the Rue Royale, midway between the Rue de la Loi and the Boulevard Schaerbeck, is situated the *Place du Congrès*, adorned with the ***Colonne du Congrès**, a monument erected to commemorate the Congress of June 4th, 1831, by which the present constitution of Belgium was established, and Prince Leopold of Saxe-Cobourg elected king. The column, of the Doric order, 175 ft. in height, is surmounted by a statue of the king in bronze, by *Geefs*. The nine figures in relief below, representing the different provinces of Belgium, are by *Simonis*. The female figures in bronze at the four corners are emblematical of the Liberty of the Press, the Liberty of Education, both by *Jos. Geefs*, the Liberty of Associations, by *Fraikin*, and the Liberty of Public Worship, by *Simonis*. The names of the members of the Congress and of the provisional government of 1830 are recorded on marble tablets. The summit, which is reached by a spiral staircase of 193 steps (trifling fee to the custodian), commands a magnificent panorama. The foundation-stone of the column was laid by King Leopold in 1850, and the inauguration took place in 1859. The substantial structures at the foot of the flight of steps which descend to the lower part of the town are destined for a *Marché Couvert*.

The traveller may now proceed by the Rue Royale, past the Park, to the church of **St. Jacques sur Coudenberg** (*Froidmont*, i. e. "cold mountain"; Pl. 11), a handsome and chaste edifice of the Corinthian order, erected by *Guimard* in 1776—85, and presenting a striking contrast to the more familiar Gothic architecture which is so universally prevalent in Belgium. At the sides of the portico are statues of Moses and David. The tympanum contains a fresco on a gold ground, by *Portaels*, completed in 1852, representing the Virgin as the comforter of the afflicted. Nothing in the interior is worthy of note. Under the French regime the church was employed for several years as a 'Temple of Reason'.

In front of the church rises the lofty equestrian **Statue of Godfrey de Bouillon*, the hero of the first Crusade, grasping the banner of the Cross in his right hand, probably the finest modern Belgian work of the kind, designed by *Simonis*. It was erected in 1848, on the spot where in 1097 Godfrey is said to have called upon the inhabitants of Brussels to participate in the Crusade, and to have concluded his appeal with the words "*Dieu li volt*" (God wills it).

The gateway nearly opposite to the statue is the entrance to the **Palais de l'Industrie** (Pl. 29), erected by the city in 1829 for the reception of technological collections. The court is adorned with a Statue in bronze (by *Jehotte*, 1846) of Duke Charles of Lorraine, who was stadtholder of the Netherlands for 40 years (1741—80) under Maria Theresa. The *Musée d'Industrie*, containing models of machinery, bridges, mills, sluices, ships, agricultural implements etc., is open to the public on Tuesd., Thursd. and Sat., 12—4, on Sundays 10—3 o'clock.

To the r. on the ground-floor is the department of the MSS. of the Royal **Library** (Pl. 6), known as the *Bibliothèque de*

Bourgogne, open to the public daily, 10—3 o'clock. It was founded in the 15th cent. by Philip le Bon, Duke of Burgundy, and contains about 22,000 MSS., the most interesting of which are a number of valuable missals embellished with beautiful miniatures by pupils of the Van Eyck's. The missal of the Dukes of Burgundy, by *Attavante* of Florence (1485), subsequently in the possession of Matthew Corvinus, King of Hungary, the chronicles of Hainault in seven folio volumes with miniature illustrations by *Memling*, and a copy of Xenophon's Cyropædia, used by Charles the Bold, should be particularly observed. These, with many other curiosities, are exposed to view in glass cases. Thus, "*Pardon accordé par Charles V. aux Gantois*" (p. 33) of 1540, MSS. as far back as the 7th cent., playing-cards manufactured at Ulm in 1594, autographs of Francis I., Henry IV., Philip II., Alva, Luther, Voltaire, Rubens etc. Most of the books in the Burgundian Library are bound in red morocco. The hall of the library is adorned with a series of portraits of the sovereigns of the country, down to Maria Theresa and Joseph II. Beautifully executed Chinese drawings are exhibited in a glass case here. The most valuable MSS. have twice been carried to Paris by the French. — The department of the printed books (234,000 vols.) is in the l. wing of the Palais de l'Industrie. The original nucleus of the collection was the library of a M. van Hulthem, purchased by the state in 1837 for 300,000 fr., and incorporated with the former civic library. The Chambers vote 60—65,000 fr. annually for the support of the Library. The admirably arranged Collection of Engravings is also worthy of notice. It contains the oldest woodcut furnished with a date (1418).

L'Ancienne Cour, a building adjoining the Palais de l'Industrie at a right angle, was the residence of the Austrian stadtholders of the Netherlands subsequently to 1713, when the old ducal palace (in the present Place Royale) was destroyed by fire. Part of the ground-floor is now fitted up as a library, the upper story contains a picture-gallery *(Musée)*, and the buildings of the court a cabinet of natural history. The sessions of the Royal Academy of Art and Science are also held here. The chapel, on the r. of the entrance, erected in 1760, was converted into a Protestant place of worship in 1803, and is commonly termed L'Eglise du

5*

Musée. Divine service in English, French and German is celebrated here every Sunday.

The ***Museum** (Pl. 26) contains about 375 pictures, all by the older masters. Twelve by Rubens are of inferior merit to those at Antwerp, the gallery of which is in all respects more valuable than that of Brussels. Excellent catalogues, 1 fr. The Museum is open to the public daily, 10—3 o'clock. The visitor ascends a staircase to the l., at the foot of which stands a Hercules said to be the masterpiece of *Delvaux* (d. 1778); and at the top of the staircase turns again to the l. (the door opposite leads to the hall of the Academy of Science).

The most valuable of the pictures are here enumerated (beginning always on the l.); the finest are indicated by asteriscs.

Entrance Cabinet: 1st Room. 107. *Backereel*, Adoration of the Shepherds; under it, 300. *Sallaert*, The Infanta Isabella at a shooting-match; opposite, 301. Procession of bridal pairs who have received dowries from the Infanta. — 2nd R.: 168. *De Crayer*, Martyrdom of St. Blaise, 153. *Champaigne*, Assumption. — Passage: *226. *Leermans*, Christ on the Cross; 166. *Craesbeke*, Flemish smoking-room. — Great Gallery. 1st Div.: Ten pictures with representations from the life of St. Benedict, by *Ph. de Champaigne;* No. 142., St. Benedict in the cave, the best. — 2nd Div.: 304. *Sassoferrato*, Madonna; 241. *Andrea di Michieli (il Vicentino)*, Marriage at Cana, a sketch (once erroneously attributed to Paul Veronese); *148. *Paolo Veronese*, Holy Family, with St. Theresa and St. Catherine; 135. *Veronese*, Entombment; 131. *Veronese*, Adoration of the Shepherds; 238. *Raphael Mengs*, Portrait of Michael Angelo; 233. *Manfredi*, Adulteress; 278. *Guido Reni*, Flight into Egypt; under it, 281. and 282. *Tintoretto*, Portraits (erroneously attributed to Titian); 234. *Maratti*, Apollo and Daphne. — 3rd Div.: *320. *Steen*, Festival of the Epiphany; 205. *Van der Helst*, Portrait of himself; 318. *Steen*, Reading aloud; 140. *Ph. de Champaigne*, St. Ambrose; **De Keyser*, Portraits of two old women; 239. *Metzu*, Midday meal; 277. *Rembrandt*, Portrait; above it, 108. *Backhuysen*, Storm on the Norwegian coast; *186. *Dow*, Portrait of himself (drawing a Cupid by lamplight; a picture said to have been purchased for 25,000 fr.); 348. *Wouverman*, Hunting scene; 293. *Rubens*, Martyrdom of St. Ursula, a sketch; under it, *Van* *de Velde*, Sea-piece; *325. *Teniers*, Village doctor (purchased in 1861 for 15,510 fr.); **Weenix*, Dead game; 338. *Veen*, Betrothal of St. Catherine; 260. *Ostade*, Repose; 121. *Bol*, Portrait; 244., 245. *Molenaer*, Interiors of Flemish cottages, two small pictures; 298. *Ryckaert*, Alchemist; 345. *Weenix*, Dutch lady; *167. *De Crayer*, Draught of fishes (the museum possesses about twelve of this master's works); 191. *Van Dyck*, Vision of St. Francis; 188. *Van Dyck*, Martyrdom of St. Peter; 190. *Van Dyck*, St. Antony and the Infant Jesus; *180. *Cuyp*, Cattle-shed; adjoining it, **Ruysdael*, Stormy sea; 319. *Steen*, Quack. — 4th Div.: 294., 295. *Rubens*, Portraits of Archduke Albert and his consort Isabella; 292. *Rubens*, Venus in the work-shop of Vulcan; *192. *Van Dyck*, Portrait of the Burgomaster Dellafaille of Antwerp; 152. *Ph. de Champaigne*, Portrait of himself; 314. *Snyders*, Dead Game and fruit; 219. *Jordaens*, Triumph of Prince Fred. Henry of Orange; 189. *Van Dyck*, Drunken Silenus; 119., 120. *Bol*, Portraits; 171. *De Crayer*, St. Paul and St. Antony; 193. *Ph. van Dyck*, Lady at her toilet. — The passage to the r. leads to the library. In the following room: 196. *Fr. Floris (de Vriendt)*, Last Judgment, a large picture with wings (the figure rising from the grave, from which Time removes the stone, is a portrait of the painter). — Three saloons with pictures of earlier Netherlandish masters are next entered. 1st Saloon: 29. *Martin Schœn* (Germ. School), Jesus is shown to the people; *Rogier van der Weyden* (?), Portrait of Charles the Bold (?). — 2nd S.: *13. *John van Eyck*, Adam and Eve, two wings of the celebrated Adoration of the Immaculate Lamb in St. Bavon at Ghent (see p. 37), sold to the government by the town as being unsuitable pictures for a church. In addition to the price, the Ghenters also received the excellent copies by Michael Coxcie of the six wings at Berlin. — 3rd S.: 14. *J. van Eyck*, Adoration of the Magi (under glass); *25. *B. van Orley*, Dead Christ mourned over by his friends, a winged picture with the donor and his family; 15. *J. van Mabuse*, Christ in the house of Simon the Pharisee. — The traveller who is desirous of becoming acquainted with some of the better productions of modern Belgian artists should endeavour to see the private collection of M. G. Couteaux (Fossé-aux-Loups 64), access to which is kindly permitted.

The **Natural History Collection** on the basement-floor (en trance to the r. in the court) is the most extensive in Belgium. The zoological department contains many examples of animals from the Dutch Indian colonies, e. g. a hippopotamus of unusual size. The mineralogical department comprises a considerable collection of minerals from Russia, presented by the Prince of Orange; also a very complete collection of the volcanic products of Mt. Vesuvius and of the fossils from the caverns of Mastricht (p. 181). Admission daily, 10—3 o'clock.

Above the Natural Hist. Collection, on the second floor, there is a *Galerie Historique*, containing pictures and busts which bear reference to events or persons of importance in the history of Belgium, many of them of considerable artistic merit. Admission daily, except Mond. and Thursd., 10—3 o'clock.

The **University** (Pl. 46), one of the *universités libres* (p. 171), is established in the former palace of Cardinal Granvella, Rue des Sols, near the Palais de l'Industrie. It was founded by a company of shareholders of the liberal party in 1834, in order to act as an equipoise to the Rom. Catholic University of Louvain (p. 163). It comprises the four faculties of philosophy, natural science, jurisprudence and medicine, and a separate pharmaceutical institution. The number of students is about 500, and the staff of professors 43. The court is adorned with a *Statue of Verhaegens* (d. 1862), one of the founders, who as the inscription records, presented a donation of 100,000 fr. to the funds.

A few paces from the university, in the same street, is situated the handsome new *Chapelle de l'Expiation*, an iron structure erected by a number of devout ladies of Brussels as an "expiation" for a theft of the host from the Cathedral of St. Gudule, committed in the middle ages.

If the traveller now return to the Place Royale and follow the street to the r. (S.), he will soon reach the *Eglise du Sablon*, or **Notre Dame des Victoires** (Pl. 12), which was founded shortly after the Battle of Worringen (in 1288), to commemorate the victory gained on that occasion by Duke John I. of Brabant over the Count of Guelders and the Archbishop of Cologne. The admirable N. Portal of the present structure dates from the 14th, the other parts from the 15th and 16th centuries. A tablet of black marble in the S. transept records that the remains of the writer *Jean Baptiste Rousseau*, who died in exile at Brussels in 1741, were transferred hither in 1842 from the church des Petits-Carmes (see below). The adjacent 1st Chapel on the S. side contains the monument of Count *Flaminio Garnier*, secretary of the Duke of Parma, consisting of six reliefs in alabaster from the life of the Virgin. The 3rd Chapel on the S. contains a monument erected in 1856 to the Marquis *de Voghera* (d. 1781), commanding general of the Austrian forces in the Netherlands. The burial-chapel of the Princes of Thurn and Taxis, in the N. transept, is sumptuously adorned with black and white marble, with sculptures of no artistic merit. A St. Ursula on the altar, by *Duquesnoy*, merits attention. The *dome* of this chapel is embellished with numerous gilded armorial bearings of the family. The church contains several pictures of little value. The best is a Last Judgment by *Fr. Floris*. A few old Flemish pictures are preserved in the Sacristy.

The Palace of the Duc d'Aremberg (Pl. 21), situated in the same Place *(Petit-Sablon*, or *Kleyne Zaevelplaets)*, erected in 1548, restored in 1753, with modern r. wing, was once the residence of the celebrated Count Egmont. It contains a small, but choice picture-gallery, comprising a fine example of every well-known Netherlandish master. Admission is, however, sometimes denied. On the wall of the staircase, a cast of *Lorenzo Ghiberti's* celebrated bronze doors of the Baptistery at Florence, representing the Days of the Creation. The pictures are all in excellent preservation, and furnished with the names of the artists: *Rembrandt*, Tobias restoring sight to his father; *G. Dow*, Old woman sitting at a table covered with gold; *H. Berckheyden*, Inner court of the Exchange at Amsterdam; *Brouwer*, Interior of a tavern; *Jan van der Meer*, Young girl; *P. Potter*, Rest in a barn; *Jan Steen*, Marriage at Cana (purchased by the Duchesse de Berry in 1837 for 21,000 fr.); *A. van Ostade*, Interior of a tavern (purchased in 1838 for 13,000 fr.); *Everdingen*, Waterfall; *Jordaens*, "Zoo de ouden zongen, zoo piepen de jongen" (when the old quarrel, the young squeak); *Gortzius Geldorp*, Portrait of the theologian Corn. Jansen (p. 27); *Teniers*, Playing at bowls; *Van Craesbeke*, His own studio. Another saloon, not connected with the above, is set apart for the works of the older masters: Madonna with saints, attributed by Dr. Waagen to *J. van Eyck;* pictures by *Martin Schön*, *Coningsloo*, *Mabuse*, *Patenier* etc. The other apartments contain magnificent old and new furniture; Etruscan vases, antique statuettes, busts in marble. The library contains a cast (the original is at one of the duke's country-residences) of the admirable head of a Laocoon, found about the year 1710 under a bridge in Florence, and purchased by an ancestor of the duke (a cast of the head of the well-known Roman Laocoon is placed beside it for comparison). King Lewis of Bavaria is said in vain to have offered 180,000 fr. for this head. The spacious and handsome riding-school, which can be converted into a ball-room on festive occasions, is employed as a conservatory in winter. The adjoining Gardens are kept in admirable order (fee 1 fr.).

A few houses above the palace, to the l., is the prison **Les Petits Carmes** (Pl. 34), the front of which was constructed in 1847 in the Engl. Gothic style. It is fitted up with cells for solitary confinement. A Carmelite monastery, demolished in 1811, formerly occupied this site. Somewhat higher stood the house of Count Kuylenburg, memorable under Philip II. as the place of assembly of the nobles of the Netherlands who began the struggle against the supremacy of Spain. Here on April 6th, 1566, they signed a petition *("Request")* to the vicegerent Margaret of Parma (natural daughter of Charles V. and sister of Philip II.), praying for the abolition of the inquisitorial courts, after which between three and four hundred of the confederates proceeded on horseback to the palace of the Duchess. At the moment when the petition was presented, Count Barlaimont, one of the courtiers of the princess, whose apprehensions had been awakened by the sudden appearance of the cortège, whispered to her, *"Madame, ce n'est qu'une troupe de gueux"* (i. e. beggars), in allusion to their supposed want of money. The epithet was overheard, and rapidly communicated to the whole party, who afterwards chose it for the name of their faction. On the same evening several of their number, among whom was Count Brederode, attired as a mendicant with a wooden goblet *(jatte)* in his hand, appeared on the balcony of the residence of Count Kuylenburg and drank success to the "Gueux", while each in token of his co-operation struck a nail into the goblet. The spark, thus kindled, soon burst into a flame, and a few years later caused the N. provinces of the Netherlands to be severed from the dominions of Spain. The Duke of Alva, in order to gratify his indignation, subsequently caused the above-mentioned house, where Counts Egmont and Horn had been arrested, and the flag of Spain again displayed, to be rased to the ground.

The *Grand Sablon*, or *Groote Zavelplaats*, the most spacious Place in the city, is adorned with an insignificant monument erected by the Marquis of Aylesbury in 1751, in recognition of the hospitality accorded to him at Brussels. Minerva is represented with the images of Francis I. and Maria Theresa; on the r. the goddess of Fame, on the l. the Schelde; beneath, the arms of the founder.

The **Palais de Justice** (Pl. 30), an unsightly and dirty-looking edifice, entered from the Rue de Ruysbroeck, stands on the N. side of the Grand Sablon. It was formerly a Jesuit monastery. The portico in front is an imitation of the temple of Agrippa at Rome. The hall of the Cour de Cassation contains two remarkably fine modern historical pictures: the *Abdication of the Emp. Charles V. (see p. 76), by *Gallait*, a master-piece of richness of composition, combined with harmony of colour and excellence of arrangement; and the *Compromise (1565), or Petition of the Belgian nobles, by *E. de Biefve*, the different figures in which are admirable, but the composition and colouring inferior. Count Horn is represented as signing the document, Egmont in an arm-chair; at the table Philip de Marnix, in a suit of armour; in the foreground William of Orange, in a blue robe; beside him, Martigny in white satin, and behind him the Duc d'Aremberg. Count Brederode, beneath the portico to the l., is inviting others to embrace the good cause. In the picture by Gallait Charles V. is represented at the foot of the throne, leaning with his left hand on William of Orange; before him kneels his son Philip II.; on the r. is his sister Mary of Hungary in an arm-chair, on the l. Cardinal Granvella. The Palais de Justice also contains the *Archives* of the kingdom. The Cour de Cassation sits on Thursd., Frid. and Sat., 10—2 o'clock, when the public are admitted. Access obtained at other times (also during the vacation, Aug. 15th to Oct. 15th) by applying to the concierge (fee 50 c.).

In the *Hoogstraet*, or Rue Haute, in the immediate vicinity, is situated ***Notre Dame de la Chapelle** (Pl. 7), a Gothic basilica, the posterior part of which was erected in the 12th, the façade in the 15th cent. To the r. of the entrance from the Rue Haute is the Chapel of the Trinity, decorated in 1852 with admirable mural *paintings by *J. B. van Eycken* (d. 1853). On the l. is an embodiment of the text: "Come unto Me, ye that labour and are heavy laden!" On the vaulting the eight Beatitudes. On the r. three female figures on a gold ground: in the centre Queen Louise Marie (d. 1850), l. the Duchess Johanna of Brabant (d. 1406), r. the Infanta Isabella (d. 1633), three princesses who won the love and esteem of the citizens of Brussels by their amiable and benevolent dispositions. A large oil-painting opposite, by the same master, represents Slaves liberated by the Christian Religion. The other chapels are embellished with a *series of pictures from the history of the Passion, also executed by *Van Eycken*, well worthy of notice, both as fine examples of modern art in Belgium, and as a proof of the public taste for such compositions. The second Chapel on the S. contains the tomb of the painter *Peter Breughel*, with a picture by that master (on the wall above: Christ giving the Keys to Peter). In the 4th Chapel, *Christ appearing to Mary Magdalene, by *De Crayer.* Adjoining the W. entrance is the monument of the painter *Lens* (d. 1822), by *Godecharles.* The 1st Chapel of the N. aisle contains the tomb of the painter *Sturm* (d. at Rome, 1844), with portrait in a medallion by *Teuerlinckx.* In the N. transept, Healing of the man possessed with a devil, by *Van Eycken.* In the N. Chapel of the choir a monument of the *Spinola* family. On the pillar a monument, with bust, to Duke *Alex. de Croy* (d. 1624). A tablet of black marble at the back of the pillar bears a long Latin inscription to the memory of *Francis Anneessens*, a citizen of Brussels, and magistrate of the quarter of St. Nicholas, who was executed in the Grand Marché in 1719 for presuming to defend the privileges of the city and guilds against the encroachments of the Austrian governor (the Marquis de Prié). — High altar-piece, Miracles of St. Boniface, by *Van Eycken.* N. side-altar, Intercession for souls in Purgatory, by *De Crayer.* S. side-altar, S. Carlo Borromeo administering the sacrament to persons sick of the plague, by *De Crayer.* The carving on the pulpit, by *Plumiers*, represents Elisah in the wilderness.

The Rue Haute is terminated towards the E. by the **Porte de Hal** (Pl. 27), the sole remnant of the former fortifications.

It was erected in 1381, and two centuries later became the Bastille of Alva during the Belgian "reign of terror". The walls having long since disappeared, and the fosse recently filled up, the old gateway now stands in an open space, a solitary relic of the middle ages. Among the pieces of ordnance preserved here a huge mortar (*"mortier-monstre"*), cast at Liège in 1834, will be observed. The gateway contains a * *Collection of Weapons and Antiquities*, open to the public on Sundays, 11—4 o'clock, at other times by payment of a fee (1 fr.). On the first floor are weapons of every description and suits of armour; a richly ornamented helmet is said to have belonged to Charles V.; the stuffed horses are those ridden in 1596 by the Governor Archduke Albert of Austria and his consort Isabella on the occasion of their public entry into Brussels; in the window-recess, artillery implements found in a well at the castle of Bouvigne (p. 152), into which they had been thrown, together with the defenders of the stronghold, by the French in 1554. — On the second floor a number of mediæval and modern objects are preserved; opposite the door is an altar-piece in carved wood, executed in 1530, representing in six sections the martyrdom of St. Ludgerus and St. Agnes; a font of 1149; tapestry of the 15th and 16th cent., on one piece of which the Battle of Nieuport (1600) is represented; the cradles of Charles of Lorraine and Charles V.; court-dress of James II. of England; model of the Bastille at Paris; the celebrated *Diptychon Leodiense*, two tablets of carved ivory executed at the commencement of the 6th cent., and recently purchased for 20,000 fr. — The third floor contains Greek and Roman antiquities; ethnographical objects, such as the cast of an Assyrian obelisk, the mummy of a priestess in its original coffin, the cloak and bow of Montezuma, emperor of Mexico. — The well-arranged catalogue (1 fr.) contains a list of 6000 objects.

A short distance hence, farther down the Boulevard, rises (r.) the Blind Asylum, an elegant structure with walls and half Gothic tower in imitation of a mediæval style, designed by Cluysenaer. It is the property of the Philanthrophic Society of Brussels.

The ***Hôtel de Ville** (Pl. 20), situated in the *Grand' Place* in the lower part of the town, is by far the most remarkable edifice in Brussels, and one of the noblest and most beautiful examples of Belgian town-halls. The magnificent façade wa completed in 1442. The sculptures and mouldings were seriousl mutilated by the sansculottes in 1792, but restored in 1853 b *Jacquet*. The graceful Tower, 364 ft. in height, which howeve does not rise from the centre of the edifice, was completed abou 1450. The first niche is filled with a statue of the architec *Jan van Ruysbroeck* (d. about 1482). The figure of the Arch angel Michael, which serves as a vane on the summit of th spire, is of gilded bronze, 17 ft. in height, but apparently o much smaller dimensions when seen from below. It was execute by *Martin van Rode* in 1454. The tower should be ascended i the afternoon (about 4 p. m.). The view is very extensive. The Lion on the field of Waterloo is distinctly recognised beyond the dark Forêt de Soignes (p. 97).

The Concierge (fee 1 fr.), who lives in the passage at the back, shows the interior of the Hôtel de Ville, which should be visited in the afternoon, as the municipal authorities hold their sessions here in the forenoon. In the W. entrance of the court is placed a large picture by *Stallaert*, representing the death of Eberhard T'serclaes (1388), a magistrate of Brussels. On the first floor, the Defeat at Châlons (451), by *Coomans*. The corridors are hung with portraits of former sovereigns, among whom are Maria Theresa, Francis II., Joseph II., Charles VI., Charles II. of Spain etc.; in the following passage, the Emperor Charles V., Philip III. of Spain, Philipp IV., Archduke Albert and his consort Isabella, Charles II. of Spain and Philip II., the latter in the robe of the Golden Fleece. In the spacious *Salle des Mariages*, where the civil part of the marriage ceremony is performed, Counts Egmont and Horn were condemned to death in 1568. The abdication of the Emp. Charles V. is sometimes stated also to have taken place in this saloon (*in* 1556), but it is well ascertained that the scene of that event was the old ducal palace in the Place Royale, burned down in 1731. The abdication is represented on a piece of Tapestry in the council-hall: in front is Charles V., beside him Mary of Hungary, before him Philip II., in the background Alva in a red cloak. Another piece represents the Coronation of Emp. Charles VI. at Aix-la-Chapelle; on the other side is the *Joyeuse Entrée* of Philip the Good of Burgundy, i. e. the conclusion of the contract of government between the sovereign, the clergy, the nobility and the people. On an adjacent table is preserved the key of the city, which on that occasion was presented to the regent. The ceiling-paintings, mythological representations by *Janssens*, are considered a masterly performance. The two fountains in the court are decorated with recumbent river-gods.

In the *Grand' Place*, or market-place, in front of the Hôtel de Ville, 25 nobles of the Netherlands were beheaded by order of the Duke of Alva in 1568. Lamoral Count Egmont, and Philip de Montmorency, Count Hoorne, were the most distinguished victims. They passed the night previous to their execution in the **Halle au Pain**, or *Maison du Roi*, formerly a seat of some of the municipal authorities, now occupied by the *Cercle Artistique Littéraire;* and they are said to have been conveyed directly from the balcony to the fatal block by means of a scaffolding, in order to prevent the possibility of a rescue by the populace. This building, erected in 1525, half in the Gothic, half in the Renaissance style, was restored in 1767 in egregiously bad taste. Beneath the statue of the Virgin is the inscription: "*A peste, fame et bello libera nos Maria pacis*", composed for the statue by the Infanta Isabella in 1624.

In front of the Halle au Pain rises the ***Monument of Counts Egmont and Hoorne**, erected at the expense of the city and the state in 1864, to the memory of these illustrious patriots, who were "unjustly executed by the Duke of Alva, June 5th, 1568", as the French and Flemish inscriptions record. The lower part is a fountain, above which rises a square pedestal in the later Gothic style. The two small bronze figures on the r. and l. are soldiers of the corps commanded by the two counts. The colossal figures in bronze above represent Egmont and Hoorne on their way to execution. The whole was designed by the eminent sculptor Fraikin.

Count Egmont, Prince de Gavre and Baron de Fiennes, a member of one of the most illustrious families of Holland, was born in 1522. He possessed great military talents, and served as commander of cavalry in the war between France and Spain. The victories gained by the Spaniards at St. Quentin in 1557, and at Gravelines in 1558, were mainly due to Egmont's impetuous valour. His frank, generous and amiable disposition rendered him an universal favourite, especially in the provinces of Artois and Flanders of which he was governor, whilst his vast hereditary estates, augmented by those of his wife, the rich heiress of the house of Luxembourg-Fiennes, secured to him a widely extended influence throughout the Netherlands. He was made a member of the council of the Duchess of Parma, the Spanish regent of the Netherlands, and employed all his influence in vindicating the liberties of the people. The well-known liberality of his principles, however, soon rendered him obnoxious to the bigoted and intolerant king of Spain. When the cruel Duke of Alva superseded the Duchess of Parma in the government, he openly showed favour to Egmont and his party, whilst secretly compassing their destruction. At length Egmont and his friend Count Hoorne, the scion of another noble family of the Netherlands, and an active member of the liberal party, were treacherously arrested at a meeting of the council and consigned to separate dungeons. The two patriots were shortly afterwards condemned to death as traitors to the Spanish government, and executed on June 5th, 1568, meeting their fate with calm fortitude. They were universally regarded as martyrs to the cause of liberty, and their judicial murder was the signal for a general revolt, which after a sanguinary war of thirty years terminated in the emancipation of the Netherlands from the Spanish yoke.

The *Guild Houses in this square are well worthy of notice. They were re-erected at the commencement of last century, after having been almost entirely destroyed by the bombardment of Louis XIV. in 1695. The former hall of the Guild of Butchers on the S. side is indicated by a swan. The Hall of the Brewers (*Hôtel des Brasseurs*, p. 56), recently restored with considerable taste, bears on its gable a gilded equestrian statue of Duke Charles of Lorraine (p. 66), designed in 1857 by *Jacquet*. On the W. side is the Hall of the Boatmen, the gable of which resembles the stern of a large vessel, with two projecting cannon. The Maison de la Louve, or Hall of the Archers, derives its appellation from a group representing Romulus and Remus with the she-wolf. The adjoining Hall of the Carpenters is richly adorned with gilding. The extensive building which occupies almost the entire S. side of the square was formerly the Hall of Weights and Measures.

In the rear of the Hôtel de Ville, about 100 yds. to the S. W. and at the corner of the Rue du Chêne and the Rue de l'Etuve, stands a diminitive figure, one of the curiosities of Brussels, known as the "*mannikin*". He is a great favourite with the lower classes, and is invariably attired in gala-costume on all great occasions. When Louis XV. took the city in 1747, the mannikin wore the white cockade, in 1789 he was decked in the colours of the Brabant Revolution, under the French regime he adopted the tri-colour, then the Orange colours, and in 1830 the blouse of the Revolutionists. He now possesses eight different suits, each of which is destined for a particular festival, and even boasts of a valet, who is appointed by the civic authorities and receives a salary of 200 fr. per annum. In 1817 the figure was carried off by sacrilegious hands, and his disappearance was regarded as a public calamity. The perpetrator of the outrage, however, was soon discovered, and the manikin reinstated amid general rejoicings.

In the vicinity of the Grande Place is situated the ***Passage,** or *Galerie St. Hubert* (Pl. 16), constructed in 1847, one of the most spacious and attractive covered arcades in Europe (650 ft. in length, 60 ft. in height, 25 ft. in width). It connects the Marché-aux-Herbes with the Rue de l'Ecuyer, and is intersected midway by the Rue des Bouchers. Many of the shops are very tempting. In the afternoon between 1 and 3 o'clock, especially in wet weather, the Passage is the Regent Street of the exquisites of Brussels, whilst at a later hour the working-classes flock hither to rejoice in the brilliant gaslight, and to gaze with admiration at the shop-windows.

About 200 yds. higher, in the Rue de la Madeleine, as well as in the Rue Duquesnoy and the Rue St. Jean, are entrances to the ***Marché Couvert,** an extensive market-place for the necessaries of life, especially fruit and vegetables, erected in 1848. A gallery in the interior, occupied almost exclusively by dealers in flowers and game, leads round the entire building. A walk here in the early morning (before 10 o'clock) will be found amusing and instructive.

The **Theatre** in the Place de la Monnaie, with a portico of eight Ionic columns, was erected in 1817. The interior was entirely remodelled after a fire in 1855. The basrelief in the tympanum, representing the Harmony of human Passions, a masterly production by *Simonis*, was completed in 1854. The *Hôtel de la Monnaie*, or Mint, is opposite to the Theatre.

The **Church of the Augustines** (Pl. 45), in the Rue Fossé-aux-Loups, near the Place de la Monnaie, used as a Protestant place of worship during the Dutch regime, is now employed as a hall for concerts, exhibitions etc. It is adorned with three large modern pictures: *Wappers*, Beginning of the Revolution of 1830; *De Keyser*, Battle of Worringen (1288); *J. Decaisne*, Belgium crowning her most illustrious men, from Charlemagne down to the 17th cent. The principal group in the picture by *Wappers* is represented in front of the Hôtel de Ville of Brussels, thronging round a lamp-post where a workman stands with the proclamation of Sept. 24th, 1830, in his hand. *De Keyser's* picture represents Siegfried of Westerburg, Archbishop of Cologne, in presence of his conquerors Duke John I. of Brabant and Count Adolph of Berg. (The building is entered through the house at the back, No. 2; fee $1^1/_2$ fr.) — The *Eglise du Béguinage* in the vicinity contains a colossal statue of John the Baptist by Puyenbroek, and an Entombment by Otto Venius.

In the Rue de Ste. Catherine, a short distance lower down, a new church is in process of erection on the site of the former Bassin de Ste. Catherine, now filled up.

The ***Martyrs' Monument** (Pl. 25) in the Place des Martyrs, a square founded by Maria Theresa, was erected in 1838 to the memory of the Belgians who fell in Sept., 1830, whilst fighting against the Dutch. It represents liberated Belgium engraving on a tablet the eventful days of Sept. (23rd to 26th); at her feet a recumbent lion and broken chains and fetters. At the sides are four reliefs in marble: in front the grateful nation; on the r. the oath in front of the Hôtel de Ville at the beginning of the contest; on the l. the conflict in the Park (in the centre Don Juan of Halen); at the back the consecration of the tombs of the fallen. The monument was designed and executed by *W. Geefs*. The marble slabs immured in the gallery below record the names of the "martyrs", 448 in number.

The old ramparts were converted into ***Boulevards** about the year 1825. They are planted with double rows of trees, and encircle the entire city. The upper part (N. and E.) is thronged with carriages, riders and walkers on fine summer-evenings, and presents a gay and animated scene. The traveller who has a few hours at his disposal is recommended to walk round the whole town by the Boulevards, a pleasant circuit of nearly 6 M. The French language and manners will be observed to be predominant on the N. and E. sides, whilst most of the frequenters of the lower Boulevards belong to the humbler classes and speak Flemish. With the exception of the Park, the Boulevards afford the most agreeable promenade of Brussels. They form the boundary between the city and the suburbs. The fosse which formerly enclosed them has been filled up, and the city gates removed since 1860, when the *octroi*, or municipal impost levied at the gates, was abolished. The sites of the gates are still known by their former names. The Porte de Cologne is that by which the town is entered from the Station du Nord, opposite the extremity of the Rue Neuve. Ascending the Boulevards hence, the traveller perceives the **Hospital St. Jean** immediately to the r., a simple, but imposing structure, admirably fitted up. (Admission 1 fr.; guide $^1/_2$—1 fr.) Patients of every rank are received here, those of the wealthier classes paying a very moderate sum for board and medical advice (4—6 fr. per day). The aged and infirm also find an asylum here. The hospital accommodates about 600 inmates.

On the slopes opposite to the hospital are the extensive grounds of the **Botanical Garden** (Pl. 23), with its spacious hothouses. The garden is open to the public on Tuesd., Thursd. and Sat., 10—3 o'clock; admission to the hothouses 30 c., to the gardens on other days also 30 c.

Near the former Porte de Schaerbeck, at the end of the Rue Royale, rises the handsome new church of *Nôtre Dame*, an octagonal edifice in the Romanesque style, designed by *Overstraeten*. The dome and each angle of the octagon are surmounted by graceful, open-work towers. The street leading to the church, being outside of the former ramparts, is termed Rue Royale Extérieure. Charming view hence of the Valley of the Senne.

On the r. side of the Boulevard, immediately above the Porte de Schaerbeck, is the *Eglise Evangélique* (Pl. 8), which is used for divine worship by a French and an English congregation. The first street on the r. above the church affords a glimpse of the *Place des Barricades*, adorned with a statue of the anatomist *Vesalius* (b. at Brussels in 1514), by *Geefs*. Higher up in the Boulevard, on the l., rises the **Observatory** (Pl. 28), erected in 1837, now presided over by *Quetelet*.

[If the Place des Barricades be crossed, the first street reached leads to the Rue de la Batterie, where (entered by No. 21) the chapel of the *Frères de la Doctrine Chrétienne* is situated. It is decorated with finely executed mural paintings by Portaels and Lagaye. — The street which descends to the l. from the former

Porte de Louvain leads to ($^1/_2$ M.) the *Shooting Gallery*, an extensive establishment, well fitted up (35 targets), and frequently an object of attraction to strangers.]

Outside the Boulevard, between the Porte de Louvain and the Porte de Namur, extends the new and handsome *Quartier Léopold*, well built, but somewhat monotonous in appearance. One of the principal streets intersecting it is the Rue de la Loi, which leads E. to the *Champs des Manœuvres*, where it is proposed to concentrate all the military establishments of Brussels. The church of *St. Joseph* (Pl. 13), a modern Renaissance building, belongs to the order of Redemptorists. The altar-piece is a Holy Family by *Wiertz*.

On the E. side of the Quartier Léopold, near the *Station du Luxembourg* (reached directly from the Boulevards by the Rue Montoyer, or by the Rue du Luxembourg), is situated the extensive ***Zoological Garden** (admission 1 fr.), beautifully laid out, and stocked with the usual inmates. Concerts here several times weekly (p. 57). The band plays in the rotunda outside the restaurant. The hothouses are kept in admirable order.

On the S. side of the Zoological Garden, rises the ***Musée Wiertz** (Pl. 47), a building in the form of an artificial ruin, situated on an eminence and surrounded with grounds. It was formerly the country-residence and studio of the painter of that name, after whose death it was purchased by the government (open to the public daily, 10—3 o'clock). It contains a number of pictures, some of them painted on the wall, and all bearing testimony to the great talent of the master, who in his power of colour sometimes resembles Rubens, and in his sense of form recals Michael Angelo. The entrance-room contains a few drawings. In the lofty studio are the following seven large pictures: One of the great of the earth; Forge of Vulcan; Contest of good with evil; The last cannon; Contest for the body of Patroclus; Conflict and Triumph of Christ. The following are some of the smaller works: Vision of a beheaded man; Lion of Waterloo; Orphans, with the inscription "Appel à la bienfaisance"; Hunger, Madness and Crime; Curiosity, in the corner; Resuscitation of a person who has been buried alive; Concierge; Box on the ear administered by a Belgian lady; Napoleon in purgatory etc.

Returning to the Boulevards by one of the streets above

mentioned, the traveller may now continue his walk, leaving the Ducal Palace (p. 61) and its garden on the r. To the l. extends the Faubourg de Namur, belonging to the parish of Ixelles, adjoining which, still farther S., is the rapidly increasing Quartier Louise in the parish of St. Gilles. The Place de Namur is embellished with a fountain and a bust of M. de Brouckere, the late able and zealous burgomaster (d. 1860), erected on the site of the former gate. A short distance farther, the broad street diverging to the l. from the *Place Louise* leads to the Bois de la Cambre, a park of considerable extent, bearing a distant resemblance to the Bois de Boulogne at Paris. Farther on in the Boulevard is the *Hospice Pacheco* on the r., a home for aged widows of officers; then the *Gendarmes' Barracks*. Finally on the l. the Porte de Hal (p. 74).

Here the Boulevard turns to the N.W. and passes the Blind Asylum (p. 75) and the spacious **Station du Midi**, which is connected by branch lines with the Station du Nord and the Station du Luxembourg. Then on the l. the *Ecole Vétérinaire*, and on the r. several large manufactories. Beyond the former *Porte d'Anderlecht* are the extensive **Abattoirs** (*Slaughter Houses*, Pl. 1) on the l., on the bank of the Senne. At the adjoining *Porte de Ninove* is the commencement of the canal, 45 M. in length, which connects Brussels with the Sambre near Charleroi. Farther on, outside the *Porte de Flandre*, is the **Etablissement Géographique** (Pl. 14) of *M. Vandermaelen*, which comprises valuable collections of maps, coins and minerals, a cabinet of natural history, hothouses etc. (admission daily, 9—11 and 1—4 o'clock). The Boulevard skirts the canal, and next passes the extensive *Barracks* and the **Custom House** (*Entrepôt Royal*, Pl. 13), with its spacious magazines.

Immediately beyond the custom-house is the commencement of the **Allée Verte**, a double avenue of limes extending along the bank of the canal of Willebroeck, which connects Brussels with Malines and Antwerp. The trees were planted in 1707, and in 1746 during the siege of Brussels in the War of the Austrian Succession were considerately spared by Marshal Saxe. This avenue was formerly the most fashionable promenade of Brussels, but is now comparatively deserted. The élite of the city, who reside in the vicinity of the Park and the faubourgs above it, at a considerable distance from the Allée Verte, seldom descend from the upper Boulevards. The concerts in the Park and the Zoological Gardens are now among the principal objects of attraction.

At the extremity of the Allée Verte, which skirts the canal for upwards of 1 M., the traveller crosses a bridge, and after a walk of a few minutes reaches **Laeken**. The churchyard of the village has sometimes been termed the Père-Lachaise of Brussels; but it will bear no comparison with the great cemetery of Paris neither in extent nor in the interest attaching to the monuments. In the small village church reposes Queen Louise Marie (d. 1850), the illustrious and benevolent consort of King Leopold I., and daughter of Louis Philippe. A handsome Gothic church, destined to contain the royal burial-vault, is now being erected here at the expense of government, aided by private contributions. The churchyard contains a small chapel with the tomb of the singer *Malibran* (d. 1836), adorned with a statue in marble by *Geefs*. Several other monuments are by the same eminent sculptor. The predominating French element at Brussels is manifest here also. The only inscription in the Flemish language is on the tombstone of an aged pastor of Laeken, erected by his parishioners.

The **Château**, $^3/_4$ M. to the N. of the church, was erected from a design by Duke Albert of Saxony for the Austrian stadtholder of the Netherlands in 1782. It was purchased by Napoleon in 1802 for the Empress Josephine, and occasionally occupied by the emperor himself, who in 1811 here formed the plan for his Russian campaign. In 1815 the château became the property of the Crown, and the grounds have since been considerably extended. The park and gardens are beautifully laid out, but the château itself contains nothing worthy of note. The latter, now the residence of the Empress Charlotte of Mexico, is not accessible. A view of it is obtained to the l. from the train to Malines, shortly after it has quitted the station at Brussels. Carriage to Laeken, see p. 57. The driver should be directed to stop at the churchyard (*"arrêtez au cimetière"*).

Brussels Lace, the most important of the products of the city, has become less expensive than formerly, as the designs are now sewn upon a ground of tulle instead of one manufactured by hand. The patterns are worked either by means of the bobbin (*fleurs en plat*), or by the needle (*fleurs en point*). Brussels annually exports lace to France alone of the value of 2—3 million fr. There are upwards of 130,000 lace-makers in Belgium, and the annual value of their manufactures amounts to about 50 million fr. (2 mill. *l.*). — The process may be witnessed at any of the numerous establishments, e. g. that of *Van der Kelen-Bresson*, Rue du Marquis 1, where visitors are generally expected to make some purchase in the ware-room. The finest qualities formerly realised as much as 10 *l.* per oz., and a veil of elaborate design was sold for 40 *l.* These expensive kinds, however, are now rarely manufactured. — The *Carriages* built at Brussels enjoy a high reputation, rivalling those of London and Paris, and at the same time somewhat more moderate in price.

10. Battle Field of Waterloo.

Railway (*Chemin de Fer du Luxembourg*, Quartier Léopold) to *Groenendael* in $^3/_4$ hr.; fares 80 or 60 c.; omnibus thence to *Mont St. Jean* (in 1 hr., fare 1 fr. 25 c.), meeting the train which leaves Brussels about 9. 30, reaching Mont St. Jean about 11, and returning to the station at 3 o'clock. For a single traveller this is the least expensive route, but the time allowed for a visit to the field is rather too limited. Should the traveller miss the omnibus he will probably be obliged to return to the station on foot, as no conveyances are to be found at Waterloo or Mont St. Jean. — On the r., after the wood is quitted, is a villa of the burgomaster of Waterloo; farther on, the château of Argenteuil with its four towers on the l., the property of Count Meeus.

Omnibus daily (except Sundays) at 9. 30 a. m. from the Hôtel de Saxe (p. 55), reaching Waterloo at 12; thence at 2, and back to Brussels at 4 p. m. — Office at *Suffel's*, 16 Rue Villa Hermosa, the first street to the r. in descending the Rue Montagne de la Cour from the Place Royale. Fare to Waterloo and back 5 fr. — Guides to the principal points of interest await the arrival of the coach at Mont St. Jean. — For a party a two-horse carriage (25—30 fr.) is far preferable to the coach. The driver should be directed to stop at the Hôtel du Musée (see below).

Those who desire to extend their excursion as far as Planchenois, and to return to Brussels in time for dinner (generally at 5 o'clock) should start not later than 7 a. m., and order the carriage to meet them at La Belle Alliance about 2. On the way back a short halt should be made at the church of Waterloo in order to inspect the memorial-tablets which it contains.

Time. A visit to the two monuments on the battle-field, the lion and the farms of La Haye Sainte and Hougomont occupies 2 hrs.; to La Belle Alliance and Planchenois 2 hrs. more. The traveller will, however, obtain a general survey of the field during the first 2 hrs.

Guides. The annexed plan and the following brief sketch of the battle will enable the visitor to form a distinct conception of the positions occupied by the respective armies without the services of a guide. The usual fee for the principal points of interest is 2 fr.; if the excursion be extended to Planchenois and the château of Frichemont, 3—4 fr.; but an agreement should invariably be made beforehand.

Relics. Old weapons, bullets, buttons etc. are offered for sale by the guides. Genuine relics are still occasionally turned up by the plough, but it need hardly be observed that most of those which the traveller is importuned to purchase are spurious.

Points of Interest. The following is the order in which they are most conveniently visited: Hanoverian Monument and that of Colonel Gordon (p. 98), farm of La Haye Sainte (p. 99), Belgian Lion (p. 98), farm of Hougomont (p. 100), Belle Alliance (p. 102), Planchenois (p. 103). If the two latter be visited, the carriage may be ordered to meet the traveller at La Belle Alliance, and La Haye Sainte may then be inspected in returning. The church at Waterloo forms the termination of the excursion.

Inns at Mont St. Jean: *Hôtel Mont St. Jean* and (to the r., where the road to Nivelles diverges from the Namur road) *Hôtel des Colonnes*. On the mound of the Lion: **Hôtel du Musée*, clean and comfortable.

Sketch of the Battle. A detailed history of the momentous events of June 18th, 1815, would be quite beyond the scope of a guide-book, but a brief and impartial outline, with a few statistics derived from the most trustworthy English and German sources, may perhaps be acceptable to those who visit this memorable spot.

The ground on which Wellington took up his position after the Battle of Quatre Bras was admirably adapted for a defensive battle. The high roads from Nivelles and Genappe unite at the village of Mont Saint Jean, whence the main route leads to Brussels. In front of the village extends a long chain of hills with gentle slopes, which presented all the advantages sought for by the Allies. The undulating ground behind this range afforded every facility for posting the cavalry and reserves so as to conceal them from the evemy. In this favourable position Wellington was fully justified in hoping at least to hold his own, even against a stronger enemy, until the assistance promised by Blücher should arrive.

The first line of the Allied army, beginning with the right wing (on the W.) was arranged as follows. On the extreme right were placed two brigades of the British household troops, consisting of two battalions of Foot-Guards under Gen. Maitland, and two battalions of the Coldstream Guards under Gen. Byng. Next came a British brigade of four battalions under Gen. Sir Colin Halkett, adjoining whom were Kielmannsegge with five brigades of Hanoverians and a corps of riflemen, Col. Ompteda with a brigade of the German Legion, and finally Alten's division. The whole of this portion of the line occupied the hills between the Nivelles and Genappe roads. Beyond the latter (i. e. farther to the E.) Kempt was stationed with the 28th and 32nd regiments, a battalion of the 79th and one of the 95th Rifles. Next came Bylandt with one Belgian and five Dutch battalions, supported by Pack's brigade, posted a short distance in their rear, and consisting of two battalions of Highlanders, with a battalion of the 1st and another of the 44th. These four battalions had suffered severely at Quatre Bras and were greatly reduced in number, but their conduct throughout the battle abundantly proved that their discipline and courage were unimpaired. Beyond the Netherlanders were drawn up Best's Hanoverians and Picton's

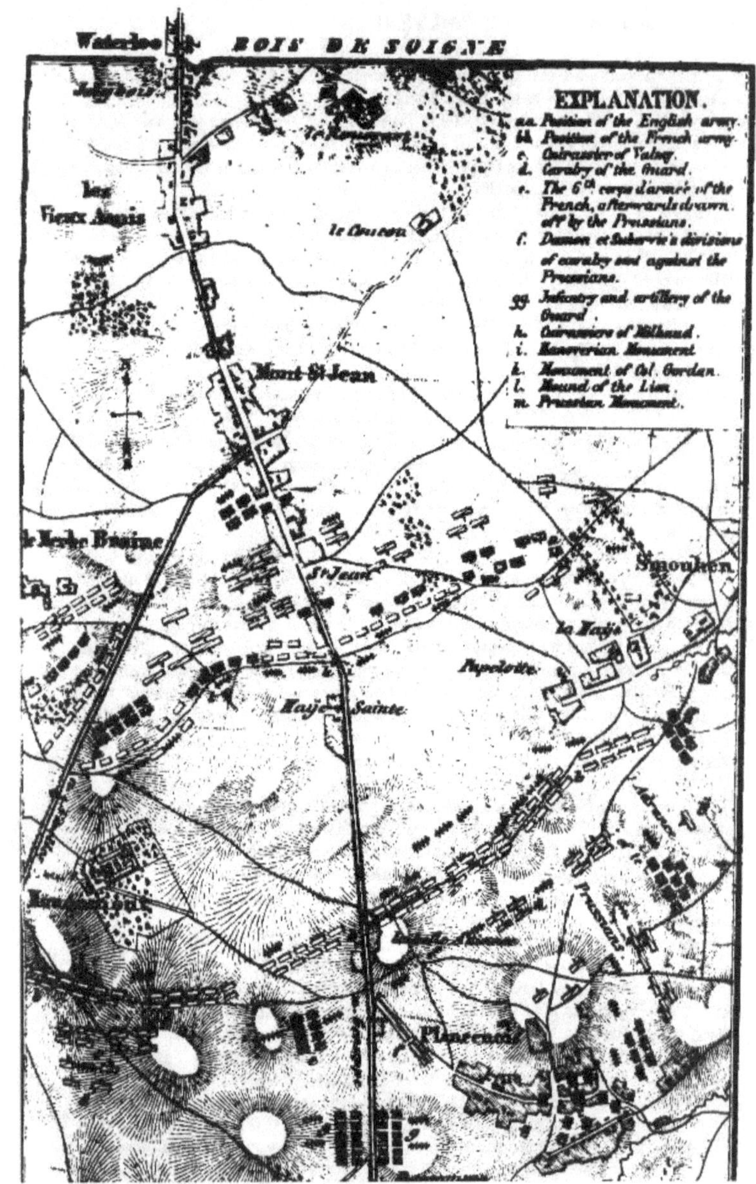
Waterloo
BOIS DE SOIGNE
EXPLANATION.
aa. Position of the English army.
bb. Position of the French army.
d. Cavalry of the Guard.
e. The 6th corps d'armée of the French, afterwards drawn off by the Prussians.
f. Domon et Subervie's divisions of cavalry sent against the Prussians.
gg. Infantry and artillery of the Guard.
h. Cuirassiers of Milhaud.
i. Hanoverian Monument
k. Monument of Col. Gordan.
l. Mound of the Lion.
m. Prussian Monument.
Mont St Jean
St Jean
Smouhen
la Haije
Papelotte
Haije Sainte
Plancenoit
Prussians

infantry division, the latter partially composed of Hanoverians under Col. von Vincke. Next to these were stationed Vandeleur's brigade, (the 11th, 12th and 16th Light Dragoons, and finally on the extreme left (to the E.) three regiments of light cavalry, consisting of the 10th and 18th British, and the 1st Hussars of the German Legion.

The first line of the Allies was strengthened at various distances by Grant's and Dœrnberg's cavalry brigades, consisting of three English regiments and three of the German Legion respectively, and posted near the Guards and Sir Colin Halkett. Next to them came a regiment of Hussars of the German Legion under Col. Arentschild; then, to the E. of the Genappe road, two heavy Brigades, the Household and the Union, to support Alten's and Picton's divisions. The former of these brigades was composed of the 1st and 2nd Life Guards and the 1st Dragoon Guards under Lord Ed. Somerset; the latter of the 1st Royal Dragoons, the Scottish Greys and the Irish Inniskillens, commanded by Gen. Sir W. Ponsonby. Besides the first line and the troops destined to cover it, various other forces were distributed as the circumstances and formation of the ground required. Thus a brigade under Col. Mitchell, Sir Henry Clinton's division, Du Plat's German brigade, Adam's light brigade and Halkett's Hanoverians were drawn up on the W. side of the Nivelles Chaussée and near the village of Merbe Braine. Finally the reserves of Brunswickers and Netherlanders, comprising infantry and cavalry, formed a line between Merbe Braine and Mont St. Jean, supported by Lambert's British brigade of three regiments, which had just arrived by forced marches from Ostende. — The artillery, consisting chiefly of British troops, were distributed as occasion required. Every battery present was brought into action in the course of the day and nobly fulfilled its duty.

In front of the centre of the Allied army lay the Château of Hougomont, which with its massive buildings, its gardens and plantations, formed an admirable *point d'appui* for the defence of the heights above. It was garrisoned by two light companies under Lord Saltoun and two under Col. Macdonnel, strengthened by a battalion of Nassovians, a company of Hanoverian riflemen, and about 100 men of the German Legion. This point holds a prominent place in the history of the battle, both on account of the fury with which it was attacked by the French, and the heroic and successful defence of its occupants. Farther to the left, and nearer the front of the Allies, lay La Haye Sainte, a farm-house which was occupied by 400 men of the German Legion under Major von Baring, but after a noble defence was taken by the French. The defence of the farms of Papelotte and La Haye on the extreme left was entrusted to the Nassovian Brigade under Duke Bernard.

Napoleon's army was drawn up in a semicircle on the heights to the E. and W. of the farm of La Belle Alliance, about one mile distant from the Allies. It was arranged in two lines with a reserve in the rear. The first line consisted of two corps d'armée commanded by Reille and D'Erlon respectively, and flanked by cavalry on either side. One corps extended from La Belle Alliance westwards to the Nivelles road and beyond it, the other eastwards in the direction of the château of Frichemont. The second line was composed almost entirely of cavalry. Milhaud's cuirassiers and the light cavalry of the guards were drawn up behind the right wing, Kellermann's heavy cavalry behind the left. A body of cavalry and a portion of Lobau's corps were also stationed in the rear of the centre, whilst still farther back the Imperial Guard, consisting of infantry and artillery, were drawn up in reserve on each side of the chaussée.

The Duke of Wellington's army consisted of 67,600 men, 24,000 of whom were British, 25,800 troops of the German Legion, Hanoverians, Brunswickers and Nassovians, and about 17,800 Netherlanders. Of these 12,400 were cavalry, 5,600 artillery with 156 guns. — The army brought into the field by Napoleon numbered 71,900 men, of whom 15,700 were cavalry, 7,200 artillery with 246 guns. — Numerically, therefore, the difference between the hostile armies was not great, but it must be borne in mind that no reliance could be placed on the Netherlanders, most of whom fled at an early stage of the battle. The staunch Dutch troops who formed part of this contingent did their utmost to prevent this dastardly act, but their efforts were unavailing. Had they formed a separate corps they would have been most valuable auxiliaries, but when mingled with the Belgian troops their bravery was utterly paralysed. Practically, therefore, the Duke's army consisted of barely 50,000 men, composed of four or five different elements. A large proportion of them were moreover raw recruits, whilst the soldiers of Napoleon constituted a grand and admirably disciplined unity, full of enthusiasm for their general, and confident of victory. The superiority of the French artillery alone was overwhelming.

After a wet and stormy night the morning of the 18th of June gave some promise of clearing, but the sky was still overcast, and rain continued to fall till an advanced hour. The ground, moreover, was so thoroughly saturated that the movements of the cavalry and artillery were seriously obstructed. This was probably the cause of Napoleon's tardiness in attacking the Allies, and of the deliberation with which he spent several of the best hours of the morning in arranging his army with unusual display. It is not known precisely at what hour the first shots were fired; some authorities mention eight o'clock, others half-past eleven or twelve, while the Duke himself in his published dispatch names ten as the hour of the commencement of the battle. It is, however, probable that the actual fighting did not begin till between eleven and twelve.

The first movement on the part of the French was the advance of a division of Reille's corps d'armée under Jérôme Buonaparte, a detachment of which precipitated itself against the château of Hougomont and endeavoured to take it by storm, but was repulsed. They soon renewed the attack with redoubled fury, and the tirailleurs speedily forced their way into the enclosure, notwithstanding the gallant resistance made by the Hanoverian and Nassovian riflemen. The British howitzers, however, now commenced to pour such a deadly shower of shells on the assailants that they were again compelled to retreat. This was but the prelude to a series of re-iterated assaults, in which the French skirmishers in overwhelming numbers were more than once nearly successful. Prodigies of valour on the part of the defenders, vigorously seconded by the artillery on the heights, alone enabled the garrison to hold out until the victory was won. Had the French once gained possession of this miniature fortress, a point of vital importance to the Allies, the issue of the day would probably have been very different.

Whilst Hougomont and its environs continued to be the scene of a desperate and unremitting conflict, a second great movement on the part of the French was directed against the centre and the left wing of the Alliés. Supported by a cannonade of 72 pieces, the whole of Erlon's corps and a division of Kellermann's cavalry, comprising upwards of 18,000 men, bristled in columns of attack on the heights above La Haye Sainte, presenting a magnificent, but terrible spectacle. Their object was to storm La Haye Sainte, break through the centre of the Allied army, and attack the left wing in the rear. At the moment when Ney was about to commence the attack, Napoleon observed distant indications of the advance of new columns on his extreme right, and an intercepted dispatch proved that they formed a part of the advanced guard of Bülow's Prussians, who were approaching from Wavre. The attack was therefore delayed for a short time, and Soult despatched a messenger to Marshal Grouchy, directing him to manœuvre his troops so as to intercept the Prussians. Owing, however, to a series of misunderstandings, Grouchy was too far distant from the scene of action to be of any service, and did not receive the order till seven in the evening.

It was about two o'clock when Ney commenced his attack. The four divisions of Erlon's corps moved rapidly in four columns towards the Allied line between La Haye Sainte and Smouhen. Papelotte and Smouhen were stormed by Durette's division, but the former was not long maintained by the French. Donzelat's division took possession of the gardens of La Haye Sainte, notwithstanding the brave resistance of a Hanoverian battalion, whilst the two other French divisions, those of Alix and Marcognet pressed onwards without encountering any obstacle. Hardly had the two latter opened their fire on Bylandt's Netherlandish contingent, when the Belgians were seized with a panic and thrown into confusion. All the efforts of their officers and the remonstrances of their Dutch comrades were utterly unavailing to re-assure them, and amid the bitter execrations of the British regiments they fairly took to flight. Picton's division, however, now consisting solely of the two greatly reduced brigades of Pack and Kempt, and mustering barely 3000 men, prepared with undaunted resolution to receive the attack of the two French divisions, numbering upwards of 13,000 infantry, besides cavalry. The struggle was brief, but of intense fierceness. The charge of the British was irresistible, and in a few moments the French were driven back totally discomfited. The success was brilliant, but dearly purchased, for the gallant Picton himself was one of the numerous slain. During the temporary confusion which ensued among Kempt's troops, who however soon recovered their order, the Duke communicated with Lord Uxbridge, who put himself at the head of Lord Edward Somerset's Household Brigade, consisting of two regiments of Life Guards, the Horse Guards and Dragoon Guards. Meanwhile, too, a body of Milhaud's cuirassiers had advanced somewhat prematurely to La Haye Sainte and endeavoured to force their way up the heights towards the left centre of the Allied line. These two movements gave rise to a conflict of unparalleled fury between the élite of the cavalry of the hostile armies. For a time the French bravely persevered, but nothing could withstand the overwhelming impetus of the Guards as they descended the slope, and the cuirassiers were compelled to fly in wild confusion. Somerset's brigade, regardless of consequences and entirely unsupported, pursued them with eager impetuosity. At this juncture two columns of the French infantry had advanced on Pack's brigade. The bagpipes yelled forth their war-cry, and the gallant Highlanders dashed into the thickest of the fight, notwithstanding the terrible majority of their enemy. This was one of the most daring exploits of the day; but the mere handful of Northmen must inevitably have been cut to pieces to a man, had not Col. Ponsonby with the Inniskillens, the Scotch Greys and the Royal Dragoons opportunely flown to the rescue. The cavalry charge was crowned with brilliant success, and the French infantry were utterly routed. Pack's troops now recovered their order and were restrained from the pursuit, but Ponsonby's cavalry, intoxicated with success, swept onwards. The Royals encountered part of Alix's division, which was advancing towards Mont St. Jean, where a gap had been left by the flight of the Belgians. A fearful scene of slaughter ensued, and the French in vain endeavoured to rally. This charge was simultaneous with that of Lord Uxbridge on the cuirassiers, as mentioned above. At the same time the Greys and Inniskillens, who were in vain commanded to halt and rally, madly prosecuted their work of destruction. Somerset's and Ponsonby's cavalry had thus daringly pursued their enemy until they actually reached the French line near Belle Alliance. Here, however, their victorious career was checked. A fresh body of French cuirassiers and a brigade of lancers were put in motion against them, and they were compelled to retreat with considerable confusion and great loss. At this crisis Vandeleur's Light Dragoons came to the rescue, the tide of the conflict was again turned; but the French, whose cavalry far outnumbered those of the Allies, again compelled the British to abandon the unequal struggle. Retreat was once more inevitable, and the loss immense, but the French gained no decided advantage. Vandeleur himself fell, and Ponsonby was left on the field dangerously wounded.

Whilst the centre and left of the Allied line were thus actively engaged, the right was not suffered to repose. At a critical juncture, when Lord Saltoun and his two light companies were suffering severely in the defence of the orchard of Hougomont, and had been reduced to a mere handful of men, a battalion of Guards under Col. Hepburn was sent to their relief and drove off the French tirailleurs, whose loss was enormous. The château had meanwhile taken fire, and the effects of the conflagration were most disastrous to the little garrison, but most fortunately for the sufferers the progress of the flames became arrested near the doorway where a crucifix hung. The sacred image itself was injured, but not destroyed, and to its miraculous powers the Belgians attributed the preservation of the defenders. There was now a pause in the musketry fire, but the cannonade on both sides continued with increasing fury, causing frightful carnage. Erlon's and Reille's corps sustained a loss of nearly half their numbers, and of the former alone 3000 were taken prisoners. Nearly 40 of the French cannon were moreover silenced, their gunners having been slain. Napoleon now determined to make amends for these disasters by an overwhelming cavalry attack, whilst at the same time the infantry divisions of Jérôme and Foy were directed to advance. Milhaud's cuirassiers and a body of the French Guards, 40 squadrons in all, a most magnificent and formidable array, advanced in three lines from the

French heights, crossed the intervening valley, and began to ascend towards the Allies. During their advance the French cannonade was continued over their heads, ceasing only when they had nearly attained the brow of the opposite hill. The Allied artillery poured their discharges of grape and canister against the enemy with deadly effect, but without retarding their progress. In accordance with the Duke's instructions the artillerymen now retreated for shelter behind the line; the French cavalry charged, and the foremost batteries fell into their possession. The Allied infantry, Germans as well as British, had by this time formed into squares. There was a pause on the part of the cavalry, who had not expected to find their enemy in such perfect and compact array; but after a momentary hesitation they dashed onwards. Thus the whole of the cuirassiers, followed by the lancers and chasseurs swept through between the Allied squares, but without making any impression on them. Lord Uxbridge with the fragments of his heavy cavalry now hastened to the aid of the infantry and drove the French back over the hill; but his numbers were too reduced to admit of his following up this success, and before long the French, vigorously supported by their cannonade, returned. Again they swept past the impenetrable squares, and again all their efforts to break them were completely baffled, whilst their own ranks were terribly thinned by the fire of the undaunted Allies. Thus failed, they once more abandoned the attack. Donzelat's infantry had meanwhile been advancing to support them, but seeing this total discomfiture and retreat, they too retired from the scene of action. The Allied lines were therefore again free, and the cannonade alone was now continued on both sides.

After this failure Napoleon commanded Kellermann with his dragoons and cuirassiers to support the retreating masses, and Guyot's heavy cavalry of the Guards advanced with the same object. These troops, consisting of 37 fresh squadrons, formed behind the shattered fragments of the 40 squadrons above mentioned and rallied them for a renewed attack, and again the French line assumed a most threatening and imposing aspect. Perceiving these new preparations, the Duke of Wellington contracted his line so as to strengthen the Allied centre, immediately after which manœuvres the French cannonade burst forth with redoubled fury. Again a scene precisely similar to that already described was re-enacted. The French cavalry ascended the heights, where they were received with a deadly cannonade, the gunners retired from their pieces at the latest possible moment, the French rode in vast numbers through the squares, and again the British and German infantry stood immovable. The cavalry then swept past them towards the Allied rear, and here they met with partial success, for a body of Netherlanders whom they threatened at once commenced to retreat precipitately. As in the earlier part of the day, Lord Uxbridge flew to the rescue with the remnants of his cavalry, vigorously seconded by those of Somerset and Grant, and again the French horsemen were discomfited. Lord Uxbridge now ordered a brigade of Belgian and Dutch carbineers who had not as yet been in action, and were stationed behind Mont St. Jean, to charge the French cavalry who had penetrated to the Allied rear; but his commands were disregarded, and the Netherlanders took to flight. A body of hussars of the German Legion, however, though far outnumbered by their enemy, gallantly charged them, but were compelled to retreat. The battle-field at this period presented a most remarkable scene. Friends and foes, French, German and British troops, were mingled in apparently inextricable confusion. Still, however, the Allied squares were unbroken, and the French attack, not being followed up by infantry, was again a failure. The assailants accordingly, as before, galloped down to the valley in great confusion, after having sustained most disastrous losses. Lord Uxbridge attempted to follow up this advantage by bringing forward a fresh regiment of Hanoverian Hussars, but he was again doomed to disappointment; for the whole troop, after having made a pretence of obeying his command, wheeled round and fled to Brussels, where they caused the utmost consternation by a report that the Allies were defeated.

During the whole of this time the defence of Hougomont had been gallantly and successfully carried on, and Du Plat with his Brunswickers had behaved with undaunted courage when attacked by French cavalry and tirailleurs in succession. The brave general himself fell, but his troops continued to maintain their ground, whilst Adam's brigade advanced to their aid. Overwhelming numbers of French infantry, however, had forced their way between them, and reached the summit of the hill, threatening the right wing of the Allies with disaster. At this juncture the Duke himself placed himself at the head of Adam's brigade and commanded them to charge. The assault was made with the utmost enthusiasm, and the French were driven from the heights. The entire Allied line had hitherto stood its ground, and Hougomont proved impregnable. Napoleon therefore now directed his efforts against La Haye Sainte, a point of the utmost importance, which was bravely defended by Major von Baring and his staunch band of Germans. Ney accordingly ordered Donzelat's division to attack the miniature fortress. A furious cannonade opened upon it was the prelude to an attack by overwhelming numbers of tirailleurs. The ammunition of the defenders was speedily exhausted, the buildings took fire, and Baring with the utmost reluctance directed the wreck of his detachment to retreat through the garden. With heroic bravery the major and his gallant officers remained at their posts until the French had actually entered the house, and only when farther resistance would have been certain death did they finally yield (see p. 99) and retreat to the lines of the Allies. After this success, the French proceeded to direct a similar concentrated attack against Hougomont, but in vain, for arms and ammunition were supplied in abundance to the little garrison, whilst the cannonade of the Allies was in a position to render them efficient service. La Haye Sainte, which was captured between 5 and 6 o'clock p. m., now became a most advantageous point d'appui for the French tirailleurs, in support of whom Ney during upwards of an hour directed a succession of attacks against the Allied centre, but still without succeeding in dislodging or dismaying the indomitable squares. Their numbers, indeed, were fearfully reduced, but their spirit was unbroken. There was moreover still a considerable reserve which had not yet been in action, although perhaps implicit reliance could not be placed on their steadiness. It was now nearly 7 o'clock p. m., and the victory on which the French had in the morning confidently reckoned was entirely unachieved.

Meanwhile Blücher with his gallant and indefatigable Prussians, whose timely arrival fortunately for the Allies prevented Napoleon from employing his reserves against them, had been toiling across the wet and spongey valleys of St. Lambert and the Lasne towards the scene of action. The patience of the weary troops was well-nigh exhausted. "We cannot go farther", they frequently exclaimed. "We *must*" was Blucher's reply, "I have given Wellington my word, and you won't make me break it!" It was about 4. 30 p. m. when the first Prussian battery opened its fire from the heights of Frichemont, about $2^1/_4$ miles to the S.E. of the Allied centre, whilst at the same time two cavalry regiments advanced to the attack. They were at first opposed by Domont's cavalry division, beyond which Lobau's corps approached their new enemy. One by one the different brigades of Bulow's corps arrived on the field between Frichemont and Planchenois. Lobau stoutly resisted their attack, but his opponents soon became too powerful for him. By 6 o'clock the Prussians had 48 guns in action, the balls from which occasionally reached as far as the Genappe road. Lobau was now compelled to retreat towards the village of Planchenois, a short distance in the rear of the French centre at Belle Alliance. This was the juncture, between 6 and 7 o'clock, when Ney was launching his re-iterated, but fruitless attacks against the Allied centre, $2^1/_4$ miles distant from this point. Napoleon now despatched eight battalions of the Guard and 24 guns to aid Marshal Lobau in the defence of Planchenois, where a sanguinary conflict ensued. Hiller's brigade endeavoured to take the village by storm, and succeeded in gaining possession of the churchyard, but a furious and deadly fusillade from the houses compelled them to yield. Reinforcements were now added to the combatants of both armies. Napoleon sent four more battalions of guards to the scene of action, whilst fresh columns of Prussians united with Hiller's troops and prepared for a renewed assault. Again the village was taken, but again lost, the French even venturing to push their way to the vicinity of the Prussian line. The latter, however, was again reinforced by Tippelskirch's brigade, a portion of which at once participated in the struggle. About 7 o'clock Zieten arrived on the field and united his brigade to the extreme left of the Allied line, which he aided in the contest near La Haye and Papelotte. Prussians continued to arrive later in the evening, but of course could not now influence the issue of the battle. It became apparent to Napoleon at this crisis that if the Prussians succeeded in capturing Planchenois, whilst Wellington's lines continued steadfast in their position, a disastrous defeat of his already terribly reduced army was inevitable. He therefore resolved to direct a final and desperate attack against the Allied centre, whilst to stimulate the flagging energies of his troops a report was spread among them that Grouchy was approaching to their aid, although Napoleon well knew this to be impossible.

Napoleon accordingly commanded eight battalions of his reserve Guards to advance in two columns, one towards the centre of the Allied right, the other nearer to Hougomont, whilst they were supported by a reserve of two more battalions, consisting in all of about 5000 veteran soldiers, who had not as yet been engaged in the action. Between these columns were the remnants of Erlon's and Reille's corps, supported by cavalry, and somewhat in advance of them Donzelat's division was to advance. Meanwhile the

Duke hastened to prepare the wreck of his army to meet the attack. Du Plat's Brunswickers took up their position nearly opposite La Haye Sainte, between Halkett's and Alten's divisions. Maitland's and Adam's brigades were nominally supported by a division of Netherlanders under Gen. Chassé, whilst Vivian with his cavalry quitted the extreme left and drew up in the rear of Kruse's Nassovians, who had already suffered severely and now began to exhibit symptoms of wavering. Every available gun was moreover posted in front of the line, and the orchard and plantations of Hougomont were strengthened by reinforcements. The prelude to the attack of the French was a renewed and furious cannonade, which caused frightful havoc among the Allies. Donzelat's division then advanced in dense array from La Haye Sainte, intrepidly pushing their way to the very summit of the height on which the Allies stood. At the same time several French guns supported by them were brought within a hundred yards of the Allied front, on which they opened a most murderous cannonade. Kielmannsegge's Hanoverians suffered severe loss, the wreck of Ompteda's German brigade was almost annihilated, and Kruse's Nassovians were only restrained from taking to flight by the efforts of Vivian's cavalry. The Prince of Orange then rallied the Nassovians and led them to the charge, but they were again driven back, and the Prince himself severely wounded. Du Plat's Brunswickers next came to the rescue and fought gallantly, but without greater success. The Duke, however, rallied them in person, and the success of the French was brief. At the same time the chief fury of the storm was about to burst forth farther to the right of the Allies. The Imperial Guard, commanded by the heroic Ney, Friant and Michel, and stimulated to the utmost enthusiasm by an address from Napoleon himself, formed in threatening and imposing masses on the heights of Belle Alliance, and there was a temporary lull in the French cannonade. The two magnificent columns, the flower of the French army, were now put in motion, one towards Hougomont and Adam's brigade, the other in the direction of Maitland and his Guards. As soon as the Guards had descended from the heights, the French batteries recommenced their work of destruction with terrible fury and precision, but were soon compelled to desist when they could no longer fire over the heads of their infantry. The latter had nearly attained the summit of the heights of the Allies, when the British gunners again resumed their work with redoubled energy, making innumerable gaps in the ranks of their assailants. Ney's horse was shot under him, but the gallant marshal continued to advance on foot; Michel was slain, and Friant dangerously wounded. Notwithstanding these casualties, the Guards gained the summit of the hill and advanced towards that part of the line where Maitland's brigade had been ordered to lie down behind the ridge, in the rear of the battery which crowned it. The Duke commanded here in person at this critical juncture. The French tirailleurs were speedily swept away by showers of grape and canister, but the column of French veterans continued to advance towards the apparently unsupported battery. At this moment the Duke gave the signal to Maitland, whose Guards instantaneously sprang from the earth and saluted their enemy with a fierce and murderous discharge. The effect was irresistible, the French column was rent asunder and vainly endeavoured to deploy; Maitland and

Lord Saltoun gave orders to charge, and the British Guards fairly drove their assailants down the hill. — Meanwhile the other column of the Imperial Guard was advancing farther to the right, although vigorously opposed by the well sustained fire of the British artillery, and Maitland's Guards returned rapidly and without confusion to their position to prepare for a new emergency. By means of a skilful manœuvre Col. Colborne with the 52nd, 71st and 95th now brought his forces to bear on the flank of the advancing column, on which the three regiments simultaneously poured their fire. Here, too, the British arms were again successful, and frightful havoc was committed in the French ranks. A scene of indescribable confusion ensued, during which many of Chassé's Netherlanders in the rear took to flight, knowing nothing of the real issue of the attack. At the same time Maitland and his Guards again charged with fierce impetuosity from their "mountain throne", and completed the rout of this second column of the Imperial Guard. In this direction, therefore, the fate of the French was sealed, and the victory of the Allies triumphant. Farther to the left of the Allied line, moreover, the troops of Donzelat, Erlon and Reille were in the utmost confusion, and totally unable to sustain the conflict. On the extreme left, however, the right wing of the French was still unbroken, and the Young Guard valiantly defended Planchenois against the Prussians, who fought with the utmost bravery and perseverance notwithstanding the fearful losses they were sustaining. Lobau moreover stoutly opposed Bülow and his gradually increasing corps. Napoleon's well-known final order to his troops — "Tout est perdu! Sauve qui peut!" was wrung from him in his despair on seeing his Guard utterly routed, his cavalry dispersed, his reserves consumed. This was about 8 o'clock in the evening, and the whole of the Allied line, with the Duke himself among the foremost, now descended from their heights, and, notwithstanding a final attempt at resistance on the part of the wreck of the Imperial Guard, swept all before them, mounted the enemy's heights, and even passed Belle Alliance itself. Still the battle raged fiercely at and around Planchenois, but shortly after 8 o'clock the gallant efforts of the Prussians were crowned with success. Planchenois was captured, Lobau and the Young Guard defeated after a most obstinate and sanguinary struggle, the French retreat became general, and the victory was at length completely won. Not until the Duke was perfectly assured of this did he finally give the order for a general halt, and the Allies now desisted from the pursuit at a considerable distance beyond Belle Alliance. On his way back to Waterloo Wellington met Blücher at the Maison Rouge, or Maison du Roi, not far from Belle Alliance, and after mutual congratulations both generals agreed that they must advance on Paris without delay. Blücher moreover, many of whose troops were comparatively fresh, undertook that the Prussians should continue the pursuit, a task of no slight importance and difficulty which Gen. Gneisenau most admirably executed, thus in a great measure contributing to the ease and rapidity of the Allied march to Paris.

So ended one of the most sanguinary and important battles which history records, in the issue of which the whole of Europe was deeply interested. With the few exceptions already mentioned, all the troops concerned fought with great bravery, and many prodigies of valour on the part of regiments, and acts of daring heroism in individuals are on record. The loss of life on this memorable day was commensurate with the long duration and fearful obstinacy of the battle. Upwards of 50,000 soldiers perished, or were hors de combat, whilst the sufferings of the wounded baffle description. The loss of the Allies (killed, wounded and missing) amounted to 11,426 men. Of these the British alone lost 6932, including 456 officers; the German contingents 4494, including 246 officers. The total loss of the Prussians was 6682 men, of whom 223 were officers. The Netherlanders estimated their loss at 4000 from the 15th to the 18th of June. The loss of the French has never been ascertained with certainty, but probably amounted to 30,000 at least, besides 7800 prisoners taken by the Allies. About 227 French guns were also captured, 150 by the Allies, the rest by the Prussians.

Napoleon's faults in the conduct of the battle were perhaps chiefly these, that he began the battle at too late an hour in the day, that he wasted his cavalry reserves in a reckless manner, and that he neglected to take into account the steadiness with which British infantry are wont to maintain their ground. The Duke of Wellington is sometimes blamed for giving battle with a forest in the rear, which would preclude the possibility of retreat, but the groundlessness of the objection is apparent to those who are acquainted with the locality; for not only is the Forêt de Soignes traversed by good roads in every direction, but it consists of lofty trees growing at considerable intervals and unencumbered by underwood. It is a common point of controversy among historians, whether the victorious issue of the battle was mainly attributable to the British or the Prussian troops. The true answer probably is, that the contest would have been a drawn battle but for the timely arrival of the Prussians. It has already been shown how the Allied line successfully baffled the utmost efforts of the French until 7 p. m., and how they gloriously repelled the final and most determined attack of the Imperial Guard about 8 o'clock. The British troops and most of their German contingents, therefore, unquestionably bore the burden and heat of the day; they virtually annihilated the flower of the French cavalry, and committed fearful havoc among the veteran Guards, on whom Napoleon had placed his utmost reliance. At the same time it must be remembered that the first Prussian shots were fired about half past four, that by half past six upwards of 15,000 of the French troops (Lobau's corps, consisting of 6600 infantry and 1007 artillery, with 30 guns; 12 battalions of the Young Imperial Guard, about 6000 men in all; 18 squadrons of cavalry, consisting of nearly 2000 men) were drawn off for the new struggle at Planchenois, and that the loss of the Prussians was enormous for a comparatively so brief conflict, proving how nobly and devotedly they performed their part. The Duke of Wellington himself in his despatch descriptive of the battle says "that the British army never conducted itself better, that he attributed the successful issue of the battle to the cordial and timely assistance of the Prussians, that Bülow's operation on the enemy's flank was most decisive, and would of itself have forced the enemy to retire, even if he (the Duke) had not been in a situation to make the attack which produced the final result". — The battle is usually named by the Germans after the principal position of the French at Belle Alliance, but it is far more widely known as the Battle of Waterloo, the name given to it by Wellington himself.

After a drive of $^3/_4$ hr. on the high road from Brussels, the **Forêt de Soignes** is reached, part of which was once presented as a gift to the Duke of Wellington by King William I. of the Netherlands. A great part of the forest, however, has been cut down since the time of the battle. In another hour the traveller reaches **Waterloo**, the headquarters of the Duke of Wellington from the 17th to the 19th of June, 1815. The small church, erected in 1855, contains two basreliefs (r. Victory in bronze, by Wiener; l. the English arms in white marble, by Geefs), Wellington's bust, presented by his family, and numerous marble slabs to the memory of English officers. One tablet is dedicated to the officers of the Highland regiments, and a few others to Dutch officers.

The garden of a peasant (a few paces to the N. of the church) contains an absurd monument to the leg of the Marquis of Anglesea (d. 1854), then Lord Uxbridge, the commander of the British cavalry, who suffered the amputation immediately after the close of the battle. The monument bears an appropriate epitaph, and is shaded by a weeping willow. The proprietor of the ground, who uses all his powers of persuasion to induce travellers to visit the spot, derives a considerable income from this source.

About half-way to Mont St. Jean, which is half-an-hour's drive from Waterloo, is the monument of Col. Stables, situated behind a farm-house on the r., and not visible from the road. The road to the l. leads to **Tervueren**, a château of the Duke of Brabant, once the property of the Prince of Orange. The royal stud was kept here till 1857, when it was transferred to the former abbey of *Gembloux* (p. 154).

The road from Waterloo to **Mont St. Jean** is bordered by an almost uninterrupted succession of houses. At the village, as already remarked, the road to Nivelles diverges to the r. from that to Namur. To the r. and l., immediately beyond the last houses, are depressions in the ground where the British reserves were stationed. To the l. rises the extensive **Farm of Mont St. Jean**, with its massive walls and numerous turrets, which was employed as a hospital during the battle.

About 1 M. beyond the village the traveller next reaches a bye-road, which intersects the high road at a right angle, leading to the l. to Wavre, and to the r. to Braine l'Alleud. Here, at the corner to the r., once stood an elm, under which the Duke of Wellington is said to have remained during the greater part of the battle. The story, however, is entirely unfounded, as it is well known that the Duke was almost ubiquitous on that memorable occasion. The tree has long since disappeared under the knives of credulous relic-hunters.

On the l., beyond the cross-road, stands an *Obelisk* (Pl. i) to the memory of the Hanoverian officers of the German Legion, in the enumeration of whose names the gallant Ompteda stands first. Opposite to it rises a *Pillar* (Pl. k) to the memory of Col. Gordon, bearing a touching inscription. Both these monuments stand on the original level of the ground, which has here been considerably lowered to furnish materials for the mound of the lion. In this neighbourhood Lord Fitzroy Somerset, afterwards Lord Raglan, the Duke's military secretary, lost his arm.

About a hundred paces to the r. rises the **Mound of the Belgian Lion** (Pl. l), about 200 ft. in height, thrown up on the spot where the Prince of Orange was wounded in the battle. The lion was cast by Cockerill of Liège with the metal of captured French cannon, and is said to weigh 28 tons. The French soldiers on their march to the siege of Antwerp in 1832 hacked off a portion of the tail, but Marshal Gérard protected the monument from farther injury.

The mound commands the best survey of the battle-field, and the traveller furnished with the plan and the sketch of the battle, and having consulted the maps at the Hôtel du Musée, will here be enabled to form an idea of the progress of the fight. The range of heights which extends past the mound, to Ohain on the E. and to Merbe-Braine on the W., was occupied by the first line of the Allies. As the ridge of these heights is but narrow, the second line was enabled to occupy a sheltered and advantageous position on the N. slopes, concealed from the eye of their enemy. The whole line was about $1^1/_2$ M. in length, forming a semicircle corresponding to the form of the hills. The centre lay between the mound and the Hanoverian monument.

The chain of heights occupied by the French is 1 M. distant, and separated from the Allied position by a shallow intervening valley, across which the French columns advanced without manœuvreing, but were invariably driven back. The Allied centre was protected by the farm of **La Haye Sainte**, situated on the r. of the road about 100 paces from the two monuments. It was defended with heroic courage by a light battalion of the German Legion, commanded by Major v. Baring, whose narrative is extremely interesting.

After giving a minute description of the locality and the disposition of his troops, he graphically depicts the furious and repeated assaults successfully warded off by his little garrison, and his own intense excitement and distress on finding that their stock of ammunition was nearly expended. Then came the terrible catastrophe of the buildings taking fire, which the gallant band succeeded in extinguishing by pouring water on it from their camp-kettles, although not without the sacrifice of several more precious lives. "Many of my men", he continues, "although covered with wounds, could not be induced to keep back. 'As long as our officers fight, and we can stand', was their invariable answer, 'we won't move from the spot!' I should be unjust to the memory of a rifleman named Frederick Lindau, if I omitted to mention his brave conduct. He had received two severe wounds on the head, and moreover had in his pocket a purse full of gold pieces which he had taken from a French officer. Alike regardless of his wounds and his prize, he stood at a small side-door of the barn, whence he could command with his rifle the great entrance in front of him. Seeing that his bandages were insufficient to stop the profuse bleeding from his wounds, I desired him to retire, but he positively refused, saying: 'A villain is he who would desert you as long as his head is on his shoulders!' He was, however, afterwards taken prisoner and of course deprived of his treasure." He then relates to what extremities they were reduced by the havoc made in the building by the French cannonade, and how at length, when their ammunition was almost exhausted, they perceived two fresh columns marching against them. Again the enemy succeeded in setting the barn on fire, and again it was successfully extinguished in the same manner as before.

"Every shot that we fired increased my anxiety and distress. I again despatched a messenger for aid, saying that I must abandon the defence if not provided with ammunition — but in vain! In proportion as our fusillade diminished, our embarrassment increased. Several voices now exclaimed: 'We will stand by you most willingly — but we must have the means of defending ourselves!' Even the officers, who had exhibited the utmost bravery throughout the day, declared the place now untenable. The enemy soon perceived our defenceless condition and boldly broke open one of the doors. As but few could enter at a time, all who crossed the threshold were bayonetted, and those behind hesitated to encounter the same fate. They therefore clambered over the walls and roofs, whence they could shoot down my poor fellows with impunity. At the same time they

7*

thronged in through the open barn, which could no longer be defended. Indescribably hard as it was for me to yield, yet feelings of humanity now prevailed over those of honour. I therefore ordered my men to retire to the garden at the back. The effort with which these words were wrung from me can only be understood by those who have been in a similar position.

As the passage of the house was very narrow, several of my men were overtaken before they could escape. One of these was the Ensign Frank, who had already been wounded. He ran through with his sabre the first man who attacked him, but the next moment his arm was broken by a bullet. He then contrived to escape into one of the rooms and conceal himself behind a bed. Two other men fled into the same room, closely pursued by the French, who exclaimed: '*Pas de pardon à ces brigands verts!*' and shot them down before his eyes. Most fortunately, however, he remained undiscovered until the house again fell into our hands at a later hour. As I was now convinced that the garden could not possibly be maintained when the enemy was in possession of the house, I ordered the men to retreat singly to the main position of the army. The enemy, probably satisfied with their success, molested us no farther."

The door of the house still bears traces of the French bullets. Several of the unfortunate defenders fled into the kitchen, adjoining the garden at the back on the left. The window was and is still secured with iron bars, so that all escape was cut off. Several were shot here, and others thrown into the kitchen well, where their bodies were found after the battle. An iron tablet bears an inscription to the memory of the officers and privates who fell in the defence of the house.

Farther to the W. are Papelotte, La Haye and Smouhen, which served as advanced works of the Allies on their extreme left. They were defended by Nassovians and Netherlanders under Duke Bernhard of Saxe-Weimar, but fell into the hands of the French about half past 5 o'clock.

The defenders of **Goumont**, or **Hougomont**, another advanced work of the Allies, situated about $^1/_2$ M. to the S.W. of the Lion, were more fortunate. This interesting spot formed the key to the British position, and had Napoleon once gained possession of it, his advantage would have been incalculable. The buildings still bear many traces of the fearful scenes which were here enacted. It is computed that throughout the day the attacks of nearly 12,000 men in all were launched against this miniature fortress, notwithstanding which the garrison (see p. 101) held out to the last. The orchard and garden were several times taken by the French, but they did not succeed in penetrating into the precincts of the buildings. The latter, moreover, caught fire, adding greatly to the embarrassment of the defenders, but happily the progress of the flames was at length arrested. Hougomont was at that time an old, partially dilapidated château, to which several outbuildings were attached. The whole was surrounded by a strong wall, in which numerous loop-holes had been made by the express orders of the Duke in person, thus forming an admirable, though miniature fortress. Notwithstanding these advantages, however, its successful defence against the persistent attacks of overwhelming numbers was due solely to the daring intrepidity of the little garrison. The wood by which it was once partially surrounded was almost entirely destroyed by the cannonade. The loop-holes, as well as the marks of bullets, are still seen, and the place presents a shattered and ruinous aspect to this day. The orchard contains the graves of Capt. Blackman, who fell here, and of Serg. Cotton, a veteran of Waterloo who died at Mont St. Jean in 1849 ($^1/_2$ fr. is exacted from each visitor to the farm).

Prodigies of valour were performed by the Coldstreams and their auxiliaries at Hougomont, and fortunately with a more successful result than that which attended their heroic German allies at La Haye Sainte, but a narrative of all the terrible scenes enacted here cannot now be given. At one critical juncture the French were within a hair's-breadth of capturing this fiercely contested spot. They forced their way up to the principal gate, which was insufficiently barricaded, and rushing against it in dense crowds, actually succeeded in bursting it open. A fearful struggle ensued. The Guards charged the assailants furiously with their bayonets, whilst Col. Macdonnel, Capt. Wyndham, Ensign Gooch, Ensign Hervey and Serg. Graham, by dint of main force and daring courage, contrived to close the gate in the very face of the enemy. — At a later hour a vehement assault was made on the back-gate of the offices, the barricades of which threatened to yield, although crowds of the assailants were swept away by a well-directed fire from the loop-holes. At the same time one of the French shells set fire to the buildings, and the flames burst forth with an ominous glare. Serg. Graham immediately requested leave of Col. Macdonnel to retire for a moment, which the latter accorded, although not without an expression of surprise. A few moments later the gallant sergeant re-appeared from amidst the blazing ruins, bearing his wounded brother in his arms, deposited him in a place of safety, and at once resumed his work in strengthening the barricades, where the danger was rapidly becoming more and more imminent. Suddenly a French grenadier was seen on the top of the wall, which he and his comrades were about to scale. Capt. Wyndham, observing this, shouted to Graham: "Do you see that fellow?" Graham, thus again interrupted in his work, instantly snatched up his musket, took aim, and shot the Frenchman dead. No others dared to follow, the attack on the gate was abandoned by the enemy, and the danger again successfully averted. Similar attacks were launched against the château with unremitting energy from half-past eleven in the morning until nearly 8 in the evening, but were all repelled with equal success. Most fortunately for the defenders their supply of ammunition was abundant. Had it been otherwise, Hougomont must inevitably have met with the same fate as La Haye Sainte, Napoleon would then have been enabled to attack the Duke's right flank, and the Allies would most probably have been defeated, or at least virtually annihilated.

The following incident, which is also well authenticated, is said to have occurred in the vicinity of Hougomont. Colonel Halkett's brigade consisted of raw levies of troops, most of whom now faced an enemy for the first time. They were exposed to a galling fire from Cambronne's brigade, which formed the extreme left of the enemy's line. Halkett sent his skirmishers to meet the van-guard of the French, somewhat in advance of whom Gen. Cambronne himself rode. Cambronne's horse having been shot under him, Halkett immediately perceived that this was an admirable opportunity for a 'coup de main' calculated to inspire his troops with confidence. He therefore galloped up alone to the French general, threatening him with instantaneous death if he did not surrender. Cambronne, taken by surprise, presented his sword and surrendered to the gallant colonel, who at once led him back to the British line. Before reaching it, however, Halkett's horse was struck by a bullet and fell. Whilst struggling to disengage himself, he perceived to his extreme mortification that the general was rapidly walking back to his own troops! — By dint of great efforts, however, he at length succeeded in getting his horse on its legs again. He then galloped after the general, overtook him, and led him back in triumph to his own line. — The troops commanded by Cambronne were a brigade of the Imperial Guard, whose boast had ever been — "*La Garde meurt, mais ne se rend pas!*"

The field-road to **Belle Alliance** from the gate of the farm skirts the wall to the l. It soon becomes narrower, and after leading about 50 paces to the r. passes through a hedge, traverses a field, and passes an embankment. After a walk of 5 min. a good path is reached, leading to the high road in 12 min. more. Coster's house (see below) lies to the r. In a straight direction the road leads to Planchenois (see below). Belle Alliance is situated on the l. This name is applied to a low white house of one storey on the road-side, now a poor tavern, 1 M. to the E. of Hougomont. A marble slab over the door bears the inscription: "*Rencontre des généraux Wellington et Blücher lors de la mémorable bataille du 18. Juin 1815, se saluant mutuellement vainqueurs.*" The statement, however, is erroneous. It is well ascertained that Blücher did not overtake the Duke until the latter had led his troops as far as *La Maison du Roi*, or *Maison*

Rouge, on the road to Genappe, about 2 M. beyond Belle Alliance, where he gave the order to halt. This was the scene of the well-known anecdote so often related of the Duke, who when urged not to expose himself unnecessarily to danger from the fire of the straggling fugitives, replied: "Let them fire away. The victory is gained, and my life is of no value now!" — The house of Belle Alliance was occupied by the French, and their lines were formed immediately adjacent to it. Napoleon's post during the greater part of the battle was a short distance to the r. of the house, and on the same level.

On the N. side of Belle Alliance a field-road diverges from the high road, and leads to **Planchenoit**, or *Planchenois*, a village situated 1 M. to the S.E. To the l. on a slight eminence near the village, rises the **Prussian Monument** (Pl. m), an iron obelisk with an appropriate inscription in German. It was injured by the French when on their way to the siege of Antwerp in 1832, but has since been restored.

The battle between the French and the brave Prussians raged with the utmost fury at and around Planchenois from half past six till nearly nine o'clock. Nine regiments of infantry, a regiment of hussars, and the cavalry of the 4th corps d'armée commanded by Prince William of Prussia were engaged in the action and fiercely contested the possession of the village. The churchyard was the scene of the most sanguinary struggles, in which vast numbers of brave soldiers fell on both sides. The village itself was captured several times by the Prussians and again lost, but they finally gained possession of it between 8 and 9 o'clock. The combatants of both armies in this conflict were all comparatively fresh, and the fury with which they fought was intensified by the bitter hostility of the two nations, and a thirst for vengeance on the part of the Prussians for previous reverses. The victory on this part of the field was therefore achieved towards 9 o'clock, and the total defeat of the French was rendered doubly disastrous by the spirited and well organised pursuit of Gneisenau.

The château of **Frichemont** lies about $2^1/_4$ M. to the N.E. of Planchenois, and the same distance from Mont St. Jean; from Planchenois to Mont St. Jean by the road also $2^1/_4$ M.

Planchenois is $^3/_4$ M. distant from the high road, which is reached near the house (on the l.) once occupied by *Coster*, a peasant who acted as Napoleon's guide during the battle.

11. From Brussels to Malines and Antwerp.

Railway to Antwerp in $^3/_4$–$1^1/_2$ hr.; fares 3 fr. 20, 2 fr. 25, 1 fr. 55 c.; by express somewhat higher. All the trains stop at **Malines**, which is nearly half way ($12^1/_2$ M. from Brussels, 14 M. from Antwerp). Travellers start from the *Station du Nord*, a handsome and commodious structure, where a spare half-hour may be employed in inspecting the interesting and admirably managed telegraph apparatus (1 fr.).

Soon after the station is left, the Royal château of *Laeken* (p. 84) is observed on an eminence on the l. Farther on, the château of the Marquis van Assche also lies to the l.

Stat. **Vilvorde**, the first important place, is a small town on the *Senne*, one of the most ancient in Brabant. Near it, on the l., is the conspicuous *Penitentiary*, an extensive building with numerous windows resembling loopholes, capable of containing 2000 convicts.

A melancholy interest attaches to Vilvorde as the scene of the martyrdom of William Tyndale, the zealous English Reformer and translator of the Bible. He was compelled to leave England on account of his heretical doctrines in 1523, and the same year he completed his translation of the New Testament from the Greek. He then began to publish it at Cologne, but was soon interrupted by his Romish antagonists, to escape from whom he fled to Worms, where the publication was completed in 1525. Copies soon found their way to England, where prohibitions were issued against them, in consequence of which most of them were burnt. "They have done none other thing than I looked for", observed the pious translator on hearing of this; "no more shall they doo if they burne me also!" Notwithstanding the vehement opposition of Archb. Warham, Card. Wolsey, and Sir Thos. More (who vainly endeavoured to refute the new doctrines in 7 vols.), four new editions rapidly found their way to England. In 1529 Tyndale began to publish the first four books of the Old Testament at Antwerp, where he now acted as chaplain to the British merchants settled there. At length, however, he was arrested in consequence of the treachery of a spy, and sent to Vilvorde, where he was imprisoned for two years. He was then tried and condemned as a heretic. On Oct. 6th, 1536, he was chained to the stake, strangled, and finally burned to ashes. His last words were: "Lord, open the king of England's eyes!" He was a man of simple and winning manners, indefatigable industry and fervent piety. His New Testament, which was translated independently of his illustrious predecessor Wickliffe, and his still more celebrated contemporary Luther, forms the basis of the Authorised Version. It is remarkable fact, that the year after his martyr-dem the Bible was published throughout England by royal command, and appointed to be placed in every church for the use of the people.

Malines, Flem. *Mecheln*.

Hôtel de la Grue, Hôtel de Brabant, both in the market-place near the Cathedral; St. Antoine, Rue d'Egmont; St. Jacques, Marché aux Grains; table d'hôte in all at 1 o'clock. *Cour Impériale, unpretending, l. side of Rue d'Egmont, near the station; the salle-à-manger contains two curious old Belgian cross-bows, a weapon once greatly in vogue in the Low Countries. '*Déjeûner de Malines*', locally a highly esteemed dish, may be ordered by those who are curious in culinary matters. — *Restaurant at the station.

The station of Malines, the focus of the four most important Belgian railways (to Brussels, to Ghent, to Antwerp, and to Liège), generally presents a busy scene. The convenience of those who have to change carriages is not much consulted here, as the passenger frequently alights in the midst of a sea of rails, at a considerable distance from the 'salle d'attente', and may easily mistake the trains. The officials, however, politely give all the necessary information. Malines is nearly equidistant from Brussels, Antwerp and Louvain.

The town, which is more than $^1/_4$ M. distant from the station, and is entered by the broad Rue d'Egmont, is situated on the *Dyle*, and has a population of 34,445 inhab. Notwithstanding its broad and regular streets, handsome squares and fine buildings, it is a dull place, totally destitute of the brisk commercial traffic which enlivens most of the principal Belgian towns. The unenterprising character of the inhabitants, somewhat emphatically recorded in the monkish lines mentioned in the Introduction (*'Mechlinia stultis'*), was first manifested in the year 1551, when the magistrates exerted all their influence to prevent the canal between Antwerp and Brussels from being constructed so as to pass near their town. The same policy was followed in the case of the canal from Antwerp to Louvain, two centuries later; and on the construction of the railway, the corporation refused to allow the station to be built within the walls. Multitudes of travellers, therefore, annually pass Malines without even obtaining a glimpse of the town and its venerable cathedral. The latter is the metropolitan church of the cardinal-primate of Belgium, whose jurisdiction formerly extended to the dioceses of Mayence, Trèves and Aix-la-Chapelle.

The *Cathedral of St. Rombold *(St. Rombaut)*, commenced

in the 12th, completed in the 15th century, is an imposing edifice, although externally far inferior to many other Belgian churches. The unfinished tower, a conspicuous object for miles around, is 326 ft. in height; the projected height was 450 ft. It was erected with money paid by the pilgrims, who flocked hither in 1452 to obtain the indulgences issued by Pope Nicholas V. on the occasion of the Turkish war. A stone in the wall of the platform bears the name of Louis XV., to commemorate the visit of that monarch in 1746. The face of the clock is 48 ft. in diameter, a fact which conveys some idea of the magnitude of the structure.

The interior of the church (nave 85 ft. high) is imposing, and worthy of its archiepiscopal dignity. It is adorned by several admirable pictures, the finest of which is an *altar-piece by *Van Dyck*, representing the Crucifixion, in the S. transept, painted in 1627, successfully cleaned in 1848. This is one of the finest of the master's works, and is worthy of the most careful inspection. The composition is extensive and skilfully arranged; the profound grief and resignation depicted in the countenance of the Virgin are particularly well expressed. (The picture is covered; sacristan's fee 1 fr.) In the N. transept: *Quellin*, Adoration of the Shepherds. Two chapels on the same side contain good altar-pieces: *Mich. Coxcie*, Circumcision, painted in 1587; *Wouters*, Last Supper. The last chapel on the N., adjoining the latter, contains a monument in marble to Archb. *Méan* (d. 1831), who is represented kneeling before the Angel of Death, executed by *Jehotte*, a sculptor of Liège. A number of large pictures in the choir are chiefly by *Herreyns* and other painters of the beginning of the present century, representing scenes from the life of St. Rombold; 25 smaller pictures, illustrations of the same subject, of the *Van Eyck School*, are curious and interesting. The Ascension in the chapel at the back of the high altar, is by *Paelinck*, one of the better masters of the 19th cent. The *Pulpit*, carved in wood, like those in the principal Belgian churches, represents the Conversion of St. Paul. Above, John and the women at the foot of the Cross; at the side, Adam and Eve and the serpent. The choir contains several monuments of bishops of the 17th cent., and windows filled with modern stained glass. A sum of 9400 fr. is annually expended by the Chapter in the restoration of the church.

The market-place still boasts of several mediæval buildings worthy of note. The Halles, with a small tower, dating from 1340, are employed as a guard-house. The Town Hall of the 15th cent. is termed the *"Beyard"*. S.W. of the Cathedral stands an old isolated building, bearing the inscription *"Musée"*, and containing a collection of civic antiquities, reminiscences of Margaret of Austria, a few old pictures etc. ($^1/_2$ fr. to the concierge, who lives in the market-place, next door to the Town Hall).

The *Statue of Margaret of Austria (d. 1530), daughter of Maximilian I. and Maria of Burgundy, celebrated as Regent of the Netherlands and instructress of Charles V., was executed by *Tuerlinckx*. The inscription alludes to Malines as her adopted mother-country. It was erected in 1849. The epitaph she jestingly composed for herself during a storm on her voyage to Spain, after her second betrothal (with the Infanta John): *"Ci-gît Margot, la gente demoiselle, qu'eut deux maris et si mourut pucelle"*, and her enigmatical motto: *"Fortune infortune fort une"* are well known.

St. Jean, near the Cathedral, is an insignificant church, remarkable only for a picture by Rubens, who considered it one of his best works: *High altar-piece with wings, an extensive and fine composition. On the inside of the wings: Beheading of John the Baptist, and Martyrdom of St. John in a cauldron of boiling oil. Outside: Baptism of Christ, and St. John in the island of Patmos, writing the Apocalypse. The two latter are in the master's best style. The pulpit in carved wood, by *Verhaegen*, represents the Good Shepherd. The church also contains several other works by the same sculptor.

Notre Dame, the first large church on the l. when the town is entered from the station, contains (in a chapel behind the high altar) *Rubens'* famous *Miraculous Draught of Fishes, a picture with wings, painted in ten days in 1618 for the Guild of Fishers, who paid the master 1000 florins for the work (about 90 *l.*).

The *Botanical Garden*, entered from the Rue d'Egmont, not far from the station, contains a bust of the botanist Dodoens, or Dodonæus, a native of Malines (b. 1517). Count Mansfield, the celebrated general in the Thirty Years' War, and Michael Coxcie, the imitator of Raphael, were also born here.

Frans Hals, born at Malines in 1584, died at Haarlem in 1666, was one of the most prolific, and after Rubens and Van Dyck, the greatest of Flemish portrait-painters. He occupies an important position in the history of art, from having been the first to introduce into Holland that freedom of style and fullness of treatment which had been developed in Belgium by Rubens and his school.

The *Dyle*, which flows through the town and falls into the *Nethe*, 6 M. distant, is affected by the rise and fall of the tide, whence 'Malines' has been erroneously supposed to be derived from 'maris linea'. — Mechlin lace, which once enjoyed a high reputation, is still manufactured here, but cannot compete with that of Brussels.

Soon after quitting Malines, the train passes stat. *Duffel*, a village on the r., and the old Gothic château of *Ter-Elst*. Then stat. *Contich*, l. of the line, and several country-residences. Finally stat. *Oude-God (Vieux-Dieu)*. *Berchem*, a village near Antwerp, was the head-quarters of the French during the siege of the city in 1832.

Antwerp, see p. 109.

Branch Railway from Contich to Turnhout in $1^1/_2$ hr., viâ *Herenthals*, a market town with 4665 inhab. (omnibus to Gheel, see below). Turnhout, the chief town of the district, with 13,002 inhab., is a prosperous place, where the rearing of leeches is an important branch of commerce.

Omnibus twice daily from Herenthals (in $1^1/_2$ hr., fare 1 fr. 80 c.; carriage 12 fr. there and back) to **Gheel** (**Hôtel de la Campine; Armes de Turnhout*), a small town which derives its principal interest from the fact of a colony of lunatics (about 800, formerly 1000) being established here and in the neighbouring villages. The district throughout which they are distributed is about 30 M. in circumference, and divided into four sections, each with a physician and keeper. Dr. Bulkens is the "médecin-inspecteur". The patients are first received into the *Infirmerie*, where their symptoms are carefully observed for a time, after which they are entrusted to the care of a *nourricier*, or *hôte*, who generally provides occupation for them. They are permitted to walk about without restraint within the limits of their district, unless they have shown symptoms of violence or a desire to escape. This really excellent and humane system, although serious apprehensions were at one time entertained as to its safety, has always been attended with favourable results, and has recently been regarded with more favour. — The *Church of St. Dymphna* (an Irish princess who was converted to Christianity, and was beheaded at this spot by her heathen father) contains a fine *altar, with the apotheosis of the saint. The choir contains the reliquary of the saint, painted with scenes from her life, probably by a contemporary of Memling. In the choir-chapels are two curious old *cabinets, adorned with finely executed carving and painting. A painted group in stone, protected by a railing, in the vicinity of the church, bears a Flemish inscription, recording that St. Dymphna was beheaded on this spot, May 30th, 600. The town originally owed its reputation for the successful cure of lunatics to this saint, whose shrine was believed to possess miraculous powers. Exorcism, however, has apparently ceased to be in vogue; and the dark chambers adjoining the church, in which patients were confined for nine days in order to be within the immediate sphere of the saint's influence, are now entirely disused.

12. Antwerp, Fr. *Anvers,* Span. *Amberes.*

Steamboats. To and from London: vessels of the Gen. Steam Nav. Co. twice, the Baron Osy once weekly; average passage 20 hrs.; fares 1 *l.* and 15 *s.* — To Harwich by the vessels of the Great Eastern Rail. Co. (new and comfortable) twice weekly in 15 hrs., thence by railway to London in $2^3/_4$ hrs.; fares to London 25, 20 and 15 *s.* — To Hull twice weekly in 30 hrs.; fares 15 and 10 *s.* — To Grimsby twice weekly in 30 hrs.; fares 15 and 10 *s.* — To Newcastle once weekly in 38 hrs.; fares 20 and 10 *s.* — To Leith once weekly in 48 hrs.; fares 30 *s.* — To Hamburg once weekly; fares 40 and 30 fr. — To Rotterdam, see p. 135.

Hotels. *St. Antoine, Place Verte, R. 3, B. $1^1/_2$, D. $3^1/_2$, A. 1 fr.; *Grand Laboureur, Place de Meir; *Hôtel de l'Europe, Place Verte. — 'S Lands Welvaert *(Hôtel du Bien Etre)*, near the Exchange; Hôtel du Commerce, Rue de la Bourse; Courier, near the Hôtel St. Antoine, unpretending, but well spoken of; *Petit Paris, Quai de Van Dyck; Hôtel du Rhin, near the latter.

Restaurants. *Bertrand, Place de Meir, one of the best in Belgium, dinner 3 fr., or à la carte; Rocher de Cancale, adjoining the Exchange and the Place de Meir. Oysters at the Croix Blanche on the Schelde. — *Cafés:* de l'Empereur, Place de Meir; Suisse and Français, both in the Place Verte. Ices at all the cafés in summer. — *Beer:* *Sodalité, opp. the Jesuits' Church, once the hall of a guild.

Newspapers at the establishment of the *Société Artistique, Littéraire et Scientifique* in the Rue Léopold, near the Malines Gate. Strangers introduced by a member. Pleasant garden, also a café etc.

Post Office, Place Verte (Pl. 36). **Telegraph Office** in the Cité (Pl. G, 5, 6).

Cabs stand in the Place Verte and Place de Meir. Drive in the town for 1 pers. $^1/_2$, 2–4 pers. 1 fr.; per hour 1 pers. $1^1/_4$, 2–4 pers. $1^1/_2$, each subsequent $^1/_2$ hr. $^1/_2$ fr. — Outside the town $1^1/_2$–2 fr. — To the railway-station or Zoological Garden $^3/_4$–$1^1/_2$ fr.

Railway to Ghent, see p. 52; station on the l. bank of the Schelde; ferry thither at the S. end of the quay. To Rotterdam, see p. 140.

Theatre (French) 4 times weekly during the winter; boxes 4, stalls $2^1/_2$, pit $1^1/_2$ fr. — *Schouwburg des Variétés* (Flemish), pit 1 fr.

Porterage from the quay into the town: portmanteau and travelling-bag 1 fr., each additional package 25 c.

English Church in the Rue des Tanneurs.

Principal Attractions: Cathedral (p. 114), Museum (p. 121), Fish-market (p. 134), Zoological Garden (p. 133). — A good survey of the city is obtained from Tête de Flandre (or *Flamisch Hoofd*), on the l. bank of the Schelde; ferry thither every 1/4 hr. 6 c.

Antwerp (from *'aen't werf'*, on the wharf), with 117,324 inhabitants, once the capital of a county of the same name, belonging to the Duchy of Brabant, was founded as early as the 7th cent. It is now the principal seaport of Belgium, and carries on an extensive traffic with Great Britain and with Germany. Its advantageous situation on the Schelde *(Escaut)*, which is here 1/3 M. broad and 30 ft. deep at high tide (60 M. from the sea) rendered it a place of great importance and wealth in the middle ages. When at the height of its prosperity in the 16th cent. it numbered 200,000 inhab. At that period thousands of vessels are said to have lain in the Schelde at one time, and many hundreds to have arrived and departed daily. Commerce, which luxury and revolution banished from other Flemish towns, especially Bruges, sought refuge at Antwerp about the close of the 15th cent. Under the Emp. Charles V. Antwerp was perhaps the most prosperous and wealthy city on the continent, surpassing even Venice itself. The great fairs held here attracted merchants from all parts of the civilised world. The Florentine Guicciardini, an excellent authority in these matters (p. 167), records that in 1566 the spices and sugar imported from Portugal were valued at 1 1/2 million ducats (750,000 *l.*, but really three or four times as much if the altered value of money be considered), silk and gold wares from Italy 3 mill., grain from the Baltic 1 1/2 million, French and German wines 2 1/2 mill., imports from England 12 mill. ducats. Upwards of a thousand foreign commercial firms had established themselves at Antwerp, among them one of the Fuggers, the merchant-princes of Augsburg, who died here leaving a fortune of nearly 2 million ducats. The Flemish manufactures also enjoyed a high reputation about the beginning of the 16th cent., and were exported from Antwerp to Arabia, Persia and India.

Antwerp's decline began during the Spanish regime. The terrors of the Inquisition banished thousands of the industrial citizens, many of whom sought refuge in England, where they established silk-factories and contributed greatly to stimulate

English commerce. The ruin of the city was completed by the atrocities committed by the Spanish soldiery in 1576, when it was unscrupulously pillaged and lost 7000 of its inhabitants by fire and sword, and finally by a siege of fourteen months and its capture by Duke Alexander of Parma. In addition to these disasters, the citizens were deprived of the greater part of their commerce by the intrigues of their Dutch rivals, who during the siege of Antwerp by the Duke of Parma (1584) used secret means to prevent assistance being given to the city, and afterwards erected forts at the mouth of the Schelde to prevent its navigation by Antwerp vessels. The maritime trade of the city received its death blow from the Treaty of Münster in 1648, by which Holland was acknowledged independent of Spain, and it was agreed that no sea-going vessel should be permitted to ascend to Antwerp, but should unload at a Dutch port, whence merchandise should be forwarded to Antwerp by river-barges only. In 1790 the population had dwindled down to 70,000 souls. In Aug. 1794 the French obtained possession of Antwerp, re-opened the navigation of the Schelde, and dismantled the forts erected by the Dutch at its embouchure. Napoleon caused the harbour and new quays to be constructed, but the wars in which he was engaged prevented him from actively promoting the interests of commerce. In 1814 the city was defended against the Allies by Carnot, but was surrendered to the British under Gen. Graham, and afterwards incorporated with the newly constituted kingdom of the Netherlands. The prosperity of Antwerp received a new impetus from the trade which it now carried on with the Dutch colonies, but it was again utterly ruined by the revolution of 1830, in which the citizens participated sorely against their will. The memorable siege of 1832, begun on Nov. 29th, terminated on Jan. 23rd, 1833, with the surrender of the city. The French besiegers under Marshal Gérard numbered 55,000 men, with 223 guns, whilst the garrison under Gen. Chassé consisted of 4500 men only, with 145 guns. The city presented a scene of frightful desolation after the siege, many of the buildings having been reduced to a heap of ruins, and all more or less damaged. For many years after this calamity, the commerce of Antwerp was totally prostrated, but a marked change has recently taken place, and the tide of prosperity has again begun slowly to set in.

About 2500 vessels, of which 140 are Belgian, trade with Antwerp annually.

Antwerp has for centuries been regarded as a model fortress. The original citadel was constructed by the Duke of Alva in 1568; it is in the form of a regular pentagon, protected by bastions ranging at progressive elevations and connected by curtains of proportionate height. In advance of these fortifications another series of extensive bastions was erected in 1701. Gen. Carnot materially strengthened the place by new works at the beginning of the present century, and several advanced works and additional defences are now in process of construction.

During the earlier period of Flemish art, the Antwerp School of Painting held a subordinate rank, and was greatly surpassed by those of Bruges and Ghent; but as these cities gradually lost their artistic, as well as their commercial importance, the fame and prosperity of Antwerp in these respects increased rapidly, until she attained the proud distinction of being one of the wealthiest cities in the world, and a cradle of art second perhaps to none but Florence. This golden era produced numerous artists of great merit, as *Quentin Massys*, *Rubens*, *Van Dyck*, *Teniers*, *Jordaens*, *De Crayer*, *Zegers*, *Neefs*, *Snyders*, *Brill* etc. (comp. Introd.). A brief sketch of the lives of Rubens, Van Dyck and Teniers (greatest genre-painter of Belgium) will probably be acceptable to the traveller who visits the venerable city which these illustrious masters so greatly contributed to immortalise.

Peter Paul Rubens was born at Siegen in Westphalia on June 29th ("St. Peter and St. Paul"), 1577. His parents were natives of Antwerp, which they had quitted for political reasons, and afterwards settled at Cologne. Rubens' father, who was a lawyer, died in 1587, and Rubens was then taken to Antwerp by his mother, and entrusted to the tuition of Otto van Veen, an eminent painter. In 1598 he became a member of the Corporation of Painters, and shortly afterwards set out for Italy, in order to acquire a more profound knowledge of his art. He studied and painted at Venice and many other Italian cities. At Mantua he entered the service of Duke Gonzaga, who in 1605 sent him on an embassy to Philip III. of Spain. In 1608 he returned to Antwerp. Rubens was twice married — in 1609 to Isabella Brant (d. 1626), and in 1630 to Helene Fourment, niece of his first wife. In 1628 he went to Madrid, where he became acquainted with Velasquez, and in 1629 to London. In 1631 he was appointed Dean of the Guild of Painters. He died in 1640, and was buried in the church of St. Jacques. The epitaph on his monument was written by his friend Gervatius. — Rubens was ennobled by Philip IV. of Spain, and knighted by Charles I. of England. He lived at Antwerp in a style of great magnificence, and possessed an extensive and very valuable collection of works of art. A portion only of the latter, sold after his death, is said to have realised half a million francs. Rubens enjoyed the advantage of an excellent education, and possessed great amiability of disposition, combined with handsomeness of person. These qualities, as well as his celebrity as an artist, procured for him the patronage and friendship of princes and men of distinction in almost every part of Europe. Rubens' style, see Introd. VIII.

Antoine Van Dyck, the son of a wealthy merchant of Antwerp, was born in 1599, became a pupil of Rubens about 1615, and was enrolled as a member of the Guild of Painters as early as 1628. He set out in 1623 to prosecute his studies in Italy, where he painted a number of beautifully executed portraits, several of which are preserved at Genoa. In 1628, after his return to Antwerp, he painted the altar-piece in St. Augustin (p. 132), and during his residence here produced most of his fine historical and devotional works. In 1632 he was appointed court-painter to Charles I. of England, who knighted him, and bestowed on him a salary of 200 *l.* per annum. Van Dyck was now in such request as a portrait-painter, that he rarely found leisure for historical works, in which it was his ambition to excel. A plan for adorning the banqueting saloon of Whitehall with a magnificent series of paintings relative to the Order of the Garter proved a failure, owing to the pecuniary embarrassment of the king. At length, in 1640, Van Dyck released himself from his numerous engagements and repaired to Antwerp, eager to find an opportunity of contesting the palm with his rivals on the continent. Hearing that Louis XIII. desired to embellish a great saloon in the Louvre with paintings, Van Dyck repaired to Paris to proffer his services, but he found that the task had already been assigned to Poussin. Mortified by his failure, and perhaps depressed by the threatening aspect of affairs at the English Court, Van Dyck returned to London, where he soon afterwards fell ill, and died in 1641 at the early age of 42. Van Dyck married Mary Ruthven, a grand-daughter of the unfortunate Earl of Gowrie who was beheaded in 1584. Style and merits of Van Dyck, see Introd.

David Teniers, the Younger (born at Antwerp in 1610, died at Brussels in 1694), was admitted to the Corporation of Painters at an early age, probably on account of his being the son of a painter (David Teniers the Elder, inferior to his son), and was elected Dean of the Guild in his 34th year. He was appointed court-painter and chamberlain by Archduke Leopold William, Stadtholder of the Netherlands, and was confirmed in these offices by Don John of Austria, the succeeding governor, who even became a pupil of the master. Teniers also enjoyed a high reputation in other parts of Europe. Philip IV. of Spain, Christina of Sweden and the Elector Palatine sent him numerous orders, which enabled him to amass a considerable fortune. He possessed an estate at the village of Perck, not far from Malines, where he resided in a comfortable style, and received visits from many of the Spanish and Flemish nobles. Teniers' first wife, whom he married in 1637, was a daughter of the painter Jan Breughel (nicknamed 'Velvet' from his partiality to that material), and niece of 'Hell Breughel' (a sobriquet derived from the character of his subjects). Rubens, to whose school however Teniers did not belong, was present at the ceremony. In 1656 Teniers married his second wife Isabella de Fren, daughter of the Secretary of State of Brabant. After a laborious and successful career he died at the advanced age of 84. Position of Teniers in the history of art, see Introd.

The city is now increasing rapidly, especially on the S. and

E. sides. The former inner ramparts have been converted into promenades, with adjoining parks. Near the station is the new *Statue of Teniers* (Pl. 47). The new Boulevard is also adorned with an **Equestrian Statue of Leopold I.**, by *Geefs*, inaugurated in 1868. The inscription records the answer of the king to the delegates of the National Congress of June 27th, 1831, when the crown of Belgium was offered to him. — A colossal statue of the Belgian chief *Boduognatus* (Pl. 45), who opposed the army of Cæsar in the year B. C. 56, was erected in 1861 in the new Boulevard Léopold in the suburb of Berchem, on the S. side of the town.

The site occupied by the city resembles the arc of a circle, of which the Schelde forms the chord. The market-place (p. 119), Place Verte (see below) and Place de Meir (formed by arching over a canal) are the finest parts of Antwerp, which on the side next to the river consists of a network of narrow streets and unattractive purlieus occupied by sailors and the lower classes. The rise of the tide at Antwerp is 12 ft., and it affects the Schelde even as far up as Ghent.

Antwerp, the most interesting town in Belgium, with an exclusively Flemish population, resembles a Dutch or a German city in many of its characteristics. The numerous master-pieces of painting which it possesses afford one of the best proofs of its former prosperity. The fascinating influence of Rubens, the prince of Belgian painters, cannot be understood by those who have not visited Antwerp, where his finest works are preserved. The present *Académie Royale des Beaux Arts* (with 16 professors) is the successor to the celebrated *Guild of St. Luke*, a corporation founded for the promotion of art by Philip le Bon, Duke of Burgundy and Count of Flanders, about the middle of the 15th cent., and richly endowed by Philip IV. of Spain.

The traveller, especially if his time be limited, should at once proceed to the Cathedral. On its S. side is the *Place Verte*, formerly the churchyard, adorned with a ***Statue of Rubens** (Pl. 45) in bronze by *Geefs*. The scrolls and books, together with brush and palette and hat, which lie at the feet of the statue, are allusions to the various functions of the master as a painter, a magistrate, a diplomatist and a statesman.

The ***Cathedral** (*Notre Dame*, Pl. 20), 130 yds. long, 72 yds.

wide, and 90 ft. in height, is the largest and most beautiful Gothic church in the Netherlands. It was commenced about the middle of the 13th cent. and completed a century later. The choir, however, is of more recent origin, the foundation having been laid by the Emp. Charles V. in 1521. In 1566 the church was seriously damaged, and robbed of its most valuable treasures of art by the puritan iconoclasts. In 1794 the French republicans even contemplated the demolition of the sacred edifice, and the sale of the materials by public auction. The interior is simple, but grand and impressive, and the harmonious perspective of the pillars very effective. It is the only church in Europe which possesses six aisles. The dome is moreover completed, as is rarely the case in Gothic churches. The entrance from the Place Verte leads to the S. transept (opp. to which the sacristan lives), which contains *Rubens'* far-famed master-piece, the **Descent from the Cross (comp. Introd. VIII), a winged picture, painted in 1612 (in Paris from 1794 to 1814, restored with great care and judgment in 1852). On the inside of the wings are the Salutation, and the Presentation in the Temple, on the outside St. Christopher carrying the Infant Saviour, and a hermit. Adjacent, *St. Francis, by *Murillo*. In the N. transept *Rubens'* *Elevation of the Cross, painted in 1610, after his return from Italy. Both pictures are covered (1 fr. for each person is exacted by the sacristan for removing the curtain), and exhibited from 12 to 4 o'clock only. The light is generally so subdued, that they cannot be seen to advantage except at an early hour. The high altar-piece, an *Assumption, is said to have been painted by *Rubens* in 16 days, doubtless with the aid of his pupils, for the sum of 1600 florins. The altar itself, which is sumptuously decorated, was also designed by Rubens.

The Descent from the Cross is the most magnificent of these celebrated pictures. The white linen on which the body of the Saviour lies is a peculiar and very effective feature in the composition, borrowed probably from a similar work by Daniele da Volterra at Rome. The principal figure itself is admirably conceived and carefully drawn, and the attitude extremely expressive of the utter inertness of a dead body. Two of the three Maries are more attractive than is usual with Rubens' female figures, but the flabby countenance of Joseph of Arimathæa exhibits neither sentiment nor emotion. The arrangement of the whole is most masterly and judicious, the figures not too ponderous, and the colouring rich and harmonious, whilst a considerable share of sentiment is not wanting, so that

8*

this work is well calculated to exhibit Rubens' wonderful genius in the most favourable light. — According to a well-known anecdote, this picture, when in an unfinished state, fell from the easel in Rubens' absence. *Van Dyck*, as the most skilful of his pupils, was chosen to repair the damage, which he did so successfully, that Rubens on his return declared that his pupil's work surpassed his own. The parts thus retouched were the face of the Virgin, and the arm of the Magdalene. — The popular story with regard to the origin of this famous picture is an invention, the foundation of which on fact is extremely slender. Rubens is said to have been employed by the Guild of Arquebusiers to paint an altar-piece for them representing their patron saint 'St. Christophorus' (i. e. "the bearer of Christ"), as a reward for which he was to receive a piece of ground which belonged to them as a site for his house. Instead of fulfilling the contract literally by painting a single picture of St. Christopher, Rubens generously determined to produce a far more noble work by representing the 'bearing of Christ' allegorically, viz. in the principal picture Christ borne by his friends, in one wing by his Virgin mother before the Nativity, and in the other by the aged Simeon in the Temple. The picture was finished and exhibited to the Arquebusiers, who could not fail to be gratified by its magnificence; but the allegorical mode in which their order was executed was entirely lost upon them, and they complained that there was no St. Christopher. In order to satisfy them, Rubens then proceeded to paint St. Christopher in person on the outside of one shutter, whilst on the other he represented a hermit with a lantern, and an owl, emblematical, it is said, of the obtuseness of the worthy Arquebusiers.

The Elevation of the Cross, although inferior, is also a magnificent work. The figures are remarkable for their easy and natural attitudes, but are inclined to be too heavy. The great animation which pervades the whole compensates to some extent for the deficiency of sentiment, and the variety of the composition is also striking. In the figures of Christ and his executioners the master displays his thorough acquaintance with the anatomy of the human frame. The horses are noble and lifelike, and a dog has even been introduced to give greater diversity to the scene. The latter was added by Rubens in 1627, when he retouched the picture. The wings form part of the same subject. On the r. a group of women and children, with horror depicted in their countenances, behind them the Virgin and St. John; on the l. mounted officers, behind them the thieves, who are being nailed to their crosses by the executioners.

The Assumption, also a famous picture, exhibiting the transcendant genius of the master in an almost equal degree, is less attractive than the two others. The Virgin is represented among the clouds, surrounded by a heavenly choir, below whom are the apostles and numerous other figures. The colouring is less gorgeous than is usual in Rubens' pictures, whilst the ponderosity of flesh somewhat mars the effect. "Fat Mrs. Rubens", irreverently observes an old author, "is planted as firmly and comfortably among the clouds, as if in an easy-chair, gazing with phlegmatic composure on the wondrous scene which she witnesses in her aërial flight, and betraying not the faintest symptom of ecstasy or emotion. Ought she not to be ashamed to sit there in her flimsy attire, and represent a goddess — and a Virgin too?"

Choir. 1st Chapel (on the S.) by the entrance from the Place Verte: altar-piece by *Zegers*. Opposite to it, Descent from the Cross, by *Kwantemann*. — 2nd Chapel: **Rubens'* Resurrection, painted for the tomb of his friend the printer Moretus (d. 1610), half life-size; on the inside of the shutters John the Baptist and St. Martina, on the outside angels. The figure of Christ emerging from the Sepulchre is very fine, and the consternation of the soldiers admirably pourtrayed. Opposite, St. Norbert, by *Pepyn*. The best view of the Assumption is obtained from this chapel. — 3rd Chapel: *O. Venius*, Crucifixion. At the sides 14 curious old scenes from the Passion on a small scale. — 4th Chapel: *De Bakker*, Last Judgment; beneath it the tombstone of Plantin, the celebrated printer (d. 1589). — 5th Chapel: Monument of a M. Verdussen, by *Geefs*. — At the back of the high altar, the Dying Mary, a large picture by *Matthyssens*. Below it, the Marriage of the Virgin, the Visitation, and the Meeting of Mary and Elisabeth, painted with great skill by *Van Bree* in imitation of half relief. — The 6th and 7th Chapels contain nothing worthy of mention. — 8th Chapel: St. Norbert, by *Van Diepenbeke;* opposite to it a copy of *Rubens'* Dead Christ *('Christ à la paille')* in the Museum (p. 123). — Raising of Lazarus, by *O. Venius*. Raising of the son of the widow of Nain, by *A. Franken*. — 9th Chapel: confessionals with large statues carved in wood, by *Verbrüggen*. Descent from the Cross, *Van Dyck* (?). — Opposite, in the choir, a monument in marble to Card. *Capello*, by *Arthus Quellyn*. — 10th Chapel: Crucifix in Parian marble, by *Van der Neer*. Confessionals, by *Quellyn*.

N. Transept: Christ and the Doctors, among whom are portraits of Luther, Calvin, Erasmus etc., by *Franken the Elder;* Madonna, after *Van Dyck*. S. Transept: Marriage at Cana, *M. de Vos;* Last Supper, *O. Venius*. 1st Chapel adjoining the S. transept: the Disciples at Emmaus, by *Herreyns* (1825).

The new *Choir Stalls and the handsome Episcopal Thrones, in the form of tabernacles, and adorned with nine groups from the history of the Virgin, are worthy of minute inspection. They are carved in wood in the richest Gothic style, and decorated with numerous small statues, admirably designed and beautifully executed. The groups on the N. side (unfinished) will represent scenes from the life of the Saviour. The architectural portions are by *W. Durlet*, the plastic by *Ch. Geerts* (p. 163). This carving, although perhaps partly copied from that in the church of St. Gertrude at Louvain (p. 163), is well worthy of comparison with the finest mediæval works of the kind. A marked contrast to these really excellent works of art is presented by the Pulpit, by *Van der Voort*, with its trees, shrubs and birds carved in wood. — Musical works by the most celebrated composers are performed at high mass (10 a. m.) on Sundays and festivals. The organ is a powerful instrument, and on grand occasions is supplemented by a full orchestra, the effect of which is beautiful and impressive. A charge of 3 cent. is made for each chair.

The **Tower** (403 Engl. ft. in height), a beautiful structure of elaborate and slender open work, was begun by *Appelmans* (d. 1434), and completed in 1530 by *Waghemakere*, whose name is inscribed on the highest gallery. The second tower has only attained one-third of the projected height. Charles V. used to say that this elegant specimen of Gothic architecture ought to be preserved in a case, and Napoleon is said to have compared it to a piece of the lace of Mechlin. The Entrance to the tower adjoins the W. portal. The crucifix over the door was cast in 1635 with the metal of a statue formerly erected in the citadel by Philip II. '*ex aere captivo*' to the Duke of Alva. The dwelling of the concierge adjoins the tower (fee for 1 pers. 75 c., 2 pers. 1 fr., 3—4 pers. $1^1/_2$, 5 or more pers. 2 fr.). The ascent is fatiguing; 514 steps lead to the first gallery, 108 more to the second and highest. The view from the latter, however, is hardly more extensive than that from the former. With the aid of a good telescope, the spectator may in clear weather follow the course of the Schelde as far as Flushing, and distinguish the towers of Bergen-op-Zoom, Breda, Brussels, Malines and Ghent. The Chimes are among the most complete in Belgium, consisting of 99 bells, the smallest of which is only 15 inches in circumference; the largest, cast in 1507, weighs 8 tons. On the occasion of its consecration, Charles V. stood 'godfather'.

An old **Well**, adjacent to the principal portal and opposite the door of the tower, is protected by a canopy of iron, and surmounted by a statue of Brabo, a mythical hero who defeated and cut off the hand of the giant Antigonus. It was executed by *Quentin Massys* (d. 1529), '*in synen tyd grofsmidt, en daer-*

naer fameus schilder' ('at one time a blacksmith, afterwards a famous painter'), as the inscription on his tombstone adjoining the entrance to the tower of the Cathedral records. This remarkable and talented man was originally a blacksmith from Louvain, who came to seek his fortune at Antwerp, where this work is one of the specimens of his skill. Here, according to the well-known romantic story (purely apocryphal, comp. p. 126), he became enamoured of the daughter of a painter, and to propitiate the father and win the daughter he exchanged the anvil for the palette. He wooed and painted successfully, and was chiefly instrumental in raising the School of Antwerp to a celebrity equal to those of Bruges and Ghent. He was one of the first of the Flemish masters who adopted the showy and effective style of the Italian schools, whilst his execution was hardly less elaborate and faithful to nature than that of his predecessors. His masterpiece is preserved in the Museum (p. 123). A slab immured at the above-mentioned spot in 1629 by his 'grateful and admiring posterity', bears the inscription: *Connubialis amor de Mulcibre fecit Apellem.*

The **Hôtel de Ville** (Pl. 34) in the vicinity, is situated in the *Grand' Place* (in the centre of which rises the 'Tree of Liberty', planted in 1830). It was erected in 1561—64 in the Italian style from designs by *Cornelis de Vriendt*, and restored in its present form in 1581, after its partial destruction by the Spaniards. It is a handsome edifice, but will not bear comparison with the superb Gothic town-halls of Ghent, Brussels or Louvain. The façade (250 ft. in length) consists of four different orders of architecture, one above the other. The lowest is a 'rustica', above which are three different ranges of columns. In the centre of the pediment, which is surmounted by a large gilded eagle, is placed a statue of the Virgin, as the tutelary saint of the city. The interior possesses little that is worthy of mention. In the chamber of the burgomaster the Chimney-piece is finely sculptured, representing the Marriage of Cana, above which are the Raising of the Serpent, and Abraham's Sacrifice. There are also a few pictures of mediocre merit. A very extensive work by *M. van Bree*, painted in 1806, is an allegory in allusion to Napoleon's scheme of converting Antwerp into a great harbour and maritime depôt. Three pictures in the council-hall represent incidents which occurred during the memorable siege of 1585. Another chimney-piece is adorned with a representation of Solomon's Judgment. Then about a dozen pictures illustrative of the history of the city, and portraits of the royal family by *De Keyser* and *Wappers*. Strangers are not admitted to the interior until the afternoon, after the departure of the officials and clerks. — The *Town Library*, also in the Hôtel de Ville, is always open to the public.

The **Guild Hall of the Archers** (Pl. 37), indicated by the bows on the gable, is a conspicuous and picturesque edifice on the N. side of the Grand' Place, where most of the houses were formerly possessed by different corporations, and date from the 16th and 17th centuries. The finest is that of the Carpenters, bearing the date 1644.

A few streets to the N. of the Hôtel de Ville is situated the church of ***St. Paul** (Pl. 25), formerly the property of the Dominicans, who occupied an adjoining monastery. The church was re-erected in 1571. Entrance in the Rue des Sœurs Noires. The court in the interior contains a '*Mt. Calvary*', an artificial elevation covered with pieces of rock and slag, garnished with statues of saints, angels, prophets and patriarchs, and surmounted by a crucifix. The grotto below is intended to represent the Holy Sepulchre at Jerusalem. The image of the Saviour is swathed in silk and cotton stuffs, and the interior hung with numerous votive tablets. At the entrance, and on the sides of the artificial rocks are half-reliefs carved in wood and rudely painted, representing souls in purgatory.

The wall of the N. aisle is adorned with fifteen pictures of which the best only need be enumerated: *Van Balen*, Annunciation; *M. de Vos*, Nativity and Purification of Mary; Scourging of Christ, after *Rubens; Van Dyck*, Bearing the Cross; *Jordaens*, Crucifixion; *Vinckenboom*, Resurrection. — In the N. transept: *Teniers*, Seven Works of Mercy, a curious collection of cripples of every description; *De Crayer*, Virgin and St. Dominicus; **Rubens*, Scourging of Christ (covered, a copy in the N. aisle). Altar-piece a copy from *Caravaggio*, the Virgin entrusts rosaries to St. Dominic for distribution (the original was sent to Vienna as a gift to the Emp. Joseph, who sent this copy as a substitute). High altar-piece: *Cels*, Descent from the Cross, a work of the present century. S. lateral altar: *De Crayer*, Body of Christ surrounded by Magdalene, St. John and angels. The fine wood-carving of the choir-stalls and the confessionals is worthy of examination. Excellent organ. Sacristan, comp. Introd. I.

The **Vieilles Boucheries**, or old flesh-market, near the church of St. Paul, erected in the 14th cent., and embellished with four hexagonal towers at the corners, is now employed as a magazine for grain.

The ****Museum** (Pl. 39), in the Rue des Récollets (*Minderbroederstraet*, or Street of the Minorites), is open to the public on Thursdays, Sundays and holidays 10—3 o'clock; on other days, 10—7 o'clock, by payment of 1 fr. for each person (tickets are issued at the outer gateway, before the court is entered). The space in front of the entrance is adorned with a *Statue of Van Dyck*, executed and presented by *Leon. de Cuyper*. M. *Nicaise de Keyser* has been director of the Academy since 1855, when a kind of corporation was instituted in connection with the School of Art. The number of members never exceeds 15, of whom 10 may be foreigners. Each fellow of the society is bound to contribute a work to the Museum. The collection now comprises 560 pictures, most of them obtained from suppressed monasteries and churches of Antwerp. The most important works are 14 by Rubens, and 6 by Van Dyck, which alone would repay a visit to Antwerp. There are, however, many other excellent pictures, whilst a considerable number form interesting links in the history of art. Excellent catalogue, with most instructive details, $3^1/_2$ fr. The artists' names are inscribed on the frames of the pictures.

"This celebrated School of Art is established in a suppressed monastery of the Minorites, and the church has furnished lofty and well-lighted galleries for the pictures. Such a spacious locality has most appropriately been dedicated to this purpose, not only on account of the great extent of many of the pictures, but also on account of their high artistic merit, and the devotional nature of most of the subjects. In the latter respect especially there is a marked contrast between this gallery and the Dutch collections. Almost all the works, moreover, were produced in the city of Antwerp itself, and the artists were either natives of the place or members of the famous Guild of St. Luke. The whole collection has remained attached to its native soil, and presents a most instructive continuity, enabling us to become acquainted with the artists, not as merely isolated individuals, but as different members of one great family. The Museum, therefore, possesses a very high historical value, and affords an admirable survey of the development of Flemish art, influenced from one generation to another by the same national, and the same local characteristics."

Entrance Hall. On the l. the *Statue of Van Bree* (d. 1839), a former director of the Academy, by *J. P. de Cuyper* (d. 1852), dedicated *'aen den kundigen en yverigen leeraer syne dankbare leerlinge en medeburgers'* (i. e. 'to the learned and zealous teacher — his grateful pupils and fellow-citizens'). On the r. the *Monument of Isabella of Bourbon* (d. 1465), wife of Charles the Bold of Burgundy (p. 13), a recumbent figure in bronze. Ceiling recently decorated with frescoes.

The enumeration of the pictures begins on the left in each saloon.

I. Saloon. 329. *Jordaens*. Last Supper. 517. *Van Bree*, Rubens' Death (May 30th, 1640), painted in 1827, colouring feeble, and expression somewhat affected. 340. *Corn. Schut*, Martyrdom of St. George, a fine and well executed composition, one of his best works.

243—246. *O. van Veen (Otto Venius, or Vaenius)*, four pictures: Zacchæus in the fig-tree, Vocation of St. Matthew, Beneficence of St. Nicholas, St. Nicholas saving his flock from death by famine.

518. *De Braekeleer*, Defence of Antwerp against the Spaniards (Nov. 4th, 1576). At the entrance to the 2nd Saloon stands the chair occupied by Rubens as Dean of the Guild of St. Luke in 1635. Above it, 515. Portrait of *Herreyns* (d. 1827); on the other side, 524. Portrait of *Van Bree* (d. 1839), two directors of the Academy of the beginning of this century (the next was *Wappers*, who was succeeded by *Nic. de Keyser*, the present director, in 1855).

*335. *Jordaens*, Adoration of the Shepherds; above it, 323. *Zegers*, Nuptials of the Virgin.

*266. *Rubens*, Adoration of the Magi, painted in 1624.

This gorgeous and imposing composition, on a similar scale with the Elevation of the Cross, but far less impressive, contains about 20 figures over life-size, besides camels and horses in the suite of the Three Kings crowded into the picture, whilst the sumptuousness of the costumes and vessels gives the whole an overloaded effect. The king holding the goblet is a somewhat awkward figure. It must, however, be admitted that the work exhibits marvellous freedom and boldness of outline, great skill in arrangement, and a wonderful variety of attitude — all genuine attributes of Rubens.

302. *De Crayer*, Elijah fed by ravens.

419. *Erasmus Quellin*, The Pool of Bethesda, a picture of vast dimensions (33 ft. in height), remarkable also for boldness of composition and accuracy of execution. The head of this picture (No. 420) hangs to the r. of the door, over 329.

II. Saloon. N. 379. *Fyt*, Two sleeping hounds, with game. — N. *303. *Corn. de Vos*, Portrait of a functionary (*knaep*, i. e. 'knave') of the Corporation of St. Luke, painted in 1620. The five artistically executed cups of gold and silver on the table at which he stands were gifts to the Academy, and prizes gained by its members. — *268. *Rubens*, 'Christ à la Paille', the body of Christ resting on a stone bench covered with straw, partially supported by Joseph of Arimathæa, and mourned over by the Virgin, with St. John and Mary Magdalene. On the wings the Virgin and Child, and St. John the Evangelist.

This most interesting altar-piece shows by its carefully executed details that it is one of the master's earlier works, produced before he had adopted his bold and dashing touch. Here, too, we have a full and flowing outline and admirable ease of attitude, but there is no symptom of the master's subsequent abuse of his power, in producing overwhelming masses of flesh and crowds of figures in forced postures. A happy mean is here observed, and there is greater beauty and sentiment than in his later works. The colouring is delicate and harmonious. The weeping Mary Magdalene is a particularly expressive figure.

N. 186. *Mart. de Vos*, Christ rebuking the doubting St. Thomas; on the wings the Decollation of John the Baptist, and the Baptism of Christ. 72. *Titian*, Pope Alexander VI. presenting the Bishop of Paphos, a member of the noble family of Pesaro, to St. Peter, on the occasion of the appointment of the bishop as admiral (this picture is a very mediocre work of the great Venetian master, but should be inspected for the sake of comparison with the Flemish masters). — **46. *Quentin Massys*, The dead Saviour, a scene (technically termed a 'Pietà') between the Deposition from the Cross and the Entombment. It was formerly an altar-piece in the cathedral, painted in 1508, and universally regarded as the master's chef d'œuvre.

Central Picture. The funeral cortège is represented as halting at the foot of Mt. Calvary, whilst on its way from the Cross to the Sepulchre. The dead Saviour is partially supported by Nicodemus, on whose right Joseph of Arimathæa supports the head with one hand, whilst with the other he removes the remaining shreds of the crown of thorns. The Mother in an agony of grief kneels near the body of her Son, and is supported by St.

John. On the left Mary Magdalene, to her right Salome. The corpse itself shows evident traces of anxiety to attain anatomical accuracy. Its attitude is rigid, the countenance distorted by the pangs of the death-struggle. The face of the Virgin is almost as pale as that of the dead body itself. The man with the turban bearing the crown of thorns, appears rather indignant than mournful. The expression of Joseph of Arimathæa is that of pain mingled with benevolence. St. John bears the rigid and almost square features, disfigured by grief, which had become the usual type of the apostle in the earlier period of art.

The Wings, which are less satisfactory than the central picture, represent the martyrdom of St. John the Bapt. and St. John the Evang. In the former Herod is represented banqueting in an open hall, whilst the daughter of Herodias brings in the head of the Baptist. The task of depicting frivolity and vanity in the countenances of the king and the hardened mother, contrasted with an expression of greater feeling in the daughter, has evidently been attempted by the master, though not very successfully. The motion of the girl, intended to be light and elastic, is hard and forced. Some of the heads, however, are admirably finished. — The other wing represents St. John in the cauldron of boiling oil. The executioners, in the costume of Flemish peasants, with their sun-burnt, muscular arms, are attending actively to the fire. In the background the Emp. Domitian appears, mounted on a white horse, and attended by eight horsemen.

N. 579. *Van de Velde*, Calm sea; *372. *Rembrandt*, Portrait of a lady, purchased from the collection of the King of Holland in 1850. — *346. *Van Dyck*, The dead Saviour ('Pietà'), painted soon after his return from Italy (1628).

The Virgin is represented supporting the head of the dead Christ on her knees; St. John shows the wound made by the nail in the left hand to two angels, one of whom veils his face. The features of Christ bear traces of intense physical suffering. St. John and the angel whose beautiful face is visible wear an expression of profound grief, which however they can still express in words, whereas the anguish of the Virgin is unutterable, her head is thrown back, her arms wildly extended. The picture is chaste, the colouring subdued (now unfortunately faded); yet the tendency of the master's school to a full and somewhat sensual outline is apparent, although the work is by no means deficient in sentiment.

*275. *Rubens*, The doubting Thomas, on the wings half-length portraits of the Burgomaster Nic. Rockox (p. 130) and his wife Adrianne Perez. — N. 306. *Corn. de Vos*, The Snoek family presenting ecclesiastical ornaments to the Abbot of St. Michael, painted in 1630; under it, 377. *Steen*, Rustic wedding. — 351. *Valentin*, Card-players. — 307. *Mart. de Vos*, Adoration of the Magi; 291. *Snyders*, Dead game; 290. *Snyders*, Swans defending themselves against dogs; 556. *Teniers*, Old woman.

S. 348. *Van Dyck*, Christ on the Cross, a small picture, of ghastly, but most effective colouring; the full outline of the body, however, hardly accords with the suffering expressed by the features. Human resignation is admirably expressed, but there is perhaps a deficiency in divine dignity.

**265. *Rubens*, Christ crucified between two thieves, one of the most celebrated, and probably the most perfect of the master's works.

Longinus, the Roman officer, mounted on a grey horse, is piercing the side of the Saviour with a lance. The penitent thief, a grey-haired man, is invoking the Saviour for the last time. To the left in the foreground stands the Virgin Mother, whom Mary the wife of Cleophas in vain endeavours to console. Farther back, St. John leans against the cross of the impenitent thief, weeping. Mary Magdalene, on her knees at the foot of the Cross, implores Longinus to spare the sacred body of her master. — This is considered by many to be Rubens' chef d'œuvre, and deserves the minutest inspection. There is no inaccurate drawing here, as in almost all the master's other works, and at the same time the composition and colouring are inimitable. The writhing agony of the impenitent malefactor, whose legs a soldier has just broken, is depicted with startling fidelity, whereas the expression of the other is composed, although worn by suffering. The profile of the Magdalene is remarkably beautiful, expressive of horror and supplication, without being distorted. The whole composition exhibits in the highest degree that marvellous boldness of imagination in which Rubens stands unrivalled.

S. *274. *Rubens*, The Virgin instructed by St. Anna, a very attractive group, colouring mellow and harmonious. — *345. *Van Dyck*, Pietà, similar to No. 346 (see above), with the addition of Mary Magdalene. This picture also presents a considerable resemblance to Rubens in all but the colouring.

S. 344. *Van Dyck*, Portrait of Malderus (d. 1633), Bishop of Antwerp. — *273. *Rubens*, Communion of St. Francis, resembling Caracci's Communion of St. Jerome. The figure of the saint, who is receiving his last sacrament, produces a most painful impression. The picture was executed in 1619, and Rubens' receipt for his remuneration is still preserved ('*seven hondert en vyftig gulden*, *tot volcomen betalinghe van een stuck schilderye door myne handt gemaeckt*', i. e. 'seven hundred and fifty florins, in full payment for a piece of painting done by my hand'). — 161. *Frans de Vriendt*, or *Frans Floris*, sometimes, although not very appropriately termed the 'Flemish Raphael': Fall of the Wicked Angels, painted in 1554, and highly esteemed by his contemporaries.

This extensive work is crowded with figures falling headlong in every conceivable attitude, and is destitute of any depth of perspective. Many of the figures are beautiful, even in their distorted positions. A fly painted on the leg of one of the falling angels has given rise to the absurd story that is was painted by Quentin Massys, and that Floris, whose daughter Massys was wooing, having been deceived by it, was satisfied with this proof of his skill, and gave his consent to the marriage. The name of the painter whose daughter Massys perhaps married (see p. 119) is unknown, while Floris was only 10 years old when Massys died.

S. 267. *Rubens*, St. Theresa delivering from purgatory the soul of Bernardino of Mendoza, founder of a convent of Theresian nuns at Valladolid; an angel on the r. prepares to withdraw Bernardino from the flames. — 343. *Van Dyck*, Christ on the Cross, at the foot of which are St. Catherine of Siena and St. Dominicus, one of the earlier works of the master. An angel with a flambeau reversed and a sepulchral lamp is seated on a stone, which bears the inscription: '*Ne patris sui manibus terra gravis esset, hoc saxum cruci advolvebat et huic loco donabat Antonius van Dyck*' — an allusion to the history of the picture. It was painted, namely, by the master in fulfilment of a promise given to his father on his deathbed, for the Convent of Dominican nuns (suppressed by Joseph II.). The form of Christ is particularly well executed. St. Catherine is represented as devoutly closing her eyes. The whole picture, although not without defects, exhibits more refined sentiment than the works of Rubens. — 192. *Martin de Vos*, Christ and the Pharisees ('Render therefore unto Cæsar' etc.), painted in 1601.

III. Saloon. 218. *A. Key*, Portrait of the Smidt family; 219. *Key*, Smidt's second wife; 393. *Gouban*, Piazza Navona at Rome. Copy of the Adoration of the Lamb at Ghent (p. 37). *M. de Vos*, Triumph of Christ, a winged picture; 162. *Fr. Floris*, Adoration of the Shepherds; *347. *Van Dyck*, Portrait of Cæsar Alexander Scaglia, the Spanish ambassador at the Congress of Münster; 604. *Verschuur*, Portrait of the painter *Herreyns*; 596. *Herreyns*, Dying Christ; under it, 284—286. *Rubens*, Two views of a Triumphal arch, designed by Rubens for the entry of Ferdinand of Austria into Antwerp in 1635, after the Battle of Nœrdlingen and the Victory of Calloo; and the Triumphal car employed on the same occasion; 400. *Murillo*, St. Francis; 283. *Rubens*, Sketch of the Descent from the Cross in the Cathedral.

IV. Saloon. 578. *L. Backhuysen*, Dutch vessel of war. — N. 282. *Rubens*, The Trinity. The dead Saviour is represented in the arms of God the Father, whilst the Holy Ghost hovers above. Above the latter, 425. *Quellin*, St. Bernhard.

S. 280. *Rubens*, Holy Family, '*La Vierge au perroquet*', so called from the parrot at the side, one of his earlier works, presented by him to the Guild of St. Luke; 281. *Rubens*, Christ on the Cross.

All the above pictures, with the exception of Nos. 72., 517. and 518., belong to the Brabant School, which attained its greatest perfection in the 16th and 17th centuries (comp. Introd. VIII). In 1840 the Museum was greatly enriched by a bequest of the burgomaster *Van Ertborn* (whose bust is in the 5th Saloon). consisting of old pictures, chiefly of the Flemish School, which flourished at Bruges in the 15th cent., and preserved in the

V. Saloon. To the r. at the entrance: *37.—40. Four admirable little pictures on a double diptych, almost resembling miniatures. On one of them Mary is represented with a lofty and rich crown, standing in the interior of a Gothic church; on her right arm the Child half wrapped in the swaddling-clothes. On the other, the Saviour in a white robe with the letters *Alpha* and *Omega*, and *P.* and *F.* *(Pater et Filius)* on a ground of red tapestry; beneath are the armorial bearings of the two donors, date 1499. The other sides of these pictures bear the portraits of the donors, Abbots of the Cistercian Monastery of Les Dunes near Bruges. These works were formerly attributed to *Memling*, but are now believed to have been executed by *Cornelius Horebout*, a master who flourished at Bruges about the close of the 15th cent.

l. 547. *Jordaens*, Portrait of a lady; 557. *Van Ostade*, The smoker; 545. *J. Breughel*, The dead Christ mourned over by the holy women and St. John; above it, 549. *Van Dyck*, Portrait of a girl; 552. *Cuyp*, Two horsemen; 583. *Berckheyden*, Amsterdam and the Town Hall; above it, 602. *Verboeckhoven*, Sea-piece; 1., 2. *Giotto*, St. Paul and St. Nicholas, two small pictures on a gold ground; 23. *Gerard van der Meire*, Bearing of the Cross, a winged picture. *11. *John van Eyck*, Virgin in a red mantle, the Child with a parrot and flowers, on the l. St. Donatus, presenting wax-tapers; on the r. the canon Van der Paelen (the donor) with a white robe, kneeling and holding a breviary and pair of spectacles in his hand; beside him St. George in full armour. This picture is a duplicate of that in the Museum at Bruges (p. 21). St. George and St. Donatus are two excellent figures, the old canon with his spectacles inferior, although perhaps a faithful portrait. Mary and the Child are less satisfactory. The heads of both and the figure of the latter are carefully executed, but there is an unusual degree of rigidity in the muscles. The features of Mary are too heavy, and the hair in disorder. All the minutiae are admirably elaborated, such as the fur of the donor, the tapestry and the gold cloth.

N. 43., 42. *Quentin Massys*, Christ and Mary, two admirable heads; 68. *L. Cranach*, Charity; 67. *Cranach*, Adam and Eve; 34. *Rogier v. d. Weyden*, Philip the Good of Burgundy, preserved under glass.

E. 18. *Stuerbout (Dirk van Haarlem)*, Madonna, a small picture; 33. *Rogier van der Weyden* (or *Roger of Bruges*), Annunciation, a small picture of most delicate execution, formerly in the Convent of Lichtenthal near Baden-Baden, once erroneously attributed to Memling (under glass). — *30. *Rog. v. d. Weyden*, Sacrament of the altar, flanked by two wings representing the six other Romish sacraments. The scene is in a spacious Gothic church, the architecture of which serves to unite the groups. This picture, the gem of the burgomaster's collection, is brilliantly executed. The different colours of the robes of the angels, who hover over each of the sacraments, are remarkable and expressive of the different orders of angels according to the komish faith. — 35. *Memling*, Praying monk. — *7., 8. *Hubert van Eyck*, a diptych, Virgin and Child, and donors.

S. 86. *Holbein the Younger*, Portrait of Erasmus of Rotterdam. — 74. *Dünwege*, Holy Family. — On the r. and l. of the last, *55., 56. *Jan Gossaert (Jean de Maubeuge)*, The Holy Women, and the Just Judges; 576. *Steen*, Samson and the Philistines; 554. *Rembrandt*, Portrait of a Jew; 553. *Rembrandt*, The young fisherman; above it, 605. *De Keyser* (p. 121), Portrait of Mme. van den Hecke; 570. *Weenix*, Harbour in Italy; above it, 593. Head of an old man; 568. *Wouverman*, Horsemen reposing.

In the Rue du Jardin is the Private Gallery of *Mme. Wuyts*, the fees for admission to which are devoted to charitable purposes.

*St. Jacques (Pl. 23), erected at the close of the 15th cent., is the principal church in Antwerp after the cathedral, which it far surpasses in the sumptuousness of its monuments and decorations in marble. Traces of the degraded taste of the 17th cent., are, however, distinctly observable in the interior. The wealthiest and most distinguished families at Antwerp here possessed their burial-vaults, private chapels and altars, the most interesting of which is that of the family of *Rubens*, in the choir, at the back of the high altar.

The principal entrance (sacristan's fee 1 fr. for 1 pers., $1^1/_2$ for 2 pers. etc.; comp. Introd. I) is on the S. side, in the Longue Rue Neuve. As most of the best pictures are covered, the attendance of the sacristan is indispensable (his house is the second at the back of the church). The best hours are 12—4 p. m., when there is no service.

On the first pillar to the r., by the W. entrance, is a Resurrection by *Van Balen*; above it, the portraits of this master and his wife, by *Van Dyck* (?). Chapels of the S. Aisle. 1st Chapel: Monument of Bogaerts, the author (d. 1851), with his portrait by *De Keyser*. 2nd Chapel: *M. de Vos*, Temptation of St. Antony. Monument of the Burgomaster Van Ertborn (p. 127). Madonna by *Guido Reni*. Verrière (glass-cabinet), painted by Pluys in 1844. 3rd Chapel: *E. Quellin*, St. Rochus cured of the plague. 4th Chapel: Altar-piece and pictures opposite, by *O. Venius*. Stained glass in the 3rd and 4th Chapels, modern. 5th Chapel: **Fr. Floris*, Women occupied with the Infant Christ and St. John. 6th Chapel: *M. Coxcie*, Baptism of Christ. *Francken*, four winged pictures. — In the S. Transept an Elevation of the Cross, a haut-relief in stone, executed by *Van der Voort* in 1719. — Chapels of the Choir. 1st Chapel: *O. Venius*, Last Supper. *Stained glass of 1626, representing Rudolph of Hapsburg giving his horse to the priest with the monstrance; below are the donors. On the wall of the choir opposite: *Van*

Dyck, Dead Christ. 2nd Chapel: *Van Balen*, Trinity. On the posterior wall: **Jordaens*, Vocation of Peter to the apostleship. On the wall of the choir opposite: *Corn. Schut*, Mary mourning over the body of Christ. 3rd Chapel: *Zegers*, St. Ivo. **M. de Vos*, Martyrdom of St. James. 4th Chapel: *Zegers*, Appearing of Christ. *Van der Voort*, Christ scourged, a group in marble 5th Chapel. *Chapel of Rubens. The tomb of the illustrious painter (d. May 30th, 1640, at the age of 64) was covered by a new tombstone in 1755, bearing a long inscription in Latin. On the r. and l. are the monuments of two female descendants of Rubens, executed by *Geefs* in 1839 and 1850. The altar-piece of this chapel is a fine work by Rubens, painted expressly for the purpose. It derives a still higher interest from the family-portraits introduced. On the l. Rubens as St. George, in front of him his two wives (the first as Martha, the second as the Magdalene) and his daughter; in the centre his father as St. Jerome; the figure in a blue robe with the child is his niece, whose portrait is also known as the 'Chapeau de Paille'; on the r. his grandfather as the god of Time. Rubens has evidently bestowed considerable care on this work, and the figures are more graceful than is usual in his pictures. The colouring, moreover, is remarkably effective and brilliant. — The beautiful **Statue of the Virgin* in marble over the altar, executed by *Lucas Faidherbe*, was brought from Italy by Rubens himself.

6th Chapel: *Jordaens*, S. Carlo Borromeo among persons sick of the plague, praying to the Virgin. 7th Chapel: *Van Lint*, St. Peter taking leave of St. Paul. 8th Chapel: *Victor Wolfvoet*, Meeting of the Women. *Moons* (d. 1845), Christ and the disciples at Emmaus. 9th Chapel: Stained glass of 1611, partially restored. On the wall of the choir, opposite: *Van Balen*, The Trinity; *Thyssens*, Abraham's Sacrifice. — In the N. Transept: *Thyssens*, Assumption of the Virgin. On the pillar, **C. Schut*, Body of Christ on the knees of the Virgin. — Chapels of the N. Aisle. 1st Chapel: *Coberger*, St. Helena giving the Cross to her son the Emp. Constantine. 2nd Chapel: *M. de Vos*, Glory, a winged picture; **Van Dyck*, Crucifixion. Above the latter, stained glass representing the Last Supper, by *Van der Veken*. 3rd Chapel: **B. v. Orley*, Last Judgment; on the wings St. George and the Burgomaster Rockox, the donor of the picture, with his three sons; and St. Catharine and the wife of the Burgomaster, with their eleven daughters. 4th Chapel: *Van Balen*, Adoration of the Magi; **Ryckaert*, Portrait of J. Doncker and his wife. 5th Chapel: Altar-piece of no great merit; *C. de Vos*, Portrait of Corn. Landschot (d. 1656); *M. de Vos*, Mary entering the Temple. 6th Chapel: Tomb of the Span. general Del Pico (d. 1693). — Over the altars on the l. and r. of the entrance to the choir: *Quellin*, Death of St. Francis; *Boeyermans*, Assumption of Mary. By the approach to the choir, life-size statues of the apostles in marble, by *Van der Voort*, *De Cuyper* and others. The high altar itself was designed by *Rubens*. Pulpit of carved wood, by *Willemsens*. Oratorio reliefs by *Geefs* and *De Cuyper*.

A few streets farther N. is situated the small church of **St. Antoine** (Pl. 16), or *Church of the Capuchins*, erected in 1589, the sole attraction of which consists of the two valuable pictures it possesses: on the l., *Christ mourned over by his friends and two angels, by *Van Dyck;* on the r., St. Antony receiving the Infant Jesus from the arms of the Virgin, by *Rubens*.

The **Jesuits' Church** (*St. Charles*, Pl. 21), near the Cathedral, with its handsome façade, was founded in 1614, but rebuilt in accordance with the taste of the 18th cent. after its destruction by a fire in 1718. The tower is considered the finest which has been constructed in Belgium since the epoch of the Renaissance. The best pictures are: High altar-piece, an Assumption of the Virgin, by *Schut;* on the l., St. Francis Xavier kneeling before the Virgin, by *Zegers;* in a chapel on the r., Presentation in the Tempel, by *Wappers*.

The **Church of the Augustines** (Pl. 17), erected in 1615, possesses a large *altar-piece by *Rubens*, representing the "Nuptials of St. Catharine with the Infant Jesus", unfortunately not in a good state of preservation. The Virgin and Child are seated on a kind of stage, behind them St. Joseph, on the r. St. Catharine receiving the ring from the Child. SS. Peter and Paul in the background, John the Baptist on the steps to the l., with the Lamb and angels. Below are several other saints, among whom St. George in full armour is the master himself. The picture is brilliantly coloured and most skilfully arranged. The head of St. Catharine is particularly fine. — Then to the r. of the

9*

principal entrance: *Lens*, Presentation in the Temple; l. *Cels*, Elisabeth and Mary, both works of the present century. Farther to the r. a copy of *Van Dyck's* Crucified Christ (p. 126), a copy of *Rubens'* 'Christ à la paille', and the Martyrdom of St. Apollonia as an altar-piece, by *Jordaens*. The horse in the latter is worthy of notice. On the l. an altar-piece by *Van Dyck*, The Vision of St. Augustine, a work of considerable reputation, but by no means one of his best. High up in the choir, Baptism of St. Augustine, by *Van Bree*. The pictures of Rubens and Jordaens were taken to Paris by the French, but restored in 1815. On the r. of the choir a modern chapel in the Romanesque style, with frescoes by *Bellemans*.

The suppressed Augustine Monastery has been converted into an arcade, termed the **Cité**, in order that Antwerp, like Brussels and Liège might also boast of its 'Passage'; but the undertaking has proved a failure. Part of it has been fitted up as a temporary exchange.

The church of **St. Andrew** (Pl. 14), erected in 1514—23, contains a very large pulpit in carved wood, by *Van Geel* and *Van Hool*. St. Peter and St. Andrew are represented in a boat on the sea, from which they are called by the Saviour. Figures life-size, finely executed. In the N. chapel of the choir: *Govaerts*, Flight into Egypt; *Zegers*, St. Anna instructing the Virgin. Modern stained glass, date 1855. Choir: *O. Venius*, Crucifixion of St. Andrew; *Quellin*, guardian angel of the youth. S. chapel of the choir: *Franck*, Last Supper (altar-piece); *Jordaens*, Adoration of the Magi; *Quellin*, Christ at Emmaus; *Quellin*, Holy Family. By the choir are two statues, l. St. Peter by *A. Quellyn*, r. St. Paul by *Zielens*. In the transepts two large modern pictures, r. Dead Saviour on the knees of the Virgin (a 'Pietà') by *Verlaf*, l. an Entombment by *Van Eycken*. Side-altar on the S.: *Pepyn*, Crucifixion; on the N., *Franck*, St. Anna teaching children, a work with numerous figures. The aisles contain a number of large modern pictures. On a pillar in the S. aisle is a small medallion-portrait of Mary Queen of Scots (by *Pourbus*), with an inscription, in memory of her two English ladies-in-waiting who are interred here. On the S. pillar of the choir a slab commemorates *Wauters* (d. 1853), one of the better painters of the present century.

The magnificent **Bourse**, or Exchange (Pl. 8), was almost entirely destroyed by a conflagration in 1858. The external walls and a few Moorish-Gothic arches are now the sole remains.

The **Royal Palace** (Pl. 41), in the Place de Meir, erected for a wealthy citizen of Antwerp in 1755 in the fantastic 'Pompadour style', is not accessible to the public.

Rubens' House (Pl. 38), in the **Rubens-Street**, near the Palace, is the largest on the l., with two gateways. The façade is new, and it now belongs to a mercantile firm.

The spacious **Theatre** (Pl. 50), completed in 1834, is handsomely fitted up in the interior. Niches over the windows contain busts of eminent dramatists and composers, among whom are Shakspeare and Schiller, Molière and Racine, Sophocles and Euripides, Mozart, Méhul etc. On the summit, the statues of the Nine Muses.

The church of *St. George*, near the theatre, consecrated in 1853, but still unfinished, is embellished with fine mural *paintings by Güffens and Swerts: St. George on horseback, Christ, the Evangelists etc.

The ***Zoological Garden** (*'Deertuin'*, Pl. 36), founded in 1843, situated on the E. side of the city, beyond the railway-station, consists of a garden and a small park, with a fine collection of animals. The arrangements are admirable, and the whole establishment one of the best in Europe. Numerous inscriptions bear testimony to the liberality with which the gardens are supported by private donations of animals, buildings etc. Admission 1 fr. (unless the visitor is introduced by a member). Concerts in summer on Tuesdays and Thursdays, 6—8 p. m., well worthy of a visit.

Grounds resembling a park extend between the Zoological Garden and the Porte de Malines, in the vicinity of which (near the Société Artistique, p. 109) are the **Botanical Gardens** (Pl. 35), with a spacious palm-house and admirably kept grounds.

If the traveller still have a few hours at his disposal, he may devote them to visiting the **Quays** on the Schelde, which were constructed by Napoleon in 1802. They extend from the Arsenal, near the S. Citadel, to the docks, a distance of nearly 1 M., and afford an entertaining promenade. A considerable number of the vessels and their crews are English and Dutch.

The street which descends from the Place Verte to the Schelde passes through a gateway adorned with sculptures, and bearing an inscription dedicated by the '*Senatus Populusque Antwerpienses*' to the '*Magnus Philippus*'. This prince was Philip IV., great-grandson of the Emp. Charles V., who reigned from 1621 to 1665, and under whom Spain entirely lost her prestige, having been deprived of Portugal in 1640, and finally of the Netherlands in 1648.

The **Marché aux Poissons** (Pl. 30), opposite the quay of the English steamboats, and adjoining the Hôtel du Rhin (p. 109), presents a busy and amusing scene between 7 and 9 a. m., when the fish-auctions take place (p. 5). The building adjoining the market on the E., flanked with towers at the corners, was formerly the seat of the *Inquisition*, the introduction of which, under the Duke of Alva, contributed so greatly to undermine the prosperity and diminish the population of the city. The court still contains a pillory and several curious old inscriptions. The dungeons are now used as cellars.

The drawbridges over the canals, which originally constituted the sole harbour, as well as the costumes and language of the people, remind the traveller of a Dutch, rather than a Belgian town. The ***Docks** at the N. extremity of the quays are now reached. The two older basins were constructed by Napoleon (1804—13), at a cost of 13 million francs, in consequence of a decree of July 21st, 1803, constituting Antwerp the principal naval depôt of the W. coast of France. In 1813 thirty vessels of war of the first class lay here, and the following year the fleet was bombarded by the English, but without decisive result. On the conclusion of the Peace of Paris the naval dockyard was demolished in accordance with the terms of the treaty. The small dock is capable of containing 100 vessels of moderate tonnage, the largest 250, and the new dock farther to the N. about 200. The graving-dock near the latter can be emptied by a steam-pump in $^3/_4$ hr. Sailors of many different nationalities are encountered here, and the signs over the shops enumerate their commodities in English, Spanish, French etc.

Between the two older docks rises the **Maison Hanséatique** (Pl. 31), a massive and venerable building originally employed as the magazine of the Hanseatic cities, and adorned with Doric and Ionic columns. It bears the inscription SACRI ROMANI IMPERII DOMUS HANSAE TEUTONICAE (date 1564), with the armorial bearings of the three cities of the League. At that time, as well as at the present day, the ambassador or consul of the League resided here. It is termed '*Oosterlingshuis*' by the Flemings. Under Napoleon it was converted into a naval barrack. In 1863 it was ceded by the Hanseatic towns to the Belgian government, as an equivalent for all river-dues exigible for the future from their vessels.

The upper dock is flanked with a row of substantial buildings, used as bonded warehouses, or **Entrepôts**, which are connected with the railway-station by several lines of rails.

The new *Fortifications*, commenced in 1859, consist of a polygonal rampart encircling the city about 1 M. beyond the original pentagon, thus affording ample space for the construction of new quarters and streets. Two citadels (N. and S.), forming the extremities of the rampart, command the course of the Schelde, as well as the city itself. Finally a series of detached forts, $3^{1}/_{2}$ M. distant from the ramparts, completes the system. The old **Citadel**, now termed Citadelle du Sud, at the S. extremity of the quays, was formerly termed *Paciotti*, after the Italian engineer by whom it was constructed for the Duke of Alva.

13. From Antwerp to Rotterdam.

Railway to Moerdijk (p. 140) in 2 hrs., thence to Rotterdam by steamboat in $2^{1}/_{2}$ hrs., in all $4^{1}/_{2}$ hrs.; fares for the whole journey 9 fr. 90, 7 fr. 90, 4 fr. 95 c. — The new railway from *Willemsdorp*, opposite to Moerdijk, viâ *Dordrecht* (where the Meuse is crossed by a bridge), to *Rotterdam* is rapidly approaching completion. — Steamboats also perform the entire journey between Antwerp and Rotterdam in $6^{1}/_{2}$—7 hrs., a pleasant trip in fine weather; fares 5 fr. 30, 3 fr. 20 c.; departure daily according to tide. Restaurant on board the vessels ('Telegraph', Nos. I. and II.), which are tolerably comfortable. Agents at Antwerp, *Van Maenen et Co.*, Quai Van Dyck 1; at Rotterdam, *Verooy et Co.*, on the quay (Boompjes).

The route by water intersects the Dutch province of Zeeland, the character of which is well expressed by its armorial bearings — a swimming lion, with the motto: *Luctor et Emergo*. The greater part of the province lies considerably below the sea-level, the only natural elevation being a few dunes, or sand-hills on the W. coast of the Islands of Schouwen and Walcheren. The rest of the province is protected against the encroachment of the sea by vast embankments, the aggregate length of which amounts

to 300 M., and the annual repairs to a million florins (
The most massive of these bulwarks are on the S. W.
the Island of Walcheren. These huge works, the c
and maintenance of which have cost enormous sums
are not unreasonably regarded by the inhabitants as w
weight in silver. Part of the embankment gave way in
consequence of which the whole island, including the
Middelburg itself (p. 139), was laid under water.

The entire group of islands has probably been formed
vial deposits, which have been gradually reclaimed from
and utilized by the construction of the embankments. Th
are separated from each other by the different embouchure
Schelde, which are frequently so broad that the low b
hardly be distinguished by the steamboat-passenger. Se
occasionally seen sunning themselves on the shore in hot
ther. The land itself is extremely fertile and admirably c
vated, producing abundant crops of wheat and other grain. U
the traveller be interested in agriculture, or contemplate a
to the sea-embankments, he will find little attraction in the to
of *Zierikzee*, *Goes*, *Middelburg* and *Flushing* (p. 139), which p
sent the usual characteristics of clean and prosperous Dutch tow

Immediately after the departure of the steamboat, the passen-ger obtains a final view of Antwerp, extending in a wide curve along the bank of the Schelde, above which rise the graceful steeple of the Cathedral, St. Paul, St. Jacques with its low, massive tower on the l., and St. Andrew, the most conspicuous church to the r. On the N. the city is bounded by the Docks (p. 134), in the vicinity of which Lieutenant van Speyk, a gallant Dutch naval officer, sacrificed his life in 1831 in vindication of the honour of his flag. A storm had driven his gunboat on shore, and a crowd of Belgians immediately hastened to the spot to secure the prize, calling on the commander to haul down his colours and surrender. The devoted Van Speyk, preferring death to capture, fired his pistol into the powder-magazine, which exploded instantaneously, involving friends and foes, as well as himself, in one common destruction.

On the opposite back lies *Fort Ostersweel* (or *Austruweel*); then, below Antwerp, the *Fort du Nord* (or. *Ferdinand*), beyond which *Fort Calloo* rises on the l. At this point, between Calloo on the

87

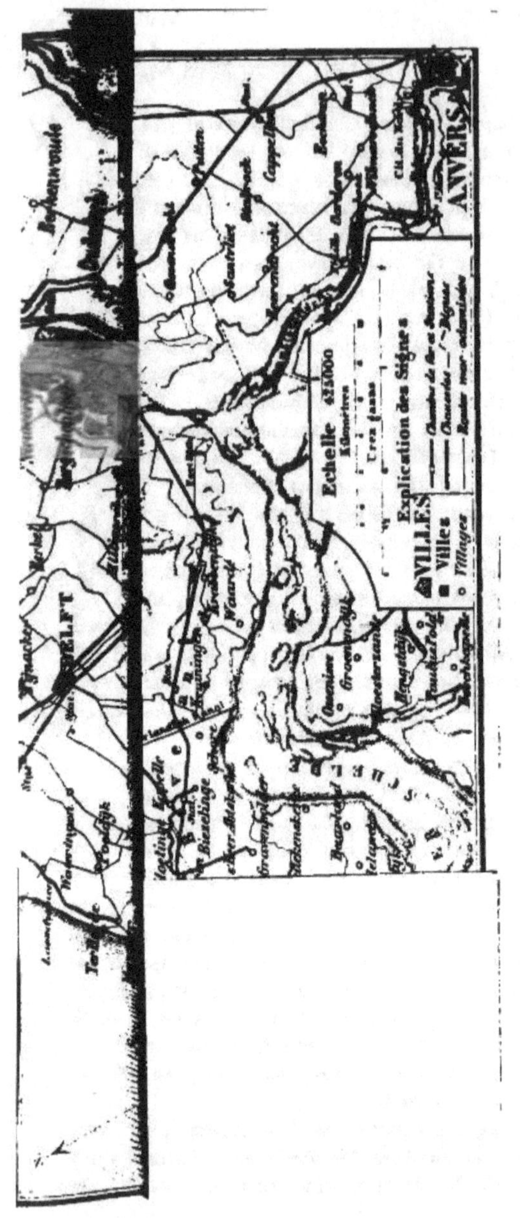

na,
ted
in
ted
ni-
nd
en
ci-
roy
he
lge
00
ely
ive
ary
ny
p,
ds
h,

ort
ed
n,
ls,
ort
tly
he

n-
art
of
It
in
of
o-
he
l,

as

to 3
The
the
and
are
weig
cons
Midd

vial
and
are
Sche
hardl
occas
ther.
vated
the t
to th
of *Zi*
sent

In
ger o
along
steepl
sive t
to the
in the
naval
honou
and a
cure t
lours
to cap
ploded
himsel

On
below
Fort C

l. and *Oorderen* on the r. bank, Duke Alexander of Parma, Philip II. of Spain's viceregent in the Netherlands, constructed his celebrated bridge across the Schelde, 2400 ft. in length, in 1585, during the siege of Antwerp, which had warmly espoused the cause of the patriotic 'Gueux' (see p. 72). All communication between the besieged and their confederates in Zeeland was thus entirely broken off. The bridge is said to have been defended by two towers and nearly one hundred guns. The citizens of Antwerp used every means in their power to destroy this formidable barrier. After numerous fruitless attempts, the fire-ships of the Italian engineer Giambelli at length set the bridge on fire, and blew up a portion of it so unexpectedly that 800 Spaniards lost their lives, and the Duke himself was severely wounded. The besieged, however, were not in a position to derive any advantage from this signal success, whilst their auxiliary fleet anchored below Fort Lillo was too weak to attack the enemy single-handed. The damage was speedily repaired, and Antwerp, notwithstanding a most obstinate defence, was shortly afterwards reduced by famine. The Spaniards entered the city on Aug. 17th, of the same year.

On the l. lower down, lies *Fort Liefkenshoek*, on the r. *Fort Lillo*, both commanding the course of the river, and both retained by the Dutch till 1839, when they were ceded to Belgium. Then, on the l. bank, *Doel*. The estuary of the Schelde now expands, and a short distance farther the Dutch frontier is crossed. **Fort Bath**, where the English fleet landed in 1809, and subsequently an important point in the Dutch-Belgian war of 1831—32, is the first Dutch station, and seat of the custom-house authorities.

The steamer now quits the main arm of the Schelde and enters a narrow channel termed the *Kreek Bak*, the navigable part of which is indicated by piles. The E. coast of the island of *Zuid-Beveland* is '*verdronken land*' (literally 'drowned land'). It was once a rich agricultural tract, but was inundated in 1532 in consequence of the bursting of the embankment, and upwards of 3000 persons perished. Operations, however, are now in progress, by which the submerged district will be reclaimed, and the present shallow and intricate channel converted into a canal, 18 ft. in depth.

Bergen op Zoom, a Dutch fortress, the tower of which has long been conspicuous, is now reached. It is the capital of a County which came into the possession of the Elector Palatine of Germany by marriage in 1722, and formed part of his dominions till 1801. The fortress, although the chef d'œuvre of the eminent Dutch engineer Gen. van Coehoorn, was taken by the French in 1747. The steamboat-pier is 2 M. from the town.

The steamboat here quits the Ooster-Schelde and enters the narrow *Rivier Eendragt*, passing a small island covered with sea-fowl. The small town of *Tholen*, and the village of *Oud-Vosmeer* situated in a small plantation, are the next stations. The *Slaak*, a broad and shallow expanse of water, the bottom of which is left dry at low tide, is next traversed. Soundings are frequently made, and the utmost attention of the steersman is requisite. The island on the l. is *Philippsland*. At the *Steenbergsche Vliet*, the *Krammer*, one of the embouchures of the Maas (or Meuse), is entered, and beyond it the *Volkerak*, the most southern arm of the river.

On the voyage from Rotterdam to Antwerp the steamer does not enter the *Slaak*, but proceeds farther to the W. To the N. in the distance rise the towers of *Nieuwe-Tonge* and *Oude-Tonge*. At *Bruinisse* the steamboat enters the narrow canal *de Keete*, towards the S.W., separating the islands of Tholen and Duiveland, and touches at *Syp*, whence an omnibus runs in 1 hr. to Zierikzee (*Hof van Holland*).

This canal is celebrated for the intrepid bravery with which it was crossed in 1575, partly by wading and partly by means of small boats, by 1700 Spanish volunteers under *Requesens*, the successor of the Duke of Alva, notwithstanding the incessant and galling fire of the Flemish defenders of the island, many of whom crowded round the assailants in boats. The capture of Zierikzee was the reward of this determined attack. The siege had already lasted a whole year, during which besiegers and besieged had alike distinguished themselves by numerous feats of valour. The difficulties of the siege were greatly increased by the opening of the flood-gates and the complete inundation of the island, whilst the besieged were reduced to great extremities on account of the shallowness of the water, which precluded the possibility of communication with their fleet under the Prince of Orange, and thus cut off all hope of fresh supplies of provisions and ammunition.

The lofty square tower of the cathedral of Zierikzee is a conspicuous point, long after the steamer has quitted the canal and begun to traverse the broad expanse of the *Ooster-Schelde*. The vessel now turns towards the S.E., and touches at *Yersekendam*, or *Jersendam*, whence it proceeds to *Bergen op Zoom*, and thence to Antwerp by the route already described.

Travellers to *Goes*, *Middelburg* (21 M.), or *Flushing* (6 M. farther) find conveyances in waiting at Yersekendam. Goes (*Korenbeurs*), sometimes termed *Tergoes*, lies on the island of *Zuid-Beveland*, separated by the *Sloe*, an arm of the Schelde, from the island of Walcheren, on which Middelburg and Flushing are situated. The ancient château of *Oostende* at Goes, now an inn, was once the residence of the beautiful Jacqueline, Countess of Holland, whose romantic and eventful career has already been briefly recorded (p. 44).

Middelburg (*Heerenlogement; Neederlandsch Logement*), the birthplace of Hans Lippersheim (according to others, born at Wesel; d. at Middelburg in 1619), the inventor of the telescope (about 1608), is the capital of the Province of Zealand, with 16,000 inhabitants. The magnificent *Town Hall*, erected in 1468 by Charles the Bold, Duke of Burgundy, is adorned with 25 statues of counts and countesses of Flanders and Zeeland. The *New Church* contains the monuments of John and Cornelius Evertsen, two Dutch naval heroes, who fell in 1666 whilst fighting under Admiral Ruyter against the English. An omnibus runs hence every hour to

Flushing, Dutch *Vlissingen* (*Duke of Wellington; Hôtel du Commerce*), a strongly fortified town with 11,000 inhab., possessing a naval dockyard and a harbour for merchant-ships. It was bombarded and taken by the English fleet under Lord Chatham in 1809, on which occasion upwards of one hundred houses, as well as the handsome town-hall and two churches, were destroyed. This was the sole and useless result of the English expedition to the island of Walcheren, untertaken by one of the finest British fleets ever equipped, the object of which was the capture of Antwerp. Napoleon afterwards caused the fortifications to be materially strengthened, so that they now, in conjunction with *Fort Breskens* on the opposite bank, completely command the mouth of the Schelde. In 1559 Philip II. embarked at Flushing, never again to return to the Netherlands. He is said to have been accompanied thus far by Prince William of Orange, and to have reproached him with having caused the failure of his plans. The prince pleaded that he had acted in accordance with the wishes of the States, to which the disappointed monarch vehemently replied: '*No los Estados, ma vos, vos!*' After the Gueux had taken Briel, Flushing was the first Dutch town which raised the standard of liberty (in 1572). — Admiral de Ruyter, the greatest naval hero of the Dutch, was born here in 1607. He was the son of a rope-maker, but his mother, whose name he assumed, was of noble origin. His greatest exploit was the ascent of the Thames with his fleet in 1667, demolishing fortifications and vessels of war, and throwing London into the utmost consternation. This triumph was principally owing to the negligence of Charles II., who spent the money destined for the support of the navy on his court and his pleasures. A few weeks afterwards, however, peace was declared at Breda, and the achievements of the Admiral thus terminated. A monument was erected to his memory in 1841 near the harbour. An observatory is also situated here.

Two hours after leaving Bergen op Zoom, the Antwerp and Rotterdam boat reaches the estuary of the Maas. The entrance to the *Hollandsch Diep*, as this broad arm is termed, is defended by two blockhouses, covered with red tiles, *Fort Ruyter* on the r., and *Fort Ooltgensplaat* on the l., both constructed by the French as defences against the English. **Willemstad**, a fortress with carefully preserved walls and ramparts, erected by Prince William I. of Orange in 1583, next becomes visible. In 1792 it was bombarded by the French during a fortnight, but without success. The lofty scaffolding on the quay is a lighthouse. Vessels of considerable size are frequently encountered here on their way from *Hellevoetsluis*, an important Dutch harbour for East India traders. The Hollandsch Diep is occasionally very rough in stormy weather, and the horrors of sea-sickness are sometimes experienced by the passengers.

Opposite *Moerdijk* (at present the terminus of the railway, the prolongation of which is nearly completed), near the small village of *Willemsdorp*, the steamer enters the *Dordsche Kil*, a very narrow branch of the Maas, with carefully kept dykes and green banks, resembling a canal. In 1711, John William, Prince of Orange, was drowned in crossing the *Diep* at Moerdijk, when on his way to the Hague to meet Fred. William I. of Prussia, with a view to adjust the difficulties of the Orange succession. At the extremity of the Kil rises a long succession of windmills, which constitute one of the most picturesque features of Dutch scenery. Most of them are saw-mills, furnished with auxiliary steam-engines, which are employed when the power of the wind is insufficient. Others are cement mills, where 'trass', a volcanic product of the Eifel in Rhenish Prussia, is reduced to powder. A number of clean and substantial houses are clustered near the mills. The steamer then touches at **Dordrecht**, near its curiously ornamented town-gate.

Dordrecht, and thence to *Rotterdam* (in 1 hr.) see p. 304.

The Railway Journey from Antwerp to Moerdijk (2 hrs.) is extremely unattractive. Fares 5 fr. 95, 4 fr. 80 c., 3 fr. — *Roozendaal*, the fifth station, is the first Dutch village, and seat of the custom-house authorities. Luggage superficially examined.

Moerdijk (*Hôtel Hofmann*, R. 1/2, B. 1/2 fl.) is a steamboat-station of considerable importance, being at present the terminus of the railway. Steamboats ply regularly hence to Amsterdam (the 'Stad Dordrecht', 'Stad Antwerpen' and 'Stad Rotterdam'); also to Rotterdam in connection with the trains, and twice daily to Dordrecht and Rotterdam independently of the railway (the 'Jan de Witt' and 'Nicholas de Witt'). Those who arrive by the last train from Antwerp must pass the night at Moerdijk, whence they may proceed by one of the latter vessels at 8 a. m. to Rotterdam, arriving there at 10 o'clock (1 hr. to Dordrecht, 1 hr. more to Rotterdam).

Branch Line from Roosendaal by *Etten* to Breda and Tilburg (in connection with which it is contemplated to open a new line of communication between the North Sea and the Rhine). To Breda in 40 min., to Tilburg in $1^1/_4$ hr.

Breda *(Hôtel de Flandre; Goude Leeuw)*, with 15,000 inhab., is a fortress on the *Merk* and the *Aa*, two small rivers which, with the marshy district around it, render the place almost impregnable, but at the same time unhealthy. The principal church contains the *monument of Count Engelbert II. of Nassau, the general and favourite of the Emp. Charles V., and his wife Mary of Baden, attributed to *Michael Angelo*. Their figures, sculptured in Italian alabaster, rest on a sarcophagus, and four statues (Cæsar, Regulus, Hannibal, and Philip of Macedon) in a half kneeling attitude bear a slab on which the admirably wrought armour of the Count is placed. The choir contains some good wood-carving, representing monks in ludicrous postures, in derision of the Romish clergy. — The *Old Palace* was erected in 1350 by Count Henry of Nassau, the *New Palace* in 1696 by William of Orange, King of England. The fortress is a quadrangle, surrounded by the river Merk. A Dutch military academy was founded here in 1826, but transferred to Medemblick in 1836.

Tilburg *(Zwaard)*, with 17,000 inhab., and an ancient château, possesses 84 cloth-factories, which annually produce upwards of 20,000 pieces of cloth, most of them of a superior quality.

14. From Antwerp to Aix-la-Chapelle.

The most direct route from Antwerp to Aix-la-Chapelle is viâ Mastricht ($4^1/_4$–$5^1/_2$ hrs.). The line is the property of a private company, and the fares (13 fr. 10, 9 fr. 85, 6 fr. 55 c.) are lower than those of the State Railway viâ Malines and Liège. The latter, however, presents far more attractions to the traveller who is visiting Belgium for the first time.

Stat. *Bouchout*, then stat. *Lierre*, where the line crosses the branch-railway from Contich to Herenthals (p. 108) and the *Nethe*. *Lierre* (Flem. *Lier*) possesses silk-factories of some importance. The church of St. Gommarius, begun in 1445, completed in 1557, contains several windows filled with fine stained glass, three of which were presented by the Emp. Maximilian. Farther on, the *Villa Regout*, the property of a wealthy citizen of Antwerp, appears on the l. The country is flat and uninteresting.

Next stations *Berlaer*, *Heyst-op-den-Berg* with leather factories and considerable traffic in cattle and grain, *Boisschot* and *Aerschot* on the *Demer*, the latter with an ancient church; the railway here crosses that from Louvain to Herenthals.

The line now follows the valley of the Demer. Stations *Testelt*, *Sichem* with several breweries, and *Diest*, a fortress of Brabant since 1838 and point of defence towards the N. The latter, a town with 8000 inhab., possesses no fewer than 28 breweries and 11 distilleries. The Demer is crossed here; then stat. *Zeelhem*, *Schuelen* and *Kermpt*.

Hasselt, the capital of the province of Limburg, with 9899 inhab., was the scene of a victory gained by the Dutch over the Belgians on Aug. 6th, 1831. At Hasselt the railway unites with the old branch-line from Landen to Mastricht.

Stat. *Diepenbeek*, *Beverst* and *Munsterbilsen*.

To Liège by a branch-line from Munsterbilsen in $1^1/_4$ hr.; fares 2 fr. 80, 2 fr. 10, 1 fr. 35 c. — Stat. *Hoesselt*, *Tongres*, *Nederheim*, *Glons*, *Liers* (whence a line to *Ans* diverges to the r., see p. 165), *Milmorte*, *Herstal* and *Liège* (p. 166).

Stat. *Eygenbilsen*, *Lanaken* and

Mastricht, see p. 179. The Meuse is crossed here. Stat. *Meerssen*, *Valkenburg* (French *Fauquemont*, with picturesque ruins peeping from the trees on the r. of the line), *Wylre*, *Simpelfeld* on the Dutch and Prussian frontier, and **Aix-la-Chapelle**, see *Baedeker's Rhine and N. Germany*.

15. From Brussels to Namur by Braine-le-Comte and Charleroi.

Although double the length of the direct route, the present journey is recommended to the traveller as by far the more interesting. The trains start from the *Station du Midi* at Brussels, and reach Namur in $2^1/_4$–$3^3/_4$ hrs. fares (not higher than by Luxemburg Railway, owing to competition) 4 fr. 35, 2 fr. 90, 2 fr. 15 c.; distance 66 M.

As the station is quitted a view of the Porte de Hal is obtained to the l. (p. 74). The train then crosses the Boulevard and traverses rich meadow-land, watered by the winding *Senne*. Near stat. *Forest* the river is crossed.

Beyond *Ruysbroeck*, the birthplace of the well-known mystic of that name in the 14th cent., the line runs parallel with the canal to Charleroi, the bed of which occasionally lies higher than the railway. Hilly district, numerous cuttings and embankments. Stat. *Loth*.

Hal *(Hôtel des Pays-Bas)*, with its popular pilgrimage-church, see p. 55. Thus far this is the direct route to Calais, already described. Then stat. *Lembecq* and *Tubize*.

Braine-le-Comte, a small town with 6336 inhab. (the name of which is supposed to be derived from Brennus, the general of the Senonian Gauls), is the junction for Mons (p. 196), and carriages are sometimes changed. Stat. *Ecaussines* possesses extensive quarries of blue limestone, which is cut in slabs and exported under the name of Flemish granite. The line next crosses the Charleroi Canal, and near Manage enters a productive coal-district.

Manage-Mons, a branch-line used chiefly for goods-traffic, intersects *Le Centre*, a valuable coal-field, comprising the important mines of *La Louvière*, *Bois-du-Luc*, *Bracquegnies* etc. *La Haine*, the rivulet whence the province derives its name *(Hainault)* is occasionally visible. Extensive colonies of miners are established at *Bois-du-Luc*. On the height near it lies the village of *Bossuoit*. All the trains between Manage and Mons (15 M. in 50 min. or 1 hr.; fares 2, 1½, 1 fr.) are slow, being employed for the transport of coal, as well as of passengers. From *La Louvière*, the first important station, a short branch-line diverges to Bascoup. At stat. *Mariemont* are the ruins of a hunting château erected by Princess Mary of Hungary in 1548, and burned down by Henry II. of France six years afterwards. In the vicinity is the handsome country residence of M. *Abel Warocqué* (d. 1868), one of the merchant-princes of Belgium. In the environs of stat. *Obourg* tobacco of a highly esteemed quality is cultivated. *Mons*, see p. 186.

Manage-Wavre is the prolongation of this line to the N., intersecting the Brussels-Namur and the Louvain-Charleroi lines at *Ottignies* (p. 154). From Manage to Wavre in 50 min. or 1½ hr.; fares 3 fr. 45, 2 fr. 65, 1 fr. 70 c. — At stat. *Seneffe*, a battle was fought in 1674 between Prince Condé and William III. of Orange. Here, too, on July 2nd, 1794, the Austrians were defeated by the French under Marceau and Olivier. Stat. *Nivelles*, a town with 9018 inhab., possesses a fine old Romanesque church *(St. Gertrude)*, dating from the 11th cent. It contains the curious shrine of the saint in the form of a church, and two fine pulpits by *Delvaux*, one in marble, the other in wood. The hours of the church-clock are struck by the colossal figure of a knight, termed Jean de Nivelles. The suppressed Abbey of St. Gertrude is adjacent to the church. Waterloo relics are said to be manufactured here, an industrial fame not appreciated by the inhabitants. Near stat. *Genappe*, in the night after the Battle of Waterloo, the Prussian troops captured the carriage of Napoleon. *Wavre*, see p. 164.

Beyond Manage the main line passes several small stations, and traverses a more hilly district, describing numerous curves, and crossing the Charleroi Canal several times. Beyond a deep cutting, a beautiful undulating and well-wooded district is entered. On an eminence is situated the town of *Gosselies*, then *Roux* and

Marchiennes-au-Pont, villages occupied by the Prussians on June 15th, 1815, the day before the Battle of Ligny (p. 149), which lies $4^1/_2$ M. to the N.E. of Gosselies.

The environs of Marchiennes and Charleroi are remarkable for picturesque scenery and industrial activity. This is by far the most interesting part of the journey. Wooded hills, prosperous villages, and well-cultivated fields are passed in rapid succession, whilst the lofty chimneys of coal-mines, iron-foundries and glass-works are seen in all directions. The numerous barges on the canal bear additional testimony to the busy traffic of the district. The line now reaches the *Sambre*, which it crosses sixteen times before Namur is reached.

Charleroi *(Hôtel Durin; Pays-Bas; Grand-Monarque)*, the most modern town in Belgium, was founded by Charles II. of Spain in 1666, in honour of whom the name (Charnoy) of the village which then occupied the site was changed to Charleroi. Under Louis XIV. it was fortified by Vauban. In 1794 it was four times besieged by the French, to whom it was ultimately surrendered on the eve of the Battle of Fleurus (p. 151), after the garrison had been reduced to the utmost extremities. On May 23rd, 1794, the French were totally defeated here by the Austrian Gen. Kaunitz, who captured 25 guns and 1800 prisoners. The following year the fortifications were demolished, but again constructed in 1816. The town itself contains nothing to interest the traveller. A handsome prison near the station, erected in 1852, resembles a Gothic castle. A view of the green ramparts is obtained from the train.

Charleroi-Erquelinnes-Paris in $5^1/_2$–11 hrs., see *Baedeker's Paris.*

Charleroi-Wavre-Louvain, see p. 164.

Charleroi-Vireux in $2^1/_2$ hrs.; fares 3 fr. 60, 2 fr. 45, 1 fr. 80 c. — From Stat. *Walcourt*, about half way to Vireux, a branch-line diverges to *Philippeville*; from stat. *Mariembourg* another to *Chimay*, where the park and château of the prince of that name are situated. *Vireux*, the French frontier-station, lies on the Meuse, above the fortress of *Givet* (p. 159). Beyond Vireux the line proceeds to Rheims and Paris.

Beyond Charleroi the train to Namur crosses the Philippeville road, and passes the numerous foundries of *Couillet* and *Châtelineau*. Opposite the latter is situated the busy little town of *Châtelet*, with 4000 inhab.

Châtelineau-Givet, a branch-line traversing (in 2 hrs.) a busy manufacturing and mining district, and connected by another branch with *Walcourt* (see above).

The indications of commercial enterprise gradually disappear. The Sambre winds peacefully through beautiful grassy valleys, occasionally skirting wooded hills. To the r. of stat. *Tamines* is situated the former abbey of *Ste. Marie d'Oignies*, now an extensive mirror-manufactory. To the r. of stat. *Floreffe*, picturesquely situated on an eminence, rises the former Premonstratensian Abbey of Floreffe, now a seminary for priests (an edifice in the 'rococo' style). The valley of the Sambre it here thickly studded with ancient châteaux, modern villas, and manufactories. The train, whence the citadel of Namur is now visible, describes a circuit round the town, and stops at the station near the Louvain Gate *(Porte de Fer)*.

Near this gate and the Porte de Bruxelles several sanguinary encounters took place between the Prussians and the retreating corps of Grouchy, the vanguard of which was commanded by Vandamme, on June 20th, 1815. The Prussians forced their way into the town, and took the bridge over the Sambre, but did not succeed in materially impeding the progress of the French. Several hundred Prussians, with two of their colonels and other officers, perished in these fruitless struggles.

Namur, Flem. *Namen (*Hôtel D'Harscamp*, diligence-office; **Hôtel de Hollande*; **Hôtel Bellevue)*, the capital of the province, with 25,883 inhab., has always been a point of great military importance on account of the natural advantages of its situation. In the time of the Romans it was the capital of the Aduatici, a race descended from the Cimbri and Teutoni. Cæsar (De Bell. Gall. II. 29) records, that, after he had defeated the Nervii on the *Sabis*, i. e. the Sambre, the Aduatici, their allies, *'cunctis oppidis castellisque desertis, sua omnia in unum oppidum, egregrie natura munitum contulerunt.'* This 'one town, admirably fortified by nature', was the ancient Namur, to the importance of which as early as B. C. 56 Cæsar thus testifies.

At subsequent periods also Namur sustained numerous sieges, in consequence of wich the greater part of the present town is of modern origin. The Beffroi, or Belfry, erected in the 11th cent. (restored in the 15th), and the Palais de Justice (formerly the monastery of St. Albinus), dating from 1464, are almost the only old buildings which have survived the destruction of their contemporaries.

The *Cathedral *(St. Aubin)*, consecrated in 1772, with a dome and Corinthian portico, is one of the finest modern churches in Belgium in the Italian style. At the sides of the high altar are statues of St. Peter and St. Paul in marble, by *Delvaux*. On the l. of the high altar a copy of *Van Dyck's* Crucifixion; on the r. a monument in marble of a Bishop de Pisani (d. 1826), by *Parmentier* of Ghent. At the back of the high altar is a tombstone erected by Alexander Farnese to his *'amatissimo avunculo'* Don John of Austria, the conqueror at Lepanto, who died in his camp near Bouge, $^3/_4$ M. to the N. E. of Namur, Aug. 20th, 1578. The pulpit is a fine specimen of carved wood, by *Geerts* (1848). The principal pictures are copies from Rubens.

The church of *St. Loup*, erected in 1621—53 in the style peculiar to the Jesuit Order, is supported by 12 pillars of marble. The choir is entirely covered with black marble, and the ceiling with sculptures. A large hole in the latter, caused by a shell during the siege by Louis XIV. in 1692, is left unrepaired in commemoration of that event.

The Citadel occupies the site of the former castle of the Counts of Namur. It was erected in 1794, and has been materially strengthened at various periods since 1817. Permission to visit it must be obtained from the commandant. The summit commands a fine view of the valleys of the Sambre and Meuse. A similar view, however, may be obtained from the table-land in the rear of the Citadel, which is accessible without permission. The situation of Namur and its Citadel resembles that of Coblenz and Ehrenbreitstein on the Rhine. The confluence of the Meuse and Sambre is at the foot of the Citadel. Both rivers are crossed by stone bridges, the newest of which was constructed in 1854.

A Penitentiary for women was erected at Namur in 1840, on Auburn's system. The prisoners work during the day together in large halls, but silence is strictly enforced. At night they occupy separate cells.

The cutlery of Namur enjoys a high reputation, and is said to be not inferior to that manufactured in England, which may however be doubted. The depôt of the royal tool-manufactory, kept by *J. F. Licot*, Rue des Fossés, is the best shop of this description at Namur.

Railway to Luxembourg and Treves, see p. 154; to Liège, see p. 183; to Dinant and Givet, see p. 151.

16. From Brussels to Namur by the High Road.

The Battle-Fields.

This route, although now almost entirely superseded by the railways, is still occasionally traversed by travellers on account of the historical associations with which it is replete. No public conveyances now run on this road.

The principal battle-fields are most conveniently reached by the Louvain-Charleroi line (p. 164), on which *Wavre*, *Ligny* and *Fleurus* are situated. — From Brussels 4 trains daily to Ottignies, junction of the Brussels-Namur (p. 154), Wavre-Mons (p. 143) and Louvain-Charleroi lines.

The district of Belgium traversed by the old road has for centuries been a theatre of war, where at various periods the principal nations of Europe have settled their differences by the sword, and where national antipathies have frequently come into fierce and sanguinary collision. *Waterloo*, *Quatre-Bras*, *Ligny* and *St. Amand*, *Wavre*, *Fleurus* and *Charleroi*, memorable names familiar to every reader of history, all lie on this route.

$9^1/_2$ M. from Brussels is the village of **Waterloo**, see p. 97.

7 M. **Genappe** is a station on the Mons-Wavre line (p. 143). The road here was completely obstructed by guns and baggage-wagons on the night after the Battle of Waterloo. Napoleon, who had probably entered his carriage at no great distance from the scene of his defeat, was here compelled to quit it in precipitate haste, leaving his sword and hat behind. These trophies, with the emperor's telescope and cloak, were taken by Blücher, and afterwards sent to Berlin. Napoleon's plate, jewels and money fell into the hands of the Prussian troops.

At **Quatrebras**, about $3^1/_2$ M. from Genappe, the 'four arms' of the road, viz. to Charleroi, Nivelles, Brussels and Namur, converge, whence the name. Here on June 16th, 1815, a battle was fought between Ney's division and a part of the British army with its German and Belgian contingents. The French numbered about 17,000 men, the Allies 18,000; but of the latter 8000 only were British and German, and on the remaining 10,000 no

10*

reliance whatever could be placed. Practically, therefore, the Allies were far outnumbered. At first, shortly after 2 p. m., the success of the French, who were opposed by the Belgians only, was complete; but their progress was soon arrested by the British and German troops, and the battle raged with the utmost fury till dusk. Prodigies of valour were, as usual, performed by the 92nd Highlanders, and most of the German troops (Hanoverians and Brunswickers) behaved with great bravery, although young and inexperienced. At one juncture the Duke of Wellington himself became involved, and only escaped by putting his horse to full gallop. About 4 o'clock the gallant Duke of Brunswick fell, whilst endeavouring to rally his troops. Towards the close of the battle the tide of success turned decidedly in favour of the Allies. Ney, to his great indignation, now learned that Erlon's corps, which had at first been ordered to support him, and would doubtless have ensured the victory to the French, had received fresh orders from Napoleon to move towards St. Amand to oppose the Prussians there. The brave marshal's discomfiture was complete, his troops were totally defeated, and under cover of the increasing darkness they retreated to their original position at Frasne.

The village of *Frasne*, the head-quarters of Ney on June 16th, lies $^3/_4$ M. beyond Quatrebras, in the direction of Charleroi. The spirited pursuit of the French by the Prussians on the night after the Battle of Waterloo extended thus far, a distance of more than 6 M. from the battle-field, notwithstanding the numerous obstacles and difficulties encountered by the indefatigable pursuers.

Sombreffe, $6^1/_4$ M. from Quatrebras, was occupied on June 15th, 1815, by the 2nd and 3rd Prussian corps d'armée under Marshal Blücher himself, who late in the evening received intelligence that Gen. Bülow with the 4th corps could not come to his assistance as originally concerted. The brave marshal accordingly resolved to fight alone, if necessary. The Duke of Wellington had agreed to co-operate with Blücher, but the British troops were too far distant to render assistance, whilst those whose position was nearest to the Prussians were fully occupied at the Battle of Quatrebras. It is well authenticated that the Duke expressed his disapprobation of Blücher's position, observing to the Marshal that 'with British troops he would have occupied the ground differently'. The chief disadvantages of the ground occupied by Blücher near **St. Amand** and **Ligny**, which he regarded as the keys of his position, were that there was too little security in the direction in which the communication with the British was to be maintained, and that the villages in advance of the line were too distant to be reinforced without enormous loss. It is also on record that the Duke, after his interview with the Marshal on the morning of the simultaneous battles, remarked to one of his staff: 'The Prussians will make a gallant fight; they are capital troops, and well commanded; but they will be beaten.' And the Prussians did fight most gallantly, well sustaining the military reputation of their country; their officers too, including the high-spirited old Marshal himself, acted their part most nobly. But their utmost efforts were fruitless; they sustained immense loss, were overmatched, and finally repulsed, but not conquered.

According to the official statistics of both sides with regard to the Battle of Ligny, the total force of the French amounted to 71,208 men, with 242 guns, that of the Prussians to 88,417 men, with 224 guns. It must, however, be remembered, that a large proportion of the French army was composed of veteran soldiers, whilst most of the Prussian troops were comparatively young and inexperienced. Moreover the French artillery was numerically superior, and far more advantageously placed. At half-past two o'clock the battle began with a deadly cannonade from the French, to which the Prussian batteries from the heights between St. Amand and Ligny vigorously responded. Under cover of his artillery Vandamme succeeded in gaining possession of St. Amand, but the Prussians soon recovered the lower part of the village, whilst the French retained the higher. The loss, however, sustained by the Prussians in sending reinforcements to the village was so enormous, that they subsequently retired from this part of the field. At the same time Ligny was the scene of a terrific struggle. The Prussians fought with the utmost fury, but the French gained the village, from which however they were soon driven by a renewed attack. Meanwhile Blücher determined to recover *St. Amand la Haye*, which he had lost at the same time as St. Amand. Two attacks failed, but a third, headed by the Marshal himself, carried everything before it, and fairly swept the French out of the village. Thus in the course of the day this village was taken and re-taken several times. At Ligny the battle raged with unremitting fury. The French re-captured the village, and established themselves in the churchyard, a most advantageous position for their artillery, notwithstanding which the Prussians continued to attack them with unabated energy. In a similar manner the villages of *Hameau St. Amand* and *Wagnele* were the scenes of fierce struggles, being several times captured and re-captured by both armies. On the whole, however, the advantage was slightly on the side of the French. As late as 8 o'clock the contest was maintained at Ligny and the environs with such obstinacy and gallantry on both sides, that the ultimate issue still appeared doubtful. At length, however, when the Prussians were well nigh exhausted, Napoleon directed eight fresh battalions of the Guard and Milhaud's heavy cavalry to advance on Ligny. At this fatal juncture, too, Lobau's corps of nearly 12,000 men arrived to reinforce the French, whilst the Prussian reserves were entirely consumed. This decided the issue of the day, and the Prussians were over-matched; and yet, notwithstanding their disadvantages, they continued to contest every inch of their ground with daring intrepidity. At the close of the battle the Marshal in person headed a final cavalry charge against the French infantry, but was repulsed by the deadly fire of an overwhelming majority. The charger of the brave old soldier was shot under him, and rolled over upon its rider, over whom several regiments of French cavalry swept in pursuit of their retreating enemy. Again, however, the indefatigable Prussians rallied, and again the French were driven back, and the Marshal, who had happily escaped notice, was rescued from his perilous situation. The resistance of the Prussians gradually became more feeble, while many thousands of perfectly fresh French troops renewed the attack. It was now almost dark, and the French remained masters of the field, but they gained no decided advantage by their triumph. The Prussian officers profited by the increasing obscurity to reorganise the wreck of their army, and the retreat was conducted with the utmost regularity. — As may be supposed from the vast number of troops engaged, and the almost unparalleled fury and pertinacity with which the contest was carried on, the loss sustained by both armies was prodigious. That of the Prussians amounted to about 12,000 men, that of the French was probably quite as severe. The fact that 21 guns only were captured by the latter affords a striking proof of the insignificance of their victory, and of the skilful manner in which the Prussians effected their retreat.

The retreat of the Prussian army on the night after the Battle of Ligny, by *Tilly* and *Mont St. Guibert* to *Wavre* (p. 143), is perhaps without parallel in the annals of military warfare. So perfect was the order and so great the skill with which it was effected, that it stands on record that the French on the following day were entirely at a loss to discover in which direction their enemy had disappeared, and at length came to the conclusion that they must have taken the direction of Namur. It was not till late in the afternoon of the 17th that the real route of the Prussians was discovered, and Marshal Grouchy was dispatched in pursuit of Blücher. The parts acted by the different armies were now interchanged. Napoleon and Ney united now proceeded to attack Wellington, while Blücher formed the 3rd corps d'armée under Thielmann at *Wavre*, in order to keep Grouchy in check, and himself hastened onwards with his three other corps towards Belle-Alliance, where he arrived on the evening of the 18th, in time to act a most prominent and glorious part in a victory of incalculable importance to the fate of the whole of Europe (p. 96).

About $1^1/_2$ M. to the S. of Ligny lies **Fleurus**, celebrated for the battles of 1622 and 1690. Here, too, on June 26th, 1794, a battle took place between the Austrian army under the Prince of Cobourg, and the French under Marshal Jourdan, in which the latter reaped an unmerited advantage. The Austrians had succeeded in storming the French intrenchments, and capturing twenty guns, and had already driven the French back to *Marchiennes-au-Pont* (p. 144), when the Prince, in consequence of some misunderstanding, and partly from having heard that Charleroi, to the aid of which he was marching, had been captured, ordered his troops to retreat. This false movement, as the event proved, ultimately contributed mainly to the loss of the whole of Belgium. It is a curious historical fact, that on this occasion a balloon was employed by the French in order to reconnoitre the Austrian position, but with what success it does not appear.

Namur, $11^1/_2$ M. from Sombreffe, see p. 145.

17. From Namur to Dinant and Givet.

Railway to (Dinant in 1 hr.) Givet in $1^1/_2$ hr.; fares 4, 3, 2 fr. — The railway unfortunately affords but little view of the beautiful Valley of the Meuse. — A small Steamboat also plies daily from Namur to Dinant in 3 hrs., but is neither very comfortable nor clean.

The valley of the Meuse above Namur is narrow, and enclosed by wooded hills and frowning cliffs. The banks are enlivened with picturesque villages and country-residences. Immediately after quitting the station, the train crosses the Meuse, remaining on the r. bank until Dinant is nearly reached.

The following villages are seen on the banks from the deck of the steamboat. l. *La Plante*, a long village, the usual limit of the walks of the townspeople of Namur. r. *Dave*; r. *Tailfer*, with iron-foundries; r. *Frêne*, with interesting grottoes; l., opp. the latter, *Profondeville*, with marble-quarries; l. *Rivière*, with the château of M. Pierrepont; r. *Godinne* (in the neighbourhood of which, near the rock Frappe-Cul, is the cavern of Chauveau); l. *Rouillon*, with the château of M. Demanet.

The scenery between Rouillon and Dinant is remarkably picturesque. Above the village rises a precipitous tuffstone-rock, termed *La Roche aux Corneilles*, from the flocks of jackdaws which generally hover around it The rock is seen to the best advantage by the traveller descending the river.

r. *Yvoir* (at the influx of the *Bocq*); l. *Moulins*, a suppressed Cistercian Abbey, now a foundry; l. *Anhée*; r. *Houx*; r. *Poilvache*, with the ruins of a fortress on a lofty rock, destroyed by the French in 1554. Somewhat higher up are the ruins of the *Tour de Monay*.

l. **Bouvigne**, one of the most venerable towns of the district, has now dwindled down to a mere village. The old ruined tower of *Crèvecoeur* is a conspicuous object here. A romantic story attaches to it in connection with the siege of the town by the French in 1554. Three beautiful women are said to have entered the tower with their husbands, who formed part of the garrison, resolved to participate in the defence and to animate the defenders by their presence. The latter, however, after a heroic resistance, perished to a man, and the three unhappy widows were now the sole survivors. Determined not to fall into the hands of the enraged and brutal soldiery, they threw themselves from the summit of the tower in sight of the besiegers, and were dashed to pieces on the rocks below.

r. **Dinant** (**Poste*; *Tête d'Or*; *Hôtel des Voyageurs*, near the stat.), a town with 7266 inhab., is picturesquely situated at the base of barren limestone cliffs, the summit of which is crowned by a fortress. Steps cut in the rock ascend from one terrace to another, leading nearly to the foot of the walls of the fortifications; but the view obtained thence is limited, comprising only the narrow streets of the town below, and the old bridge over the river. The narrowness of the valley and the projections of the rocks entirely exclude the distant view. The bold position of the fortress, crowning the lofty and precipitous rock, imparts a very picturesque and imposing appearance to the town and its environs. The most convenient ascent is through the garden of the casino, to which, however, strangers must be introduced by a member (perhaps the landlord of their hotel). — The grotto of *Monfat*, one of the local curiosities, possesses no great attraction.

In 1467 the inhabitants of Dinant, having roused the anger of Philip le Bon, Duke of Burgundy, by acts of insubordination, paid dearly for their temerity. The Duke, accompanied by his son Charles the Bold, who succeeded him a few years later, marched against the town, besieged and captured it, and treated the townspeople with great cruelty. He is said to have caused 800 of them to be drowned in the Meuse before his own eyes. The unfortunate town itself was pillaged and burned, and the walls demolished. In 1554 a similar fate overtook it, when it was taken by storm by the French under the Duc de Nevers, and plundered. In 1675 the town was again taken by the French.

The church of *Notre Dame*, a handsome Gothic edifice of the

13th cent., possesses a fine portal. The tower is a curious structure, 210 ft. in height. In the rear of the church are the steps in the rock, 410 in number, by which the citadel is reached.

About $^3/_4$ M. above Dinant, on the r. bank of the river, the high-road to Givet leads through a species of natural gateway, formed by rugged cliffs on the l., and an isolated pinnacle of rock rising boldly on the r., and termed *La Roche à Bayard*. In the vicinity are quarries of black marble, adjoining which lies the picturesque village of *Anseremme*, at the foot of overhanging rocks. The *Lesse* here falls into the Meuse.

From Dinant to Givet the railway follows the course of the river. The *Château of Freyr*, the property of the Beaufort-Spontin family, is situated at the foot of wooded hills (in which there is an interesting cavern), on the l. bank of the river, and possessing well-kept gardens. On the opposite bank rugged and singularly contorted rocks rise abruptly from the river, occasionally overhanging it. Farther on, the river is enclosed by lofty escarpments of rock on both sides, and as far as *Falmignoul* the scenery is romantic. Stations *Hastière* and *Agimont*.

Givet *(Cygne; Mont d'Or)*, situated on both banks of the Meuse which are connected by a bridge, is the first French town on the line, and seat of the *Douane* officials. *Givet-St-Hilaire* is on the l. bank, at the base of the hill on which *Charlemont* is situated, *Givet-Notre-Dame* on the r. bank. Both parts of the town are strongly fortified, and almost entirely surrounded by moats. Popul. 4000. The composer *Méhul* (d. 1818) was born here, and a statue has been erected to his memory.

Givet is connected with Charleroi by two railways, the line Vireux-Charleroi, and that by Morialmé-Châtelineau (p. 144); by the former the journey occupies $4^1/_4$, by the latter $2^1/_4$ hrs.

18. From Brussels to Luxembourg and Treves.

Railway to Luxembourg in $6^1/_2$ hrs.; fares 17 fr. 60, 13 fr. 20, 8 fr. 80 c. — From Luxembourg to Treves in $1^1/_2$—$2^1/_2$ hrs.; fares 5 fr. 75 c., 4 fr. 25 c., 3 fr. — The station from which the trains start is at the extremity of the Rue de Luxembourg, in the Quartier Léopold.

The first stations, *Boitsfort* and *Groenendael* (omnibus hence to Waterloo, see p. 85), with their pleasant woods, are both favourite resorts of the citizens of Brussels for picnics and excursions. From the next stat. *La Hulpe*, a glimpse is obtained to the r. of the Mound of the Lion (p. 98) on the field of Waterloo in the distance. On the l., near *Rixensart*, is the château of Count Merode. *Ottignies* is the point of intersection of the Louvain-Charleroi (p. 164) and Louvain-Manage-Mons (p. 143) lines. Then *Mont St. Guibert* with beautiful environs. On the r. the château of *Birbaix* with well-kept gardens. At *Chastre* the Province of Brabant is quitted and that of Namur entered. At *Gembloux*, in 1578, Prince William of Orange, who had formally ceased to recognise the Spanish supremacy, was defeated by Don John of Austria, the Spanish governor. A few months later the Don's victorious career was cut short by his sudden death near Namur (p. 146). An old abbey here contains the royal stud and an agricultural institution. Stations *St. Denis-Bovesse* and *Rhisne*. Several cuttings in the blue limestone rocks are passed through, and a strikingly picturesque view obtained of

Namur, see p. 145.

The line now intersects the Forest of Ardennes, a wild, mountainous district, still richly wooded in many parts, and a suitable field for the robust pedestrian. The forest still contains deer and wild boars, and even wolves are not entirely exterminated. The delicious mutton of the Ardennes is the best in Belgium, but the traveller must not always expect such fare at the poor village inns.

Immediately after quitting Namur, the train crosses the Meuse, and a remarkably fine panorama is again enjoyed of the town and its citadel. As the train proceeds, it affords many picturesque glimpses of the valleys and woods of the Ardennes. The next stations are *Naninne*, *Assesse* and *Natoye*. Before *Ciney* is reached, the château of the eminent geologist Halloy is seen on the l. Ciney was formerly the capital of the Condroz (Condrusi of the Romans), as the district between the Meuse and Ourthe was once called. Stations *Haversin* and *Aye*. From the latter an omnibus (in 1/2 hr., 1/2 fr.) runs to

Marche (*Cloche d'Or*), the chief town (2319 inhab.) of the *Famenne*, a productive agricultural district. Here in 1577, Don John of Austria, the Spanish governor of the Netherlands, confirmed the Pacification of Ghent (p. 35) by the so-called Perpetual Edict; but his subsequent conduct soon proved that he entertained no real intention of abandoning the intolerant and unscrupulous policy of his bigoted master Philip II. Marche was formerly a fortress. Lafayette was taken prisoner by the Austrians here in 1792.

The train descends gradually from Aye to *Jemelle*, and affords to the l. a fine view of the valley of the *Wamme*. Jemelle lies at the confluence of the latter with the *Homme*, a tributary of the Lesse.

A small hut adorned with shells near the station indicates the entrance to the **Grotte de la Wamme** (admission for 1 pers. 3, 2 pers. 5 fr.). This cavern, which penetrates the limestone rocks near the railway, is smaller than the Trou de Han (see below), but is curious on account of its numerous long and narrow passages. A number of relics found here appear to indicate that the grotto was once inhabited.

Jemelle, which possesses limestone and marble quarries, and lime-kilns, is the station for the venerable town (3 M.) of *Rochefort* (Hôtel de Londres; Etoile), once the capital of the County of Ardennes, situated on the Homme. The old castle is the principal reminiscence of its former importance. — An omnibus is usually in waiting at Jemelle to convey travellers to Han (in 1 hr.; 3 fr. there and back). A visit to the grotto requires at least 4 hrs.; fee 5 fr. for each person.

Near Han the valley of the Lesse is closed by a wall of rock extending across it, whilst the river pours itself into a cavern at the foot of the rock, termed the ***Trou de Han**, or **de Belvaux**, thus forcing for itself a passage. The subterranean course of the river is about $1^1/_2$ M. The cavern consists of a series of chambers, opening into each other, varying in height, and some of them supported by natural pillars. The numerous stalactite-formations have been named fancifully in accordance with their forms, *Trône de Pluton*, *Boudoir de Proserpine*, *Galerie de la Grenouille* etc. The entrance to the grotto is at a considerable height on the slope of the hill, and visitors emerge at the farther extremity in a boat. A visit to the cavern, the recesses of which have been more thoroughly explored within the last few years, occupies 4 hrs., and is occasionally accompanied with some difficulty and fatigue, owing to the wet and slippery nature of the ground. The expedition, however, is extremely interesting, and should by all means be undertaken. The guide, who provides torches, lives in the neighbourhood; the landlord of the inn at Han also acts in that capacity. The entrance to the cavern may also be reached from Jemelle direct (an ascent of $^3/_4$ hr.).

Beyond Jemelle is stat. *Grupont*. The train follows the sinuosities of the *Homme*. To the l., on a bold rocky buttress rises the strikingly picturesque *Château Mirwart*, with its four towers. From stat. *Poix* an omnibus runs (in 1 hr., 75 c.) to **St. Hubert** (*Post; Hôtel de Luxembourg*), a poor town with 2649 inhab., celebrated for the chapel which contains the relics of the saint who has given his name to the place. The former abbey has been converted into a Reformatory for youthful criminals.

The *Church*, in the Flamboyant style, with its double aisles and interesting crypt, dates from the 16 cent. (façade and towers erected in 1700). A chapel on the l. near the choir contains a sarcophagus adorned with 8 basreliefs by *Geefs*, presented by King Leopold.

St. Hubert, the tutelary saint of sportsmen, was once a profligate and impious prince, who did not scruple to indulge in the pleasures of the chasse even on the solemn fast-days appointed by the Church. Whilst thus irreverently engaged on the holy fast of Good Friday, he suddenly beheld the miraculous apparition of a stag, with a cross growing from its forehead between its antlers. Thus warned by Heaven itself of the danger of adhering to his sinful courses, he at once desisted from the hunt, voluntarily relinquished all the honours and advantages of his noble rank, and determined thenceforth to devote himself to a life of piety and self-abnegation. He accordingly delivered up the whole of his fortune to the Church, became a monk, and founded the abbey and church which are still called by his name. The holy man is said to have enjoyed miraculous powers during his life-time, and long after his death numerous miracles were wrought by means of his relics. Unfortunately the latter, which once conferred their benefits on crowds of pious pilgrims who flocked hither to be cured of their diseases, were burned together with the church by the fanatical iconoclasts of the 16th cent. Notwithstanding this irreparable loss, however, a peculiar sanctity still attaches to the former scene of the saint's pious labours.

Libramont, the watershed between the Lesse and the Semoy, is the station for *Recogne*, a village to the r., on the road to Bouillon and Sedan. *Longlier* is the station for *Neufchâteau*, a small town once fortified, which lies $^3/_4$ M. to the r. Then *Marbehan*, with handsome new church, and *Habay-la-Neuve*.

Arlon, Flem. *Arel (Hôtel de l'Europe; Hôtel du Nord)*, a prosperous little town with 5708 inhab., situated in a well-cultivated plain, 1245 ft. above the sea-level, is the capital of the Belgian province of Luxembourg. It was the *Orolaunum Vicus* of the Antoninian itinerary, and in the middle ages a fortress. A branchline diverges here to *Longwy* and *Longuyon*, where it unites with the Ardennes Railway (Thionville-Mezières).

Then *Sterpenich*, *Bettingen* (Luxembourg douane; luggage, however, not examined till after arrival at Luxembourg), *Capellen*, *Mamer* and *Bertringen*.

Luxembourg, formerly *Lützelburg (Hôtel de Cologne; Hôtel de Luxembourg; Hôtel de l'Europe; Hôtel des Ardennes)*, until 1866 a fortress of the Germanic Confederation, is the capital (with 13,800 inhab.) of a small Grand Duchy of the same name, under the supremacy of the Dutch. The Oberstadt, or upper part of the town, Luxembourg properly so called, is of considerable extent, situated like a mountain-stronghold upon a rocky table-land, which is bounded on three sides by precipices 200 ft. in height. In the narrow ravine of the *Petrusbach* and the *Alzette*, a second quarter of the town has sprung up. This Unterstadt consists of *Pfaffenthal* on the N., *Clausen* on the E., and *Grund* on the S., separated by the *Bock* (se below), all remarkable for their commercial activity. The valley of the Alzette, forming a natural moat for the fortress, is sprinkled with houses, and occasionally intersected by the walls of the fortifications. This combination of mountain and valley, enlivened with numerous groups of trees and gardens, and diversified with indented cliffs and imposing military structures, presents a strikingly beautiful appearance, especially when seen from the Treves road, near *Fort Dumoulin*.

The grandeur of the scene is considerably enhanced by the vast *Viaducts* of the railways to Treves and Diekirch, and the colossal Petrus Bridge, which spans the ravine between the railway-station and the S. side of the Oberstadt.

The fortifications, the demolition of which is about to take place, are now all accessible. They are partly hewn in the rock, bearing a distant resemblance to those of Gibraltar. The Bock, a narrow ridge of rock projecting far into the valley of the Alzette, is honeycombed with casemates and loopholes, which command the valley towards the N. and S. The high road to Treves winds over this ridge. On the E. slope stands a tower belonging to old fortifications of the 14th cent.

The fortifications have been added to at various periods during the last five centuries, and the different parts of the defences have derived their names from the successive occupants of the town who constructed them. Thus Henry IV., Count of Luxembourg (d. 1312 as Henry VII., Emp. of Germany), and his warlike son, the blind King John of Bohemia (d. 1346), and subsequently the Burgundians, Spaniards, French, Austrians and Prussians. In 1684 the fortress was besieged and captured by Louis XIV., after which Vauban re-constructed a great part of the works. On June

7th, 1795, the Austrian Marshal Bender surrendered Luxembourg to the French republicans. Carnot, the eminent general of engineers, terms Luxembourg *'la plus forte place de l'Europe après Gibraltar, le seul point d'appui pour attaquer la France du côté de la Moselle'.*

Beyond the fortifications and the romantic nature of the situation, Luxembourg offers no inducement to the traveller to make a prolonged stay. The Spanish governor Count Mansfeld (1545—1604) once possessed a magnificent château here, but every vestige of the building has disappeared, with the exception of a few fragments of the walls and two gateways. The once celebrated gardens and parks which surrounded the château have survived in nothing but the name, which is now applied to a well-shaded promenade on the slope of a hill near the Treves Gate, worthy of a visit on account of the remarkably fine view it commands. The visitor who has sufficient leisure will be amply rewarded by a walk through the entire valley.

Railway from Luxembourg by Thionville to Metz in 3 hrs.; fares 6 fr. 70, 5 fr., 3 fr. 65 c. (comp. *Baedeker's Paris*).

At stat. *Oetringen* the line enters the charming valley of the *Sire*. On a wooded hill to the l. are the remains of an ancient structure of heathen origin; at the base of the hill lies the château of *Villers*, with its park, the property of the family of that name. On the r. *Schuttringen*, with a château. Then stat. *Roodt*. From *Ollingen* to *Betzdorf* the line runs on the r. bank of the Sire.

Stat. *Wecker*. The line now crosses the Sire four times within a very short distance, and at stat. *Mertert* enters the valley of the Moselle. Beyond stat. *Wasserbillig*, the Luxembourg frontier-station, at the confluence of the *Sauer* and Moselle, lies the village of *Igel*, where a **Roman Monument*, the finest on this side of the Alps, erected by the family of the Secundini, is situated.

Opposite to *Cons* the line unites with the Saarbrücken-Treves Railway. The station at **Treves** is on the l. bank of the river. (Hotels at Treves: *Hôtel de Trèves*, *Maison Rouge*, *Luxemburger Hof*, *Stadt Venedig;* the two last are good second class inns). For a description of this very interesting town and the excursions to

Louvain. Löwen

1 Hotel de Ville
2 Halles. local de l'Université
3 St. Pierre
4 St. Michel
5 St. Quentin
6 St. Jacques
7 St. Gertrude

Places
a. Grand' Places
b. Vieux Marché
c. Place du Peuple
d. Marché aux Grains
e. Place St. Jacques

Heverlé
Commune de Winxele
Commune de Herent
Commune de Wilsele
Commune de Kessel-Loo
Commune
Chemin de fer de Namur
La Dyle
Porte de Namur
Porte de Bruxelles
Kaserne

be undertaken from it, as well as of the journey to Coblenz by the romantic Moselle, or by the hardly less picturesque railway, see *Baedeker's Rhine and N. Germany*.

19. From Brussels to Liège.

Express trains in 2 hrs. (5 fr. 40, 3 fr. 60 c.), ordinary in 3 hrs. (4 fr. 50, 3 fr., 2 fr. 25 c.). Finest views on the left.

Saventhem, one of the first small stations, has frequently been mentioned in connection with the name of Van Dyck, who having got thus far on his way to Italy is said to have fallen in love with a fair village damsel, and to have been so infatuated as to be unable to proceed farther, until Rubens heard of the affair, and succeeded in opening the eyes of his pupil to the folly of thus sacrificing his prospects, and induced him to continue his journey. The story, however, with all its romantic details, has proved to be without the slightest foundation. The best existing authority in these matters is the Catalogue of the Antwerp Museum, the compilers of which have made the lives of the principal masters the subject of the most anxious investigation, and have declared the above anecdote purely apocryphal. — The train does not now, as formerly, proceed by Malines, but by a new and more direct line. The country traversed is not unlike many districts in England, excepting that hedges are rarely seen. The first important place is

Louvain, Flem. *Leuven* (*Hôtel de Suède, in the Place du Peuple; Cour de Mons, Marché aux Poissons; Sauvage, Marché au Beurre. — *Café* in the Grande Place. *Louvain Beer*, which is highly esteemed by the Belgians, is a very sickly beverage. — *Vigilantes*, as at Liège; omnibus ½ fr. — *Attractions:* Exterior of Hôtel de Ville (p. 160); St. Peter's, with the aid of the sacristan (p. 161); Halles, exterior (p. 163); Choir-stalls in St. Gertrude's (p. 163)). The name of the town is believed to be derived from *Loo*, signifying a wooded height, and *Veen*, a marsh. *Venloo* has the same etymology. In the 14th cent., when Louvain was the capital of the Duchy of Brabant, and residence of the princes, it numbered 44,000 inhab. (now 32,371). Of these a large proportion were engaged in the cloth-trade, and the town contained no fewer than 2000 manufactories. Here, as in other Flemish towns, the weavers were a very turbulent class, and always manifested great jealousy of the influence of the nobles in their civic administration. During an insurrection in 1378, thirteen magistrates of noble family were thrown from the window of the Hôtel de Ville, and received by the populace below on the points of their spears. Duke Wenceslaus chastised the citizens for their rebellious conduct, by taking the city by force of arms, and compelling them to crave his pardon with every token of abject humiliation. The power of the nobles soon regained its ascendancy, and their tyrannical sway caused thousands of the industrious citizens to emigrate to England, whither they transplanted their handicraft. The decay of Louvain began at that period, and its effects are apparent to this day.

Louvain is a dull place, possessing little or no commercial traffic, and most of the inhabitants are engaged in agricultural pursuits. The walls, constructed in the 14th cent., enclose a large area unoccupied by houses, and employed almost exclusively as arable land. The former ramparts, by which the walls were encircled, are converted into promenades, forming a circuit of 5 M. The old market-place and the Grande Place are the only animated parts of the town. The latter, with the Hôtel de Ville, the church of St. Peter, and the Halles in a side-street, presents a very imposing aspect. It is reached by the new Rue de la Station, in a straight direction.

The ****Hôtel de Ville** (Pl. 1), one of the richest and most beautiful existing examples of late Gothic architecture, resembles the town-halls of Bruges, Ghent (in the older part), Mons and Oudenarde, but surpasses them in elegance and harmony of design. It was erected in 1448—63, probably by *M. de Layens*, a skilful architect of that period. The secular edifices in Belgium, of which this is perhaps the most remarkable, are far more elaborately decorated than the ecclesiastical. The delicately executed carving of the exterior, which had suffered greatly from exposure to the weather, was restored in 1842 with the utmost care by the sculptor *Goyers*. Portions of the decorations are entirely new, but the ancient models have been scrupulously imitated, and valuable assistance has been derived from the original drawings. The numerous prominent corbels, which it is intended to provide with statues, are embellished with admirably executed, and almost detached groups of miniature figures. Below are celebrated natives of Louvain (upwards of 80 statues have already been executed.

On the first floor, figures emblematical of the privileges of the city; above, the sovereigns of the land. — The interior is comparatively insignificant. Most of the apartments are fitted up in a modern style, and adorned with pictures of little merit. A winged picture by *Mich. Coxcie*, representing the Ascension, is, however, worthy of notice. On the upper floor a model of the towers of St. Pierre is preserved.

The Gothic church of *St. Pierre (Pl. 3), opposite to the *Hôtel de Ville*, a noble cruciform structure, was erected in the 15th cent. It originally possessed a wooden tower, burned down in 1458, and replaced by another which was destroyed by a storm in 1604. The celebrated Justus Lipsius is said to have invented the chronogram oMnIa CaDVnt, in order to commemorate the catastrophe.

Interior. The 1st Chapel of the S. aisle contains an altar-piece copied from the original of *De Craeyer*, which disappeared during the French Revolution, representing S. Carlo Borromeo administering the Eucharist to persons sick of the plague. An old winged picture by *Van der Baeren* (1594), the Martyrdom of St. Dorothea; statue of St. Charles, by *Geerts*, a sculptor of Antwerp (d. at Louvain, 1855). 2nd Chapel: a curious, blackened image of Christ here is regarded with great veneration on account of the legend attaching to it, that it once caught a thief who had entered the church with sacrilegious intent. The railing is adorned with armour and cannon.

The Pulpit *(Chaire de Vérité)*, carved in 1742 by *Bergé*, represents Peter's Denial on one side, and the Conversion of St. Paul on the other. The life-size figures, hewn out of solid blocks of wood, are finely executed. The whole is surmounted by lofty palm-trees.

The 3rd Chapel of the aisle contains a picture of *Memling's* school, representing the consecration of a cook as bishop, under Gregory V. The choir is separated from the nave by a rich and elaborate *Rood Loft*, or *Jubé*, in the florid Gothic style, executed at the close of the 15th cent., consisting of three arches adorned with small statues, and surmounted by a lofty cross. The candelabrum is said to be the workmanship of Quentin Massys (p. 118).

5th Chapel, in the choir: *Stuerbout*, surnamed *Dirk van Haarlem* (d. at Louvain, 1479), Martyrdom of St. Erasmus, a painful subject, in the background the Emperor with three attendants, richly attired; the whole is represented in a carefully executed landscape with blue mountains in the distance. 6th Chapel: *De Craeyer*, The Holy Trinity. **Stuerbout*, Last Supper, painted at the same time as the Martyrdom of St. Erasmus (1467). These two pictures, which possess very great value in the history of art, were formerly attributed to Memling. They have been recently cleaned and retouched. Their Gothic rigidity is to some extent counterbalanced by the beautiful drawing and delicate colouring, and the details are admirably executed.

7th Chapel: **Quentin Massys*, Holy Family (carried off during the French Revolution, restored in 1815), one of the greatest treasures of which the church boasts. The principal picture *represents* the Virgin and Child, with two other holy women, and children who appear to be learning to read. Behind them, four men, standing by an edifice in the Italian style, through the arches of which a distant landscape is seen beyond. On the wings, the Death of St. Anne, and the Expulsion of Joachim from the Temple, of which the former especially is worthy of examination. This work differs very materially in its character from the celebrated Pietà at Antwerp (p. 123). Its tone is sprightly and animated, whilst in drawing and colouring it is hardly inferior.

Near the high altar is a Tabernacle (35 ft. in height), elaborately executed in stone, in the form of a Gothic tower, by *Layens* (in 1433), the architect of the Hôtel de Ville. The 8th Chapel (N. side of choir) contains a *Descent from the Cross by *Rogier van der Weyden*, a winged picture on a golden ground, at the sides of which are the donors. This is a small duplicate of a picture in the Museum at Berlin. The same chapel contains the tombstone of Henry IV., Duke of Lorraine, the founder of the church; the basement is modern.

The reliefs in the chapels on the r., and the carved woodwork of the principal portal are worthy of careful inspection. The chapels containing the above celebrated pictures are generally closed (sacristan $^1/_2$ fr.; more for a party).

The church of **St. Michael** (Pl. 4), erected by the Jesuits in 1666, was converted into a 'Temple of Reason' during the Revolution. It contains twelve tolerable pictures by modern artists. On the r. an Entombment, by *Wappers*; l. Christ before Pilate, by *Van Bree*.

The church of **St. Gertrude** (Pl. 7), formerly the court-chapel of the Dukes of Brabant, contains *choir-stalls executed in the florid Gothic style at the close of the 15th cent., and considered the finest in Belgium. They have been recently restored by *Goyers.*

The church of **St. Quentin** (Pl. 5), situated on an eminence near the Porte de Namur (founded in 1206, re-erected in the 15th cent.), and **St. Jacques** (Pl. 6) possess several pictures of the school of Rubens. The choir of the latter is adorned with four tolerable modern works.

The **Halles** (Pl. 2), erected as a warehouse for the Cloth-makers' Guild in 1377, and fitted up in 1679 for the purposes of the university, still bears testimony to the wealth and taste of the founders. The *Library*, one of the most valuable in Belgium, is adorned with a sculptured group representing a scene from the Flood, executed by *Geerts* (p. 161), who was subsequently the director of the Louvain Academy. The entrance-hall contains a number of portraits of former professors, and a large picture by *Van Bree*, Christ healing the blind, painted in 1824, and presented by King William I.

The **University** was founded in 1426. In the 16th cent. the theological faculty especially was considered the most distinguished in Europe, and adhered with inflexible tenacity to the orthodox dogmas of the Church. The number of students is said to have exceeded 6000 at the period when the celebrated Justus Lipsius (d. 1606) taught here. Under Joseph II. its reputation somewhat declined, but it continued to exist until the close of last century. So extensive were its privileges, that no one could formerly hold a public appointment in the Austrian Netherlands, without having taken a degree at Louvain. After having been closed by the French republicans, the university was re-established by the Dutch government in 1817. A philosophical faculty was afterwards instituted, notwithstanding the determined opposition of the clergy, and complaints to which it gave rise are said to have contributed in some degree to the Revolution of 1830. Since 1836 the university has been re-organised, and has assumed an exclusively ecclesiastical character. It is one of the 'Universités Libres', independent of government, and supported entirely by the church. It is usually termed the 'Catholic' in contradistinction

11*

to the 'free' university of Brussels. It now possesses five faculties and about 850 students.

Insignificant traces only now remain of '*Caesar's Castle*', the ancient stronghold of the counts and dukes, situated on an eminence near the Porte de Malines. It derives its appellation from an unfounded tradition that it was originally erected by the great Roman general. The Emp. Charles V. and his sisters were educated in this castle by the learned Adrian Dedel, who was afterwards elevated to the papal throne as Adrian VI.

From Louvain to Charleroi by railway in $2^1/_4$—3 hrs., viâ *Wavre* and *Ottignies*. Near stat. *Villers-la-Ville* are the remarkably picturesque and interesting ruins of the abbey of that name, destroyed in 1796. Stat. *Tilly* is supposed to have been the birthplace of the celebrated Imperial general of that name. *Ligny* and *Fleurus*, both celebrated battle-fields, have been already mentioned (p. 149). *Lodelinsart*, a large and flourishing village, possesses coal-mines and manufactories of considerable value. *Charleroi*, see p. 144.

The first important station beyond Louvain is

Tirlemont, or *Thienen* (*Quatre Saisons*, near the station; *Plat d'Etain; Hôtel de Flandre*, these two in the market-place. *Restaurant* at the station), a clean and well-built, but dull town with 12,188 inhab., once like Louvain occupied by a far more considerable and wealthy population. The walls, which form a circuit of nearly 6 M., now enclose a large extent of arable land. The market-place is spacious and imposing. Here is situated the church of *Notre Dame du Lac*, founded in the 13th cent., enlarged in the 15th, but not yet completed. It contains some pictures and wood-carving of little merit. The adjacent *Hôtel de Ville* will not bear comparison with the structures of this description in the principal Belgian towns. The great attraction at Tirlemont is the **Church of St. Germain*, situated on an eminence, probably dating from the 9th cent., and the most ancient in Belgium. The well-preserved tower is unquestionably of Roman origin. The high-altar-piece is a Pietà, by *Wappers*. The celebrated Jesuit Bollandus (d. 1655) was a native of Tirlemont. He was the first compiler of the *Acta Sanctorum*, and his successors who continued the work styled themselves Bollandists.

As the train proceeds on its way, an extensive retrospect, embracing the town and its environs, is enjoyed. To the r. (S.W.), in clear weather, the Lion and the Prussian Monument on the Field of Waterloo are sometimes visible. As Landen is approached, the line intersects the plain of *Neerwinden* (the village lies to the l.), the scene of two great battles. The first of these was fought between the French under Marshal Luxembourg, and the Allies under William III. of England, and terminated in the defeat of the latter, July 29th, 1693. In the second the French under Dumouriez and Louis Philippe (then '*General Egalité*', afterwards king of the French) were defeated by the Austrians under the Prince of Cobourg (great-uncle of the late king Leopold), and driven out of Belgium.

Stat. *Landen*, now a mere village, possesses an historical interest as the native place of Pepin, the majordomo of the royal domains of the Frank monarch Clotaire II. He died here about the year 640, and was buried beneath a hill which still bears his name. His remains were afterwards removed to Nivelles (p. 143), where his daughter Gertrude (d. 659) founded a convent. His fifth lineal descendant was Charlemagne, who ascended the throne of the vast Frank empire 128 years later.

From Landen to Aix-la-Chapelle by a branch-line in 3–4½ hrs.; fares 8 fr. 15, 6 fr. 15, 4 fr. 5 c. — This route is somewhat shorter than the main line viâ Liège, but presents fewer attractions. *St. Trond*, the most important station, is a town with 11,573 inhab. and eleven churches, several of which are of ancient origin. *Mastricht*, and thence to Aix-la-Chapelle, see p. 179.

Next stat. *Gingelom*, *Rosoux* and *Waremme*, beyond which the line intersects an ancient and well-preserved Roman road, termed by the country-people *Route de Brunhilde*, which extended from Bavay *(Bavacum Nerviorum)*, near Mons, to Tongres, 9 M. to the N.E. of Waremme. The latter was the capital of the ancient province of *Hesbaye*, the natives of which were once remarkable for their personal strength and bravery, as the old proverb, '*Qui passe dans le Hesbain est combattu l'endemain*' testifies. The land of the Brabanters, a somewhat phlegmatic race of Germanic origin, is now quitted, and that of the active and enterprising Celtic Walloons entered. A smiling and highly cultivated district is exchanged for a scene of industrial enterprise. Numerous coal-mines, foundries and manufactories are passed in the vicinity of **Ans**, which lies 450 ft. higher than Liège.

The line now descends rapidly (1 : 30), affording a fine view of the populous city of *Liège* and the beautiful and animated valley of the Meuse. An extensive brick building on the hill to the l. is a military hospital.

20. Liège and Seraing.

Flem. *Luik.*

Hotels, all near the theatre. *Hôtel de Suède (Pl. a), comfortable, R. 2–3, B. 1½, D. 3, A. 1 fr.; *Hôtel d'Angleterre (Pl. b) and Hôtel de l'Europe (Pl. c), at the back of the theatre. Hôtel Schiller, Place du Théâtre (Pl. d), a good second-class inn. — Pommelette, Rue Souverain-Pont (Pl. e), starting-point of the diligences, noisy; Grand Cerf (Pl. f) (R. and B. 2½, D. 2, A. ½ fr.) and Hôtel de France (Pl. g), both in the Rue du Dragon d'Or.

Restaurants. Pommelette, Deux Fontaines, ascent to the l. by the theatre; Hôtel Schiller etc. — *Cafés:* Venise, Midi, Divans, all near the theatre. Renaissance, in the Passage. Maure, Rue du Pont d'Avroy, Bavar. beer.

Vigilantes 1 fr. per drive; to the station 1 fr. 25 c. — Per hr., 1½ fr. for the first, and 25 c. for each succeeding ¼ hr.

Steamboats to *Mastricht* (R. 21) three times daily in summer. Mastricht, which has been celebrated for its caverns for about a thousand years, may conveniently be visited from Liège. The Mastricht boats start a few paces below, those to Namur above the *Pont des Arches*, adjacent to the university. From Mastricht to Rotterdam daily, in two days, one night being spent at *Venlo*. From Liège to *Seraing* once every hour at least in summer, fares 50 or 35 c.

Railway Stations. *Station des Guillemins*, on the l. bank (for Aix-la-Chapelle and Brussels), and *Station de Longdoz*, on the r. bank (to Namur and Paris).

Weapons. Lepage, Rue Hors-Château 73; Collette etc. — *Horticulture.* The hothouses of M. *Makoi*, a nursery-gardener near the station, contain a fine collection of exotic plants.

Principal Attractions: Palais de Justice, the court (p. 168); Church of St. Jacques (p. 168); St. Paul's (p. 169); view from the citadel (p. 173).

Liège, with 104,905 inhab., the capital of the Walloon district, and formerly the seat of a principality of the name, lies in a strikingly picturesque situation. The ancient city with its numerous towers rises on the lofty bank of the broad Meuse, into which the *Ourthe* here flows. The numerous chimneys bear testimony to the industry of the inhabitants, whilst the richly cultivated valley contributes greatly to enhance the picturesque effect. The scenery around Liège is unsurpassed in Belgium. The city itself, too, has recently been greatly embellished by the construction of new streets, quays and promenades. The coal-mines in the environs form the basis of the commercial prosperity of Liège. They are worked in a scientific and systematic manner, and many of them are said to extend beneath the houses and the river itself. One of the most important branches of industry is the manufacture of weapons of all kinds. Liège is at once the armoury and the Sheffield of Belgium.

The Walloons (p. 165) are an active, intelligent and enterprising race. "*Cives Leodicenses sunt ingeniosi, sagaces et ad quidvis audendum prompti*" is the opinion pronounced by *Guicciardini* with regard to the Liégeois. Indefatigable industry and a partiality for labour of the most arduous description are among their strongest characteristics, but they have frequently manifested a fierce and implacable spirit of hostility for those who have attempted to infringe their privileges. On such occasions they have never scrupled to wield the weapons for the manufacture of which they are justly celebrated. The history of Liège records a series of sanguinary insurrections of the turbulent and unbridled populace against the oppressive and arrogant bishops by whom they were governed. Foreign armies have frequently been invoked by the latter to chastise their rebellious subjects, but such intervention served but to give rise to renewed and embittered struggles for independence. The bishops, however, who had been constituted temporal princes of Liège by the German emperors as early as the 10th cent., retained their supremacy till the French Revolution in 1794, when the city was finally severed from the German Empire. In ancient times the bishops possessed a Walloon body-guard of 500 men, and Walloon soldiers, like the Swiss, were in the habit of serving in the armies of Spain, France and Austria. They enjoyed a high reputation for bravery, which has been justly extolled by Schiller in his 'Wallenstein'. Their language is a very corrupt patois of French, mingled with words of Celtic and Teutonic origin. They claim descent from the Eburones, a warlike tribe who occupied the district between the Rhine and Meuse, and were severely chastised by Cæsar for having rebelled against the Romans, B. C. 54. There is, however, also reason to believe that they are partly of Celtic extraction.

A short distance from the station are situated the broad quay and the Square d'Avroy, the principal promenade of Liège, bounded on the r. by the Bassin de Commerce. At the extremity of the Quai Cockerill rises the *Equestrian Statue of Charlemagne* (Pl. 35), by Jehotte, in reminiscence of the tradition that the great emperor granted their earliest privileges to the citizens.

The ***Palais de Justice** (Pl. 40), a somewhat heavy example of Renaissance architecture, the finest secular edifice at Liège, and formerly the residence of the prince-bishops, was erected in 1508—33 by Cardinal Eberhard de la Mark, a scion of the family of the 'Wild Boar of Ardennes', whose turbulent career is so admirably described by Sir Walter Scott in his 'Quentin Durward'. The façade towards the Place St. Lambert was re-erected in 1737 after its destruction by fire. The courts of the interior appertain to the original structure, and the sixty stunted columns of the colonnade exhibit traces of the Venetian, Gothic and Moorish styles. Each column is adorned with different sculptures, such as Moorish heads, grotesque faces, entire figures, luxuriant foliage etc., all chiselled with admirable skill and precision. The court and colonnades present a quaint and picturesque appearance. The latter serve as a shelter for shops and stalls of all kinds. On the W. side a new *Hôtel du Gouvernement* (Pl. 15) was erected in 1852, an imposing structure in the same style of architecture as the adjoining older building.

The spacious *Place de St. Lambert* in front of the Palais de Justice derives its name from the ancient church of St. Lambert, which was totally destroyed by the French sansculottes and their brethren of Liège in 1794. The ruins were removed in 1808, and the stones employed in the construction of the Quai de la Sauvenière.

The church of ***St. Jacques** (Pl. 11), on the S. side of the city, a magnificent florid Gothic structure, was founded in 1014, as is recorded by the tombstone of the Bishop Balderic in the S. transept. The present edifice dates from 1522—38, a period when Gothic architecture had begun to degenerate, and to exhibit traces of a transition to the Renaissance. The unsuitable N. portal was subsequently added, in accordance with the degraded taste of the 18th cent. The groined vaulting of the interior is adorned with foliage and arabesques. The fine stained glass windows of the choir, dating from the beginning of the 16th cent., represent the Crucifixion, the donors, their armorial bearings and tutelary saints. The elaborate stone-carving in the choir, and the organ-case, carved by Andreas Severin of Mastricht (d. 1673), should not be overlooked. The interior has recently been entirely restored in a style of great magnificence, tempered however with considerable taste, and producing a most striking and harmonious effect.

In the vicinity is the ***Cathedral** *(St. Paul*, Pl. 15), of which the choir dates from the close of the 13th cent., the nave and other parts from 1557. The vaulting of this church too is adorned with painted arabesques and foliage. The 1st Chapel of the S. aisle contains a Resurrection, by *Ansiaux*; in the 2nd, Christ in the sepulchre, executed in marble by *Delcour* in 1696. To the l. of this is the pulpit (see below); 3rd Chapel, Martyrdom of St. Lambert, by *Tahan*. The two altar-pieces were carried off during the French Revolution, but subsequently restored. That on the S. side, representing SS. Gregory, Jerome, Ambrose and Augustin, the four Fathers of the Church, is by *Quellin*; that on the N., the Assumption, by *Lairesse*. The stained glass in the choir and S. aisle is of the 15th cent.; that of the N. aisle modern, by Capronnier of Brussels. In the 4th Chapel (on the N.), Baptism of Christ, painted by *Carlier* in 1600. During the recent restoration of the church several old frescoes were discovered in the N.W. corner. One of the chief ornaments of the sacred edifice is the modern *Pulpit, carved in wood under the direction of the eminent sculptor *Guil. Geefs* of Brussels. This specimen of carving in wood, as well as the choir-stalls in the cathedral of Antwerp etc., testifies to the high perfection which the art has attained in Belgium, and far surpasses most of the earlier works of the kind. Five figures in marble, also by *Guil. Geefs*, representing Religion, SS. Peter and Paul, SS. Lambert and Hubert, serve to support the pulpit. The fallen angel at the back is by *Jos. Geefs*, brother of the principal master. The tower contains a set of chimes.

On an eminence commanding the city rises the church of **St. Martin** (Pl. 13), erected in its present form about the middle of the 16th cent. The festival of Corpus Christi *(Fête de Dieu)* was first instituted in this church in the year 1246, in consequence of a vision beheld by S. Juliana, Abbess of the neighbouring convent of *Cornillon*; and eighteen years afterwards its celebration throughout Christendom was ordained by Pope Urban IV., who had been a canon at the cathedral of Liège at the time of the 'vision'. A marble slab under the organ bears an inscription commemorating the 500th anniversary of the festival. On Aug. 4th, 1312, the church was destroyed by fire, having become ignited during a fierce conflict between the burghers and the nobles; 200 of the adherents of the latter, who had been forced by the infuriated populace to take refuge in the church, perished in the flames. The first lateral chapel on the r. is adorned with 14 small circular reliefs, well executed in marble, by *Delcour*. Four reliefs in the choir by *Franck* represent the history of St. Martin. The interior of the church is hardly a sufficient attraction to repay the fatigue of ascending the hill, but the tower commands an admirable prospect (visitors apply at the house No. 47, nearly opp. the chief portal; fee 50 c. for each pers.).

***Ste. Croix** (Pl. 9), which may be passed on the way to St. Martin's, is a small and simple, but interesting church, consecrated as early as 979 by the celebrated Bishop Notger, and recently restored, after having undergone many alterations since the period of its foundation. The nave and aisles (14th cent.), supported by slender round, as well as clustered columns, are remarkable for their light and graceful effect. The pillars are of the blue-limestone so common in this part of Belgium, the walls and vaulting of yellowish sandstone. The pointed arches in the transept are filled with 14 medallion-reliefs, which serve as oratorios. The stained glass in the choir (by *Kellner* of Munich, and *Capronnier* of Brussels), executed in 1854, represents scenes from the Passion.

St. Barthélemy (Pl. 7), a basilica of the 12th cent., with nave and double aisles (originally single only), and two Romanesque towers, is totally disfigured in the interior by stucco and painting. The Baptistery, to the l. by the choir, contains an admirable *font in bronze, resting on twelve oxen, and representing the Baptism of St. John and the Apostles in relief. It was executed in the 12th cent., a period when the art of bronze-casting was in its infancy, and is therefore of great historical value.

St. Denis (Pl. 10) was founded in 987, but the present edifice dates from the 13th and 14th centuries. The Baptistery contains a large altar adorned with numerous figures carved in wood, executed about the end of the 15th or beginning of the 16th cent., and representing the Passion, and the Martyrdom of St. Denis. The statues of the Virgin and St. Denis at the sides of the high altar are by *Delcour*. The stained glass in the choir is modern.

Liège and Ghent possess the only Belgian universities endowed by government, those of Brussels and Louvain, as already mentioned, are dependent on private and ecclesiastical support. The **Palais de l' Université** (Pl. 44), erected in 1817, is well adapted for its purposes. The principal court contains a handsome detached structure, with Ionic colonnade, lighted from above, and used as an Aula, or hall, "*Universis Disciplinis*". The buildings comprise lecture-rooms, academic collections, library (about 100,000 vols.), excellent apparatus for instruction in physical science, and finally a museum of natural history of inconsiderable extent, but well arranged. The latter contains a fine collection of the bones of antediluvian animals, found in the numerous caverns in the environs, especially in that of Chokier (p. 183). The *Ecole des Mines*, an excellent institution attended by numerous students, an *Ecole des Arts et Manufactures*, and a training-school for students who contemplate a scholastic career (*Ecole Normale des Humanités*) are establishments connected with the university, which possesses a staff of 41 professors. The average number of students is between eight and nine hundred, of whom nearly half attend the mining and polytechnic schools.

The Place in front of the university is embellished with a *Statue* in bronze, of *André Dumont* (Pl. 36), an eminent geologist, member of the Belgian Academy, and author of the Carte Géologique of Belgium. Opposite to the university is the *Conservatoire* or School of Music.

The original *Pont des Arches* over the Meuse, constructed in 1657, was superseded by the present bridge of that name in 1860. The Bishop Maximilian (Elector of Cologne, and Duke of Bavaria) caused a strongly fortified tower, termed *La Dardanelle*, to be erected on the old bridge in 1685, in order to prevent communication between the two quarters of the city during civic revolts. At that period the bridge was the great rallying-point of the seditious citizens, who were here harangued by their demagogues. On July 27th, 1794, it was the scene of a fierce and bloody struggle between the Austrians and the French, in which the former were compelled to retire to the shelter of the batteries of the Chartreuse. — In 1468, when Charles the Bold of Burgundy was invoked by the Bishop to suppress an insurrection of his turbulent subjects, the barbarous conquerors wreaked their vengeance on many of the wives and daughters of the unfortunate citizens by placing them in open boats, and sinking them in the middle of the river.

The house of Count Asseburg on the broad *Quai de la Batte* below the bridge, which was tenanted by Blücher in the spring of 1815, was attacked by the mutinous Saxon soldiers on May 2nd, 1815. The marshal, however, quitted the house by a door at the back, and effected his escape on horseback.

About $^{1}/_{2}$ M. above the Pont des Arches is the **Pont de la Boverie,** constructed in 1843. It crosses the Meuse in four graceful arches, and the Ourthe by a single span. On the r. bank, near the bridge, is the *Ecole de Natation*, or swimming-school. In the vicinity, extending along the bank of the river, is the **Zoological Garden** (Pl. 31), recently founded by the Liégois in order that their city may in no respect be behind those of Brussels and Antwerp. The collection of animals is at present insignificant, but the grounds afford a fine panorama of the town and environs. The best point of view is the bears' den. — Higher up, the river is crossed by the *Pont du Val Benoît*, a handsome railway-bridge, one half of which is used for the ordinary traffic of carriages and foot-passengers.

The **Passage Lemmonier,** an arcade with shops on each side, constructed in 1837—39, connects the Rue de l'Université with the Rue Vinave d'Ile.

The handsome and spacious *Place du Théâtre* is adorned with a fine bronze **Statue of Grétry** (Pl. 37), the celebrated composer (d. 1813), designed by *Geefs*. The heart of the master is deposited beneath the marble basement. The monument is chaste and pleasing, and the statue is free from the cumbrous masses of drapery which too often disfigure modern works of the kind. The house in which Grétry was born (1740), in the Rue des Récollets, Quartier d' Outremeuse (the quarter on the r. bank of the river), is indicated by a marble tablet recording the fact.

The **Theatre** (Pl. 43), erected in 1818 (performances from Oct. 1st to May 1st), and completely restored and re-decorated in the interior in 1861, at a cost of a million francs, is a remarkably handsome and spacious edifice.

The **Hôtel de Ville** (Pl. 29), erected in 1714, is unattractive. The *Grand-Marché* in front of it is adorned with three *Fountains* of questionable taste. That in the centre, the *Fontaine des Trois Grâces*, was erected in 1696 from designs by *Delcour*. The two others, which date from 1719, bear the arms of the burgomasters of Liège, and those of the Bavarian Palatinate.

The *Bourse*, with its large dome, on the other side of the Grand-Marché, was originally a church of St. Andrew. It formerly contained the *Musée Communal*, now removed to the old cloth-hall, Rue Feronstrée 65, which however need not detain the traveller.

The **Cannon Foundry** (Pl. 21), the property of government, is situated on the bank of the Meuse, in the suburb of St. Leonard. Near it is the extensive royal **Gun Manufactory** (Pl. 33), erected in 1840. Both of these establishments are well worthy of the attention of the professional visitor.

The **Citadel** (486 ft. above the sea-level) commands an admirable survey of the extensive city with its numerous towers and chimneys, and of the populous and industrious valleys of the Meuse, the Ourthe and the Vesdre. The view is bounded towards the S. by the mountains of the Ardennes; towards the N. it extends to the Mont de St. Pierre near Mastricht, beyond which stretch the broad plains of Limburg. The ascent to the citadel is by the old Brussels road through the suburb of St. Walburgis; after reaching the summit of the hill, the visitor turns to the r. The inhabitants of this quarter of the city came into fierce collision with Dutch troops, who had been sent from Tongres to reinforce the garrison during the revolution, in September, 1830. The latter, thus thwarted, were compelled to retreat without effecting their purpose. The citadel still preserves nearly the same form as when it was originally erected by Bishop Maximilian in 1650. Permission to visit it must be obtained at the office of the commandant, Quai de la Sauvenière 50. The inspection of the fortifications, however, will hardly interest the ordinary traveller, who may enjoy an almost equally fine view of the town and environs, from the heights near the fortress, without entering its precincts.

The heights of the **Chartreuse** on the opposite bank of the Meuse, which derive the name from a former monastery of that order, and are now strongly fortified, also command a charming prospect. Still higher than the Chartreuse lies *Robermont*, where the Prince of Cobourg was defeated by Marshal Jourdan, Sept. 19th, 1794. This was the last battle fought by the Austrians on Belgian ground. A fortnight later the victorious French entered Cologne with little opposition. The cemetery of Liège is in the neighbourhood of Robermont. — A fine view may also be enjoyed (no fee) from the terrace of the barracks of *St. Laurent* (Pl. 14).

The **Casino Garden** (Pl. 2) is another locality on the r. bank of the river which should if possible be visited. It is situated near the *Longdoz* station (Namur Railway), and affords a complete survey of the valley of the Vesdre as far as Chaudfontaine. Strangers are introduced to the garden by a member of the club (e. g. the landlord of their hotel).

Liège is now connected with Luxembourg by means of two railways: the Ourthe Line following the picturesque valley of that river as far as *Marloie*, near stat. *Aye* on the Brussels and Luxembourg line (R. 18), and the railway viâ Pepinster and Spa (R. 24). — Beautiful excursions to the château of *Colonster* and *Tieff*, 3 M. from stat. Chenée (p. 166) on the Aix-la-Chapelle line; and to *Esneux*, the third station on the Ourthe Railway (by train in 1/2 hr.).

Excursion to Seraing. The traveller who has half a day at his disposal, after having inspected the attractions of Liège, is strongly recommended to employ it in visiting the machine-factory of Seraing, one of the most extensive and interesting in the world.

Railways to Seraing: by the Liège and Namur line (from the *Station de Longdoz*), on the r. bank of the Meuse in 1/4 hr. (comp. R. 22); by the line on the r. bank (from the *Station des Guillemins*) in 1/4 hr. to *Jemeppe*, the station for Seraing, 1/2 M. from the entrance to the factory.

Steamboats, see p. 166. A trip to Seraing by water (40 min.) is very pleasant in favourable weather. The deck of the steamer affords a fine survey of this picturesque district, with its numerous indications of commercial enterprise and prosperity. The landing-place at Seraing is by the slender suspension-bridge across the Meuse.

Two hours at least must be devoted to the inspection of the works. Visitors are not admitted without a special introduction to Mr. Pastor, the director, who either conducts them in person through the establishment, or places them under the guidance of one of the higher officials (of course no fee). The present difficulty of obtaining admission was introduced in consequence of the continual interruptions occasioned by the multitudes of strangers who formerly flocked hither to gratify their couriosity.

Seraing was formerly the country residence of the Bishops of Liège, whose palace and its gardens were converted in 1817 by

John Cockerill, an enterprising English engineer, aided chiefly by German miners, into one of the most celebrated industrial establishments in the world. One half of the works were the property of William I., King of the Netherlands; but, after his expulsion from Belgium by the revolution of 1830, Cockerill purchased the royal share, and was sole proprietor till his death at Warsaw in 1840. After that event, the gigantic establishment, the vast extent and comprehensiveness of which were due solely to the enterprise and talent of the founder, was purchased by a company, part of the funds having been contributed by the Belgian government. Mr. Pastor, the present director is a relative of the former proprietor. — As the steamer approaches Seraing, a good survey is obtained of the numerous chimneys with their lurid flames, and dense clouds of murky smoke. The natural beauty ' the situation is of course totally gone. The magnificent ectacle presented by the works at night should by all means be witnessed by those who are not already familiar with such scenes.

The episcopal palace, which was occupied by the bishops till 1794, situated on the r. bank of the Meuse, now serves merely as the entrance to the works. The prelates fomerly retired hither in quest of the rural tranquillity of which there is now no vestige. The château was surrounded by a smiling and well-cultivated district, and possessed an extensive garden in the French style, adorned with statues, fountains etc. The latter is now a chaotic waste of coal, slag, tramways, heaps of rubbish etc., whilst the rustic village has been superseded by a smoke-begrimed town with upwards of 22,000 inhabitants.

The establishment, which is admirably organised, and conducted on the most scientific principles, occupies an area of 45 acres, and comprises three distinct departments, viz. coal-mines, iron-foundries, and machine-factories. Within this limited space there are 3 coal-mines, 41 forges and furnaces of various descriptions, a number of coke-kilns, 81 smithies, a brass-foundry, a vast workshop for the manufacture of boilers, another for the construction of locomotives, and a third for other kinds of machinery; finally, extensive turning-apparatus, carpenters' sheds, drawing and modelling saloons, offices etc. The buildings occupied by the magazines, mechanical workshops and offices form two spacious courts. The works are connected with the Meuse by means of a canal, the harbour of which always presents a busy scene. The most productive coal and iron districts in Belgium communicate with Seraing by means of the Meuse, the Ourthe and the Sambre, so that the necessary materials are abundantly supplied to the works from a number of different sources.

In addition to the above works, there are 16 stationary steam-engines constantly in operation, of between seven and eight hundred horse-power in the aggregate, whilst a network of miniature railways, of a total length of nearly 5 M., unite the various departments. Upwards of 1000 miners and 5000 workmen are employed here, under the direction of three superintendents, one for each of the above-mentioned departments. The average quantity of coal consumed amounts to 206 tons daily, and about 80 tons of iron are daily consigned to the two great blast-furnaces.

These imperfect data will suffice to convey an idea of the imposing dimensions of the works. Before quitting them the visitor should inspect the models, the overwhelming variety of which recals the scene presented by the machinery departments at the great exhibitions of London and Paris.

In the vicinity of Seraing are the extensive coal-mines and blast-furnaces of the *Espérance* company; farther distant, the glass manufactory of *Val-St-Lambert*, established in a suppressed Cistercian Abbey, one of the largest establishments of the kind in Europe. Farther down the river are the furnaces of *Sclessin* on the l., and the iron-works of *Ougrée* on the r. bank of the river.

21. The Meuse from Liège to Mastricht.

Railway from Liège to Mastricht in 1 hr. 5 min.; fares 2 fr. 40, 1 fr. 80, 1 fr. 20 c. — *Visé* is the last Belgian, *Eysden* the first Dutch station.

Steamboat daily in summer in 3 hrs., returning in 4 hrs.; fares 2 or 1 fr., half-fares returning against the stream. The steamboat-pier is below the new bridge (p. 171). Another steamer plies between Liège and Mastricht on the *Liège-Mastricht Canal*, twice daily, at the same fares (in 2 hrs.), recommended for the return-journey. — A steamer also plies six times weekly on the canal between Mastricht and Hertogenbosch (p. 302). Steamboats to Venloo and Rotterdam, see p. 186. Railways from Mastricht to Aix-la-Chapelle and to Landen, see p. 182.

The steamboat-trip on the Meuse from Liège to Mastricht is so attractive, and the caverns of the Mont St. Pierre, or the Petersberg, so remarkable, that the traveller should on no account omit to make this excursion. As the steamer starts at an early hour, the whole expedition can be accomplished in one day, so that a night need not be spent at Mastricht. Breakfast may be obtained on board of the steamers, where it will probably be more satisfactory than a hasty meal before starting.

Travellers from Liège to Mastricht, intending to return the same day, should leave their luggage at Liège, in order to avoid the double formalities of the Dutch and Belgian douane in going and returning.

Soon after the steamboat starts from the *Quai de la Batte* (p. 172) at Liège, it passes two conspicuous buildings on the l. bank, the *Mont-de-Piété*, or pledge-office, built of red brick, and the royal cannon-foundry, above which the citadel rises in the background. The vine appears to thrive on some of the neighbouring hills, but this district will probably never attain the rank of a wine-producing country. A short distance below Liège the river describes a long curve.

l. A stunted round tower, the remains of an old windmill.

r. *Jupille*, peeping from the midst of trees, a picturesque place with a loftily situated church. The village, which is of very ancient origin, was once a favourite residence of Pepin of Herstal, who died here in 714, and was also frequently visited by Charlemagne.

The heights on the l. bank now recede, retaining the same elevation until they terminate in the Petersberg near Mastricht. The plain is abundantly sprinkled with villages, manufactories and country-houses. Numbers of tall chimneys bear testimony to the industrious character of the inhabitants. The upper part of the hills on the r. bank are picturesquely wooded, whilst the land at their base resembles a vast orchard.

r. *Souverain-Wandre*, a village hidden by trees. The l. bank now becomes better cultivated and more attractive.

l. **Herstal** was the birthplace of Pepin of Herstal, 'le Gros', the 'maire du palais', or rather regent of the empire, especially as the Merovingian monarchs had already lost much of their original power. His son Charles Martel did not succeed in realising the ambitious schemes of his father; but his grandson Pepin the Little, having secured the approval of the Church and the entire kingdom, at length superseded the half imbecile Childeric III., surnamed l'Insensé, and thus usurped the throne of the vast

Frank empire. He was crowned by Archbishop Boniface in 752, and died here in 768. *Charlemagne* himself is said to have been born at Herstal, but the truth of the tradition cannot now be ascertained. Charles the Bald of France concluded an important treaty here with Lewis the German in 870, concerning the partition of Lorraine. The village, which is nearly 3 M. in length, has gradually extended so far as almost to become a suburb of Liège. The inhabitants belong almost exclusively to the working classes, who are employed at the numerous manufactories of this district. About the beginning of the 18th cent. the village came by inheritance into the possession of Prussia, but was sold by Frederick the Great to the Bishop of Liège for $^1/_2$ million francs.

l. *Chertal*, appertaining to Herstal.

r. *Chératte*, an unimportant village.

r. The château of *Argenteau*, recently restored, belongs to a count of that name, the cousin and heir of the distinguished Austrian diplomatist, who died in 1794. The picturesque château stands on a bold rock, clothed on the summit with oak-plantations. The court of the building is connected by means of a lofty bridge with another rock, where the pleasure-grounds are situated. The park, from which a chapel peeps forth, extends for a considerable distance to the N. The curious formations of the sandstone rock somewhat resemble those of the 'Saxon Switzerland' near Dresden. Argenteau is by far the finest point on this part of the river.

l. *Hermalle*, a village opposite to Argenteau.

r. **Visé** *(Hôtel de Brabant)*, with 2648 inhab., once a fortified town, was the head-quarters of Louis XIV. when he besieged Mastricht in 1673. The works were demolished in 1675. Remains of the town-walls are still visible.

r. *Navagne*, at the influx of the *Berwinne* into the Meuse. During the sieges of Mastricht in the 17th cent., the Spaniards constructed a fort here, which afterwards fell into the hands of the Dutch. It was then taken by the French, and existed till the beginning of the 18th cent., but no trace of the works now remains.

l. *Lixhe*, seat of the Belgian douane.

r. **Eysden**, the first Dutch station, and seat of the customhouse, is situated in an extensive plantation of fruit-trees, and surrounded by luxuriant pastures. The castle is of considerable antiquity. The small building adjoining the custom-house was a freemasons' lodge previous to 1830, down to which period Eysden had been a favourite residence for retired officers. Since the Revolution, however, the freemasons and veterans alike appear to have deserted the place. The Dutch custom-house officials cause a short detention here.

The Petersberg, with its sandstone cliffs, rising nearly 400 ft. above the river, bounds the view towards the N. The château of *Caster* on the summit is the country-seat of a citizen of Liège. The ruins of the '*Caesar's Tower*', or *Lichtenberg*, a venerable stronghold of Roman origin, next become visible. Immediately before it, one of the principal outlets of the sandstone quarries (p. 181) is seen from the deck of the steamboat. The citadel on the N. slope of the hill now comes in sight, and the steamer stops at the quay above the nine-arched bridge, which was constructed by a Dominican monk in 1683.

l. **Mastricht**, from '*Maes-trecht*', i. e. Trajectum ad Mosam, was the *Trajectum Superius* of the Romans.

Hotels. *Lévrier, or Hasenwind (i. e. greyhound), in the Boschstraat; Zwarte Arend, or Aigle Noir, a good second-class inn; table d'hôte in both at 1. 30 p. m., $3^1/_2$ fr. — Near the Petersthor and the church of Notre Dame, Mauel, a hotel with restaurant, unpretending. These inns are all at a considerable distance from the river.

Guides. Five or six experienced guides to the caverns live at Mastricht, one of whom (*François Courtens*, '*eerste kenner van de onderardsche wege*') lives in the street leading to the Petersthor, opposite the Arsenal. Fee for the services of a guide, incl. lamps, 6 fr. — Carriage from Mastricht to the upper entrance to the galleries 6 fr.

Mastricht, the capital of the small portion of the province of Limburg which belongs to Holland (the rest of the province belongs to the N. Germanic Confederation), with 32,000 inhab., is connected with the suburb of Wijk by means of the bridge already mentioned. It was formerly one of the strongest fortresses in Europe, defended by very extensive works, and undermined by a labyrinth of subterranean galleries, whilst the surrounding country can be laid under water by means of sluices. The modern fortifications on the l. bank, which are designed for protection on the Belgian side, are a model of careful and scientific construction. The *Citadel*, situated on the N. slope of the Petersberg, is also modern.

Mastricht was besieged by the Spaniards, under the Duke of

12*

Parma, during four months, in 1579. The garrison consisted of 1000 soldiers (French, English and Scottish), 1200 of the towns-people, and 2000 peasants from the environs. Notwithstanding the tenfold numerical superiority of the Spaniards, they were repulsed nine times by the sallies of the intrepid defenders. At length, greatly reduced in numbers, and exhausted by famine, the latter were compelled to succumb, although the defence was obstinately continued even after the besiegers had entered the town. The victors wreaked their vengeance on the ill-fated burghers with savage cruelty. The greater part of the population, which is said to have comprised 10,000 weavers alone (?), perished by fire and *sword, or in the waters of the Meuse. The value of the spoil was estimated at upwards of a million ducats, but the success of the Spaniards was purchased by a sacrifice of 8000 men.

The fortress has sustained numerous other sieges, three of which are especially memorable and terminated with its capitulation, viz. that of 1632 by Prince Henry of Orange, that of 1673 by Louis XIV., and that of 1748 by the French under Marshal Saxe. Mastricht was the only town in the S. part of the Netherlands which was successfully defended by the Dutch against the Belgian insurgents after the eventful month of September, 1830.

The *Hôtel de Ville*, or *Stadhuis*, situated in the great market-place, and provided with a clock-tower, contains several valuable pictures of the Dutch School. The well-executed tapestry in the *Salle des Princes* represents the history of the Israelites in the wilderness. The town-library is also established in this building.

Several of the churches of Mastricht boast of great antiquity. That of *Onze Vrouw*, or *Notre Dame*, rests on Roman substructures. The façade exhibits several incongruous styles of architecture.

The *Cathedral* of *St. Servaes* is believed to date from the Carlovingian epoch, and a considerable part of the present structure belongs to the 11th and 12th centuries. One of the altar-pieces is a Descent from the Cross by Van Dyck. The modern statue of Charlemagne by W. Geefs was executed in 1845.

The principal attraction at Mastricht is the subterranean labyrinth of sandstone quarries which honeycomb the ***Petersberg** in every direction, and have been worked for upwards of a thousand years. The services of a guide in these bewildering mazes are indispensable (see above). It will be found most convenient to enter them near the house of the burgomaster of the village of St. Peter, $^3/_4$ M. from Mastricht, and to ascend gradually to the upper outlet, near a suppressed Servite monastery (*Slavanden*, now the Casino, and property of a private society); or the excursion may be undertaken in the reverse direction, and may be indefinitely extended by those who care to explore the more remote recesses.

The formation of the Petersberg, extending from Mastricht to Liège, consists of a soft, yellowish, sandy and calcareous stone (sometimes termed 'chalk-tuff'), which has been deposited by the water of the ocean, and contains numerous conchylia, fragments of coral, sharks' teeth, fossil turtles, bones of a gigantic marine monster resembling a crocodile, and other traces of its remote subaqueous origin. Many of these interesting fossils are preserved in the collection at Liège (p. 171), and others may be inspected at the Athenæum at Mastricht. The so-called *orgues géologiques*, cylindrical openings of 1—7 ft. in diameter, and generally vertical, perforating the formation to a vast depth, and now filled with clay, sand and rubble, are a singular phenomenon which has not yet been satisfactorily explained. It is conjectured that they were originally formed by submarine whirlpools, the action of which is known to produce circular orifices in rocks of much harder consistency, and that they were afterwards enlarged by the percolation of water impregnated with carbonic acid.

The commercial value of the stone consists in the facility with which it is sawn into symmetrical blocks, and its property of hardening on exposure to the atmosphere. The galleries, which vary from 20 to 50 ft. in height, are supported by pillars of 12—14 ft. in diameter, left for the purpose. The first excavations are believed to have been made by Roman soldiers, and the same systematic mode of working has been observed even since that period. *Guicciardini's* (p. 167) description of the quarries three centuries ago is so accurate even at the present day, that it is well worthy of repetition:

'Viscera montis scatent lapide quodam molli, arenoso, et parvo negotio sectili, cujus ingens assidue hic effoditur copia, idque tam accurata conservandi et montis et fodientium cura, tamque altis, longis, flexuosis, et periculosis quoque meatibus.'

The galleries constitute a vast labyrinth, of 10—12 M. in length, and 6—7 M. in breadth, and are all so exactly similar in appearance, that their intricacies are known to a few experienced guides only. Most of the entrances are closed, as adventurous travellers have not unfrequently perished in the foolhardy attempt to explore the quarries alone. The dead bodies, which have occasionally been found in the less frequented recesses, have been preserved from decomposition by the remarkable dryness of the air, and the lowness of the temperature. Thousands of names are rudely scratched on the pillars, and a genuine inscription of the year 1037 is even said to have been discovered. The quarries served as a place of refuge for the inhabitants of the neighbourhood during the sanguinary wars of the 17th cent., and have remained alike unaffected by the horrors of that period and the action of the elements.

One of the phenomena pointed out by the guides is the gradual formation of a small natural reservoir in the roots of a fossil tree, by the dropping of water from the branches, which still remain imbedded in the ceiling, the intermediate part having been removed in the course of the excavations.

The invariable temperature in the quarries is about 55° Fahr., but even in hot weather the visitor soon becomes accustomed to it; whilst the remarkable dryness of the interior renders the walk far more agreeable than most other subterranean expeditions. On emerging from these gloomy depths, the traveller enjoys a charming view of the river and its serpentine course for many miles through the broad and fertile plain, of the town with its picturesque towers and bridge, and of the pleasing and cheerful environs, — forming a delightful termination to the excursion. The terrace of the Casino (refreshments) already mentioned is the finest point of view.

Railway from Mastricht towards the E., to *Aix-la-Chapelle* in 1 hr.; towards the W., by *Hasselt* and *St. Trond* (p. 165) to *Landen*, a station on the Louvain-Liège line, in $1^3/_4$ hr.

On the Meuse, about 7 M. below Mastricht, is situated the small town of **Maaseyck** (4528 inhab.), the birthplace of the Van Eycks (see p. 32), to whom a handsome monument in marble was erected in 1864.

22. From Liège to Namur.

Railway (constructed by an English company, now the property of the Compagnie du Nord) in $1^1/_4$—$2^1/_2$ hrs.; fares 5 fr., 3 fr. 80, 2 fr. 50 c.; express 6 fr. 20, 4 fr. 70 c. — Trains start simultaneously from both stations at Liège and meet at Flémalle Junction.

The steamers have ceased to ply on this part of the river, and glimpses only of its picturesque and rocky scenery are obtained from the train. The traveller should endeavour to secure a seat in the last compartment of a first-class carriage, with seats on one side only, and windows across the entire end.

This portion of the valley of the Meuse is remarkably picturesque and attractive, and at several points well worthy of comparison with that of the Rhine. Bold cliffs, ruined castles, rich pastures, and thriving villages are passed in uninterrupted succession, and numerous foundries and manufactories with their lofty chimneys bear testimony to the enterprising character of the inhabitants. The entire district is densely populated, the land well cultivated, and the scenery pleasantly diversified with hop-gardens, corn- fields and meadows. Several quarries on both banks yield excellent marble, which is largely exported to Holland, where it is used for paving and decorative purposes.

Ougrée and *Seraing* (p. 175) are stations on the r., *Tilleur* and *Jemeppe* stations on the l. bank of the river, all remarkable for their picturesque situation, and their numerous manufactories and coal-mines.

Flémalle, a village of some importance, is the junction of the lines of the r. and l. banks. The bridge which here crosses the river, and the branch-line (that of the r. bank) were constructed chiefly with a view to connect the valuable coal-mines on the l. bank with the great iron-works on the opposite side of the river, and the latter with the main line between Brussels and Cologne.

Farther on, to the r., on a precipitous rock rising almost immediately from the river, stands the château of *Chokier*, of ancient origin, but dating chiefly from the previous century. The red tower and substantial walls present a very picturesque appearance. Baron Surlet de Chokier, a member of the noble family to whom the château belongs, was regent of Belgium during five months previous to the election of King Leopold. Then, at some distance from the river, on the l., the castle of *Aigremont*, with its white walls, rising conspicuously on the summit of a lofty ridge, the property of Count d'Outremont. It is said to have been originally erected by the Quatre Fils Aymon, four traditionary heroes of the middle ages. In the 15th cent. it was the central point of the warlike exploits of William de la Marck, the 'Wild Boar of the Ardennes'. To the l., opposite stat. *Engis*, stands the château of *Engihoul*, at the base of a limestone rock. Stat. *Hermalle*, with a handsome château and park, is another picturesque spot, between which and Neuville the scenery is less attractive, and the banks are flatter.

Stat. *Amay* is a market-town at some distance from the river, possessing a Byzantine church and several conspicuous towers. *Neuville* is a modern château, beyond which the bank traversed by the railway becomes bolder and more picturesque. It lies nearly opposite stat. *Ampsin*, where a ruined tower and fragments of walls are seen on the bank of the river. The train continues to skirt the base of the hills on the l. bank, of which no view is obtained. The first important station on the line is

Huy, Flem. *Hoey (*Aigle Noir; *Poste)*, a town with 10,755 inhab. The *Citadel*, constructed in 1817, forms a square, with bastions and numerous casemates, rising from the river in terraces of batteries. The works are partially hewn in the solid rock, and command both banks of the river. The hills on the l. bank are here more than $^1/_2$ M. distant from the river. The *Collegiate Church* is a fine structure, dating from 1311. The old gateway by the choir is adorned with quaint reliefs of the 11th cent., representing the Nativity, the Adoratien of the Magi, and Herod. The large statues of the Virgin, St. Maternus and St. Dominicus, and the rose-window of the same early period are still more interesting.

The abbey of *Neufmoustier*, founded by Peter the Hermit (d. 1115), formerly stood in one of the suburbs of Huy, and the great preacher of the Crusades was himself buried here. A statue has been erected to him in the garden of the old abbey. This was one of no fewer than 17 conventual establishments which Huy possessed under the regime of the bishops of Liège, although the population of the town at that period was less than half of what it is at the present day. — Charming excursions may be made hence into the valley of the *Hoyoux*, a brook which falls into the Meuse at Huy.

Stat. *Bas-Oha*, with an old castle restored as a country-residence, boasts of a few vineyards. On the height opposite are the ruins of the castle of *Beaufort*, destroyed in 1554.

Stat. **Andenne**, a small town with 6370 inhab., is a busy place, with several extensive paper, fayence, and other manufactories. The fine white clay dug in the vicinity is exported in great quantities to Holland, where it is used for making tobacco-pipes. Down to 1785 a religious establishment of 32 sisters, exclusively of noble family, and not bound by any vow to abstain from matrimony, had existed here for upwards of a thousand years. It is said to have been founded by St. Begga, daughter of Pepin of Herstal (p. 177), and the order is thought to be identical with that of the Béguines, who are also permitted to marry. The establishment was transferred to Namur by Emp. Joseph II.

Andenne is connected by a modern iron bridge with *Seilles* on the l. bank, a straggling village of considerable extent, the last in the district of Liège. There are several lime-kilns here, and a handsome château restored in the style of the 15th cent. The columns of the Palais de Justice at Liège (p. 168) are of the blue limestone which is quarried in this neighbourhood.

Sclaigneaux is the station for *Sclayn*, a prosperous and picturesquely situated village on the opposite bank. Stat. *Namèche*, another pretty village, lies opposite *Samson*, a village at the foot of a magnificent and precipitous white cliff of limestone. Above Samson are situated the ruins of an ancient castle, once the residence of Sibylla of Lusignan, mother of Baldwin V., the last king of Jerusalem. A long breakwater here projects into the river in order to deepen the navigable channel. The rocks between Sclayn and Namur are not unlike the curious formations of the 'Saxon Switzerland'. On the opposite bank, farther on, rises the château of *Moisnil*; then that of *Brumagne*, the property of Baron de Woelmont.

Stat. *Marche-les-Dames*, adjoining which are the iron-works of *Enouf*, is charmingly situated. The château of the Duc d'Aremberg, which peeps forth from amidst groups of trees on the cliff, occupies the site of an ancient abbey, founded in 1101 by 139 noble ladies whose husbands had joined the Crusade and accompanied Godfrey de Bouillon to the Holy Land. The rocky bank is so precipitous and barren in many places, as to resemble the ruins of a gigantic wall. Unfortunately, however, many of the finest points of this remarkable and attractive scenery are entirely lost to the railway-traveller.

Namur, see p. 145.

23. From Liège to Aix-la-Chapelle.

Railway in $2^1/_4$—4 hrs.; fares to Verviers 2 fr., 1 fr. 50, 1 fr. 5 c.; express 2 fr. 80, 2 fr. — Fares from Verviers to Aix-la-Chapelle (express) 5 fr. 7 c., 3 fr. 62 c. *Through*-tickets upwards of one-third higher (comp. Introd. VII.). Carriages are changed at Verviers, where there is generally a detention of 20 min. or $^1/_2$ hr. — Herbesthal is the Prussian frontier-station, where the small articles of luggage taken by the traveller into the carriage are examined. All the packages in the luggage-van are examined at the termination of the journey.

The district traversed by the line as far as the Prussian frontier is remarkable for its picturesque scenery, its busy manufactories, its beautiful country-residences, and for the engineering skill with which the line itself has been constructed. Precipitous hills of considerable height are penetrated by about twenty tunnels, profound ravines are crossed by means of lofty bridges, whilst embankments, cuttings and viaducts are passed in rapid succession. The construction of this portion of the line, about 25 M. in length, is said to have cost upwards of 25 million francs. The picturesque stream which the line crosses so frequently is the *Vesdre*, and pleasant glimpses of its well-wooded banks are obtained on both sides of the train. The rock-formation penetrated by most of the tunnels is a bluish limestone, frequently veined with quartz, and often employed for building purposes. This, the most beautiful portion of the journey between England and Germany, is of course missed by those who travel by the night-express; but travellers to whom it is not already familiar should by all means see it by daylight.

The train starts from the *Station des Guillemins* at Liège, situated about 1 M. from the principal hotels, crosses the handsome *Pont du Val Benoît*, and soon passes the extensive zinc-foundry of the *Vieille Montagne Co.*, the exhalations from which are extremely prejudicial to the vegetation in its environs. The *Ourthe* is now crossed near its confluence with the *Vesdre*. Stat. **Chênée** is a busy manufacturing place. Beyond it, the village of *Vaux-sous-Chèvremont* lies to the l. of the line.

Stat. **Chaudfontaine** (**Grand Hôtel des Bains; Hôtel d'Angleterre*), a small and beautifully situated watering-place, attracts numerous visitors from Liège. The thermal spring (104° Fahr.) which supplies the baths is situated on an island in the Vesdre, and is pumped up by means of a powerful water-wheel. The river is here crossed by a handsome suspension-bridge. Chaudfontaine, like the great German watering-places, boasts of the amenities of a 'Cursaal' situated near the station, in the garden of which concerts are given in summer. In the rear of the church a pleasant path, provided with seats, leads to the top of the hill (a walk of 10 min.), at the base of which the village lies. A fine view of the Vesdre is enjoyed thence.

On the height to the l., beyond the tunnel stands the picturesque château of *La Rochette*. Farther on, immediately to the r. of the railway, rises the turreted old castle of **Le Trooz,** perched upon a precipitous rock, and employed for upwards of a century as a manufactory for boring gun-barrels. Beyond it, the station of the same name is passed. The château of *Fraipont* next becomes visible on the r. Then stat. *Nessonvaux*.

Above the next tunnel an artificial ruin is situated. A short distance farther, to the r. of the line, lies the modern *Château de Masures* (*masure* = old hut, or ruined wall), erected by M. Biolley, a wealthy Belgian manufacturer, who was ennobled in 1846. This picturesque Gothic villa, approached by a suspension-bridge, is said to occupy the site of a hunting-seat of Pepin the Little, father of Charlemagne, which stood here upwards of a thousand years ago. Beyond the next tunnel, the train reaches

Stat. **Pepinster,** junction for Spa and Luxembourg (see R. 24). The name is said to be derived from 'Pepin's terre', the district having anciently belonged to the ancestors of Charlemagne.

Stat. *Ensival* on the l. of the line, is an extensive village near Verviers, of which it has become almost a suburb.

Verviers (*Hôtel du Chemin de Fer*, at the station, R. 2, D. 2, B. 1 fr.; *Pays-Bas*, in the town), the last Belgian station, is a town (popul. 28,284) of entirely modern origin, consisting exclusively of extensive manufactories, the substantial dwellings of their proprietors, and the humbler habitations of the artisans. Cloth is the stable commodity of the place. Upwards of 350,000 pieces are manufactured annually in Verviers and the environs, the value of which is estimated at 80 million francs. The principal manufacturers (*Biolley*, *Simonis* etc.) possess depôts in Italy, and even export their wares to America. The uniforms of the Belgian army are made of cloth manufactured here. The water of the Vesdre is said to be peculiarly well adapted for the purposes of dyeing.

To the r., as the town is entered from the station, is situated the '*Harmonie*', the property of a private society, and adorned with a colonnade. A simple fountain on the l. is adorned with a bust of *Napoleon*, erected as a token of gratitude to the emperor under whose auspices the prosperity of Verviers first took its rise. The *Eglise des Recollets*, or *Church of the Franciscans*, the first on the l., is uninteresting. The church of *St. Remacle*, on the E. side of the town, erected in 1834 at the cost of the principal manufacturers, is totally destitute of decoration, resembling a Lutheran place of worship. The mural paintings in the choir, representing Christ surrounded by angels, are by Bellemans of Antwerp. The *Hôtel de Ville* in the market-place bears the inscription: '*Publicité sauvegarde du peuple*'. Near it is the *Theatre*.

During the working hours Verviers has an almost deserted appearance. Its pallid population is visible only at the hours of meals, or late in the evening, especially on the E. side of the town. Two hours are allowed for dinner in the middle of the day (12—2), but work is begun at an early (6 or 7 a. m.), and terminated at a late hour (7 or 8 p. m.)

Beyond Verviers the train passes through seven tunnels, and crosses several bridges within a distance of 6 M. Stat. **Dolhain**, a modern place, picturesquely situated in the valley of the Vesdre, occupies the site of the lower part of the ancient city of Limburg. On the height above it stands the conspicuous castle of **Limburg**, once an important defence of the capital of the fertile Duchy, of which but few traces now remain. The city possessed a cathedral and five other churches, a massive stone bridge over the Vesdre, and strong fortifications, occupying the entire breadth of the valley of Dolhain. Limburg suffered its first serious calamity in 1288, when it was sacked by Duke John I. of Brabant after the Battle of Worringen. It was subsequently captured and pillaged at different periods by the Dutch, the Spaniards and the French, notwithstanding which it appears from the '*Topographia Germaniae Inferioris*', published in 1659, to have been a flourishing and populous place down to that date. It was at length indebted for its utter annihilation to the 'most Christian' monarch Louis XIV. in 1675. The substructures only of the huge towers of the castle on the E. side of the hill are still recognisable. This was the ancestral seat of the powerful ducal family of Limburg, from which the Counts of Luxembourg and the German Emperors Henry VII., Charles IV., Wenceslaus and Sigismund were descended. A number of well built houses have sprung up within the walls of the ancient fortifications, from which the old Gothic *Church of St. George* peeps forth. The walls and buttresses of the sacred edifice, as well as a finely executed tabernacle have survived the vicissitudes of the ill-fated city. The tombstone of a Princess of Baden (d. 1672), wife of Prince Francis of Nassau, the Spanish governor of Limburg, who surrendered the fortress to the French in 1675, is also preserved. The interior is modern. The heights command a fine view of the green valley and the bridge over the Vesdre. — Pedestrians, proceeding in the opposite direction, may quit the train at Dolhain, and walk thence vià Verviers to Liège, a distance of 24 M. The scenery is interesting and picturesque the whole way.

Herbesthal, the first station in the Prussian dominions, is the junction for *Eupen*, a small town about 4 M. distant (by train in $^1/_4$ hr.). The formalities of the douane, generally very lenient, cause a detention of about 10 min.

Beyond stat. *Assenet*, the train crosses the *Goehl Valley* by means of a viaduct of 17 double arches, 117 ft. in height. On the l. lies the village of *Lontzen*, with the château of *Welkenhausen*, which was formerly held by the Prebendary of Aix-la-Chapelle as a vassal of the King of Prussia and the Elector Palatine, by whom alternately the investiture was granted.

Farther on, to the l., on the slope of the wooded hills, is situated the *Eineburg*, or *Emmaburg*, once a country-residence of Charlemagne, where his secretary Eginhard is said to have become enamoured of the emperor's daughter Emma, whom he afterwards married. In the vicinity of the Emmaburg, on the Belgian and Prussian frontier, is situated the so-called neutral territory of *Moresnet*, a tract about 3 M. in length, and $^3/_4$ M. in breadth, containing the valuable zinc-mines of the *Altenberg*, or *Vieille Montagne*, the property of a company whose works are near Liège (p. 186). Owing to some difficulties in adjusting territorial questions at the beginning of the present century, this community was left in an anomalous position of neutrality, or perhaps rather of amenability to the jurisdiction of both countries, as it pays a trifling tax to Belgium as well as to Prussia.

Then, to the l., the village of *Hergenrad*, beyond which the train passes through a short tunnel, and then a longer one, 720 yds. in length. The train next reaches stat. *Ronheide*, and descends an inclined plane to

Aix-la-Chapelle (see *Baedeker's N. Germany*). Railways hence to *Mastricht* (p. 179), *Cologne*, *Düsseldorf*, etc.

24. Baths of Spa.

From Spa to Luxembourg.

Railway from Pepinster (p. 187) to Spa in $^1/_2$ hr.; fares 1 fr. 80, 1 fr. 35, 90 c. Seats on the top of the carriages pleasant in fine weather. During the bathing season an express train runs from Brussels to Spa daily, travellers by which do not change carriages.

Hotels. Hôtel d'Orange, good table d'hôte (everywhere at 4 o'clock) $4^1/_2$ fr.; Hôtel de Flandre; Pays-Bas; Bellevue; York etc. — Hôtel des Etrangers, a good second-class inn.

Cafés: de la Redoute (p. 192); Paris et Rocher de Cancale, on the Promenade de Sept Heures (p. 192).

Horses, or rather ponies, are much in vogue here, being used by visitors even for the shorter excursions. The small 'Américaines' will be found comfortable vehicles for longer distances. Invalids who make a prolonged stay generally hire a pony or Américaine for the entire duration of their visit (charges according to arrangement). A ride or drive to all the springs and back (5—6 fr.) occupies about 3 hrs.

English Church Service during the season.

The valley of the *Hoëgne*, which the railway traverses, is enclosed by picturesque and wooded hills, and enlivened by a succession of country-residences, gardens and manufactories. Near stat. *Juslenville* is the château once occupied by Queen Hortense Beauharnais (d. 1837), the mother of Napoleon III. The chapel, perched on a lofty wooded rock above the line, belongs to the same estate.

Stat. **Theux**, a dull place with 3858 inhab., was once the capital of the County of Franchimont. On Oct. 29th, 1468, whilst Charles the Bold of Burgundy and Louis XI. of France were besieging Liège, a band of 600 daring and patriotic adventurers marched from Theux to the camp of the besiegers, with the design of capturing the two princes in person, and thus causing the siege to be raised. Their attempt, however, failed, and to a man they paid for their temerity with their lives. Excellent black marble is quarried in the vicinity. On an eminence on the l., beyond the village, rises the extensive ruined castle of *Franchimont*, destroyed as early as 1145 by a Bishop of Liège. The last proprietor is said to have been a robber-knight, and to have possessed vast treasures which he buried in the vaults beneath his castle, where they remain concealed to this day. The tradition is gracefully recorded by Sir Walter Scott in his lines on the Towers of Franchimont,

"Which, like an eagle's nest in air
Hang o'er the stream and hamlet fair.
Deep in their vaults, the peasants say,
A mighty treasure buried lay,
Amass'd through rapine and through wrong
By the last lord of Franchimont." etc.

The line now follows the course of the *Wayai*, a brook which falls into the Hoëgne at Franchimont. *La Reid* is the next station.

Spa, with 5282 inhab., consists, like all watering-places, almost exclusively of hotels and lodging-houses, whilst the numerous shops and bazaars, with their tempting display of souvenirs and trinkets, the pleasure-seeking throng in the promenades, and the importunities of valets-de-place and other members of the same fraternity, all combine to indicate that character which occasioned the introduction of its name into the English language as a generic term. This, the original and genuine 'Spa', the oldest European watering-place of any importance, has flourished for a century and a half. It was the Baden-Baden of the 18th cent., but has been gradually superseded by the more modern and attractive watering-places of Germany. The annual number of visitors is still considerable (13—14,000), but about one-half of their number are Belgians of the middle classes, whilst Spa was formerly the fashionable resort of crowned heads and nobles from every part of Europe. Peter the Great was a visitor here in 1717, Gustavus III. of Sweden in 1780, the Emp. Joseph II. and Prince Henry of Prussia in 1781, and the Emp. Paul, when crown-prince in 1782; a long enumeration might also be given of members of the noble families of England, France, Germany and still more distant countries, who have patronised Spa and benefited by its waters. After the French Revolution the reputation and prosperity of Spa began steadily to decline, and at the present day, although the efficacy of the waters and the charms of the scenery continue unchanged, it enjoys a comparatively subordinate rank among European watering-places, and would probably sink into insignificance but for the subtle attractions of the gaming-table, an institution tolerated in no other part of Belgium. The small town, which has several times suffered severely from conflagrations, is a modern, well-built place. The rocky and wooded environs are picturesque, but without pretension to grandeur.

The *Redoute*, corresponding to the 'Cursaal' of German baths, near the Pouhon Spring, comprises ball, concert, reading, dining and gaming rooms. The *Vauxhall*, a similar establishment, lies to the S. of the town, on the way to the Géronstère Spring.

The *Promenade de Quatre Heures* near the Redoute, where a band plays in the afternoon, is a favourite resort of visitors; whilst the *Promenade de Sept Heures*, shaded by magnificent old lime-trees, finds more favour, as its name suggests, at a later hour in the day. The latter is on the way from the station to the town. The band does not play in the morning, as the patients are then engaged in walking in the woods and drinking the waters. Pleasant paths ascend the neighbouring hills, leading through the woods to fine points of view.

The principal Chalybeate Springs are sixteen in number. The most important is the *Pouhon Spring* (the Walloon word *pouhir* = *puiser* in French, i. e. to draw), rising in the middle of the town, and covered by a species of pump-room erected by William I., King of the Netherlands, in 1820, '*à la mémoire de Pierre le Grand*'. The bronze bust of the emperor was presented by the Russian Prince Demidoff in 1853. The water of this spring is largely exported to all parts of Europe, as well as to England, the E. and W. Indies, and America. Being strongly impregnated with iron, it possesses highly tonic and invigorating properties. Other equally powerful springs in the neighbourhood are not used by the public. The temperature of the water seldom exceeds 50° Fahr. — The customary *Tour des Fontaines* next brings the traveller to the two *Tonnelets* ($1^1/_2$ M. to the E. of Spa), which are reached by shady and well-kept avenues of lime-trees, commanding a succession of pleasing views. The next spring is the *Sauvenière*, near which is the *Groesbeck*. In the beautiful plantations in the vicinity stands a *Monument*, erected in 1787 by the Duc de Chartres (Louis Philippe), to commemorate the recovery of his mother, the Duchess of Orleans, from a serious illness, the result of taking the waters of La Sauvenière. It was inaugurated by a 'fête champêtre' described by Madame de Genlis in her memoirs, destroyed by the French republicans in 1792, but subsequently restored by the Orleans family. At the Fontaine de Groesbeck, women are frequently observed devoutly drinking the water on their knees, thus showing their simple *faith* in its miraculous virtues. About $1^1/_2$ M. distant is the *Géronstère Spring*, formerly the most celebrated. Its properties were tested by Peter the Great, whose physician extols them in a document still preserved at Spa. — Returning from the Géronstère, the visitor proceeds to the *Barisart*, which derives its name from the restaurant established on the spot. Bath-houses and *cafés* have sprung up at all the principal springs, and at Spa itself a new establishment for warm baths is in course of construction.

Those who make some stay at Spa may visit the **Cascade of Coo**, 9 M. to the S. of Spa, and 3 M. from Stavelot. The route thither is by the Géronstère, and the villages of *Bu* and *Roanne*. The waterfall is formed by the *Amblève*, which is precipitated over rocks about 60 ft. in height. Above the waterfall the stream is crossed by a bridge, where beggars occasionally assail the traveller, and have been known to throw a dog into the waterfall for the amusement (?) of the spectator.

The **Grotto of Remouchamps** (carriage 15 fr.), 9 M. to the W. of Spa, is a stalactite-cavern which has frequently been described by geologists. The road leads from *La Reid* (p. 191) across a precipitous hill and bleak moor, and then descends to Remouchamps. Blouses to protect the clothes and candles, as well as guides, are procured at the little inn. A trifling charge is made by the parish authorities for opening the door of the grotto. The path in the interior is wet and slippery. The cavern is traversed by a stream, supposed to be that which disappears at *Adeuseux*, and after a subterranean course of 3 M. emerges at Remouchamps.

On the summit of a precipitous rock, nearly opposite to Remouchamps, rises the old château of *Mont Jardin*, surrounded by pleasure-grounds, and still inhabited.

About 3 M. to the W., near the village of *Amblève*, are situated the scanty ruins of a castle termed *Les Quatre Fils Aymon*, from these four chivalrous heroes of mediæval lore. William de la Marck, the 'Wild Boar of the Ardennes', who was executed at Mastricht in 1485 (comp. p. 194), and whose savage exploits are so admirably depicted by Sir Walter Scott in his 'Quentin Durward', is said once to have resided here. The true history of this turbulent adventurer is as follows:

William de la Marck, the scion of an ancient and noble family of Westphalia, born about 1446, was educated by Louis de Bourbon, Bishop of Liège, who watched with deep interest the development of his protégé's impetuous and warlike disposition. William distinguished himself at an early age in the Pays-Bas by the ferocity, rather than by the bravery of his conduct, which procured for him his unenviable sobriquet of the 'Wild Boar of the Ardennes'. After having been guilty of numerous acts of violence and oppression, he at length had the audacity to assassinate Richard, Keeper of the Seal to the Bishop, who had ventured to censure his behaviour, in the palace, and almost before the eyes of his benefactor. Justly incensed at this outrage, the Bishop banished the offender from his court, and William sought an asylum at the court of Louis XI. of France, determined to embrace the first possible opportunity of being revenged on his former master. He accordingly instigated a revolt in the Bishop's dominions, and received money and troops from the French king to aid him in his enterprise. Soon after his arrival in the Province of Liège, he entrapped the Bishop into an ambuscade, and slew the unfortunate prelate with his own battle-axe. The Liégeois, ever prone to rebellion, and rejoicing in the fate of their lawful sovereign, whose severity had occasioned general dissatisfaction, now created William their commander-in-chief. He next invaded Brabant, where he committed many atrocities, but having been defeated by the Archduke Maximilian, he was compelled to return to Liège. William soon afterwards allied himself with René of Lorraine, with a view to prosecute the war against Austria, and Maximiliam, having failed to disembarass himself of so formidable a foe in open fight, resolved to have recourse to treachery. He succeeded in corrupting Frederick of Horn, William's friend and confidant, who accordingly betrayed his master to the Austrians. The 'Wild Boar' was conducted to Mastricht, where he terminated his blood-stained career on the scaffold at the early age of 39 years. He died, as he had lived, with unflinching courage and resolution, and met his merited fate with composure.

From Spa to Luxembourg.

114 M. Railway in $4^1/_2$ hrs.; fares 12 fr. 10, 9 fr. 10, 6 fr. 45 c.

The train at first proceeds in an E. direction, traversing a hilly, and in some places well wooded district, and afterwards turns to the S. — Stat. *Francorchamps*, then

Stavelot (*Hôtel d'Orange*), a thriving manufacturing town with 4000 inhab., on the *Amblève*, and down to the Peace of Luneville in 1801 the seat of abbots of princely rank and independent jurisdiction. The Benedictine Abbey was founded as early as 651, and its possessions extended as far as Malmedy, which since 1815 has been within the dominions of Prussia. A small portion of the tower only of the abbey-church, an ancient structure in the Romanesque style, is now extant. The parish-church contains the *Chasse de St. Remacle*, Bishop of Liège 652—62, a reliquary of embossed copper, gilded, enamelled and adorned with precious stones. The niches at the sides are filled with statuettes of the twelve Apostles, St. Remaclus and St. Lambert, in silver. During the French Revolution this costly and highly revered receptacle of the relics of the saint, which it is said still to contain, was preserved from destruction by being submerged in the water of the Amblève.

The line follows the valley of the Amblève as far as stat. *Trois-Ponts*, where it enters the picturesque ravine of the *Salm*. Stations *Grand-Halleux*, *Viel-Salm*. Farther on, to the r. of the line, are situated the ruins of the castle of *Salm*, the ancestral seat of the princely family of that name. The line now quits the valley of the Salm, and at stat. *Gouvy* crosses the watershed between the Meuse and Moselle, which is at the same time the Luxembourg frontier. Stat. *Trois-Vierges* lies in the valley of the *Wolz*, which the line now traverses. Several unimportant stations, *Maulusmühle*, *Clervaux*, *Wilwerwiltz*, *Kautenbach*; then *Goebesmühle*, at the confluence of the Wolz and the *Sure*, or *Saur*. The most beautiful scenery on the line lies between this point and *Ettelbrück*, the following station, and a number of tunnels and bridges are passed in rapid succession. A branch-line connects Ettelbrück (train in 10 min.) with *Diekirch* (Hôtel des Ardennes), a small town prettily situated on the Sure. About 9 M. lower down the same stream lies *Echternach*, a favourite place of pious resort, celebrated for the singular 'Leaping Procession' which takes place here annually on Whit-Tuesday. The abbey enjoyed an independent jurisdiction till 1801.

At Ettelbrück the train enters the valley of the *Alsette*, at first narrow and picturesque, and follows the course of the stream as far as Luxembourg. Stations *Colmar-Berg*, *Mersch*, *Lintgen*, *Wolferdange*, *Dommeldange*, and finally

Luxembourg, see p. 156.

25. From Brussels to Paris.

A. By Mons, Valenciennes, Douai, Arras and Amiens.

Belgian Railway to Quiévrain, where the line enters the French dominions. From Brussels to Paris in 10—11 hrs.; no express trains by this route beyond Mons. Fares to Paris 36 fr. 5, 27 fr., 19 fr. 45 c.

As far as *Braine-le-Comte*, see p. 142. **Soignies**, a town with

6759 inhab., possesses a venerable abbey-church *(St. Vincent)* in the purest Romanesque style, founded in the 7th cent., and probably the most ancient structure in Belgium, erected in its present form by St. Bruno, Archbishop of Cologne, in 965. Many of the tombstones in the churchyard date from the 13th and 14th centuries. Extensive quarries of mountain-limestone in the neighbourhood. The line then describes a wide curve, pursuing for some distance a direction nearly opposite to that of Mons, until it reaches stat. *Jurbise*, where the line to Tournai and Courtrai diverges. The château of *Belœil*, situated 6 M. to the W. of Jurbise, the seat of the Prince Ligne, may also be conveniently visited from Ath, on the direct line from Brussels to Tournai (see p. 54).

Mons, Flem. *Bergen (Hôtel Garin; Hôtel Royal)*, the capital of *Hainault*, with 26,943 inhab., owes its origin to a fortress erected here by Cæsar during his campaigns against the Gauls. The fortifications were dismantled by the Emp. Joseph II., but were reconstructed in a superior style in 1818. They consist of a polygon, surrounded by 14 bastions, and are regarded as a model of engineering skill. The facility with which the surrounding district can be laid under water from the river *Trouille* contributes materially to the strength of the place, whilst it is protected on the E. by two lakes of considerable extent. The works are, however, again doomed to destruction, and will shortly be entirely demolished.

The coal-mines in the environs of Mons are very productive, yielding between seven and eight million tons annually, valued at 84 million francs. The total produce of the coal-mines of Belgium is estimated at 10 million tons annually, of the value of 105 million francs; of the 78,232 miners employed, 60,734 belong to the province of Hainault alone. The average yield of the Belgian mines between 1836 and 1841 amounted to $3^1/_2$ mill. tons only, three-fourths of which were obtained from this district. The most valuable coal-field is the *Bassin du Flenu*, in the vicinity of the town, to the l. of the road to Jemappes.

The most interesting edifice at Mons is the Cathedral of Ste. Waltrude, situated on the l. as the town is entered from the station. The construction was commenced in 1460, but not completed till 1582. The tower was never erected, and the church possesses a small spire only. The exterior is somewhat disfigured by subsequent additions, but the interior is a model of boldness and elegance. The slender clustered columns are without capitals, rising immediately to the vaulting and keystones. Several reliefs in marble of the 16th cent., by *Dubrucque*, are worthy of inspection. One of the lateral chapels contains a large and curious representation of the Resurrection. A modern painting on the W. wall, by *Isendyk*, represents *St. Waudru*, or St. Waltrude, healing the sick. The church formerly appertained to a semi-ecclesiastical establishment, founded by St. Waltrude, for ladies of noble rank, who devoted one half of the day to religious, and the other half to secular pursuits, and were permitted to marry. Orders of this practical character appear to have been common in Belgium in the middle ages (orders of St. Begga at Andenne, of the Béguines at Ghent, Bruges etc., see pp. 185, 45, 22.

To the I. of the cathedral, and occupying the highest ground in the town, rises the Beffroi, or belfry, appertaining to the former palace, which is now fitted up as a lunatic asylum. The tower, which is said to stand on the ancient site of the castle of Cæsar, was erected in 1662, and contains a 'carillon', or set of chimes.

The Hôtel de Ville, erected in 1440, with a tower added in 1718, is greatly inferior to those of Brussels, Louvain etc., although of the usual Belgian type.

A handsome monument, by *Frison*, was erected here in 1853, to the memory of the celebrated composer *Orlando di Lasso*, or *Roland de Lattre*, who was born at Mons in 1520.

The direct line to Paris viâ Hautmont and Maubeuge (p. 202) diverges at Mons from the route at present described.

Near *Malplaquet*, 3 M. to the S.E., Marlborough and Prince Eugene gained a signal victory over the French in 1709, but not without a loss of nearly 20,000 men. In the vicinity, Pichegru defeated the Duke of York on May 18th, 1794, capturing 60 guns and 1500 men.

At *Jemappes*, 3 M. to the W., Dumouriez and the Duc de Chartres (Louis Philippe), with an army of 50,000 men, defeated 22,000 Austrians under the Duke of Saxe-Teschen, who was compelled to retreat beyond the Meuse, Nov. 6th, 1792.

Stat. *St. Ghislain* lies on the canal by means of which the produce of the coal-mines of Mons is transported to Condé.

Hornu, a large village to the l. of the railway, nearly opposite the latter, is an extensive colony of miners and artisans, who occupy large buildings resembling barracks.

Near *Boussu*, on the l. of the line, on April 29th, 1792, the Austrian Gen. Beaulieu surprised and defeated the French under Biron, whose disastrous flight and 'sauve qui peut' are so well known.

Thulin lies on the r.; then, on the l., *Quiévrain*, the seat of the Belgian, and *Blanc-Misseron*, seat of the French douane. The examination of luggage, however, frequently does not take place until the train arrives at Valenciennes. The transition from the picturesque, populous and industrial district of Hainault to the flat and monotonous agricultural tracts of this part of France is here very perceptible.

Valenciennes *(Poste; *Hôtel des Princes; *Railway Restaurant)*, an ancient fortress on the *Schelde*, or *Escaut*, with 24,000 inhab., is a dirty and uninviting town, with narrow, old-fashioned streets. The principal building is the *Hôtel de Ville*, in which Gothic is combined with modern architecture. If the traveller have occasion to make Valenciennes a resting-place, he may devote a few hours to the civic *Museum*, which contains a few pictures by Rubens, and the church of *St. Géry*, with a fine Descent from the Cross by the same master. A monument was erected in 1856 to the celebrated historian *Froissart*, a native of the town.

Valenciennes formerly appertained to Hainault. In 1656 it was unsuccessfully besieged by Turenne. By the Peace of Nymegen it came into the possession of France, and was fortified anew by Vauban. In 1793 it was taken by the Austrian, Hanoverian and British Allies under the Duke of York and the Prince of Cobourg, but was retaken by the French in the following year. The lace manufactured here has lost much of its ancient reputation.

Immediately after quitting the station, the train crosses the *Schelde*. In the vicinity, to the l. of the line, are the celebrated coal-mines of *Anzin*.

At *Raismes* the line enters an extensive wood. Then several small stations in an unattractive district.

Douai *(Hôtel de Flandre)*, on the *Scarpe*, with 22,000 inhab., situated at some distance from the railway, has been a fortress of considerable importance for many centuries. In the interior the town is far more prepossessing than Valenciennes. The *Hôtel de Ville*, with *Beffroi* and five towers, is a fine example of the Flemish secular architecture of the 15th cent. The central tower is still surmounted with the Flemish Lion as a weathercock.

Douai possesses an important artillery school, and a cannon-foundry where a large proportion of the ordnance of the French army is cast.

The Ghent-Courtrai-Lille line here unites with the present route.

The following stations are *Vitry* and *Roeux*, both in the department Pas-de-Calais, the capital of which, **Arras** (*Hôtel de l'Europe*), with 25,271 inhab., formerly the chief town of the County of Artois, is next reached. The town, situated on the *Scarpe*, and fortified by Vauban, is now a prosperous, manufacturing place, the seat of one of the three great French schools for engineers, and an episcopal see. The *Grande Place* and the *Place de l'Hôtel de Ville*, with the Hôtel de Ville and Belfry, and several venerable buildings of the 15th—17th cent., all of which still retain their mediæval exterior, are very picturesque.

In 1640, when Arras was garrisoned by the Spaniards and captured by the French, the victors on entering the town found the following inscription over one of the town-gates:

'Quand les Français prendront Arras,
Les souris mangeront les chats'.

They suffered the inscription to remain, but by simply deleting the letter *p* in the fourth word they appropriated the boast to themselves. — The tapestry to which Arras has given its name was formerly extensively manufactured here.

Corbie, the fourth station beyond Arras, possessing a handsome abbey-church, which bears some resemblance to Notre Dame at Paris, was formerly a fortress, but was dismantled by Louis XIV. The line crosses the *Somme* several times.

Longdeau (*Rail. Restaurant), near Amiens, is the junction of the Amiens-Boulogne and the Paris lines. Travellers proceeding to Amiens quit the Paris train here, and are conveyed to the station of Amiens in 10 min. (*Rail. Refreshment-rooms).

Amiens *(Hôtel de France; Hôtel de Paris; Hôtel du Rhin,* with a small garden, near the station, unpretending; *Hôtel de l'Univers),* with 58,780 inhab., situated on the Somme, formerly the capital of Picardy, now that of the Department of the Somme, is one of the most important manufacturing towns in France. Cotton goods form the staple commodity. The well-known peace between France and England was concluded here in 1802.

The * *Cathedral*, one of the most beautiful Gothic structures in Europe, was erected in 1220—88 by the architects Robert de Luzarche, Thomas de Cormont, and Renault, son of the latter. The slender spire which rises over the transept is constructed of wood, having been erected in 1529 to replace the original tower, destroyed by lightning two years previously. The towers of the W. façade are uncompleted; that on the N. side dates from the 15th, the other from the 13th cent. The flying buttresses have been restored recently.

The three lofty and receding *Portals* of the W. façade are richly adorned with reliefs and statues. The reliefs of the central portal represent the Last Judgment, the statues the twelve Apostles. The admirable figure of the Saviour, which separates the doors of the central portal, is known as 'le beau Dieu d'Amiens'. On the r., above the portal, the Entombment, Assumption and Coronation of the Virgin; on the l. the history of St. Firmin, the tutelary saint of Picardy.

The nave is of the imposing height of 130 ft., the aisles 60 ft. only. The choir, with its double aisles, is flanked by a series of seven chapels. The lateral chapels of the aisles were added at a comparatively recent period, openings having been made between the buttresses for the purpose, as in Notre Dame at Paris. The magnificent wheel-windows are 35 ft. in diameter. The piers which support the church taper slightly, so that the pavement appears narrower than the vaulting.

The triforium, or arcade beneath the windows of the nave, affords a fine survey of the interior of the church. If the visitor have ascended thus far, he should not omit to walk round the external galleries, and to ascend the steeple, both of which will be found interesting.

The sacristan's dwelling adjoins the N. portal of the W. façade (fee 1 fr.) The interior of the cathedral is shown by the

Suisse, or verger, whose services, however, may well be dispensed with.

The S. transept contains reliefs of the beginning of the 16th cent., gilded and painted, representing in four sections the history of St. James the Great. Beneath are tablets bearing names of members of the 'Fraternité du Puy'; above, several small modern reliefs in marble.

The N. transept contains similar reliefs of the same period, also in four sections, representing the expulsion of the money-changers from the Temple, and other events from the history of that sacred edifice. The adjoining sarcophagus of stone, believed to date from the 11th cent., probably once served as a font.

By the N. wall of the choir, the history of John the Baptist; by the S. wall the history of St. Firmin, and the discovery of his body, executed in 1489 and 1530.

At the back of the high altar is the monument of the canon Lucas, by Blasset, erected at the beginning of last century. Between the statues of the Virgin and the canon, a weeping angel is represented. The merits of the monument, and especially of the '*enfant pleureur*' are often greatly overrated.

The choir-stalls, carved at the beginning of the 16th cent., are worthy of notice.

The two large statues in marble at the entrance to the choir represent St. Vincent de Paule, and S. Carlo Borromeo.

Amiens possesses little else to interest the traveller. The statue in the large *Place*, on the way from the station to the town, is that of the linguist *Dufresne Ducange* (d. 1688), who was a native of Amiens.

The traveller proceeding to Paris now returns to *Longdeau* (p. 199).

Near *Boves*, the next station, are the ruins of a château where Henry IV., '*ce vert galant*', frequently resided with the beautiful Gabrielle d'Estrées. A pleasing view of the valley of the *Noye* is obtained, beyond which the district offers little attraction, until Clermont is reached.

Next stations *Ally-sur-Noye*, *Breteuil*, *St. Just*; then *Clermont* (Hôtel du Croissant), a town with 5144 inhab., picturesquely situated on a green hill, which is crowned by an old château, now employed as a prison. Beyond this point the scenery is very pleasing, and the country well populated.

Liancourt still possesses an old château founded by the Duchess of Liancourt, a member of the same family as Marshal Schomburg, whose ancestral castle of Schönburg is situated near Oberwesel on the Rhine. The handsome church was erected in the 16th cent.

Nicholas du Plessis d'Armerval, Seigneur de Liancourt, a man of weak intellect and deformed in person, was married by Henry IV. to Gabrielle d'Estrées, on condition that he should quit her immediately after the marriage ceremony, and never presume to enter his wife's residence.

Near *Creil* (*Rail. Restaurant) the line approaches the *Oise*. An extensive manufactory of porcelain is situated on an island in the river.

Branch-Line from Creil towards the N.W., to **Beauvais**, which possesses a remarkably fine Gothic cathedral, still uncompleted, but of very imposing dimensions. Height of nave 140 ft.

Stat. *St. Leu* boasts of a church of the 12th cent.; then *Précy*, *Bovan*, and *Beaumont-sur-Oise* with a fine Gothic tower. *Isle-Adam* is one of the most beautiful points on the line. Stat. *Pontoise* is commanded by the ancient church of St. Maclou, situated on a rocky eminence. Stations *Herblay*, *Franconville*, *Ermont*, *Enghien-les-Bains* and *Montmorency*.

The train now passes the *Fort de la Briche*, one of the advanced defences of Paris, and reaches the *Seine*. It then crosses the Canal de St. Denis, halts at *St. Denis*, with its celebrated abbey-church and royal burial vaults, passes the Montmartre, and finally enters the Station du Nord at Paris, opposite to the extensive Hôpital Lariboissière. (Hotels at Paris: *Cailleux* and *St. Quentin*, both near the station; **Grand Hôtel*, Boulevard des Capucines; **Grand Hôtel du Louvre*, Rue Rivoli; **Hôtel du Rhin*, Place Vendôme 4; **Hôtel Meurice*, Rue de Rivoli 228, etc., see *Baedeker's Paris*).

B. By Mons, Hautmont and St. Quentin.

Express trains from Brussels to Paris always take this route ($6^1/_2$—$7^3/_4$ hrs., ordinary trains 10—11 hrs.). Express fares, 34 fr. 60 c., 28 fr.; ordinary, 32 fr. 55, 24 fr. 40, 17 fr. 60 c.

The journey as far as Mons has already been described (R. 25, A.).

Stat. *Cuesmes* and *Frameries*, two populous villages with coal-mines in the neighbourhood. Stat. *Quévy*, then *Feignies*, the first French station. At stat. **Hautmont** the line unites with that from Cologne to Paris, vià Liège, Namur, Charleroi, Erquelines and Maubeuge. *Landrecies* is a small fortress on the Sambre. At *Le Cateau Cambresis* a peace was concluded between France and Spain in 1559. From *Busigny* a branch-line diverges to Cambrai and Douai. The next important place is

St. Quentin *(*Hôtel du Cygne)*, with 27,000 inhab., formerly a fortified town, situated between the Somme and the Canal of St. Quentin, the *Augusta Viromanduorum* of the Romans. It is now a manufacturing place, woollen and linen goods being the staple commodities. The fine Gothic cathedral, and the magnificent Gothic Hôtel de Ville are well worthy of a visit. The Musée contains a collection of drawings in chalk by De Latour. Here in 1557 Duke Emman. Philibert of Savoy defeated the French under Coligny and Montmorency. About 6 M. to the W. of the next stat. *Montescourt*, the castle of *Ham*, celebrated for the political prisoners who have been confined within its walls, is situated. *Tergnier* is the station for *La Fère*, a small town situated on the Oise, about 3 M. to the E. of the railway. *Chauny*, with 7654 inhab., is a place of some importance. **Noyon**, a small town, possessing a handsome church in the transition style, was the birthplace of the Reformer Calvin.

The line follows the course of the Oise, through a cheerful, well-cultivated district. Three small stations, then

Compiègne *(Cloche; France; Soleil d'Or)*, a town with 10,364 inhab., which has always been a favourite residence of the sovereigns of France. The present palace, erected during the reign of Louis XV., was greatly extended by Napoleon I. Near the bridge over the Oise here, Joan of Arc fell into the hands of the English.

Stat. *Verberie*, *Pont St. Maxence*, *Creil*. Hence to Paris, see p. 202. — (Farther particulars in *Baedeker's Paris).*

Travellers from Brussels to Paris may select many other routes besides the above, so as to combine the journey with a visit to various other poin t of interest. On the whole, however, R. 25, A. will be found the most interesting. The two following routes may be preferred by some:

1. Brussels, Alost, Ghent (p. 51), Courtrai, Mouscron, Lille (pp. 24, 54), Douai etc., see p. 199 et seq.

2. From Brussels to Namur (see RR. 15, 18), from Namur to Charleroi, and thence to Hautmont, whence the Route 25, A. is followed. The portion of this route between Charleroi and Maubeuge leads through the valley of the Sambre, and passes the small town of *Thuin*, the picturesque ruins of the Abbey of *Lobbes*, then *Erquelines* (Belg. frontier), *Jeumont* (Fr. frontier), and *Maubeuge*, a fortified town on the Sambre, with 8700 inhab.

HOLLAND.

Plan of Tour and Travelling Expenses. The following tour is recommended to the traveller whose time is limited:

	Days
From Antwerp to *Rotterdam* by steamboat	1
Ascent of the tower at Rotterdam, Erasmus Monument, walk through the city, and along the quays; *Delft*, Tomb of Prince William; *Hague*, walk through the streets	1
To *Scheveningen* at 6 or 7 a. m., bath, breakfast in bath-house. Drive to *'T Huis in 'T Bosch*. Potter's Bull and Rembrandt's Anatomy in the Museum. Curiosity Cabinet. Back to Scheveningen to dinner at 4 p. m.; evening on the beach, or in the theatre at the Hague	1
To *Leyden*, Siebold's Museum, Museum of Antiquities, Nat. Hist. Museum; in the evening to *Haarlem*	1
Church at Haarlem, picture-gallery in the Pavilion; in the evening to *Zaandam*	1
Morning at Zaandam, evening at *Broek*	1
To *Amsterdam*, harbour, Zoolog. Garden, paintings in the Museum, Exchange, evening at the theatre	1
To *Utrecht*, walk through the town, and ascend tower of cathedral; thence by railway to Arnheim, Düsseldorf and Cologne, or back to Rotterdam, or to Amsterdam	1

A hasty glance at the principal places in Holland may thus be obtained in a week or ten days, but the traveller whose time permits will prefer to devote a longer period to this really interesting country, and to avail himself of the steamboats on the canals and rivers, as well as on the open sea in fine weather. The following will be found an instructive and agreeable tour of a fortnight:

	Days
From Antwerp to *Rotterdam* by steamboat	1
Rotterdam and *Delft*	1
The *Hague* and *Scheveningen*	2

	Days
Leyden and *Haarlem*	1
Alkmaar; Helder and back by steamer; *Zaandam*	4
Broek and *Amsterdam*	3
Utrecht and back to Amsterdam	1
By steamer to *Kampen*, thence by railway (or by steamboat on the Yssel) to *Arnheim*	1

Hôtels in Holland are inferior to those of Belgium and Germany, as a rule; the charges as high, whilst the cuisine and attendance are often defective. At the same time they are generally scrupulously clean, and in some of their characteristics more nearly resemble the hotels of England than those of other parts of the continent. The usual charge for a bedroom is $1^1/_2$ fl., breakfast 70 cents, table d'hôte $2^1/_2$ fl., attendance $^1/_2$ fl. Luncheon is generally taken at 1, dinner at 4 or 5 o'clock. As a nation, the Dutch are extremely enlightened and well-educated, but the class with whom the traveller comes in contact will perhaps impress him less favourably with regard to their manners and address.

Fees at museums, churches etc. should not exceed 2 fl. per day. Hotel expenses amount to 7—8 fl. daily, travelling and other expenses to 4—5 fl., so that the total cost of a tour in Holland will be 14—15 fl. a day. The 'voyageur en garçon' may reduce his expenditure to one half of this sum by taking breakfast at the cafés, dining at unpretending restaurants, and avoiding the more expensive hotels. It may also be remarked that the steamboats on the canals, the Rhine, Meuse, Yssel etc. afford a cheaper, and often pleasanter conveyance than the railways.

Money, Passport, Customs-Dues. Silver-pieces of $2^1/_2$ *(ryksdaalder)* and 1 florin, 50 *(dubbeltje)* and 25 *(kwartje)* cents. The Dutch florin, gulden, or guilder (of the same value as the Rhenish florin, i. e. about 2 fr. 15 c., or 1 *s.* $8^1/_2$ *d.*) is divided into 100 cents, or 20 *Stuivers* (pronounced stoiver). A stuiver (no longer current), or 5 cents, is therefore nearly equivalent to 1 *d.* — Gold pieces of 5 and 10 fl., termed half and whole Willemsd'ors respectively, fluctuate in value. The average exchange for a Willemsd'or is 9 fl. 70 cents, for a Napoleon 9 fl. 30 cents, for a sovereign 11 fl. 70 cents.

Passports are now dispensed with in Holland, but the traveller may occasionally find one of these documents useful, and should be provided with one in case he contemplates a tour of considerable duration. — The Dutch Custom-house Officials are generally lenient in their examination of the luggage of English travellers. It should, however, be borne in mind, that all new articles, especially if not wearing-apparel, are liable to pay duty according to their value, which must be declared beforehand. In order to prevent evasion of the duties by travellers, one of the regulations of the douane provides, that, if too low a value be named by the traveller, the officials are empowered to buy the article at the price named, with the addition of 10 per cent. New articles found in passengers' luggage, which have not been previously declared, are liable to confiscation.

Language. A slight acquaintance with the Dutch language (pronunciation, see Introd. IV) will contribute greatly to the instruction and enjoyment afforded by a tour in Holland. Those who have a knowledge of German, Swedish, or Danish will recognise the identity of the roots of the great majority of the words in these languages with those of the Dutch, to which Flemish is still more nearly allied. The following lines from two popular ballads will serve as a specimen:

Wien Neêrlandsch bloed in de aadren vloeit,
Van vreemde smetten vrij,
Wiens hart voor land en Koning gloeit,
Verhef den zang als wij:
Hij stel met ons vereend van zin,
Met onbeklemde borst,
Het godgevallig feestlied in
Voor Vaderland en Vorst.
(Tollens.)

(Literal translation: "Let him, in whose veins Netherlandish blood flows, free from every stain, and whose heart glows for country and king, raise the song with us, united in sentiment, with unburdened breast, in the festal song, pleasing to God, for Fatherland and Sovereign.")

Wij leven vrij, wij leven blij
Op Neêrlands dierbren grond,
Ontworsteld aan de slavernij,
Zijn wij door eendragt groot en vrij;
Hier duldt de grond geen dwinglandij
Waar vrijheid eeuwen stond.
(Brand.)

(Literal translation: "We live free, we live blithe, on Netherlands' dear ground; delivered from slavery, we are through concord great and free; here the land suffers no tyranny, where freedom has subsisted for centuries".)

The Dutch language is highly cultivated and developed, and totally free from that vague and arbitrary character which stamps the Flemish as little else than a mere patois. Like other languages of purely Teutonic origin, it has admitted a considerable number of words of the Romanic stock to the rights of citizenship; e. g. *Kantoor* (comptoir), *kwartier* (quartier), *katoen* (coton), *kastrol* (casserole), *rekwest* (requête) etc. Words of foreign origin, however, have been imported into Dutch from motives of convenience or fashion, rather than absolute necessity, the language itself being remarkably rich and full of vital energy. Words of purely native growth are to be found in almost every branch of science and art; thus affording a striking proof of the enlightened and industrious character of the nation.

Railways. The remarks made with regard to those in Belgium apply to Holland also, except that the fares on the Dutch lines are considerably higher (comp. Introd. VII).

Diligences are managed by private companies in Holland, and government only undertakes to control the letter and parcel departments. A Dutch post is about $4^3/_4$ M., accomplished by these cumbrous, but not uncomfortable vehicles in $^3/_4$ hr., at a fare of $^1/_2$ fl. The Dutch generally reckon distance by 'uren gaans', hours of going, or walking, one of which is about 3 M.

Diligence and steamboat time-tables are contained in the 'Reiswijzer', which is published monthly, and is to be found at all the hotels.

Carriages, roomy and comfortable, with two horses, may be hired at 15 fl. a day, including tolls and other expenses. If the journey terminates at a distance from the place where the vehicle was hired, the driver is entitled to charge for the days he requires in order to return home.

The Roads in Holland are excellent. As stone is unknown in the greater part of the country, small and well hardened bricks (*'klinkers'*) are used as a substitute, forming a smooth and hard surface which rivals that of the best macadamized roads. The original cost of the construction of these Dutch roads is estimated at 6000 fl. per English mile, a considerable sum when the perfectly level character of the country is considered; and high tolls are consequently levied. As, however, the heavy traffic is carried on almost exclusively by water, the roads are generally frequented by light vehicles only, and are maintained at a comparatively moderate expense.

The **Trekschuit** (*ch* with a guttural sound, *ui* pron. oi), literally 'draw-boat', was formerly a conveyance universally employed in Holland, where canals are as common as roads in other countries. All the principal towns, however, are now connected by railways, and the canal-boats still in use are often drawn by small screw-steamers instead of by horses (e. g. from Amsterdam to Haarlem, and from the Hague to Delft).

Dutch Peculiarities. The picturesqueness of the national costumes, which have retained their ground longer in Holland than in most other countries, is well known. They are now seen to the best advantage in the islands of Urk and Marken.

Canals (*'Grachten'*) intersect most of the Dutch towns, as well as the country. in every direction, and are generally enlivened with numerous barges. The different quarters of the towns are connected by means of draw-bridges (*'ophaalbrug'*). The roads and streets skirting the canals are usually planted with trees, which contribute greatly to their picturesque aspect.

The houses are generally lofty and narrow, and constructed of red brick and white cement. The beams occasionally seen projecting from the gables are used for drawing up goods to the lofts, which are used as magazines. The windows of the ground-floor are generally of imposing dimensions, and polished with the scrupulous care which characterises the Dutch of all classes, thus imparting to the houses a far more cheerful and prosperous appearance than is usual in large towns. At the cellar-doors in the side-streets, sign-boards with the words *'water en vuur te koop'* (water and fire to sell) are frequently observed. At these humble establishments boiling-water and red-hot turf are sold to the poorer classes of the community for the preparation of their tea or coffee. Many of the houses and public buildings are considerably out of the perpendicular, a circumstance due to the soft and yielding nature of the ground on which they stand.

The Chimes in the towers of the churches, or other public buildings, proclaim the quarters of every hour by playing a few bars of some popular or operatic air, a pleasing custom, of which however the effect is destroyed by the too frequent repetition.

The 'Gaper' (gaper), a painted Turk's or Moor's head, is the customary sign of the druggists' shops. A large crown, decorated with box-leaves and gilding, suspended beneath the Dutch flag, is an indication that new herrings have arrived in the shop thus adorned. *'Tapperij'* (tap-room), or *'hier verkoopt man sterke dranken*' (strong drinks are sold here), are the common signs for taverns. '*Dit huis is te huuren*' (this house is to hire, or let) is also frequently observed.

Stoofjes, or foot-warmers, are universally employed by the female members of the community, and are seen in great numbers in the churches.

The Village Feasts ('*kermis*', literally 'church-mass', i. e. the anniversary of the foundation of the church) form a substitute for the Carnival of Roman Catholic countries, but the gaieties on these occasions too frequently degenerate into scenes of drunken revelry. The popular refreshments at these festivities are 'Hollands' and '*broedertjes*', a kind of cake sold in the numerous booths erected for the purpose.

In many Dutch towns the custom prevails of affixing bulletins to the doors of houses in which persons are sick, in order that their friends may be apprised of the state of their health without knocking or ringing. At Haarlem and Enkhuizen the birth of a child is announced by means of a small placard adorned with red silk and lace, and the friends of the family are entertained on these occasions with '*kandeel*' (a species of mulled wine) and '*kaneel-koekjes*' (cinnamon-cakes). Betrothals are celebrated by an extensive consumption of '*bruidsuiker*' ('bridal sugar', or sweet cakes) and '*bruidstranen*' ('bridal tears', as the spiced wine is figuratively termed).

The Dutch love of cleanliness sometimes amounts almost to a monomania. The scrubbing, washing and polishing which most houses undergo once every week, externally as well as internally, are occasionally somewhat subversive of comfort. Spiders appear to be regarded with especial aversion, and vermin is fortunately as rare as cobwebs.

Country Residences *(buitenplaatsen* or *buitens)*. Although nature has not bestowed her charms lavishly on Holland, the careful cultivation of the fields, gardens and plantations imparts a picturesque and prosperous appearance to the country. In the vicinity of the larger cities, especially on the Vecht between Utrecht and Amsterdam, also at Arnheim, Haarlem etc., numerous tastefully constructed villas and country-seats are seen near the roads and canals, frequently enclosed by carefully kept gardens, parks and pleasure-grounds. These paradises of the Dutch gentry and retired merchants usually bear inscriptions characteristic of the sentiments of their occupants, and breathing a spirit of repose and comfort. Thus: *'Lust en Rust'* (pleasure and repose), *'Wel Tevreden'* (well content), *'Mijn Genoegen'* (my satisfaction), *'Mijn Lust en Leven'* (my pleasure and life), *'Vriendschap en Gezelschap'* (friendship and sociability), *'Vreugde bij Vrede'* (joy with peace), *'Groot Genoeg'* (large enough), *'Buiten Zorg'* (without care). Many villas rejoice in much lengthier titles, which perhaps appear peculiarly appropriate to the proprietors, but cannot fail to excite a smile when read by strangers. Few of these country-houses are seen from the railway, and the traveller should therefore endeavour to pay a visit to some of the more attractive, which are mentioned in the following pages.

Windmills *(molens)* are a characteristic of almost every Dutch landscape, and often occupy the former ramparts and old bastions of the towns, which they appear to defend with their gigantic arms. Many of them are employed in grinding corn, sawing timber, cutting tobacco, manufacturing paper etc., but one of their most important functions is to transfer the superfluous water from the low ground to the canals, by means of which it is discharged into the sea. This is usually accomplished by means of large water-wheels, the mechanism of which is far simpler and less expensive than that of pumps. The highly cultivated state of the country bears testimony to the efficiency of this system of drainage. Many of the windmills are of vast dimensions, the towers often resembling fortifications, and the sails exceeding 100 ft. in length.

Dykes. Holland is probably the lowest country in the world, the greater part of which lies many feet below the sea-level. Upon the dykes, or embankments, therefore, by which the encroachments of the sea are prevented, the safety of the entire kingdom depends. In many places these vast and costly structures are equally important and necessary to prevent inundation by the rivers, the beds of which are gradually raised by alluvial deposits.

The first care of the constructors of the dykes is to lay a secure and massive foundation, as a preliminary to which the ground is stamped or compressed in order to increase its solidity. The dykes themselves are composed of earth, sand and mud, which when thoroughly consolidated are entirely impervious to water. The surface is then covered with twigs of willows, interwoven

14*

with elaborate care, the interstices of which are filled with clay, so as to bind the whole into a solid mass. The willows, which are extensively cultivated for the purpose, are renewed every three or four years. Many of the dykes are, moreover, planted with trees, the roots of which contribute materially to the consolidation of the structure. Others are provided with bulwarks of masonry, or protected by stakes against the violence of the waves, whilst the surface is covered with turf.

The most gigantic of these embankments are those of the Helder, and of West-Cappel on the W. coast of the island of Walcheren (p. 135). The annual cost of the maintenance of the latter alone amounts to 75,000 fl. annually, whilst the total expenditure throughout Holland for works of a similar description is estimated at 6 million florins. A corps of engineers, termed *De Waterstaat*, is occupied exclusively in superintending these works. The constantly imminent nature of the danger will be thoroughly appreciated by the stranger, if he stand at the foot of one of the great dykes at high tide, and hear the breakers dashing against the other side of the barrier, at a height of 16—18 ft. above his head.

Canals intersect the country in every direction. They serve a threefold purpose: (1) as a means of communication, with which almost every town and village in the kingdom is furnished; (2) as drains, by which superfluous water is carried off from the cultivated land; (3) they form substitutes for hedges and walls, which are not more common enclosures for houses, fields and gardens in other countries, than canals are in Holland. The Dutch canals differ from those in most other countries in generally being considerably broader, whilst the width is by no means invariable; and locks are rare, as the level of the water is nearly always the same. Those, however, which are directly connected with the sea are closed at their extremities by massive flood-gates, to prevent the encroachment of the sea when its level is higher than that of the water in the canal.

The principal canals are about 60 ft. in width, and 6 ft. in depth. Not only the surface of the water, but the bed of the canal is frequently considerably above the level of the surrounding country. The great North Canal (p. 273), the broadest and deepest in Europe, is a marvellous monument of Dutch skill and perseverance in undertakings of this description. It will, however, be surpassed by the new canal now in course of construction, which will connect Amsterdam with the N. Sea. This magnificent channel of communication will be 17 M. in length, 190—320 ft. in breadth, and 23 ft. in depth. The cost is estimated at 18 million florins. The new Willems-Canal in N. Brabant is also worthy of mention.

Polder is a term applied to a morass or lake, the bed of which has been reclaimed by draining. A great part of Holland and Flanders has been thus reclaimed, and rendered not only habitable, but extremely valuable for agricultural purposes.

The first step in the process of drainage consists in enclosing the marsh to be reclaimed with a dyke, to prevent the admission of water from without. The water is then removed by means of water-wheels of peculiar construction, driven by windmills or steam-engines. A remarkable feature in these undertakings is, that the marsh or lake to be reclaimed is sometimes too deep to admit of the water at once being transferred to the main canals, and thus carried off. In these cases a system of dykes, one within the other and each provided with a canal on its exterior, forms an ascending series of levels, from the lower of which the water is gradually transferred to the higher, and thence finally into the principal channels. An excellent example of this is seen in the Schermer-Meer, where four different levels have been formed. These canals, although entirely separate from one another, are all provided with means of communication, by which in case of necessity the water from the higher can be discharged into the lower.

The extraordinary fertility of the land thus reclaimed is accounted for to a great extent by the fact, that every superfluity of water can be removed by means of the water-wheels on the shortest notice, whilst in dry seasons an admirably efficient system of irrigation is constantly available.

The aspect of these polders differs materially from that of the rest of the country. The speculators by whom they are drained map them out with mathematical precision into parcels, separated by canals and rows of trees at right angles, and furnished with houses of precisely uniform construction, all affording manifest indications of the artificial nature of the ground. The polders often lie under water during the winter, but this by no means impairs the fertility of the soil, provided the water is not salt.

Dunes, or downs, are the low sand-hills, 50—60 ft. in height, which extend along the coast of Holland and Flanders, and have been thrown up by the action of the wind and waves. Those nearest the sea are of very unsubstantial consistency, and frequently altered in shape by the wind, affording little or no sustenance to vegetable life. Between the central downs (the highest and broadest) and those still farther inland, is situated an uninterrupted tract of pasture and arable land, occupied by numerous cottages, and producing excellent potatoes. In many of the downs there are rabbit-burrows of vast extent, where excellent sport may often be enjoyed.

In order to prevent the sand from the downs from covering the adjacent land, they are annually sown with the plants that will take root in such poor soil, especially the reed-grass *(arundo arenarea)*. In course of time the roots spread and become entwined in every direction, thus gradually consolidating the sand, which then becomes capable of supporting richer vegetation. A substratum of vegetable soil once formed, the arid and useless sand-hill is converted into a smiling and fertile agricultural district, in which even plantations of pines appear to thrive.

History and Statistics †. The earliest inhabitants of the district at the embouchures of the Rhine are said to have accompanied the Cimbri and Teutoni in their expedition against Italy. Several banished tribes of the Catti, who settled in the deserted island of Betuwe (p. 306), were conquered by the Romans, whose supremacy over this part of the country continued till the 4th cent., when the Salic Franks, the inhabitants of the banks of the Yssel, took possession of the Betuwe, and established themselves between the Schelde, Meuse and Lower Rhine. The district to the N. E. of the Salic Franks was occupied by the Frisians, to the E. of whom were the Lower Saxons. The supremacy of Charlemagne extended over the whole of the Netherlands.

Under his successors the system of investing vassal-princes with the land gradually developed itself. The most powerful of

† 'Nederland, zijne Provincieën en Kolonien, Land en Volk, beschreven door J. Kuyper', published in 1868, is recommended to those who possess some acquaintance with the language as an excellent book of reference.

these were the Bishops of Utrecht and the Counts of Holland. In 1274 Count William II. was elected King of Rome through the influence of Pope Innocent IV. In 1512 the Dutch provinces were enrolled as a part of the Burgundian section of the Germanic Empire.

Under the Emp. Charles V. the whole of the Netherlands were united, and enjoyed a golden era of prosperity, in consequence of the powerful protection accorded by that monarch to commerce and navigation. Under his bigoted son and successor Philip II. of Spain, after the Duke of Alva's arrival at Brussels (1568), that memorable, and at first apparently hopeless struggle commenced, which lasted for 80 years, and terminated in the recognition of the Northern Netherlands as an independent state by the haughty Spaniards, and the establishment of the powerful Dutch Republic.

The great founder of Dutch liberty was William of Nassau, 'the Silent', Prince of Orange, a nobleman of German extraction. He fell in 1584 by the hand of an assassin at Delft (p. 226). On the day of his death his son Maurice was elected stadtholder by the states.

Under his auspices the power and wealth of the Republic rapidly increased, and the E. Indian trading company was formed (1602); but the judicial murder of Oldenbarneveld (1619) is a foul blot on the memory of this prince, and the pernicious theological controversies of the *Arminians* and *Gomarists* (p. 305) were productive of many evil effects during this period. Maurice died in 1625, and was succeeded by his brother Frederick Henry (1625—47), under whom the unity of the Republic became more consolidated, and the prosperity of the States reached its culminating point. The Dutch commerce of that period was the most widely extended in the world.

Their great navigators *Houtman*, *Heemskerk*, *Davis*, *Schouten*, *Lemaire*, *Hartog*, *Edels*, *Schapenham*, *Nuyt*, *Vianen*, *Caron*, *Tasman*, *De Vries*, *Van Campen* and *Berkel*, explored the most distant coasts in the world during this period, and the E. Indian factories, especially that of Batavia, which had been established in 1619, yielded a rich harvest. The Dutch school of painting, too, had now attained its culminating point; *Rembrandt* flourished as an historical, a portrait, and a genre-painter; *Van der Helst*, historical; *Backhuizen* and *Van de Velde*, sea-pieces; *Steen*, *Dow* and

Teniers, genre and humorous scenes; *Wouverman*, horses and battles; *Potter*, animal-pieces; *Berchem*, *Waterloo* and *Ruysdael*, landscapes; *Huysum*, flowers and fruit. The sciences were also highly cultivated during this prosperous epoch, as the well-known names of *Grotius*, *Vossius*, *Heinsius*, *Gronovius* etc. abundantly testify.

Frederick Henry died in 1647, a short time before the Peace of Westphalia, by which the independence of the United States of the Netherlands was formally recognised, and was suceeded by his son William (d. 1650), then in his 21st year.

On the death of the latter, who by the commission of several arbitrary acts had rendered himself unpopular, especially to the powerful aristocratic party, the States resolved not to elect a new stadtholder; and the reins of government were now entrusted to the Grand Pensionary Cats, the celebrated John de Witt, and other able and energetic senators.

During this period the navigation acts were passed which gave rise to the war with England, and called into activity the talents of *Van Tromp*, *De Witt*, *De Ruyter*, and other naval heroes, whose memory is still fondly cherished by the Dutch. Within the brief period of sixteen months as many as ten great naval battles were fought, in most of which the arms of the Republic were crowned with success. In 1667 De Ruyter even entered the estuary of the Thames with his fleet, endangering the safety of London itself, to the great consternation of the citizens.

In consequence of the murder of the Grand Pensionary John de Witt (p. 230), and the invasion of Holland by the French under Louis XIV., Condé and Turenne in the spring of 1672, the office of stadtholder was revived, and conferred by a decree in 1674 on the Princes of Orange as an hereditary right.

The French war was terminated by the Peace of Nymegen in 1678, the stadtholder William III. (1672—1702) having been the means of asserting the liberties of Europe against the usurping encroachments of the ambitious 'Grand Monarque'. William, the son-in-law of James II. of England, ascended the English throne in 1689, in consequence of which his native country became estranged from him, and in conjunction with Austria and Spain engaged in a new war with France, terminated at length by the Peace of Ryswijck in 1697.

William III. died in 1702 without issue, and was succeeded by his brave cousin John William Friso, Prince of Orange, who had commanded the army of the Republic during the war of the Spanish succession. He was accidentally drowned at Moerdijk in 1711.

The events of the 18th cent. scarcely require special mention. The Republic had lost its prestige, and a revolution which broke out towards the close of the century terminated in the expulsion of the Stadtholder William V., who was reinstated in his office by the Prussian army which had advanced almost unopposed to the gates of Amsterdam itself.

The importance of the Republic had now dwindled to a mere shadow. In 1795 the French Republicans, led by Dutch exiles, took possession of the country, founded the 'Batavian Republic', and at the same time caused heavy taxes to be levied. Schimmelpenninck, an able statesman, was created president of the new Republic, under the old title of Grand Pensionary, but in 1805 was compelled to yield up his authority to Louis Bonaparte, the brother of Napoleon I., the emperor having created him King of Holland. This semblance of independent existence came to an end in 1810, when Napoleon annexed Holland to France, declaring it to have been formed by the alluvial deposits of French rivers.

At length in November, 1813, the French were expelled from Holland by the Dutch, aided by the Russians and Prussians; and the Prince of Orange, son of William V., the last stadtholder, who died in exile in 1806, ascended the throne of Holland as an independent sovereign.

By the Congress of Vienna, the southern, or Belgian provinces of the Netherlands, were united with the northern into a single Kingdom, and the Prince of Orange was created King of the Netherlands, under the title of William I. This bond of union between two races differing materially in language, religion and character was severed by the Belgian Revolution of 1730 (comp. Introd. IX). Ten years later William I. abdicated in favour of his son William II., who died in 1849, and was succeeded by William III., the present king (born in 1817, married Princess Sophia of Würtemberg in 1839; their eldest son William, Prince of Orange, was born in 1840).

The Kingdom of the Netherlands, which including the Province of Limburg is 13,600 sq. M. in area, has a population of 3,500,000 (1/3rd Rom. Cath., 100,000 Jews), of whom about 2 millions are of Batavian, or Dutch, half a million of Frisian, and nearly as many of Flemish origin. On an average, therefore, each square mile is occupied by 277 souls (maximum in N. Holland 560, minimum in the Province of Drenthe 93). The Netherlands are divided into nine provinces: N. Brabant (capital Hertogenbosch), Guelderland (Arnheim), N. Holland (Amsterdam), S. Holland (Hague), Zeeland (Middelburg), Utrecht (Utrecht), Friesland (Leeuwarden), Over-Yssel (Zwolle), Groningen (Groningen), Drenthe (Assen). Besides these provinces, the district of Limburg (210,023 inhab., capital Maastricht), is governed by the king of Holland as grand-duke, and that of Luxembourg (202,203 inhab., capital of the same name) by the same monarch as duke. Limburg now bears a share of the payment of interest (31 million florins) on the national debt, in the same proportion as the other provinces. The ducal house of Nassau, connected with the royal family of Holland by bonds of agnation, possesses a contingent interest in the succession to the Duchy of Luxembourg; it formerly was also interested in like manner in the succession of the Grand Duchy of Limburg, but has relinquished all right to make any claim to the latter, in consideration of a pecuniary compensation. Limburg may, therefore, be regarded as now forming an integral part of the Kingdom.

The colour of the national flag is red, white and blue, placed in horizontal lines (the French are placed vertically); the motto, 'Je maintiendrai'.

The most important Dutch Colonies in the *E. Indies* are Java (capital Batavia), Sumatra, Borneo, Celebes; in the *W. Indies* Surinam, St. Eustache and Curaçao; to which must be added a number of factories on the coast of Guinea. The total area of these possessions amounts to 660,000 sq. M., the population to 18 million souls.

The Merchant Fleet of Holland numbers upwards of 7000 vessels, 2500 of which trade with distant parts of the world.

The Army consists of 1 Regiment of grenadiers and riflemen, 8 Regiments of infantry, 5 Regiments of dragoons, 5 Regiments of artillery, 1 Batallion of engineers. Prince Frederick is the '*groot-*

meester', or commander of the artillery. Total number 61,000 men. An army of 30,000 men is moreover distributed throughout the colonies.

The Royal Navy consists of 154 vessels of war of various descriptions, and is commanded by Prince Frederick, the uncle of the King, 3 admiral-lieutenants, 1 vice-admiral, 4 contre-admirals, 20 captains, 40 commanders etc.

Executive Power: a state-council, consisting of 12 members nominated by the King, and 8 responsible ministers. — Legislative Power: two Chambers, the members of which are elected by the States General. The first consists of 39 members, elected by the provinces for a period of 9 years; the second of 74 members, elected by the electors of the districts.

---

26. Rotterdam.

London to Rotterdam viâ *Harwich* in 20 hrs. (sea-passage 14 hrs.); fares 25, 20, 15 *s.*; return-tickets one fare and a half. Tickets issued at Bishopsgate station, and at all the important stations of the Great Eastern Railway at the same fares. Passengers also booked from *any* station on the G.E.R. to Rotterdam at the above fares, on giving 24 hrs. notice to the station-master. The boats on this route are new and well fitted up. Service three times weekly.

The *Gen. Steam Nav. Co.*'s steamboats also ply between London and Rotterdam two or three times weekly, in 20—22 hrs.; fares 20 or 15 *s.*

The *Batavier*, the property of the Netherlands Steamboat Co., plies once weekly (fares 25 or 15 *s.*), and the Fyenoord (15 *s.*) also once weekly between London and Rotterdam.

The vessels of these two companies run in connection with the Rhine-steamers of the Cologne and Düsseldorf, and the Netherlands companies respectively. Tickets at very moderate fares may be procured from London to any station on the Rhine as far as Mannheim.

Hull to Rotterdam four times weekly, in 28 hrs.; fares 20 or 10 *s.* — Steamboats also ply from Grimsby, Newcastle, Leith etc. to Rotterdam, but the accommodation they afford is not always of the most comfortable description.

Hotels. New Bath Hotel, on the Boompjes on the Maas, near the steamboat-piers, R. 1 fl. and upwards, L. 30 c., B. 60 c., D. 1½ fl., A. 40 c.; *Hôtel des Pays-Bas, in the Korte Hoogstraat, well fitted up, similar charges. — *Hôtel Lucas (R. and L. 1½ fl., D. incl. wine 2 fl.), and *Hôtel Oelschlaeger (R. and B. 1½ fl., A. 25 c.), both in the Hoogstraat. Hôtel Weimer and Hôtel Verhaaren, both on the Spanish Quay, unpretending.

Cafés etc. Zuid Hollandsch Koffijhuis, Korte Hoogstraat; Café Français, opp. the latter; Nederlands Wapen (also a restaurant), in the same street; Café de Hollande, near the railway. — Café Lutz, Zuidplaats, and Eisele, Hoogstraat, are restaurants where beer may be procured. — Café Frascati is a '*café chantant*' in the Torentstraat, adjacent to the Groote Kerk (Pl. 10); concerts and humorous entertainments every evening.

Shops. The best are in the Hoogstraat.

Bookseller. O. Petri, Oppert 6.

Cabs. For 1—4 pers. 60 c. per drive without luggage, per hour 1¼ fl. The station of the Dutch railway is 1¼ M. from the Boompjes; that of the Rhenish line, on the Maas, in the vicinity of the Boompjes. Omnibus to the hotels 25 c.

Steamboats several times daily to *Nymegen* (p. 300), in 8—10 hrs.,

Arnheim (p. 288) in 10, *Briel* in 2, *Dordrecht* (p. 304) in 1, *Gouda* (p. 285) in 2, *Hertogenbosch* in 8, *Middelburg* in 9, *Moerdijk* in $2^1/_2$ (pp. 135, 140); to *Antwerp* in 9–10 hrs. daily.

Screw Steamers to Delft and the Hague every hour.

Zoological Garden (Pl. 35), adjacent to the Dutch railway-station, at the Delft Gate. Animals fed in summer at 7 p. m., from Sept. 1st at 2. 30 p. m.

English Church Service performed by a resident chaplain. — *English Presbyterian Church* in the Haringvliet. — *Scotch Presbyterian Church* on the Schotsche Dijk.

Principal Attractions: Church of St. Lawrence (p. 222), Erasmus (p. 222), Boymans Museum (p. 223), walk along the Boompjes (p. 222).

Rotterdam, with 114,025 inhab. ($^1/_5$th Rom. Cath., 4000 Jews), the second commercial town in Holland, situated on the r. bank of the *Maas*, near its confluence with the *Rotte*, about 14 M. from the N. Sea, occupies a site in the form of a nearly equilateral triangle, the base of which is the Maas, and the vertex the Delft Gate. The city is intersected by numerous canals *(grachten* or *havens)*, such as the *Leuvehaven*, *Oude Haven*, *Nieuwe Haven*, *Scheepmakershaven*, *Wijnhaven*, *Blaak*, *Haringvliet* etc. The first three of these, however, are more strictly speaking arms, or bays of the Maas, connected by the numerous canals which intersect the town. The ordinary rise of the tide in the Maas is 6—8 ft. Communication between the different quarters of the town is maintained by means of drawbridges *(ophaalbrug)*.

A huge dyke or embankment, running through the centre of the town, protects the *Binnenstad*, the quarter situated behind it, from inundation during high tide. The *Hoogstraat*, or high street, $^1/_2$ M. in length, is situated on this embankment, whilst the *Buitenstad*, the most modern and attractive part of the town, lies in the space between the Hoogstraat and the Maas. Owing to changes in the course of the stream, and the deposit of alluvial soil, this new quarter of the town has gradually extended, and the handsome houses of the *Willemskade* were erected in 1850 on ground thus reclaimed from the river.

The numerous vessels lying in the canals and harbours, which are so deep as to accommodate those of heavy tonnage, and admit of their discharging their cargoes in the very heart of the city, always present a busy and picturesque scene. The names of many of the vessels (*Samarang*, *Sumatra*, *Borneo*, *Java* etc.) indicate that they are engaged in the Indian trade. The voyage from

Holland to the E. Indian colonies and back generally occupies about 9 months, and the most common cargoes consist of coffee, sugar, tobacco, rice and spices. A number of vessels are also moored opposite to the ***Boompjes**, whence upwards of 100 steamboats start for the neighbouring Dutch towns, the Rhine, England, France, Russia, and the Mediterranean. This handsome quay, which derives its appellation from the trees with which it is planted, extends for a distance of $1^1/_4$ M. along the bank of the Maas, and will not fail to strike the stranger as far more attractive and cheerful than similar localities in most other seaport-towns. Notwithstanding its considerable size and important traffic, Rotterdam is on the whole one of the cleanest, most smokeless and pleasing of all commercial towns. The average number of vessels which enter the port is 2500.

The great market-place, a considerable part of which is constructed on vaulting over a canal, is adorned with the insignificant statue in bronze of the illustrious **Erasmus of Rotterdam** (Pl. 4), who was born at Rotterdam, and died at Basle in 1536. The monument, which bears long Dutch and Latin inscriptions, was erected by the citizens of Rotterdam in 1622. The house in which he was born, in the Breede Kerkstraat, is adorned with a small statue, and bears the inscription: *"Haec est parva domus, magnus qua natus Erasmus"*.

The ***Church of St. Lawrence** (*Groote Kerk*, Pl. 10), recently restored, is a brick structure of 1472 in the later Gothic style. The interior is of fine proportions, but will not bear comparison with the magnificent Gothic edifices of Belgium and Germany. The chief objects of interest are the marble monuments of vice-admiral *Witte Cornelisszoon de Witt* (d. 1658), vice-admiral *Cortenaer* (d. 1665), contre-admiral *Van Brakel* (d. 1690) and other dutch naval heroes, bearing long Latin or old Dutch inscriptions. The armorial bearings in this, as in almost all the other churches in Holland, were destroyed by the French republicans. The brazen screen which separates the choir from the nave is finely executed. The large *Organ* is considered by some to rival the celebrated instrument at Haarlem. It possesses three key-boards, 72 stops and 4762 pipes, the largest of which is 32 ft. long, and 17 in. in diameter. The organist may be engaged to play for an hour, and to show the internal mechanism, for a fee of 10 fl.

The *Tower*, 288 ft. in height, consisting of three broad and tapering stories, has been built into the façade of the church. It was formerly surmounted by a wooden spire, removed in 1645, and replaced by a flat roof. Any degree of attractiveness it may once have possessed was totally destroyed by the construction in 1650 of a massive support, extending across the entire façade. The summit affords a characteristic view of Dutch scenery. Canals, country-houses, windmills, perfectly straight avenues, and perfectly flat green pastures and arable land are the principal features of the environs, and it sometimes appears doubtful whether land or water is the predominating element. The towers of Briel, Schiedam, Delft, the Hague, Leyden, Gouda and Dordrecht are all visible in clear weather. The tower is ascended by a convenient flight of 320 stone steps. The sacristan, who lives on the S. side of the church, receives a fee of 10 c. from each person for showing the church, and 60 c. from each visitor to the tower.

The **Zuiderkerk** (Pl. 18), with its lofty Gothic tower, situated between the Wijn Haven and Scheepmakers Haven, was erected in 1849.

The **Exchange** (Pl. 1), built of sandstone in 1722, contains a spacious court, flanked by colonnades, and covered with glass. The exterior is of very simple construction. Business-hour 1 o'clock. The upper rooms contain a good collection of physical instruments (the property of the *Bataafsch Genootschap*, or Batavian Society). The tower contains a set of chimes.

The following five buildings are the only others worthy of mention: the **Schieland Palace** (*Gemeenlandshuis van Schieland*, Pl. 5), in the Korte Hoogstraat, seat of the authorities who superintend the embankments (the *Hoogheemraadschaf van Schieland*); the new **Stadhuis** or town-hall (Pl. 27), with a Corinthian colonnade towards the Hoogstraat, and principal façade towards the Botersloot; the modern **Palace of Justice** (Pl. 22), formerly a public rifle-gallery; the **Hospital** or *Gasthuis* (Pl. 7) in the Koolsingel, worthy of a visit on account of the excellence of its organisation; the **Yacht Club** (Pl. 34).

The **Boymans Museum** (Pl. 5), a collection of about 450 pictures, most of them by Dutch masters, which became the property of the town in 1857, although inferior to the galleries of the Hague and Amsterdam, is well worthy of a visit. The building was burned down in 1864, but most of the pictures were saved, and the gallery has been re-erected.

Entrance Room, beginning on the r.: 147. *Nason*, Portrait of a man in rich costume; 230. *Simon de Vos*, Portrait; *175., *176. *Pynaker*, Two large landscapes; 231. *De Vos*, Portrait. I. Room, r. of the staircase: r. 133. *Molenaer*, Scene of merriment; under it, 28. *Breughel 'the Old'*, Dutch Village; 146. *Mytens*, Portrait of the Grand Pensionary Jac. Cats and his niece; 92. *G. Honthorst*, Soldier lighting his pipe; 27. *Breughel*, Dutch village; 245. *Willaerts*, Embouchure of the Maas at Briel, with vessels of war and numerous figures; by the door, *47. *Cuyp*, Head of an ox; 129. *Miereveld*, Prince Maurice of Nassau; 134. *Molenaer*, Three peasants at a fire; 255. View of Rotterdam in the 17th cent.; 78. *Hannemann*, Portrait of John de Witt; 93. *Honthorst*, Head of an old man. — II. Room: r. *53. *Dürer*, Portrait of Erasmus; 200. *Schoreel*, Portrait of a boy; 256. Erasmus in his study; *84. *Van der Helst*, Portrait of Daniel Bernard; 229. *C. de Vos*, Time crowning the husbandman with a rich harvest; higher up, 208. *Snyders*, Wild boar hunt; *269. *Salvator Rosa*, Monk praying; *270. *Salv. Rosa*, Woman defending herself against a Satyr; *128. *Miereveldt*, Portrait; 21. *Bol*, Lady with red dress; *183. *Rubens*, Portrait; 217. *Van de Velde*, Equestrian. — III. Room: r. *45. *Cuyp*, Dead game; 43., 44. *Cuyp*, Fruit; 41. *Cuyp*, Repast of shell-fish; above it, 37. *J. G. Cuyp*, Three children in rich costume of the 17th cent.; *42. *A. Cuyp*, Cock and hen; *251. *Wouverman*, Rider on a grey horse; 56. *Eeckhout*, Portrait of a child; 166. *Ostade*, Man reading; 82. *Van der Helst*, Gentleman and lady richly attired; 185. *Ruysdael*, Landscape; 186. *Ruysdael*, Fish-market at Amsterdam. — IV. Room (beyond the staircase): r. 11. *Berckheyden*, The old exchange at Amsterdam; 118., 119. *Maas*, Portraits of the ambassador Nieuwpoort and his wife; *88. *Hondekoeter*, Poultry; *Backhuysen*, Stormy sea; *89. *Hondekoeter*, Dead fowls; 167. *Ostade*, Village tavern; *250. *Wouverman*, Soldiers engaged in plundering; 83. *Van der Helst*, Clergyman; *206. *Steen*, St. Nicholas; *4. *Backhuysen*, Frigate in a storm; *207. *Steen*, Operation on a 'malade imaginaire'; 9. *Beerstraten*, Old town-hall of Amsterdam; *239. *Weenix*, Dead swan; 107. *Koning*, Old man weighing gold. — V. Room: r. 8. *Backhuysen*, Fruit and flowers; 18. *Bloemers*, Flowers; portrait of Hogendorp (see below). — VI. Room (chiefly modern masters): r. *6. *Backhuysen*, Dutch landscape; 64. *Eysden*, Portrait of the burgomaster Hoffmann; 204. *Spoel*, Reception of Prince William IV. on his arrival from England; 156. *Nuijen*, River view by sunset; 125. *Meijer*, Sea-piece; 191., 192. *Ary Scheffer*, Count of Würtemberg and his son after the Battle of Reutlingen; *98. *Kate*, Council of war in the 17th cent.; 13. *C. Koekkoek*, Forest scene; *Molijn*, The artist among gipsies; *105. *H. Koekkoek*, Sea piece, with threatening storm.

At the back of the Museum stands the statue of *Gysbert Karel van Hogendorp* (b. 1762, d. 1834), the 'promoter of free trade', and the 'founder of the laws affecting the tenure of land in the Netherlands', as the inscription records. The statue was executed by *Geefs*, the eminent Belgian sculptor.

To the W. of the Nieuwe Werk (pl. A, 6) is the *Park*, which affords a pleasant promenade, adorned with a **Statue* in white marble of *Tollens* (b. 1778, d. 1856), the most popular Dutch poet, designed by Strackée.

The **Botanical Garden** (Pl. 6), to the l. of the Delft Gate, contains some fine cacti, and rare exotics from the E. and W. Indies (fee 25—50 c.).

27. From Rotterdam to the Hague.

Railway (*'Hollandsche Yzeren Spoorweg'*) in $^3/_4$ hr.; fares 1 fl. 20, 1 fl., 60 c. — Passengers are particularly cautioned against leaning out at the windows, as the carriages pass very close to the railings of the numerous bridges.

Flat pastures, numerous windmills and straight canals, stagnant water covered with green weeds, and occasionally a few plantations and thriving farm-houses are the principal features of the country. On the l., immediately after the station is quitted, is *Delfshaven* on the Maas; on the r. the village of *Overschie*, the birthplace of the naval hero Piet Hein (d. 1629).

Schiedam *(Doelen)*, a town on the *Schie*, with 16,559 inhab., is celebrated for its 'Hollands' and 'Geneva' (so called from the *Jenever*, or juniper-berry with which it is flavoured, and not from the town of that name), of which there are no fewer than 221 distilleries. Upwards of 30,000 pigs are annually fattened on the refuse of the grain employed in the process.

Rising beyond Schiedam are seen the towers of **Vlaardingen**, the principal Dutch depôt of the 'great fishery', as the herring-fishery is called by the natives, in contradistinction to the whale-fishery. This small town possesses upwards of 70 fishing-smacks, some of them of considerable size. As much as 700 fl. is frequently paid for the first ton of herrings, but the price generally soon falls to 25 fl.

Delft *(Hôtel Casino)*, with 21,732 inhab. ($^1/_3$ Rom. Cath.), situated on the *Schie*, is connected by means of that river with Delfshaven, and thus with the sea. The town was totally destroyed by fire in 1536, with the exception of five houses, and in 1654 suffered serious damage in consequence of the blowing up of a powder-magazine. The pottery and porcelain of Delft were once celebrated throughout Holland, and the name is even familiar to English ears, but most of the manufactories have ceased to exist, and the town is now a dull place, destitute of all commercial importance. The venerable and dignified aspect of the place, however, presents a not unpleasing scene of repose to the traveller who has just quitted the busy streets of Rotterdam. The canal is generally clear, and undisturbed by traffic, and some of the streets are shaded with fine old lime-trees.

Delft has attained a melancholy celebrity in the annals of Holland as the scene of the assassination of William of Orange, the founder of Dutch liberty (b. in 1533 at Dillenburg in Germany, d. 1584). The **Prinsenhof**, or palace, where the murder was committed, situated in the street leading from the Rotterdam to the Hague Gate, nearly opposite to the old church, is now a barrack (fee to sergeant who shows the building 25—50 c.). The visitor is conducted across the court, and through a door on the r. to the spot where the tragedy was enacted. The marks left by the fatal bullet are still pointed out. Five weeks after this event the States-General assembled here, and appointed Prince Maurice, the son of their illustrious and ill-fated liberator, their stadtholder in the place of his father, although then in his 18th year only.

The **Nieuwe Kerk** in the great market-place, erected in 1381, contains a magnificent *Monument (executed in marble by *De Keyzer* and *Quellin* in 1621) to the memory of Prince William. His effigy in marble lies upon a sarcophagus beneath a canopy, also in marble, supported by 14 columns, and adorned with small obelisks. On one of the four columns, Liberty is represented with a sceptre and hat as her insignia; on a second, Justice with her scales, beside which William's favourite motto, '*Saevis tranquillus in undis*', is inscribed; on the third column Prudence, with a twig of thorn in her hand; on the fourth, Religion, with the Bible in one hand, and a miniature church in the other, whilst her foot rests on a corner-stone, which is emblematical of Christ. At the head of the statue is placed a second statue in bronze, representing the prince in full military accoutrement. At the feet of the recumbent figure is a dog, in remaininiscence of the prince's favourite dog which was the means of saving his life in 1572, when he was attacked in the night by two Spanish assassins in his camp at Malines. The goddess of Victory, with outspread wings, 6 ft. in height, a figure in bronze resting on the ground on the point of the left foot only, is usually regarded as the most remarkable part of the monument. The inscription records that the prince was murdered by an assassin hired by Philip II. of

Spain. Beneath the same stone his wife and his son Prince Maurice (b. 1567, d. 1625) are also interred. The church afterwards became the burial-place of all the princes of the House of Orange. King William I. (d. 1843), his queen (d. 1837), who was a sister of Fred. William III. of Prussia, and their son William II. (d. 1849) were the last members of the family interred in the vaults. — The church also contains a simple monument to *Hugo Grotius*, who was a native of Delft (d. at Rostock in 1645). — One of the pillars bears an inscription to the memory of two officers who fell at the siege of Antwerp in 1832.

The handsome **Town Hall** *(Stadhuis)*, on the W. side of the market-place, erected in 1618, contains a collection of pictures and historical curiosities.

The **Oude Kerk**, with a somewhat leaning tower, erected in the 11th. cent., contains the monument of admiral *Van Tromp* (d. 1653), the victor in 32 naval battles, the last of which, fought against the English, and the occasion of his death, is represented on the monument. After defeating the English fleet under Blake near the 'Dunes', he caused a broom to be hoisted to his masthead, to signify that he had swept the channel clear of his enemies. *Piet Hein*, the admiral of the Indian Company, who in 1628 captured the Spanish 'silver fleet', with its precious freight valued at 12 million florins, also has a monument in this church. — The naturalist *Leeuwenhoek* (d. 1723) is interred here, and a monument with medallion figure was erected to him by his daughter.

The *Polytechnic School* is attended by about 285 students. The once celebrated *Model Chamber* of the dockyard of Amsterdam, comprising models of ships, mills, machinery etc., has been transferred hither.

At the Rotterdam Gate, near the landing-place of the canal-boats from Rotterdam, rises a large and gloomy building, adorned with the arms of the old Dutch Republic. It was originally a warehouse of the E. India Company, but was subsequently converted into an **Arsenal**. The entire equipment of the artillery, with the exception of the guns cast at the Hague, is manufactured in this establishment, which is connected with an artillery-laboratory and a powder-magazine outside the town.

Delft is $4^1/_2$ M. distant from the Hague; by railway in $^1/_4$ hr. The traveller, however, who has sufficient leisure, should by all

15*

means avail himself, for this part of the journey at least, of the '*Trekschuit*', or canal-boat, a conveyance peculiar to Holland. The trip (1 hr.) will be found very agreeable in fine weather, and the scenery pleasing, although monotonous. Numerous country-residences, the communication between which is maintained by means of the canal, and a succession of attractive and well-kept gardens are passed, whilst the passenger-traffic itself affords an interesting and busy scene. On the l. appears the spire of *Rijswijk*, where the celebrated peace between England, France, Holland, Germany and Spain was concluded in 1697. The palace of the Prince of Orange, where the treaty was signed, no longer exists, but its site is indicated by an obelisk erected in 1792 by the stadtholder William V. The poet Tollens is interred in the churchyard of Rijswijk.

28. The Hague.

Dutch *'S. Gravenhage*, or *'S. Hage*, French *La Haye*.

Hotels. *Bellevue, in the Park, well fitted up, of the hi hest class, with corresponding charges; *Hôtel de l'Europe, Lange Houtstraat 64; *Hôtel de Turenne, Nieuwe Markt, R. and B. 1 fl. 70, L. 30, D. 2 fl., A. 25 c.; *Oude Doelen, Turnoiveld 240, near the theatre (*doel*, a common sign for inns in Holland, means 'target'; *doelen*, guilds of riflemen); Twee Steden, in the Buitenhof, well spoken of. — Of the 2nd class: Toelast, in the Groenmarkt, R. and B. 1 fl. 60 c.; Paulez, opposite to the theatre; *Hôtel Bassjou, in the Spui Straat, R. and B. 1 fl. 70, D. 2 fl., A. 50 c.; Pays-Bas, near the railway station; Bois-le-Duc, Spui 405; Heeren Logement, Voorhout, opp. the theatre; Lion d'Or, Hofstraat; Keizershof, Buitenhof.

Cafés. Zuid-Hollandsch, in the Groenmarkt, near the town-hall; Café Français, on the S. side of the Plein; Belvedere, in the Buitenhof; *Van der Pijl, Plaats 27, dinner at 1 fl. and upwards, Bavar. beer; *Müller, Wagenstraat, a good 'bierhuis'; *Erlangen, Wagenstraat 4, of which the spécialité is the beer from the German town of that name.

Confectioner: Mœnchen, Lange Houtstraat.

**De Boer's Grand Bazar Royal*, in the Zeestraat (prolongation of the Noord-Einde), to the l. on the way to Scheveningen, is a most attractive emporium of curiosities and fancy-articles of every description.

Theatre. Mond., Thursd. and Sat. French, Tuesd. and Frid. Dutch, the latter in winter only. *Stalles* of the parterre, reserved, 3 fl.; front seats in boxes 2½ fl.; pit 1 fl. 20 c. etc. Performances commence at 7 p. m.

Omnibus per drive 20 c. without luggage. To Scheveningen, see p. 238.

Carriages. *Vigilante*, or cab, from the station to the town 60 c.; to Scheveningen 1½ fl. for 1—4 pers., there and back 2 fl.; to the bath-house at Scheveningen 2, there and back $2^1/_2$ fl. — *Horse Railway* and *Canal Boat* to Scheveningen, see p. 238. — Carriages may be hired of Koens in the Groenmarkt, Starrenburg at the Scheveningen Gate etc. One-horse carr. to Scheveningen by the new road, and back by the old, including the drive to the Huis in 't Bosch' (p. 237), 3 fl., an excursion of 3—4 hrs. If the traveller, therefore, start at 6 a. m., he will have time to enjoy a bath at Scheveningen, visit the fish-auction (p. 240), inspect the Huis in 't Bosch on the way back, and reach the Museum at the Hague between 10 and 11 o'clock.

English Church, chaplain resident throughout the year.

Principal Attractions: Museum (p. 231), statues (p. 235), excursion to Scheveningen. The Museum is 1 M. distant from the railway-station. At the S.E. Gate, near the station, is the extensive *Iron foundry of Enthoven*, near which casts of the statues of Rembrandt (p. 268) and Coster (p. 249) are placed.

The **Hague** (85,689 inhab., $^1/_3$ Rom. Cath.) was originally a hunting-seat of the Counts of Holland, whence its name *'S Graven Hage* (i. e. 'the count's enclosure', from the same root as the Engl. 'hedge'). It has for many centuries been the favourite residence of the Dutch princes, but continued to be a mere market-borough until Louis Bonaparte, when king of Holland, accorded to it the privileges of a town. Its present aristocratic and prosperous appearance is due solely to the presence of the court and the numerous nobles and diplomatists who reside here, and not to the internal resources of the town itself.

No town in Holland possesses so many broad and handsome streets, lofty and substantial houses, and spacious and imposing squares as the Hague. The N.E. quarter of the town is the finest part, where on the *Vijverberg*, the *Kneuterdijk*, the *Voorhout* and the *Noordeinde* a series of magnificent palaces is situated. The *Prinsengracht*, on the S. side of the town, is also a handsome street which merits a visit.

The vicinity of the *Vijver* (i. e. fish-pond), a sheet of water nearly in the centre of the town, enlivened by an island and a number of swans, is the most fashionable locality, where several members of the royal family, the ambassadors, ministers, and other persons of high rank reside.

The *Buitenhof*, the large *Place* on the S. side of the Vijver, is adorned with a ***Statue of William II.** (d. 1849) (Pl. 23), in bronze; the four figures at the sides are emblematical of princely rank, history, prosperity and military glory. The names of the victorious battles at which the king was present are inscribed on the pedestal *(Bajados, Vittoria, Salamanca, Quatre-Bras, Waterloo, Hasselt, Leuwen).*

On the N. side of the Vijver is situated the **Binnenhof** (Pl. 21), an irregular pile of buildings, some of them of mediæval origin. surrounded with a moat and resembling a fortress. The square formed by these buildings is entered by means of drawbridges. Several of the municipal and ministerial offices are situated here. The most conspicuous building, opposite to the visitor approaching from the Buitenhof, contains a spacious hall (where the numbers of the lottery are now drawn), with a fine Gothic roof. The wings of the edifice contain the halls where the two Chambers of the States-General hold their sessions.

During the glorious period of the Republic, the Buitenhof and Binnenhof were witnesses of two dark tragedies which sully the pages of its history. The influence of *John van Oldenbarneveld*, the Grand Pensionary, or prime minister, of Holland, the chief founder of the Republic, and the highest official after the stadtholder, had become distasteful to Prince Maurice of Orange, who made the then prevailing theological controversies between the Arminians and Gomarists a pretext for ruining that noble-minded statesman. The stadtholder accordingly, during a meeting of the States-General, caused Oldenbarneveld to be arrested, together with his learned friends *Grotius* and *Hogerbeets*, the Pensionaries of Rotterdam and Leyden. The two latter were conducted to the castle of Loevenstein (p. 303), whilst the Grand Pensionary himself, who had declared himself in favour of the Arminian doctrines, was condemned to death, 'for having conspired to dismember the States of the Netherlands, and greatly troubled God's Church'. On May 24th, 1619, the unfortunate minister, then in his 72nd year, was executed on a scaffold erected in the Binnenhof, after having written a touching vindication of his innocence to his family, and solemnly declared on the scaffold that 'he had ever acted from sincerely pious and patriotic motives'.

The *Gevangepoort*, a tower with a gateway leading from the Buitenhof to the Plaats, is the locality where the second of these tragedies was enacted. In 1671 *Cornelius de Witt*, who was falsely accused of a conspiracy against the life of the stadtholder William III., was imprisoned here. His brother *John de Witt*, Grand Pensionary and president of the Republic, having received intelligence that his brother's safety was endangered, hastened to the tower to afford him protection. The enfuriated populace, who had been stirred up by the enemies of the two brothers, and induced to believe in their guilt, availed themselves of this opportunity, and, having forced their way into the prison, seized the persons of their ill-fated victims, whom they literally tore to pieces with savage cruelty. The modest dwelling of the Grand Pensionary de Witt is in the Kneuterdijk, opposite the Hoogenieuwstraat, within a few paces of the scene of this deed of violence. The house of Oldenbarneveld now forms part of the offices of the minister of finance.

The ***Museum** (Pl. 12), established in an isolated building erected by Prince Maurice of Nassau (d. 1663), contains a collection of curiosities on the lower, and a picture-gallery on the upper floor. The latter is open to the public daily from 9 to 3 o'clock, except on Saturdays, when (10—12 a. m.) visitors may apply to the concierge for tickets to admit them on Sunday. No fees. About two-thirds of the pictures (300 in all) belong to the Dutch school, which attained its highest consummation in the 17th cent. (catalogue 50 c.).

North.

Drawings in Chalk. | III. | Director's Room.
I. | Staircase. | IV.
II. | Vestibule. | V.

South.

Vestibule (beginning on the l.): 134. *Schalken*, Lady at her toilet, lighted by a wax-candle; 32. *Van Dyck*, The Huygens family; 61. *Hondekoeter*, Birds, among them a raven attacked by the others; *74. *Jordaens*, Gardener and girl, offering fruit. — r. 139. *Snyders*, Stag-hunt, landscape by *Rubens;* under it, 174. *Wouverman*, A camp; 180. *Wouverman*, Riders and carriage drawn by six grey horses; 25. *J. Breughel*, Paradise, figures by *Rubens;* 170. *Weenix*, Dead game; 138. *Schalken*, William III., Prince of Orange and King of England; 268. Prince

Maurice, 269. Prince William II., both by unknown masters; 15., 16. *F. Bol*, Admiral de Ruyter and his son. The other portraits of members of the House of Orange are destitute of artistic merit.

I. Saloon (beginning on the l.): 120. *Rembrandt*, Portrait of a young man; 104. *Netscher*, Small portrait; 163. *Van de Velde*, Beach at Scheveningen; 140. *Snyders*, Kitchen with vegetables and game, figure by *Rubens*; 31. *G. Dow*, Woman with a lamp; 142. *J. Steen*, The painter and his family; *41. *Everdingen*, Portraits of the family of the Grand Pensionary Steyn, in a picture where Diogenes is represented seeking for a man in the market-place at Haarlem; 106. *A. van Ostade*, Interior of a rustic tavern; 17. *Both*, Large Ital. landscape; 153. *Teniers*, Alchimist in his laboratory. — 266., 267. William I., Prince of Orange, before and after death, by unknown masters; *146. *J. Steen*, Poultry-yard; 86. *Metsu*, Lady writing, a man behind her, and a mandoline-player in the background; *181. *Wouverman*, Landscape, known as the 'hay-wagon'; *141. *P. Potter*, Landscape with cows; **116. *Rembrandt*, School of Anatomy, formerly in the Anatom. School at Amsterdam, purchased by King William I. for 32,000 fl. — The picture represents Professor Tulp, surrounded by his pupils, about to dissect a corpse, and is one of the great master's finest works, although the subject is unpleasing. 39. *A. Moro*, Man sitting at a table; 93. *W. Mieris*, Grocer's shop; 171. *Van der Werff*, Flight to Egypt; 145. *J. Steen*, Dentist.

II. Saloon: *30. *Dow*, Lady with a child in the cradle and attendant, a carefully executed picture; 144. *Steen*. Physician feeling a girl's pulse; 12. *Berchem*, Cavalry-fight in a defile; 35. *Van Dyck*, Portrait of the artist Quint Simons; 155. *Terburg*, Portrait of the artist in his costume as burgomaster; 52. *De Heem*, Flowers and fruit; 121. *Rembrandt*, Old man; 131. *Ruysdael*, Sea-shore; *119. *Rembrandt*, An officer; *154 *Terburg*, An officer holding a letter which appears to have been delivered to him by a trumpeter; 173. *Wouverman*, Battle; *123., *124. *Rubens*, Catharine Brant and Helena Fourment, the master's first and second wife, both admirably executed; 130. *Ruysdael*, Waterfall; 147. *Steen*, Physician at the bedside of a patient; *33., 34. *Van Dyck*, Portraits, known as those of the Duke and Duchess of Buckingham, but more probably those of members of a Dutch family, as the armorial bearings in the corner appear to indicate; 90. *F. Mieris*, Portrait of the painter and his wife; 118. *Rembrandt*, Susanna bathing; *92. *Mieris*, Boy blowing soap-bubbles; **117. *Rembrandt*, Presentation in the Temple, Simeon holds the Infant Jesus, whom the high priest blesses. This is perhaps the most perfect of the master's works; the effects of light and shade are admirable.

III. Saloon (beyond the staircase): 62. *Hondekoeter*, Menagerie of William III. at the palace of Loo (p. 307). — 169. *Weenix*, Swan, stag and dead game in a landscape; 125. *Rubens*, Portrait of his father-confessor; *143. *J. Steen*, Representation of human life (as this picture is termed in the catalogue). — 265. William I. of Orange, master unknown. — **112. *Paul Potter's* far-famed Bull, the gem of the whole collection, remarkable as one of the few animal-pieces which the master painted on so large a scale. The picture was carried off to Paris by the French, and was regarded as fourth in point of value among all the pictures in the Louvre. The three which ranked before it were Raphael's Transfiguration, Domenichino's Communion of St. Jerome, and Titian's Martyrdom of St. Peter. This celebrated picture was purchased in 1749 for 630 fl., but before it was restored by the French the Dutch government offered 50,000 fl. to Napoleon for its restoration. It is alleged that documents have been discovered, proving that the picture was painted by the master of Potter, and not by that artist himself. 6. *Backhuysen*, Sea-piece; 5. *Backhuysen*, Return of William III. of England at Maasluis (in 1691); above it, 13. *Bloemart*, Banquet of the gods; 152. *Teniers*, Kitchen. (The adjoining apartment contains a number of drawings in chalk of the 18th century.)

IV. Saloon: 209. *Murillo*, Spanish herdsman; 55. *Memling* (or *Rogier van der Weyden*), Descent from the Cross; above it, 229. *Guido Reni*, Death of Abel; 210. *Velasquez*, Charles Balthasar, son of Philip IV. of Spain; *208. *Murillo*, Virgin and Child.

V. Saloon: 195. *Holbein*, Portrait of Rob. Cheesemann, holding a falcon; 187. *Dürer*, Portrait; 194. *Holbein*, Portrait of Sir Thomas More(?); 196. *Holbein*, Portrait of Jane Seymour, Queen of Henry VIII.; 238., 239. *Salvator Rosa*, Prometheus chained to the rock, and Sysiphus rolling the stone. — 247. *Tintoretto*, Portrait of a magistrate; 220. *Cignani*, Adam and Eve. — *Dürer* (?), Elisabeth, daughter of Emp. Ferdinand I. Most of the other pictures are copies from celebrated Italian masters.

The ground-floor of the same building contains the ***Cabinet of Curiosities**, accessible to the public at the same time as the Picture Gallery (admission free). Those who desire to examine the collection very minutely should purchase a catalogue (50 c.); a few only of the 750 objects which the cabinet comprises can be here enumerated. Several rooms are devoted to curiosities from China and Japan, others to objects of interest from the Dutch colonies and other parts of the world. The collection of historical relics begins with the celebrated wooden goblet of the Gueux, or first revolutionary party in the Netherlands, and comprises the remnants of the gallant Van Speyk's gunboat (see p. 136). The visitor is recommended to visit the room to the l. first, and finish with the historical relics in the first room on the r. A minute inspection of the Chinese and Japanese curiosities will be found very fatiguing; the pictures and curiosities should therefore, if possible, be visited on different days.

I. Room (l.): Cabinet with Chinese costumes. In the corner: 41. Mandarin 'en petit costume'. 270. Stained glass, representing the rice and tea harvest, views of Canton, review of troops etc.; 156. Chinese court of judicature and execution of the sentence (in a glass-case); 8. Portrait of the emperor, with moveable head. In a glass-cabinet in the centre, 273. Chinese fruits in wax.

II. Room: Japanese objects. 413. Cabinet with Japanese tools, apparatus of a copper-mine; 414. Figures of soldiers; 415. Musical instruments and weapons; 416. Armour of a general; 421. Caricatures etc. from Japan; 423. Japanese costumes, masks. In the centre: 417. Saloon of the Daïri, the spiritual emperor of Japan, with different figures; 427. Japanese letters, printing ink, paper etc. in a glass-case.

III. Room: Japanese fancy articles, toys, porcelain, rich costumes, specimens of artistic workmanship etc. In a cabinet by the wall, 412. Model of a Japanese temple. In the centre, 455. Glass-case with a model of the island Desima, the Dutch factory, beautifully executed in all its details by Japanese artificers.

IV. Room: Costumes from the E. and W. Indies, and from

Zeeland; 427. Domestic arrangement of the natives of Surinam; 743. Idol from the island of Ceylon. On the wall of the chimney-piece Indian weapons; 488. Cap of the sultan of Java; 480. Relief panorama of Mont Blanc, the Valley of Chamouny and the Simplon.

V. Room: 721. Cabinet of tortoise-shell containing a large model-house, constructed by order of Peter the Great (p. 276), who purposed taking it to Russia, in order to present to the Empress a view of the interior of a house at Amsterdam. The work is said to have occupied 25 years, and to have cost 30,000 fl. — 722. Chair and goblet used by Gen. Chassé at the siege of Antwerp (p. 111); 647. Chair from the prison in which Oldenbarneveld was confined (p. 230); 660. A cannon, gilded and plated with silver, presented by the Handels-Maatschappy, or Trading Company, to Admiral de Ruyter. In the central glass-cabinet. 720. Reminiscences of Prince William of Orange (p. 226), articles of dress worn by him on the day of his assassination; 691. Armour of Admiral Ruyter, with the gold chain and medal presented to him by the States-General; 694. Baton of Admiral Hein (p. 227); 713., 714. Bowl and goblet of the Gueux (p. 72); 732. Reminiscences of Van Speyk (p. 136) etc.

The *Plein*, an extensive square on the E. side of the Museum, is adorned with the ***Statue of Prince William I.** (Pl. 24), in bronze, by *Royer*, erected in 1848. The statue is represented with one finger slightly raised, in allusion to his well-known taciturnity. His favourite motto, '*saevis tranquillus in undis*', and the dedication of the monument by '*the grateful people to the father of their fatherland*' are inscribed on the pedestal.

An ***Equestrian Statue** (Pl. 25) to the same prince was erected in 1845 by his descendant King William II., opposite to the palace of the present king in the Noord-Einde. The pedestal is adorned with the arms of the seven provinces. It now stands opposite the garden-gate of the palace of the late king, a handsome modern Gothic building, which once contained a celebrated picture-gallery, the chief ornament of Brussels previous to the Belgian revolution, and subsequently the greatest attraction of the Hague. This fine collection was sold by public auction in 1850.

The **Royal Palace** (Pl. 15), situated opposite to the latter, is handsomely fitted up, and contains several fine family-portraits. It was erected by the stadtholder William III.

Near these palaces, on the E. side of the Lange Voorhout, is situated the **Ministerie van Marine** (Pl. 21), or offices of the minister for naval affairs, where a collection of models of vessels and objects of nautical interest is preserved (fee 1 fl. for 1—2 pers., 2 fl. for a party). The models of Dutch men-of-war, Chinese and Indian ships, machinery, nautical instruments etc. are the principal objects of interest. The specimens of 'camels' are also worthy of notice. These were vessels filled with water, and attached to each side of ships of heavy tonnage when unable to pass over the shoals of the Zuiderzee; the water was then pumped out, and the ship thus raised 5—6 ft. higher out of the water. This apparatus has been disused since the construction of the Nord-Canal.

Farther distant, on the W. side of the Lange Voorhout, is a spacious edifice containing the royal **Library** (Pl. 1), open to the public daily except Sundays and holidays. The miniatures in the prayer-book of Philip le Bon of Burgundy, painted in grisaille, are of great artistic value; several of them, such as the Annunciation and Coronation of the Virgin, are probably by *Memling*. The prayer-books of Marie de Medicis, Catharine of Arragon etc. also merit inspection. A valuable addition to the library was made in 1850 by a bequest of the books and antiquities of Baron Tiellandt, which now form a separate department, and are deposited in a building in the Boschkant.

The collection of **Coins, Medals** and **Gems** contained in the same building is very valuable and extensive. The cameos, 300 in number, are principally of ancient origin; that representing the Apotheosis of the Emp. Claudius is one of the largest known. The following are among the finest: Head of Hercules; bust of Bacchus; Faun attempting to rob a Bacchante of her robe; reversed lyre with horns representing two dolphins, which crown the head of Cupid with roses, grouped artistically with the panther of Bacchus, holding the thyrsus in its front paw; mask with large beard and open mouth; Venus and Cupid; Cybele riding on the lion; giant dragging a griffin from a cavern; helmeted head in profile, with long beard; Homer as a statue; several portrait-heads; head of Medusa, in the most beautiful cornelian, a modern work. The catalogue of the director gives full particulars about every object in the collection.

Among the denizens of the **Fish-Market** (Pl. 40), at the back of the fish-halls, a number of storks may generally be seen walking about, apparently interested in the busy scene. The stork belongs to the armorial bearings of the Hague, and these birds are maintained by the town for the same reason as the bears by the Bernese, and the eagles by the citizens of Geneva.

The *Groote Kerk* (Pl. 9), or principal church, adjoining the fish-market, is a Gothic edifice of the beginning of the 14th cent. The interior contains nothing worthy of note. The other churches are also uninteresting.

The water in the canals, being entirely destitute of fall, would become impure and injurious to health unless artificially replenished. This is effected by means of a steam-engine on the Dunes, by which fresh water is pumped into the pond and the canals. An imperceptible current thus occasioned causes the water to flow towards Delft and Rotterdam, where it is finally pumped out into the Maas.

The *Cannon Foundry* (Pl. 8) and the *Esplanade* are near the N.E. gate of the town, whence the road to Leyden issues. Outside this gate extends the celebrated and beautiful ***Park** *(het Bosch)*, a plantation intersected by avenues in different directions. On Sundays from 2 to 4 o'clock, on Wednesdays from 6 to 8, and almost daily in summer, a band plays here and attracts numerous visitors. On the N. side the forest is converted into a deer-park; near the road there are regular avenues of stately old trees, whilst the more remote parts are in a more primitive and natural state.

In the Park, about $1^1/_2$ M. from the Hague, is situated the **Huis in 't Bosch**, i. e. the 'House in the Wood', a royal villa, erected by the widow of Prince Ferd. Henry of Orange in memory of her husband, the stadtholder of the Netherlands during the Thirty Years' War. (Visitors ring at the door in the r. wing; fee 1 fl. for 1—3 pers., 2 fl. for a larger party.) In the drawing-room are two mural paintings in grisaille, by de Witt (1749), representing Meleager and Atalante, Venus and Adonis. The Chinese and Japanese saloons contain sumptuous silk tapestry, with representations of the birds of these countries with their brilliant plumage, admirably executed. It is said to have been a gift from the emperor of Japan to the stadtholder William V. The *Orange Saloon*, an octagon painted by celebrated masters of the school of Rubens with scenes from the life of the prince, is considered the principal attraction of the villa. The best of these paintings is by *Jordaens*, and represents the young prince as triumphing over vice, sickness and other enemies of youth. The others present several bold and finely conceived groups, but exhibit numerous traces of the inaccurate drawing of Rubens' school, whilst the aggregate effect can hardly be called pleasing. The light falls from the lofty cupola above, and from the side. To a height of 40 ft. the walls are covered with canvas, above which the paintings are on wood.

The Queen's apartment adjoining the vestibule contains a fine picture by *Gallait*, *Philip le Bel on his death-bed, visited by his insane consort. Opposite to it, The last time of going to Church, by *E. de Block* (both were at the London Exhibition of 1862), and several other pictures.

29. Scheveningen.

There are three modes of communication between the Hague and Scheveningen: (1) Horse Railway every hour (in $^1/_2$ hr.) from the Kneuter Dijk to the Bath-house, fare 20 c. — (2) Omnibus every hour (in $^1/_2$ hr.), to the village 30, to the Bath-house 40 cents, starting from the Plaats at the Hague (W. side of the Vijver), and from the Bath-house at Scheveningen. There is unfortunately no direct omnibus communication between the railway-station at the Hague and Scheveningen. Cabs and other vehicles, see p. 228. — (3) Canal Boat on the new canal six times daily in 25 min., fare 15 c.; landing-place at the Hague at the Princess Gracht, near the Bosch.

Hôtels. *Bath House, the property of the city of the Hague, an extensive winged building on the Dunes, about $^3/_4$ M. from Scheveningen, containing upwards of 100 rooms at $1^1/_4$ fl. and upwards per day, B. 60 c., D. at 4. 30 o'clock $1^3/_4$ fl. (2 fl. for occasional visitors), A. 25 c.; board and lodging for a servant $1^1/_2$ fl. per day, each horse $1^1/_2$ fl. A band plays every evening on the terrace, from $6^1/_2$ to $8^1/_2$ o'clock, for which each inmate of the bath-house is charged $1^1/_2$ fl. weekly. Reading-room per day 15 c., week 60 c., fortnight 1 fl. During the height of the season rooms are seldom to be obtained at this establishment, unless previously ordered. Crowds of Dutch visitors from all parts of the country dine and spend the evening here on Sundays. — Hôtel Garni, adjacent to the Bath-house, the property of a company; R. 75 c. and upwards, most of the charges the same as at the Bath-house, excellent cuisine. — Hôtel Zeerust (small bath-house), also situated on the Dunes, at the end of the main road from Scheveningen; charges somewhat lower than the above, R., B., D. and S. about 4 fl. per day. — The traveller may prefer to take up his quarters at the Hague, and visit Scheveningen for the purpose of bathing only; but in order that this arrangement may be satisfactory he should have a carriage at his disposal. The full benefit of the sea-air can of course be enjoyed only by those who reside on the Dunes.

Lodgings may also be procured in the village (*Van der Gryp*, *Van der Duyn-Mooiman* etc.), and it is advisable in this case to procure a written contract; but the air is far less refreshing than that of the beach, and the stranger will hardly find really comfortable quarters elsewhere than in the two principal establishments mentioned above. The smaller bath-house is frequented principally by Dutch visitors of the middling classes.

Baths. Machine with awning 50, without awning 30 c.; small machine, which is conveyed to the water's edge only, 15 c.; fee 10 c. for each bath. Gentlemen bathe on the N., ladies on the S. side of the Bath-house.

Living at Scheveningen is about one-third more expensive that at Ostende or Blankenberge, the favourite Belgian watering places, but the attractions of the Hague and the beautiful woods in the neighbourhood render Scheveningen far preferable.

Warm Baths of salt-water, vapour-baths etc. at the Bath-house, well fitted up.

Physician of the Baths, Dr. *Mess;* usual fee 2 fl. for each consultation.

Carriages must be ordered at the Hague (p. 228), either by the visitor personally, or through the porter at the Bath house. — Chairs and tents may be hired by loungers on the beach. — Le 'Petit Courier' contains a list of visitors.

Boats. Scheveningen at present boasts of a single small yacht only, which may be hired at a somewhat exorbitant charge.

Donkeys. Per $^1/_2$ hr. 20 c., $^1/_2$ day 1 fl. 25 c.; with small carriage 50 c. per hour, 2 fl. for $^1/_2$ day; carriage and pair of donkeys 75 c. per hour, $2^1/_2$ fl. for $^1/_2$ day.

Scheveningen, or more correctly *Schevelingen*, a large fishing village with 7436 inhab., is connected with the Hague by a well-paved road, which is said to have been constructed by the Emp. Charles V. The distance from De Boers Bazaar (p. 228) at the Scheveningen Gate at the Hague to the new Rom. Cath. church at the entrance to the village of Scheveningen is $1^1/_2$ M., to the beach $2^1/_4$, to the Bath-house 3 M. The road is shaded by a beautiful avenue the whole way, and bordered with plantations of venerable oaks and other trees. On the l., about half-way, is the royal château of *Zorgvliet*, once the residence of the poet Cats.

At the extremity of the avenue stands the clean and prosperous village, with its well-built brick houses, protected from the sea by the Dunes. According to a probably unfounded tradition, the church with its pointed spire stood in the centre of the village about the middle of the 16th cent., but the sea having made extensive encroachments since that period, it now forms the W. extremity of Scheveningen. Behind the village the ground gradually rises, so that no view of the sea is obtained until the traveller stands on the summit of the Dunes or sand-hills.

On the way from the village to the Bath-house, the traveller passes the loftily situated *Restaurant*, and beyond it the *Pavilion of Prince Frederick* and the *Hôtel Garni*. In the vicinity of the *Bath House* a number of handsome villas have been erected by wealthy Dutchmen. A *Terrace* paved with brick, or 'klinkers', leads past the Bath-house and villas as far as the lighthouse, and the *Obelisk* erected to commemorate the return of King William I. after the French regime. The intervening space between these buildings and the village will probably be gradually filled up, and Scheveningen will then become a very important, as well as an attractive watering-place. The beach itself, although admirably adapted for bathing, is monotonous and unpicturesque, but the magnificent woods a short distance inland afford a great variety of walks, and contribute materially to the advantages of the place. Scheveningen possesses about 100 fishing-boats *(pinken)*, the cargoes of which are sold by auction on the beach immediately on their arrival, an event which is announced by a public crier. The scene on such an occasion is often remarkably picturesque and entertaining. The herring-fishery is also prosecuted with considerable success, many of the 'pinken' occasionally venturing as far as the N. part of the coast of Scotland.

In 1673 Admiral de Ruyter defeated the united fleets of France and England off the coast near Scheveningen.

30. Leyden.

Railway from the Hague to Leyden in 20—25 min.; fares 80, 60, 40 c. — Stations *Nieuw Oosteinde* and *Voorschoten*. Immediately before reaching Leyden, the train crosses the narrow arm of the Rhine which retains the name of the principal river, although less important than the arm which falls into the N. Sea below Rotterdam. *Fiacre* into the town 60 c.

Hotels. *Hôtel de Zon (Pl. 1), in the Noble Straat, opposite to the Raadhuis; *Lion d'Or (or *Hôtel Verhaaff*), in the Breede Straat, adjoining the Antiquarian Museum (Pl. 11); Heerenlogement den Burg (Pl. 2), see p. 241.

Café. *Zomerzorg, by the railway-station, with pleasant garden,

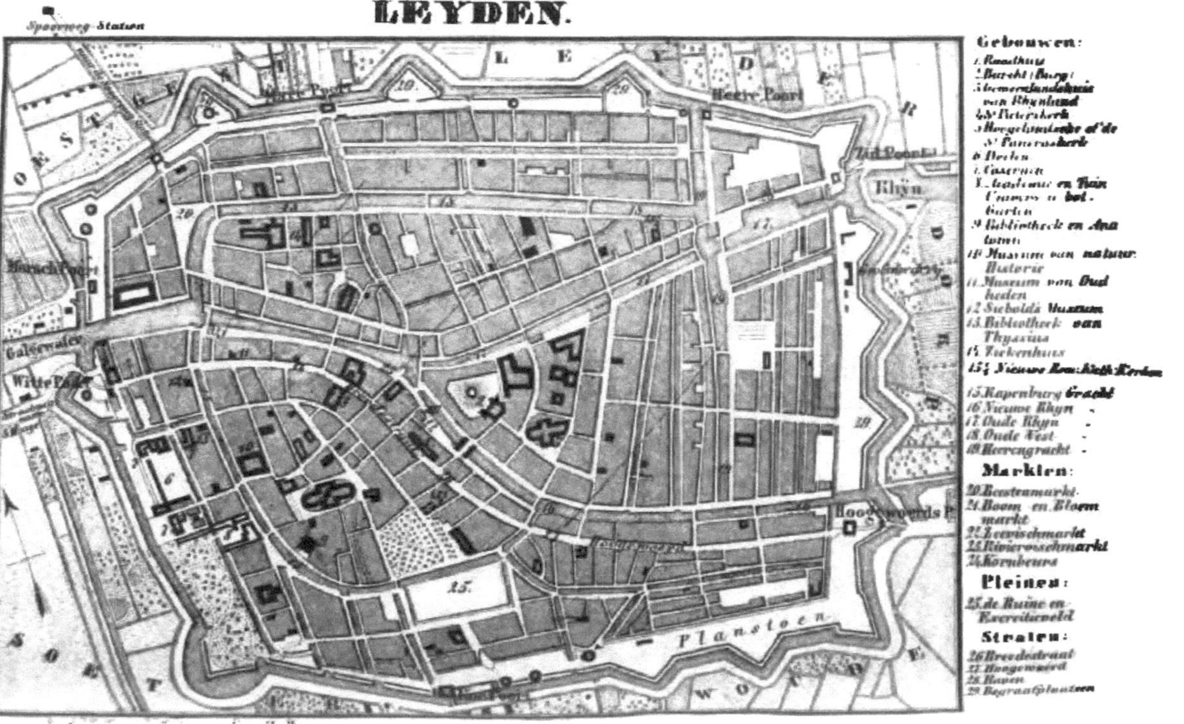
LEYDEN.
Spoorweg-Station
Heere Poort
Witte Poort
Rhyn
Hoogewoerds P.
Plantsoen
Gebouwen:
1. Raadhuis
2. Burcht (Burg)
3. Gemeenlandshuis van Rhynland
4. St. Pieterskerk
5. Hooglandsche of de St. Pancraskerk
6. Doelen
7. Casernen
8. Academie en Hortus botan.
9. Bibliotheek en Anatomie
10. Museum van natuur. Historie
11. Museum van Oudheden
12. Siebolds Museum
13. Bibliotheek van Thysius
14. Ziekenhuis
15. Rapenburg Gracht
16. Nieuwe Rhyn
17. Oude Rhyn
18. Oude Vest
19. Heerengracht
Markten:
20. Beestenmarkt
21. Boom en Bloem markt
22. Leewisch markt
23. Riviervischmarkt
24. Korenbeurs
Pleinen:
25. de Ruine en Exercitieveld
Straten:
26. Breedestraat
27. Hoogewoerd
28. Haven
29. Begraafplaatsen

containing a large pond with gold fish, which are protected by wires from the attacks of gulls. Beer at the restaurants of Müller, Breede Straat, and De Jong, Nieuwe Rijn.

Principal Attractions. Antiquities (p. 243), Siebold's (p. 244) and Natural History (p. 244) Museums.

Leyden, the most ancient town in Holland, the *Lugdunum Batavorum* of the Romans, has a popul. of 37,007, but is sufficiently extensive to accommodate 100,000 inhab., a number it boasted of during its most prosperous period. The *Rhine*, or rather the comparatively unimportant arm of that river which alone retains the name (p. 240), flows through the town, resembling a canal, and destitute of current except at low tide when the sluices at Katwijk are opened (p. 247).

Leyden still presents many picturesque mediæval features, and although most of the quaint old decorations are in the questionable taste of the 17th cent., they bear testimony to the former prosperity of the citizens, and their appreciation of artistic forms.

The most ancient structure in Leyden is the **Burcht**, or *Burg* (Pl. 2), situated on a mound of earth in the centre of the town, and commanding a survey of the town and the environs as far as the Dunes. It is of circular form, and was originally a castle of Drusus, although it is sometimes stated that the foundations were laid by the Anglo-Saxon Hengist. The building, which has been restored and adorned with pinnacles, now belongs to the Hôtel Burg.

Near the Burg is situated the **St. Pancras-Kerk**, or *Hooglandsche Kerk* (Pl. 5), erected in 1280, with singular-looking spires in front and at the back. The nave is in the round-arch, the transept, aisles and choir in the pointed style. The interior, which is spacious and handsome, but totally destitute of decoration, is supported by 38 massive buttresses. By one of these is the insignificant monument of the burgomaster Van der Werff (d. 1604), who in 1571 gallantly and successfully defended the town during a determined siege by the Spaniards of 5 months.

A few paces to the W. of the Burg, a bridge with covered halls, used as a *Corn Exchange*, leads to the *Breedestraat*, the principal street in Leyden. Here, on the r., rises the long **Stadhuis** (Pl. 1), a quaint, but picturesque structure in the style of the 16th. cent., with a lofty flight of steps, and somewhat clumsy ornamentation. Over the side-entrance on the N. is the following inscription: "*nae sWarte hVngernoot geLraCht had tot de doot bInaest zes dVIzent MensChen, aLs't God den Heer Verdroot gaf hI Vns Weder broot, zo VeeL WI CVnsten WensChen*" (i. e. literally: When the black famine had brought to the death nearly six thousand persons, then God the Lord repented of it, and gave us bread again as much as we could wish). This inscription, which refers to the siege of 1574, is a chronogram, the larger letters (among which W is reckoned as two V's) recording the date, and the 131 letters the number of days during which the siege lasted. The accuracy of this enigmatical record is undisputed, but the traveller will probably be somewhat puzzled, if he attempt to verify it for himself.

The Stadhuis contains two pictures of value in the history of art. The older of these, preserved in the hall of the tribunal is by *Cornelius Engelbrechtsen* (1468—1533), representing the Crucifixion, with numerous figures, and on the wings the Sacrifice of Abraham and the Miracle of the Brazen Serpent. The other picture, in the apartment of the burgomaster, is a Last Judgment by *Lucas of Leyden*, a pupil of Engelbrechtsen. A large modern picture in the council-chamber, painted in 1817 by *Van Bree*, who afterwards became the director of the Antwerp Academy, represents an incident from the siege of 1574: Van der Werff (p. 241), the intrepid burgomaster of Leyden, offers his own body to satisfy the hunger of the despairing citizens, but declares that he will not break the oath by which he had bound himself to defend the city to the uttermost. There are also several portraits of no great interest. The table on which the fanatical Baptist John of Leyden once worked as a tailor is shown as a curiosity.

St. Peter's (Pl. 4), erected in 1315, with double aisles, is the largest church at Leyden, and the last resting-place of many distinguished men. The monument of the celebrated physician *Boerhave* (d. 1738) bears the modest inscription: '*Salutifero Boerhavii genio sacrum*'. Other monuments bear the names of *Dodonæus*, *Spanheim*, *Meerman*, *Clusius*, *Scaliger* and other Dutch savants. The inscription on that of Prof. *Lusac* records that he perished in the explosion of 1807 (p. 245).

According to a popular tradition, Prince William of Orange, after the siege of 1574, offered to reward the citizens for their gallant conduct in the defence by exempting them from the payment of taxes for a certain number of years, or by the establishment of an university in their city. The latter alternative is said to have been preferred, and a *High School*, or **University**, was accordingly founded in 1575. Its fame soon extended to every part of Europe. Hugo Grotius and Cartesius (Descartes), the greatest scholars of their age, Salmasius, Scaliger, Boerhave, Wyttenbach and others resided and wrote their works here, and Arminius and Gomar, the founders of the theological sects named after them, were professors at the university. Lord Stair (d. 1695), the celebrated Scottish jurist, spent several years in exile at Leyden, whence he accompanied his friend and future sovereign William of Orange to Great Britain in 1688. Leyden still enjoys a high reputation as a seat of learning, especially as a school of medicine and natural science, owing to the very extensive and instructive collections which it possesses. Most of the professors (26, students 616) teach at their private residences (some of them still in Latin), a few only deliver lectures in the university-building itself (*Academie*, Pl. 8). The hall of the senatus is adorned with portraits of all the professors, from Scaliger down to those last deceased. Niebuhr in his Roman History expresses his opinion that no locality in Europe is so memorable in the history of science as this venerable hall.

The **Botanical Garden** (Pl. 8), open to the public daily till 1 o'clock, is arranged according to the systems of Linné and Jussieu, and kept in admirable order. The collection of exotics, especially from the E. Indies, is of great value. The hothouses contain examples of the cinnamon-tree, the quinine tree, the coffee plant, the cotton-tree, the mahogany-tree, the New Zealand flax-plant, the papyrus-tree, the bamboo, the sago-shrub, the camphor-tree, the 'flycatcher', the arrowroot-plant, the tamarind-shrub, palms etc. The trunk of a tree sawn through the middle, with an iron tool resembling a pitchfork imbedded in the heart, is also shown as a curiosity.

The ***Natural History Museum** (Pl. 10), open to the public daily, except Sundays, 12—3 o'clock, is established in a building on the farther side of the canal, and admirably arranged. It is one of the finest collections of the kind in Europe, comprising many valuable specimens of the products of the Dutch colonies in the E. and W. Indies, and other interesting curiosities. The

16*

cabinet of stuffed birds includes the collection of M. Temmink, one of the greatest European ornithologists. The cabinet of *Comparative Anatomy* is considered one of the most complete in the world.

***Siebold's Museum,** a collection of Japanese curiosities of great value, is now preserved in a house in the Nieuwe Hoogewoerd, the prolongation of the Breedestraat. It is accessible in summer daily, 9—7 o'clock, in winter till dusk (50 c. each person). Colonel v. Siebold (d. 1866), a native of Würzburg in Germany, was originally a physician, and resided in Japan from 1822 to 1830, where in his professional capacity he enjoyed rare opportunities of obtaining an insight into the habits of the interesting inhabitants of that island. After various adventures, not unattended with danger, he succeeded in bringing his collection to Europe, where it is probably the most extensive of the kind. It is now the property of the Dutch government, and comprises a domestic altar, the only one in Europe, figures of saints, images in bronze, surgical instruments, fans, parasols, magnets, toys, bons-bons, musical instruments, numerous objects in bamboo, anatomical figures, two suits of armour, flags, pictures, an idol, carefully wrought nets, numerous Japanese books, models of a country-house etc., beautifully embroidered articles of dress, ornaments, pipes, knives, scissors, amulets, paper, playing card's, articles manufactured of straw, travelling-boxes, brooms, silk, fancy-articles, model of a burial-ground, altar from Tibet, paintings in curiously carved gilt frames etc. The whole collection bears testimony to the great skill of Japanese workmanship, which in articles of the above description is hardly surpassed in any European nation. The custodian offers Japanese (?) articles for sale from a private collection of his own.

The ***Museum of Antiquities** (Pl. 11), in a building at the commencement of the Breedestraat, is open on Sundays 12—7, on Tuesd., Thursd. and Sat. 11—4 o'clock, but may be visited at other times on payment of a fee (50 c. for 1—2 pers.). It contains numerous and valuable relics and curiosities, most of which are Egyptian, some of them historical, and others illustrative of the manners and customs of that people in ancient times. The collection of sarcophagi, domestic utensils, reliefs, statues, mummies, papyrus scrolls, ornaments etc. is one of the richest in the world. The Punic relics are also extremely interesting, consisting of numerous sculptures and reliefs, most of them from Carthaginian tombs.

Ground Floor. Room I. (r.). Indian idols in stone, Brahma, the 'Creator', Wischnu with the trunk of an elephant, the 'Destroyer', resting on skulls, in numerous examples of various sizes (sun, water, fire or power, wisdom, justice, or the past, the present, the future, the Indian Trinity, often represented as a body with three heads); an idol in the form of a bull of lava; relics from Carthage; custodian of a temple, a quaint figure with a sword. — Rooms II. and III.: Greek and Roman antiquities, statues and inscriptions. — Room IV.: Egyptian antiquities, hieroglyphics, sarcophagi, statues, four statues from the entrance to the catacombs, votive tablets, Sphinx, captive Jews escorted by armed Egyptians, sun-dials. — First Floor, Room I.: Household gods of the Egyptians, papyrus scrolls, coffins, mummies, dogs, cats, fishes, crocodile, ibis, well-preserved heads of mummies, with teeth, earrings and hair. — Rooms II. and III.: Egyptian mummies, trinkets, scarabæi, necklaces, bracelets, rings, mirrors, etc.,all believed to be about 3000 years old. — Halfway up the next staircase is an extensive collection of Egyptian MSS. on papyrus. — Room IV.: Roman sarcophagi and inscriptions, numerous Greek sculptures. — Second and Third Floors: Temple of Minerva and several others, modelled in cork; casts of celebrated reliefs (Parthenon, Column of Trajan etc.; model of a 'giant's grave' in the County of Drenthe (p. 311), with Teutonic idols and relics from the tumulus itself; Roman weapons, Greek and Etruscan vases; clay-lamps from Africa, Greece and Italy; Greek seals, numerous Etruscan bronzes, Greek weapons, helmets etc.

The **Ruine** (Pl. 25) consists of two large open spaces (on one of which a laboratory has recently been erected), planted with trees, situated on the r. and l. of the Rapenburger Gracht, and partially used as an esplanade. It was formerly covered with houses, and derives its present appellation from an appalling calamity, which took place on Jan. 12th, 1807. In consequence of some act of negligence, a barge laden with 70 casks of gunpowder, lying in the neighbouring canal, took fire and exploded with fearful violence about half past 4 p. m. Numerous houses and streets were instantaneously converted into a heap of ruins, whilst human beings, horses, carts etc. were hurled into the air and dashed to atoms. Three schools with their pupils and teachers were entirely destroyed, and many hundreds of the other inhabitants also perished. In addition to this disaster a conflagration also broke out, and raged in this quarter of the town with the utmost fury, having unfortunately extended to several large magazines of train-oil. Upwards of 800 of the finest houses in Leyden were either totally destroyed, or taken down in consequence of the damage sustained.

In proportion to its population, Leyden occupies a higher rank than any other town in Holland in the history of art.

Rembrandt van Ryn, the son of a maltster or miller, was born near Leyden in 1606. His principal master was Van Swanenburg of Leyden, of whom nothing is known, except that he was considered a skilful painter by his contemporaries. Rembrandt's education as an artist appears to have been completed at a very early period, for he settled at Amsterdam in 1630, and painted some admirable works shortly afterwards. In 1634 he married Jaskia Uilenburg, the daughter of a citizen of good position, and lived happily with her till her death in 1642. This appears to have been the brightest period of the master's life, during which he enjoyed the society and patronage of many persons of rank, among them his well-known friend the Burgomaster Six. Notwithstanding the considerable sums he received for his paintings (first dated 1627) and his not less celebrated etchings (first dated 1628), and the then high annual premium of 100 florins paid to him by each of his pupils, his affairs gradually became involved after the death of his first wife, and at length in 1656 he was declared bankrupt. This catastrophe was mainly attributable to his mania for collecting curiosities and works of art, a taste which frequently led him into extravagant expenditure. All his highly prized treasures were publicly sold by the Court of Bankruptcy, and realised a miserably insignificant sum. Rembrandt, however, must have been endowed with no ordinary degree of fortitude, for after this disaster he continued to labour with the same indefatigable perseverance, and as brilliant success as before. He even contracted a second marriage shortly after his bankruptcy. After a successful, but chequered career, he died in Oct., 1669. It is now well ascertained that the stories told about Rembrandt's avarice and sordid disposition are totally unfounded. His principal faults appear to have been an insatiable love of collecting curiosities, and a too great partiality for the society of those beneath him in rank. His industry and perseverance were his chief merits. His misfortunes alone appear to have deprived him of the rank and popularity he enjoyed in early life. — Rembrandt has the great merit of having developed a hitherto unexplored field of art, which may be described as the concentration of light and shade and colour. The effects he represents are rare and beautiful, but perfectly natural. His style is one of striking contrasts. His chief excellence is his power of portraiture. His works are often grotesque in design, defective in drawing, and coarse in sentiment, but in his consummate mastery of 'chiaroscuro' he stands unrivalled.

Gerard Dow, or Dou, the son of a glazier, was born at Leyden in 1613, and became a pupil of Rembrandt in his 15th year. He resembled his great master in his appreciation of the charms of chiaroscuro, but widely differed from him in the minuteness and delicacy of his execution. Such was his reputation that Van Spiring of the Hague, one of his patrons, is said to have paid him 1000 florins annually for the mere right of having the first offer of his pictures. Notwithstanding the elaborateness of his style, he produced upwards of 200 highly finished works, many of them almost miniatures, and yet of a free and easy touch. Most of his subjects are derived from humble life, pervaded with a sentiment of placid kindliness, but rarely animated in action. He died at Leyden in 1675, and was interred in the church of St. Peter.

Gabriel Metsu (born at Leyden in 1615, died at Amsterdam about 1670) was a genre-painter of great merit. Most of his scenes are derived from humble life, and are generally remarkable for geniality of sentiment. In warmth of colouring, drawing, arrangement and keeping he is almost unrivalled.

Frans van Mieris, the Elder (born at Leyden in 1635, died in 1681), a pupil of Gerard Dow, was an admirable painter of conversation-pieces. His works, sometimes almost miniatures, are noted for the beauty of their execution. Unlike most of his compatriots, Mieris evinced a marked preference for refined subjects.

Katwijk *aan Zee (Hôtel des Bains)* lies at the embouchure of the Rhine, 8 M. to the N. W. of Leyden. A canal closed with huge gates here assists the sluggish river to empty itself into the sea. The mouth of the Rhine was completely obstructed by sand in consequence of a hurricane in the year 839, and from that period down to 1807 its waters formed a vast swamp, termed the Haarlemer Meer, which is now almost entirely drained. At length at the latter date the evil was remedied by the construction of a large canal with three locks, the first of which was furnished with two, the second with four, and that next to the sea with five pairs of gates. During high tide the gates are closed in order to exclude the water, which rises to the height of 12 ft. on the external side, whilst the level of the canal is far lower. At low tide the gates are opened during 5—6 hours in order to permit the accumulated waters of the Rhine to escape, and the masses of sand thrown up by the sea are thus again washed away. It is computed that 100,000 cubic ft. of water issue from the gates in a second. In stormy weather, when the wind blows towards the land, the tide does not fall sufficiently to admit of the gates being opened. The dykes constructed at the entrance to the canal and on the sea-shore are of most imposing dimensions. The foundation consist of piles driven into the loose sand, upon which a massive superstructure of masonry is placed. These magnificent works, undertaken during the reign of King Louis by the engineer M. *Conrad* (p. 249), are the finest of the kind in Europe, and have recently been strengthened in consequence of an outlet of the Haarlemer Meer having been conducted hither. — The neighbouring kilns convert the heaps of shells thrown up by the sea into lime, which is used in the construction of the dykes. — **Katwijk** is much frequented by the citizens of Leyden as a sea-bathing place in summer.

Endegeest, a country-residence with attractive grounds, halfway between Leyden and Katwijk, was for many years occupied by Descartes (Cartesius), who wrote his most important mathematical and philosophical works here.

31. Haarlem.

Railway from Leyden to Haarlem in 1 hr.; fares 1 fl. 50, 1 fl. 20, 76 c. — Stations: *Warmond* (on the l. rises the extensive seminary of that name for Rom. Cath. priests), *Piet-Gyzenbrug* (on the l. is the new church of *Noordwijkerhout*), *Veenenburg*, *Hillegommerbeek*, *Vogelenzang*, with a modern Gothic church. The railway here intersects a portion of the sterile sand-hills which form the E. slope of the Dunes of the N. Sea (p. 214). About $1^1/_2$ M. to the E. of stat. Vogelenzang, near the village of *Bennebroek*, is situated *Hartenkamp*, a country-residence, where Linné, the celebrated Swedish naturalist, resided in 1736—38 with his wealthy patron George Clifford who was English ambassador at that time. Linné wrote his 'Hortus Cliffordianus' and his 'Systema Naturae' here, and also devoted much of his time to horticulture. The beautiful gardens once attached to the house have long since disappeared.

Hotels. *Kroon, near the Groote Kerk (Pl. 6); *Funckert, the nearest to the station ($^1/_2$ M.); a few paces beyond it, Leeuwerik, a second-class inn, both in the Kruisstraat which leads from the station into the town. — On the r., at the egress from the station, are several cafés, where accommodation for the night may also be procured.

Fiacre from the station into the town 50 c., luggage extra; to the Pavilion (p. 250) 60 c., to Zandvoort (p. 279) 4 fl., Bloemendael 4 fl., Brederode 6 fl., Velsen 6 fl. (and fee of 50 c. to 1 fl. for each of the longer excursions). — *Diligence* to Zandvoort daily, fare 50 c.

Principal Attractions. Organ in the Groote Kerk, modern pictures at the Pavilion, Teyler's Museum.

Haarlem (with 29,268 inhab.), which during a long period was the residence of the Counts of Holland, is one of the cleanest and most attractive towns in Holland. Like Leyden, Haarlem sustained a most calamitous siege during the Spanish War. The besiegers were commanded by Frederick of Toledo, son of the Duke of Alva, who succeeded in capturing the town after a siege of seven months (in 1572—73). Upwards of 10,000 of the burghers perished on this occasion, and the commandant, the Protestant clergy and 2000 of the townspeople were executed by order of the victor. Four years later the Spaniards were again expelled.

The modern *Rom. Cath. Church* is near the railway-station.

The **Groote Kerk** *(St. Bavo)*, erected at the close of the 15th

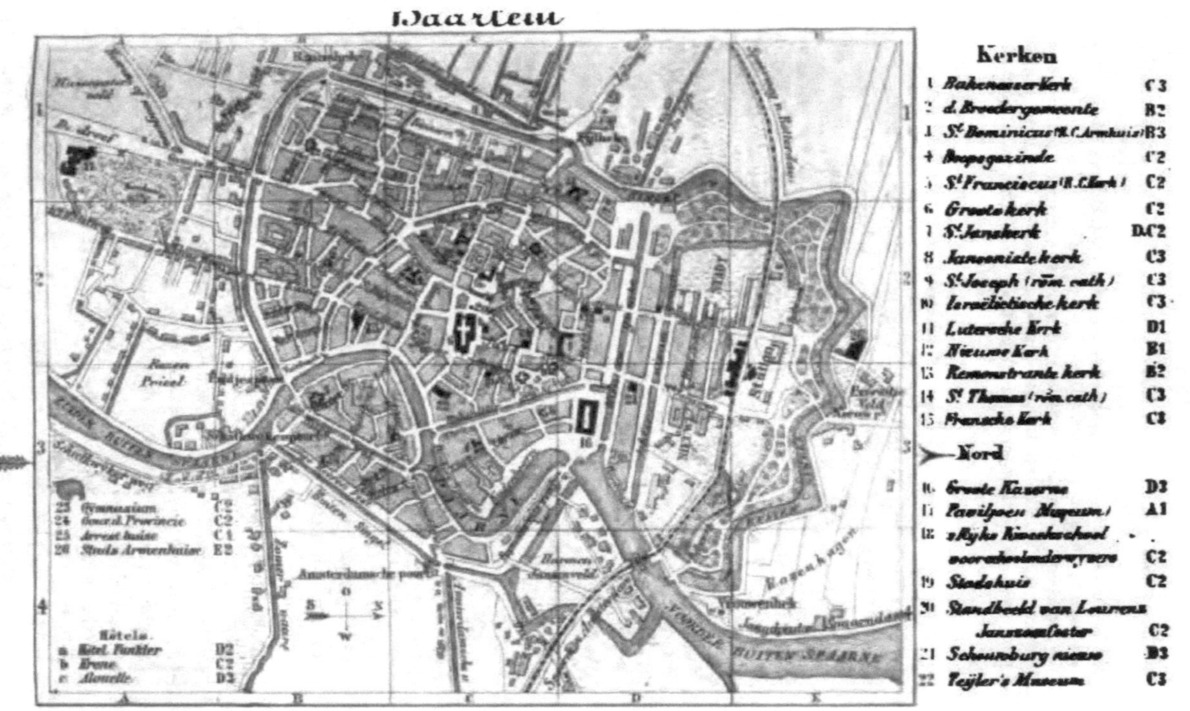
Haarlem
Kerken
6 Groote kerk C2
11 Lutersche Kerk D1
12 Nieuwe Kerk B1
14 St Thomas (röm. cath) C3
15 Fransche Kerk C3
Nord
16 Groote Kazerne D3
19 Stadshuis C2
20 Standbeeld van Lourens Janszoon Coster C2
22 Teyler's Museum C3
23 Gymnasium C2
25 Arrest huise C1
Hôtels
Amsterdamsche poort

cent., is a spacious and lofty edifice. The nave, resting on 28 columns, is separated from the choir by a brazen screen, adorned with figures and foliage. A cannon-ball in the wall is still pointed out as a reminiscence of the Spanish siege. The group in marble beneath the organ represents ecclesiastical poetry and music, expressing their gratitude to Haarlem for the erection of the organ. A monument in the centre of the church is sacred to the memory of *Conrad* (d. 1808), the engineer who constructed the locks of Katwijk (p. 247), and his coadjutor *Brunings* (d. 1805). By the choir is the tomb of *Bilderdijk* the poet (d. 1831). The small models of ships suspended beneath an arch between the nave and the S. aisle commemorate the 5th Crusade, under Count William I. of Holland. They date from 1668, the originals having fallen to decay.

The pulpit in carved wood, with handsome railings of brass, dates from 1435. A slab on a pillar near it marks the tomb of *Coster* (see below).

The *Organ, constructed in 1735—38 by Müller, was long considered the largest and most powerful in the world, but is now surpassed by several in England (Birmingham, York etc.). It was taken to pieces in 1868, and is now undergoing thorough repair, but will shortly be re-erected. It possesses 4 keyboards, 64 stops and 5000 pipes, the largest of which is 15 inches in diameter and 32 ft. long. Under the skilful hand of the organist the tone ranges from an exquisite 'piano' to the most overwhelming 'thunderstorm' with which the performance generally concludes. The hautbois, piano-forte, trumpet, whistle etc. are imitated with marvellous accuracy, and the audience are often tempted to doubt whether the mimic chimes are really produced by means of organ-pipes. Public performances on Tuesdays and Thursdays, 1—2 o'clock, on which occasions the true capabilities of the vast instrument are rarely brought into action. Private performances at any time on application to the organist, 12 fl. for a single visitor or a party. — The tower, 239 ft. in height, erected in 1516, commands an extensive view.

The large market-place in front of the church is adorned with a ***Statue of Coster**, in bronze, designed by *Royer*, erected in 1856. The inhabitants of Haarlem claim for their fellow-citizen *Lourens Janszoon*, surnamed *Coster* (i. e. sacristan, from the office be held in the Groote Kerk), the honour of having been the real inventor of printing. It is proved by old documents that Coster discovered the art of cutting letters on wooden tablets and taking impressions from them, as early as 1423. The *"Spiegel onser Behoudenis"*, preserved in the Stadhuis at Haarlem, was printed in this manner. Coster then proceeded to employ separate and moveable types made of wood, and subsequently of lead and zinc. Although there is little doubt, therefore, that he was the first inventor of printing, there is no foundation for the story that the secret was betrayed by an assistant of Coster to Gutenberg (1440) at Mayence; and it is probable that the latter arrived at the same results by his own independant efforts.

The **Stadhuis** contains a tolerable collection of old and modern pictures, most of them by natives of Haarlem (open daily 10—3, Sundays 12—3 o'clock, admission 25 c.; catalogue 25 c.). I. Room (Council Chamber): Portraits of Counts and Countesses of Holland. — II. Room: Portraits. — Corridor (beyond the staircase): *Heemskerk*, Adam and Eve; *Grebber*, Banquet of the Arquebusiers; *Veyts*, The Evangelists. — III. Room: (large saloon): Pictures by *Cornelissoon*, *Verspronk*, *Soutman*, *Hals*, *Holstein*, *Van Loo*, *Roosentael* etc., most of them representing meetings of the Arquebusiers and directors of charitable and other institutions. — IV. Room: Pictures by *Van der Ulft*, *Wyck*, *De Heem*, *Heemskerk*, *Schooreel*, *Adrian van Utrecht*, *Berckheyden*, *De Bray*, *Aertsen*, *Vroom* etc. — The saloon on the farther side of the great picture-saloon contains antiquities and various relics, among which is the flag used by the besieged town in 1573 (p. 248).

The *Hout* (i. e. *wood)* or ***Park of Haarlem**, on the S. side of the town, is a beautiful and extensive plantation of fine old beeches, intersected by walks, enlivened by tame deer, and provided with cafés and other places of holiday resort. A monument was erected here in 1823 on the spot where Coster first cut his wooden types.

In this wood, about $^1/_2$ M. from the *Houtpoort* (i. e. 'wood gate'), and $1^1/_4$ M. from the railway station, is situated the ***Pavilion** *(Paviljoen Welgelegen)*, erected by the wealthy banker Mr. Hope of Amsterdam in the Italian style. The château was afterwards purchased by Louis Napoleon, ex-king of Holland, and now belongs to the government. The entrance is on the S. side. The court is adorned with a copy of the well-known Laocoon group, in lead. The picture-gallery, containing 250 works of Dutch and Belgian artists, is open to the public on Fridays and Saturdays 9—4 (in winter 10—4) o'clock; access obtained on other days, except Sundays, at the same hours by payment of a fee (25—50 c.). The following pictures are among the most interesting (the enumeration begins on the l. by the entrance): 109. *Lebroussart*, Savoyard; 105. *Kruseman*, Elisha and the Shunamite woman; 257. *Weiss*, Fruit; 193. *Pieneman*, Portrait of his father, the painter of the Battle of Waterloo (see below); 228. *Schouman*, Naval battle near Palembang; 192. *Pieneman*, Battle of Waterloo at the moment when the Prince of Orange, afterwards King William II. (d. 1849), is wounded, Wellington and his staff in the centre, a very large picture, 30 ft. in length, 20 ft. in height. On each side of the latter, 173. *Payen*, Ten views of Java; 106. *Kruseman*, Girl reposing; 145. *Van Os*, Lion, life-size; 148. *Van Os*, Dutch National Guard on the lunette near Vaarden, Apr., 1814; 55. *Eekhout*, Savoyard with dog and ape; *246. *Versteegh*, Effects of light and shade; 234. *Van Stry*, Woman scouring a kettle; *3. *Assche*, Waterfall in the Ardennes; 38. *Cuijlenburg*, Admiral Zoutman; 208. *Riquier*, Rubens introducing the painter Brouwer to his wife; 99. *Kremer*, Vondel (see p. 268) at the castle of Muiden; 127. *Nicolié*, Interior of the church of St. Jacques at Antwerp; 250. *Verveet*, St. Peter's at Rome. — 2nd Room (r.): *104. *Kruseman*, Italian women and guitar-player; 28. *V. d. Burgh*, Interior of a cottage; 94. *Knoll*, Stable; 259. *Winter*, Sheep-fold; 21. *Bosboom*, Tomb of Engelbert II. of Nassau in the church at Breda (p. 141); *102. *Kruseman*, Parting of Philip II. from William of Orange in 1559 (see p. 139); 221. *Schotel*, Scene on the coast of Zeeland; 16. *Beduff*, Assembly of the States at Dordrecht in 1572, Philip de Marnix enumerates the services rendered to the country by William I.; *103. *Kruseman*, Persons praying to the Madonna; 95. *Kobell*, Herd of cattle; 129. *Noël*, Wester Kerk at Amsterdam, with figures of intoxicated men; 113. *Maas*, Good Samaritan; 225. *Springer*, Town-hall of Verre; 68. *Haanen*, Fruit; 126. *Navez*, Meeting of Isaac and Rebecca; 125. *Navez*, Elisha raising the son of the Shunamite woman from the dead; 112. *Lindhorst*, Fruit; 219. *Schotel*, Stormy sea; 213. *Raden Saleh* (a Javanese prince), Buffalo fighting with a lion; 217. *Schelfhout*, Winter scene; 50. *Schoenmaker*,

Irate schoolmaster. — 3rd Room (r.): 253. *Voogd*, Herd of buffaloes in a storm; *56. *Eckhout*, Nuptials of John IV., Duke of Brabant, with the beautiful Jacqueline, Countess of Holland (see p. 44); 207. *Regenmorter*, The painter Steen sending out his son to sell his pictures; *114. *Meyer*, Sinking of the steamboat 'Wilhelm I.' on the coral-reef of Lucipara in 1837, a very large picture; 249. *Verveer*, View of Noordwijk; 153. *Paelink*, Psyche; 225. *Waldorp*, Agitated sea; 25. *Bree*, The Prince of Orange in the Orphan Asylum of Amsterdam after the inundation of 1825; 214. *Saligo*, Portrait of himself; 54. *Eekhout*, Sick woman visited by a physician; 41. *Decoene*, Peasants returning home; 141. *Van Os*, Landscape with cattle; 191. *Pieneman*, Portrait of the actor Snoek; 190. *Pieneman*, Portrait of the actress Wattierziezenis; 286. *Leickert*, Winter scene; 239. *Trigt*, Catechising in Norway; 150. *Van Os*, Flowers and dead game; 27. *Brice*, Poultry-dealer and cook; 45. *Deventer*, View of Katwijk.

Teyler's Museum in the Damstraet, in the rear of the Groote Kerk, contains collections of chemical, optical, hydraulic and other instruments, the most powerful electric batteries in Europe, a laboratory, fossils, coins, books, a few modern pictures, valuable MSS., a cabinet of natural history etc. The Museum was founded in consequence of a bequest of *Peter Teyler van der Hulst*, a wealthy merchant of Haarlem, who, although not remarkable for his intellectual pursuits during his lifetime, left half of his property to be devoted to the promotion of science, and the other half to the poor. A certain sum is annually set apart for the purchase of prizes to be competed for by scientific essayists.

The **Seminary for Teachers** *(Kweekschool voor Schoolonderwijsers)* enjoys a high reputation.

The **Bleaching Grounds** of Haarlem were a source of great emolument to the inhabitants before the discovery of bleaching linen with chlorine, and derived their advantage from the peculiar properties of the water in the neighbourhood. The linen brought to them from different parts of the continent was afterwards exported as 'Dutch linen'.

Haarlem is celebrated for its **Horticulture**. The flower-beds of the numerous nursery-gardens display their gayest colours, and diffuse their most delicious perfumes about the end of April and the beginning of May. Whole fields of hyacinths, tulips, auriculas, carnations etc., grouped in every variety of colour, are seen on the S. and W. sides of the town. *Krelage's* gardens, situated in the Kleine-Houtweg, comprise a beautiful winter-garden, as well as a profusion of beds of geraniums, ranunculuses, anemones, camellias, cacti, auriculas, tulips etc. Many of the finest gardens in Europe are supplied with roots from Haarlem, and Holland justly claims the merit of having promoted horticulture to a far greater extent than any other country in the world. In the years 1636 and 1637 the flower-trade in Holland assumed the form of a mania, and tulips became as important an object of speculation as railway-shares and the public funds at the present day. Capitalists, merchants, and even private individuals entirely ignorant of floriculture, traded extensively in roots, and frequently amassed considerable fortunes. The rarer roots often realised enormous prices. It is recorded, for example, that a single 'Semper Augustus' was sold for 13,000 fl., an 'Admiral Enkhuizen' for 5000 fl., an 'Admiral Liefkenshoek' for 4000 fl. etc. A single Dutch town is said to have gained upwards of 10 million fl. by the sale of tulip-roots in one year, and a speculator at Amsterdam realised 68,000 fl. in four months in the same manner. At length, however, a corresponding reaction commenced, the mania speedily subsided, the prices fell so rapidly that many of the bolder speculators were totally ruined, and before long a root of the highly-prized 'Semper Augustus' might be purchased for 50 fl. At the present day a root of the rarest variety of tulip seldom costs above 10 fl.

Frans Hals (see p. 108), one of the greatest portrait-painters of the Netherlands, spent the greater part of his life at Haarlem, and the celebrated Wouvermans lived and died here.

Philip Wouvermans (b. 1620, d. 1668) was one of the most prolific and successful of Dutch painters. He excels in horses, and is especially prone to introduce a white horse into his works as the principal mass of light. His compositions exhibit great taste for the picturesque, his figures and animals are well drawn and life-like, and his touch is easy and spirited. No fewer than 800 pictures are attributed to him, but many of these were probably the work of his younger brother and skilful imitator Peter. Jan, another younger brother, generally painted views of canals, plains and water-scenes, enlivened by figures and animals. Winter-scenes, too, are said to have been one of Jan's favourite themes, and many of those attributed to Philip are probably by the younger brother, who was also an artist of considerable reputation.

Bloemendael, a beautiful village with numerous country-residences, and park-like environs, situated 3 M. to the N. W. of Haarlem (fiacre, see p. 248) in the rear of the Dunes, attracts numerous visitors. The sand-hills, which here form a chain nearly 3 M. in breadth, resemble a vast rabbit-warren, and the ancient inhabitants of the district were known as the 'rabbit-eaters'. The highest point of these hills is the *Brederode'sche Berg*, or *Blauwe Trop*, which rises immediately behind the lunatic asylum of *Meerenberg*, to the height of 250 ft. above the sea-level. The path to it ascends to the l., at the end of the wooden fence. The extensive view embraces the admirably cultivated and partially wooded plains of N. Holland, Haarlem, the Haarlemer and Wijker Meer, the Y, Amsterdam, the innumerable windmills of Zaandam, the undulating and sterile sandhills and the sea. At the base of these hills are situated the picturesque red brick ruins of the château of *Brederode*, once the seat of the powerful counts of that name, who acted so important a part in the history of Holland (p. 73). From the Dunes near the village of Overveen ($1^1/_2$ M. to the W. of Haarlem) a similar prospect may be enjoyed, but the interesting ruins of Brederode are not visible hence.

Railway to Zandvoort, Alkmaar and the Helder, see R. 35.

Railway to Amsterdam in $^1/_2$ hr.; fares 1 fl., 70 c., 45 c. — The railway, canal and high road run parallel to each other in a straight line the whole way. The new *Foort aan de Liede* is seen on the r., immediately after the train has quitted the station. On the r. extends a broad and well cultivated plain, studded with numerous cottages. So recently as 1840 this was the *Haarlemer Meer*, a lake 18 M. in length, 9 M. in breadth, and about 14 ft. in depth, formed in the 15th. cent. by the bursting of an embankment, and subsequently increasing so considerably in extent as to imperil the towns of Amsterdam, Haarlem, Leyden and Utrecht. The operations for draining the lake were commenced in 1840, and completed in 1853, at a cost of 8 million florins. The area of this new and vast 'polder' (see p. 213) is about 72 sq. M., and the land thus reclaimed realised an average price of 1434 fl. per acre. It is entirely encircled by canals, used for purposes of drainage and irrigation as already explained. The population of this district is now 7249. The engines with their lofty chimneys, which are employed in pumping up superfluous water from the 'Meer', are worthy of the notice of professional men.

At *Halfweg* (i. e. 'halfway'), the only station between Haarlem and Amsterdam, there are strong sluice-gates which separate the waters of the Y (pronounced I) from the Haarlemer Meer, and if opened would inundate the country for 30 M. round, and even lay the dykes themselves under water. The danger has been greatly diminished by the draining of the lake, but this is still regarded as a point which requires the constant attention of the water-engineers. The old château of *Zwanenburg* near the railway, dating from the 17th cent., is now the residence of the inspector of the canals. The four birds (*'armoiries parlantes'*) over the pillars of the gateway belong to the armorial bearings of the former proprietor. The Inn *ter Hart* is adjacent. About 250 years ago the château (now partly converted into a beetroot-sugar manufactory) lay 1/2 M. from the Haarlemer Meer, which before it was drained had advanced to the very walls of the building.

Amsterdam, with the conspicuous windmills erected on the old bastions of the fortifications, now becomes visible. Fiacres etc., see below.

32. Amsterdam.

Hotels. Near the station of the Rhenish Railway, *Amstel Hôtel, the property of a company, R. 1 1/2 fl. and upwards, B. 75, L. 50, A. 50 c., a tariff of charges in every room; *Pays-Bas, Doelenstraat 21, R. from 1 fl., D. 2 1/4 fl., A. 40 c.; *Oude Doelen (p. 228) and Rondeel, both in the Doelenstraat; *Keizerskroon, Kalverstraat; *Old Bible, Warmoesstraat; Oude Graaf, Kalverstraat; Hôtel Polonais, Kalverstraat; *Hôtel Haas, Papenbrugsteeg; Elberfeld, a commercial inn; Munt, in the Schapenplein; Oldewelt, on the Nieuwendijk, in the centre of the town; Nieuwe Stadsherberg (tolerably comfortable), close to the steamboat-quay.

Restaurants etc. These establishments are often crowded in the afternoon, and the traveller will probably prefer to dine at his hotel. Ebel, *Jonge, Graaf, Diligentia, Café Suisse, all in the Kalverstraat. *Hannier, in the Rokin, French cuisine, D. 1—1 1/2 fl.; *Van Laar, Kalverstraat, near the Dam, oysters 30 c. per doz. — *Beer:* Schwab, *Pollman, *Lourau, München, all in the Warmoesstraat; Roetemeier, in the Amstelstraat; Roscamm, in d'Water. — *Cafés:* Poolsche Koffyhuis, Café Suisse, Café Français, Nieuwe Koffyhuis, all in the Kalverstraat. Near the Tollhuis, on the tongue of land formed by the Noord-Kanal and the Y (or Ij), is situated a café to which the citizens flock on summer evenings; steamboat thither every half-hour.

Swimming Bath in the Y, near the W. Dock; others beyond the lock and by the Osterdok-dyk. Bath-establishment (also for ladies) in th Rokin.

Shops. The best are on the Nieuwendyk (pron. Neevendyke) and i the Kalverstraat.

Theatres (closed from the beginning of May to the end of August Stads Schouwburg (Pl. 60) in the Leyden'sche Plein; Grand Théâ tre des Variétés (Pl. 50) in the Amstelstraat. The former is devote almost exclusively to the Dutch drama; opera once weekly; ballet also Performances begin at 8 p. m. The charges for admission vary. — Salo des Variétés (Pl. 71), in the Amstelstraat, is a place of popular reso *Het Paleis voor Volksflyt (i. e. Palace of National Industry), ne the Utrecht Gate, and not far from the l. bank of the Amstel, is a spacio establishment where concerts (50 c.) etc. are frequently given. Frasca (Pl. 12), concerts and refreshments. Music in the park on Sundays from to 4 o'clock, and on summer-evenings by gas-light. Tivoli, an open-a theatre outside the Leyden Gate, where German plays are generally acted.

Steamboats daily to Alkmaar (p. 279) 7 times, to Enkhuizen (p. 28 twice, to the Helder (p. 282) 5 times, to Zaandam (p. 275) nearly eve hour; Purmerend (p. 284) 6 times. — To Harderwijk (p. 294) 3 tim weekly; to Leyden daily, except Sunday; to Rotterdam (p. 220) daily; t Hoorn (p. 284) daily, except Sunday; Harlingen (p. 312) twice daily; t Hamburg twice weekly, to London twice weekly; to Hull every five days.

Cabs to or from the station, for 1–4 pers. 1 fl. — Drive in the tow 75 c., for which however the vehicle must be ordered beforehand. — Om nibus from the station to all the hotels, 20 c., luggage 10–20 c.

Post Office (*Postkantoor*, Pl. 53), in the Vorburgwall, at the back of th Paleis.

Church Festival, or Kermis (p. 210), commences on the second Monda in September, and lasts a fortnight.

English Church (Pl. 19). — *Presbyterian Church* in the Begyn Straat.

Principal Attractions: *Museum in the Trippenhuis (p. 261), Museum van der Hoop (p. 264), Zeemans Kweekschool (p. 260), Entrepô (p. 260), Exchange (p. 267) at the business hours, Paleis (p. 266) and espe cially the view from the tower, *Zoological Garden (p. 261), *Walk on the Buitenkant (p. 259), the Ooster and Westerdok.

Amsterdam, the commercial capital of Holland, consisted about the end of the 12th cent. of a few fishermen's huts on the Zuiderzee, at the mouth of the Amstel. In 1290 it was presented by Count Florence V. to John van Persijn, one of his barons. The count was afterwards murdered by Gijsbrecht van Amstel and his fellow-conspirators, an event which forms the subject of a tragedy by the talented Dutch dramatist Vondel, and Amsterdam was burned down. In the 14th cent. the town began to assume greater importance, and was sought as an asylum by exiled merchants of Brabant. In 1421 one-third of the town was destroyed by a con-

by the com-
ecome a very
corded to the
the crest in
prosperity of
., when the
of the Inqui-
s and skilful
en the years
nt, and was
ce concluded
India Com-
direction, all
period to the
rnal circum-
e to occupy
reatened by
ly affect the
gh somewhat
s for several
the dissolu-
ne the resi-
ly the third

he Y (or Ij,
forms the
58 are Rom.
The city is
n. Amster-
synagogues,
nicircle, the
mference is
at or canal,
s within the
l the Singel.
nten (70 in
constructed
in length,
kably hand-

Swimmin
and by the
Rokin.
Shops.
the Kalverstr
Theatres
Stads Scho
tre des Va
almost exclus
Performances
des Variét
*Het Palei
the Utrecht G
establishment
(Pl. 12), con
to 4 o'clock,
theatre outsi
Steambo
twice, to th
hour; Purm
weekly; to I
Hoorn (p. 28
Hamburg twi
Cabs to
75 c., for wh
nibus from t
Post Offi
Paleis.
Church I
in September
English
Princi
Museum van
(p. 260), Exe
cially the vie
Buitenkant (
Amsterd
the end of
derzee, at
by Count I
The count
his fellow-c
gedy by the
burned dow
importance,
Brabant. I

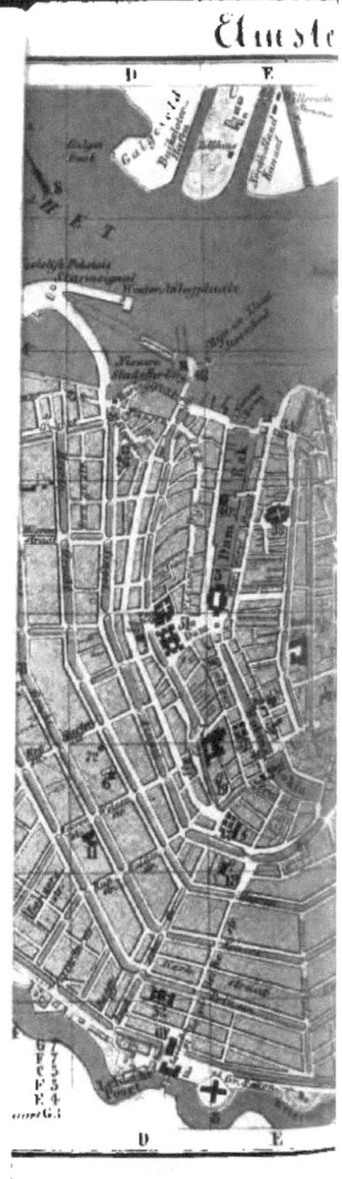

l by the com-
become a very
accorded to the
s the crest in
d prosperity of
nt., when the
of the Inqui-
nts and skilful
ween the years
tent, and was
eace concluded
E. India Com-
y direction, all
period to the
xternal circum-
nge to occupy
threatened by
usly affect the
ough somewhat
has for several
r the dissolu-
came the resi-
ntly the third

the Y (or Jj,
ich forms the
,158 are Rom.
. The city is
oen. Amster-
9 synagogues,
emicircle, the
cumference is
moat or canal,
nals within the
nd the Singel.
achten (70 in
, constructed
M. in length,
arkably hand-

Swimmin and by the Rokin.

Shops. the Kalverstr

Theatres Stads Scho tre des Va almost exclu Performances des Variét *Het Palei the Utrecht G establishment (Pl. 12), con to 4 o'clock, theatre outsi

Steambo twice, to th hour; Purm weekly; to I Hoorn (p. 28 Hamburg twi

Cabs to 75 c., for wh nibus from t

Post Off Paleis.

Church in September

English

Princi Museum van (p. 260), Exc cially the vie Buitenkant (

Amsterd the end of derzee, at by Count I The count his fellow-c gedy by the burned dow importance, Brabant. I

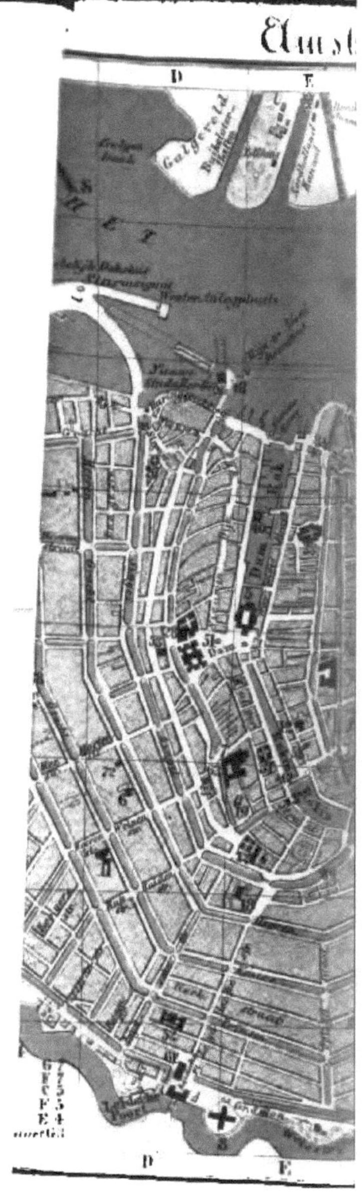

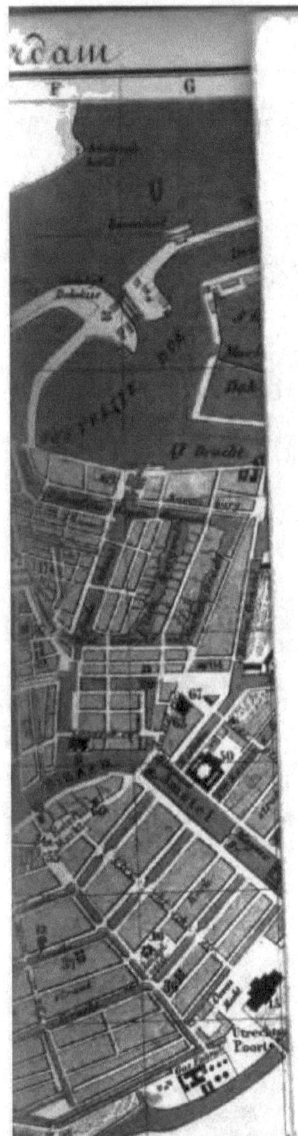

d by the com-
l become a very
accorded to the
as the crest in
d prosperity of
ent., when the
s of the Inqui-
nts and skilful
ween the years
tent, and was
peace concluded
E. India Com-
ry direction, all
t period to the
xternal circum-
ange to occupy
threatened by
ously affect the
ough somewhat
has for several
er the dissolu-
came the resi-
ently the third

the Y (or Ij,
ich forms the
7, 158 are Rom.
s. The city is
men. Amster-
9 synagogues,
emicircle, the
cumference is
moat or canal,
als within the
nd the Singel.
achten (70 in
s, constructed
M. in length,
arkably hand-

some and picturesque appearance, and will bear comparison with the finest streets in any other European city. Canals of various sizes intersect the city in every direction, and divide it into 90 islands, which are connected by means of 280 bridges. The cost of the works connected with the bridges, canals, dykes etc., is estimated at several thousand florins per day. The safety of the entire city depends on the security of these works, any defect in which would expose Amsterdam to the risk of being laid many feet under water.

The houses are all constructed on foundations of piles, a fact which gave rise to the jest of Erasmus of Rotterdam, that he knew a city whose inhabitants dwelt on the tops of trees like rooks. The upper stratum of the natural soil consists of nothing but mud and loose sand, upon which no permanent building can be erected unless a solid substructure be first formed by driving piles into the more solid sand beneath. The operations of the builder below the surface of the ground are frequently as costly as those above it. In the year 1822 the great corn magazine, originally built for the E. India Company, literally sank into the mud, the piles having been inadequate to support the weight of the 3500 tons of grain which were stored in the building at the time. About the middle of the last century the city was threatened with total ruin by the alarming ravages of wood-worms, by which many of the subterannean piles were completely honeycombed. Fortunately, however, the insect, which appears to have been brought by foreign vessels from a warmer climate, did not thrive long in its northern home, and gradually became nearly extinct. In 1858 it again made its appearance, but there is probably no ground for serious apprehensions. Naturalists who are desirous of seeing living examples of the worm should apply to the Counsellor Kater at Nieuwendam ($1^1/_2$ M. to the N. W. of Amsterdam).

The Amstel Canal is 9 ft. in depth, the others generally 3—4 ft. only, whilst the bottom generally consists of a thick layer of mud, which is stirred up by almost every barge that passes. Dredging machines are constantly engaged in removing the mud, which forms a valuable kind of manure. In order to prevent the entire stagnation and consequent unhealthiness of these vast volumes of water, a supply of pure water from the Y is constantly introduced into the canals by means of a shaft which passes beneath the Exchange (Beurs, Pl. 5).

The entire want of spring-water at Amsterdam is a serious disadvantage to so large a city. The houses are all provided with cisterns for rain-water, which is used by the citizens of all classes for culinary purposes. The water used for drinking is conducted to Amsterdam by means of pipes from a reservoir, 7 acres in area and 20 ft. deep, situated in the Dunes $4^1/_2$ M. above Haarlem, and $13^1/_2$ M. from Amsterdam. An additional supply is also conveyed to Amsterdam from the Vecht, a small river above Weesp, about 9 M. from the city, by means of *'leggers'*, or water-barges constructed for the purpose, out of which it is pumped and retailed to the consumers.

The ***Harbour**, or *'Buitenkant'* (i. e. 'outside'), from the Westerdok to the Sailors' Home, about $1^1/_2$ M., always presents a busy and entertaining scene. The massive piers which run nearly parallel to the city are important barriers against the encroachment of the tide, and form the two spacious **Docks**, the *Oosterdok* and *Westerdok*, where nearly 1000 vessels of considerable tonnage can be accommodated. The mouths of the canals and the Amstel are closed by massive flood-gates.

At the commencement of the Westerdok is the *Haringspakkerij*, where herrings were formerly packed for exportation under the supervision of a government official. A bridge crosses the harbour hence to the *Nieuwe Stads-Herberg* (p. 255), an inn opposite to the steamboat-quay. The view from the upper windows of this house is very extensive, embracing the Y and a considerable part of the Zuiderzee. The view from the *Nieuwe Brug*, a bridge across the mouth of the Damrak, one of the broadest canals, is also fine.

Farther to the E., at the extremity of the Geldersche Kade (i. e. Quay), rises the **Schreyershoekstoren** (literally "criers' corner tower", built about 1482), situated on the wharf whence vessels formerly sailed to all parts of the world, and deriving its name from the tears so frequently shed here by persons parting from their friends. A rude relief at the side is an allusion to the origin of the name. Farther to the E., on the Y-gracht, or Buitenkant, is situated De Ruyter's (p. 269) house (No. 80), on the gable of which is placed his portrait in relief.

At the extremity of the quay is situated the **Kweekschool*

17*

voor de Zeevaart (Pl. 41), or **Seamen's Institution,** where about 80 boys are educated for the merchant-service. Mathematics, navigation, astronomy, modern languages etc., as well as practical matters connected with the profession, are carefully taught. The establishment contains various models and apparatus, and a vessel of war anchored in the Oosterdok is also used for purposes of instruction. A kind of drill or review takes place several times a month, and visitors are admitted by previously applying at the institution. The interior of the building is fitted up in a nautical style. Each pupil has his hammock, and under it a chest which must contain the whole of his personal effects. One of the rooms contains models of vessels and busts of celebrated naval commanders of the 17th cent., with a few relics and curiosities. The Kweekschool is accessible daily, except Sat. and Sund.; fees are deposited in a box at the entrance.

Beyond the bridge rises the substantial **Zeemanshuis** (Pl. 44), or *Sailors' Home*, to which access is permitted daily. To the l., in the vicinity, is the extensive naval **Dock Yard,** occupying the entire island of Kattenburg, where everything that is necessary for the equipment of vessels of war is manufactured. Strangers are only admitted to the great magazines on showing their passports.

A short distance hence is the **Entrepôt** (*'s Entrepot Dok*, Pl. 10), or custom-house harbour and bonded warehouses. Visitors apply at the office at the entrance, where they are provided with a guide (50 c.). The canal is 22 ft. in depth, admitting vessels of large tonnage. The names of different countries and cities, such as America, Africa, Cuba, Archangel, St. Petersburg, Smyrna, Hamburg, London etc., are inscribed over the entrances to the magazines on the S. side, whilst those on the N. are destined exclusively for the reception of the products of Batavia. It will be more apparent to the traveller here than in any other place in Holland, that he is in the dominions of an industrious and wealthy sea-faring nation. Vast quantities of wine, corn, sugar, coffee, rice and indigo are stored in these warehouses, and the sales of coffee, indigo etc. which take place several times annually attract purchasers from every part of Europe. Here, too, may be seen a considerable number of barges from the Rhine, Moselle, Main and Neckar, by means of which upwards of 100,000 tons of goods are annually conveyed hence to different parts of Germany.

Adjoining the Entrepôt is the **Plantaadje** ('plantation'), a kind of suburb between the Entrepôt and the Muider Gracht, planted with trees, and divided by a canal into two squares. The *Park*, on the W. side, belongs to a private society; concerts frequently take place here on summer evenings at 8 o'clock (admission 1 fl.). Opposite to the principal entrance of the Park is the **Botanical Garden** (Pl. 13, admission 25 c.), remarkable for the numerous species of palms which it contains.

The ***Zoological Garden** (Pl. 47), popularly termed the '*Artis*' (being the property of the society '*Natura Artis Magistra*'), situated near the Botanical Garden, is one of the finest in Europe (admission 75 c.; open daily from 6 a. m. till 10 p. m.; it contains a good *café*, where a band plays on Wednesday evenings). With the aid of the annexed plan, the visitor may obtain a glimpse at all the principal objects of interest in about 2 hrs. The rarest animal here is the *Cryptobranchus Japonicus*, or great salamander (in the snake-house), of which even the Zoolog. Gardens of London do not possess an example. The *Museum*, a large building within the precincts of the garden, comprises a collection of stuffed animals and an *Ethnological Museum*, the former of which is entered from the garden, the latter from the street. Some of the Chinese, Japanese and Indian curiosities are worthy of inspection. The handsome structure opposite the Museum is an asylum for the aged poor.

The **Museum** (Pl. 45), established in the *Trippenhuis* (so called from its former proprietor, the burgomaster *Trip*), on the Kloveniersburgwall, is open to the public daily (Sat., Sund. and holidays excepted; admission on Sund., 12—3 o'clock 50 c.), 10—3 o'clock. The collection of pictures here is a national gallery in the true sense of the word, comprising many interesting and valuable works of the Old Dutch School. Excellent catalogue (1 fl. 25 c.), with numerous facsimiles of monograms. There is also a considerable collection of engravings (3700 impressions).

First Floor. I. Saloon (l. of the staircase): **121. *Barthol. van der Helst*, The Arquebusiers (or '*Schutters*') of Amsterdam celebrating the conclusion of the Peace of Münster, on June 18th, 1648, by a banquet. The picture, which is considered by some to be the finest in the collection, comprises 25 life-size figures, all portraits, sitting at a table, easy in attitude, and skilfully grouped (height 8, width 18½ ft.). On the opposite side: **286. *Rembrandt*, 'Nocturnal Patrol', probably a company of Archers, headed by their captain, and on their way to practise shooting at a target (12½ by 15 ft.). These two pictures occupy almost the entire N. and S. walls.

On the W. wall (to the visitor's l. on entering), lowest row: 118., 119. *Van der Helst*, Portraits; 435. *Rembrandt's School*, Portrait of P. van Uitenboogard, treasurer of the Province of Holland; 115. *Van der Helst*, Portrait of Admiral Cortenaer (p. 222). Above it, at the top: 13. *Barendsen*, Alva; 294. *Schalken*, William III. of England. Upper row: 150., 151. *Honthorst*, Prince Fred. Henry of Orange and his consort.

By the windows are several portraits of historical interest; among them, 401. Earl of Leicester, 402. Admiral Coligny, both by unknown masters.

Wall on the r. of the entrance: 203. *Mierevelt*, Phil. William Prince of Orange; 200. Prince William I. of Orange, 'the Taciturn': 95. *Aart de Gelder*, Peter the Great.

II. Saloon (r. of the staircase): *285. *Rembrandt*, Directors of the Guild of the Clothmakers engaged in deliberation; l. of the latter, higher up, 34. *F. Bol*, Portrait of the sculptor A. Quellyn. Below the latter, on the r. and l., 123., 124. *Van der Helst* and *Backhuysen*, Portraits of Admiral Aart van Nes and his wife. Above: 300. *Van Schuppen*, Prince Eugene of Savoy; 225., 226. *Mytens*, Portraits of Admiral van Tromp and his wife. Wall on the l.: *165. *Karel du Jardin*, Five directors of the spinning-factory sitting and standing at a table, life-size. On the r. and l. of the latter: 116., 117. *Van der Helst*, Portraits of Bicker, burgomaster of Amsterdam, and his corpulent son. By the window: 138. *Holbein*, Erasmus of Rotterdam; 139. *Holbein*, Robert Sidney; 185. *Lucas van Leyden*, Philip of Burgundy, Count of Holland.

Upper Floor. L. of the staircase, I. Room: *366. *Weenix*, Dead game, poultry and fruit, with an ape and a dog. — 23. *Berchem*, The three flocks; *279. *Ruysdael*, Great waterfall; 312. *J. Steen*, Quack; 209. *F. v. Mieris*, Lady writing; 68. *G. Dow*, Girl looking out of a window, with a lamp in her hand; 208. *F. v. Mieris*, Lute-player; 20. *Berchem*, Italian landscape; 251. *Potter*, Straw-cutter. On the opposite side: 163. *K. du Jardin*, Portrait of himself; 313. *Jan Steen*, Lady feeding a parrot; 386.

Wouverman, The shying grey horse; 199. *Metsu*, Old toper; 363. *A. de Vos*, Merry fiddler; 143. *Hondekoeter*, Peacock and hen; 223. *Murillo*, Annunciation; 82. *Van Dyck*, Children of Charles I. of England; 144. *Hondekoeter*, Ducks; *147. *Hondekoeter*, Pelican, ducks and peacock (known as '*la plume flottante*'). — II. Room: l. *142., 143. *Hondekoeter*, Poultry and Game; 81. *Van Dyck*, Portrait of Van der Borcht, burgomaster of Antwerp; 347., 348. *Van de Velde*, Naval battles (between the Dutch Admiral Ruyter and the Engl. Adm. Monk, 1666); 198. *Metsu*, Repast; *160. *Huysum*, Flowers; 379. *Wouverman*, Riding-school; 237. *Ostade*, Peasants smoking and drinking; *311. *J. Steen*, Baker's shop; **70. *G. Dow*, Evening school, effects of light and shade, under glass (purchased in 1808 for 17,500 fl.); *367., 368. *Weenix*, Game; *25. *Berchem*, Italian landscape; *71. *G. Dow* and *N. Berchem*, Lady and gentleman with a dog in a landscape; *315. *Steen*, Eve of St. Nicholas. — III. Room: 110. *Hals*, Portrait of himself and his wife; ***G. Flink*, Civic Guard ('*Schutter*') of Amsterdam after the conclusion of the Peace of Westphalia ($17^1/_2$ by 9 ft.), some of the portraits the same as in Van der Helst's large picture; *122. *Van der Helst*, Directors of the Guild of Goldsmiths (or of Arquebusiers?) examining a gold goblet and chain (formerly in the '*doelen*', or House of the Archers).

On the r. of the staircase at the entrance: 84. Dying Saviour, after *Van Dyck*. 1st Room (beginning on the l.): 296. *Massys*, Madonna and Child; 171. *Jordaens*, Landscape and satyr; 254. *A. v. d. Venne* and *J. Breughel*, A curious representation of different religious sects, with numerous figures, '*evangelici piscatores*', according to the inscription; 276. *Rubens*, Old man in fetters receiving sustenance from the breast of his daughter; opposite to it, *253. *Potter*, Boar-hunt; l. of the latter, 299. *Schooreel*, Daughter of Zion; 1. *Allori*, Judith with the head of Holophernes. — 2nd Room: 120. *Van der Helst*, Mary Henrietta Stuart, widow of Prince William II. of Orange. On the opposite side: 33. *Van Dyck*, Magdalene; l. of it, 62. *Cuyp*, Cock fighting with a turkey cock; 88. *Flink*, Isaac blessing Jacob; 5. *Backhuysen*, The Grand Pensionary J. de Witt (p. 230) embarking in order to issue commands to the Dutch fleet; 305. *Snyders*, Deer, wild boar and vegetables; 310. *J. Steen*, Merry peasants embarking in a boat; 57. *De Crayer*, Adoration of the Shepherds. — 3rd Room:

323. *Terburg*, Conclusion of the Peace of Westphalia in the townhall at Münster, the heads being portraits; 356. *Pourbus*, Elisabeth of England; *349. *Van de Velde*, View of Amsterdam from the Y, a large sea-piece (6 by $10^1/_2$ ft.); *109. *Huysum*, Fruit; 321. *Teniers*, Temptation of St. Antony; 254. *Potter*, Orpheus as a harp-player in top-boots; 35. *Bol*, Admiral de Ruyter; *298. *Schalken*, Boys eating, old man looking on; 314. *Jan Steen*, Rustic wedding; 297. *Schalken*, Young smoker; 318. *Teniers*, Guard-room; *210. *W. v. Mieris*, Poultry-dealer; *172. *Kalf*, Handsome dishes full of oranges and lemons; 141. *Hondekoeter*, Plants, birds and butterflies; 58. *De Crayer*, Descent from the Cross. — 4th Room: 230. *Neefs*, Interior of a church; 278. *Ruysdael*, Landscape and cattle (a duplicate in the Dresden Gallery); *255. *Potter*, Landscape with cattle and sheep; 384. *Wouverman*, Plundering; 304. *Snyders*, Game and fruit; *211. *F. v. Mieris*, Praying hermit; 33. *Bol*, Portrait of himself; 374. *Van der Werff*, Two girls decking a statue of Cupid with flowers; 373. *Van der Werff*, Girl drawing a statue of Venus; 229. *Neefs*, Interior of the cathedral at Antwerp; 195. *Maas*, Girl looking out at a window.

The ***Museum van der Hoop**, a bequest by a banker of that name (in 1854), consisting of 198 pictures, some of which are modern, is established in the Academy of Art (the former *Oudemannenhuis*, to the S. of the Trippenhuis, on the opposite side of the canal), and is accessible daily from 10 to 3 or 4 o'clock (Sund. after 12 o'clock only, admission 10 c., on Mond. 25 c., at other times 50 c.). I. Saloon: 77. *Minjon*, Still life; 100. *Rachel Ruisch*, Flowers. — *164. *Jac. Schoemaker Doijer*, The women of Haarlem, led by Kenau Hasselaer, defend the walls of their city against the Spaniards (p. 243); 179. *Leys*, Lady in a satin dress, and man reading; 194. *Wouterus Verschuur*, Trotting match (p. 280) on the Zaan; 183. *S. Opzoomer*, Valdez and Magdalena Moens at the siege of Leyden (p. 243); *196. *Versteeg*, A woman, effects of light and shade; 27. *Cuyp*, Black horse and accessories; 18. *Bloemart*, Egg-dealer; 157. *Span. School*, Knight and squire; 99. *Ruysdael*, Mill and woodcutter. — 190. *Schotel*, The Willems-Lock on the Y (p. 277); 117. *Teniers*, Dice-players; 177. *Kruseman*, Poets of the Netherlands, in the centre Joost van den Vondel, on the l. Cats. Over the door: 186. *Portman*,

The Crown Prince Alexander (now Emp.) of Russia visiting the cottage of Peter the Great at Zaandam (p. 276). — II. Saloon: 143., 144. *Van der Werff*, Hercules and Bacchus; 60. *Huysum*, Flowers; *94. *Rubens*, Marie de Medicis, Queen of Henry IV. of France; 136. *Weenix*, Poultry. — 115. *Teniers*, Village feast; *125. *A. van Utrecht*, Still life; *106. *J. Steen*, Musicians ('*soo de ouden songen, piepen de jongen*', i. e. 'when the old quarrel, the young squeak'); *97. *Ruysdael*, Landscape with windmill. — 108. *J. Steen*, Drunken men; *20. *Both*, Rocky landscape with waterfall; 105. *J. Steen*, Sick girl and physician; 3. *Backer*, Chief members of a Guild sitting at a table; 54. *Hoogstraten*, Sick woman and physician; 57. *Huysum*, Flowers. — 33. *K. Du Jardin*, Gentleman with dog and hare; 144. *Wouverman*, Landscape; 107. *J. Steen*, Feast of the Epiphany; *58. *Ruysdael*, Northern landscape; 31. *G. Dow*, Hermit; 90. *Potter*, Horse-piece. — *30. *G. Dow*, Woman with a bobbin in her hand; *95. *Rembrandt*, Jewish bride; 68. *Metsu*, Room with a lady in red velvet and a gentleman returning from the chasse; 66. *Maas*, Old woman spinning; *93. *Rubens*, Portrait of his wife Helen Fourment; *96. *Ruysdael*, Landscape with waterfall; *35. *Van Dyck*, Portrait of J. B. Franck; 46. *Hobbema*, Mill.

The **Fodor Museum**, on the Keizersgracht, was bequeathed to the city by a wealthy merchant of that name in 1860. It consists of a valuable collection of paintings by ancient and modern masters, preserved in a building erected with the funds left by the donor for the purpose (open daily, except Tuesdays, 10—4 o'clock, admission 50 c.; Sundays 11—4, 25 c.). Entrance-room, r. 156. *Lindlar*, Lake of Lucerne. 2nd (long) room: l. 80. *Ary Scheffer*, Exiled Greeks; 160. *Wieschebrink*, Grandmother's interruption; 103. *Springer*, Market at Haarlem; *27. *Gallait*, Gipsy-woman resting; *38. *De Keyser*, Francis I. and Benvenuto Cellini; 52. *Koekkoek*, Sea-piece; *81. *Ary Scheffer*, Christus Consolator, a large picture; 131. *Decamps*, Flock of sheep in a storm; 78. *Pieneman*, Portrait of William III., the present king of Holland; 26. *Dijckmans*, Old woman; *129. *Decamps*, Turkish School; *Bosboom*, Administration of the sacrament in the Groote Kerk at Utrecht; *124. *Rosa Bonheur*, Horses; 59. *Madou*, Poacher detected. — 3rd Room: water-colours. 4th (passage) Room: Father and mother of the founder, opposite them the founder himself. 5th Room:

Handsome clock with a small statue of Rembrandt; opposite to it a bust of Vondel.

Private Collections. That of the family of Six van Hilligom, consisting of very valuable old Dutch pictures, has been celebrated for upwards of a century, but is now divided between M. van Six and M. van Loon, by whom amateurs are kindly admitted. *M. de Vos* in the Heerengracht also possesses a valuable collection of paintings.

Felix Meritis (Pl. 11), the property of a society of that name, which has existed since 1777 (Keizersgracht, 556), contains a few pictures, casts, physical and mathematical instruments, a library, an observatory and a handsome concert-room. Scientific men who make a prolonged stay at Amsterdam will probably find this establishment useful in many respects; an introduction is easily obtained through a member. — The *'Linnæus'* botanical garden, situated outside the Muider Poort, although still in its infancy, is recommended to the notice of floriculturists.

The ***Palace** (*Het Paleis*, Pl. 51), erected by *Jac. van Kampen* in 1648 as a town-hall, at a cost of 30 million florins, is the finest edifice at Amsterdam. It rests on a foundation of 13,659 piles; length 282, width 235, height 116 ft. In 1808 it was presented by the city to King Louis Napoleon as a residence. The building was admirably adapted for its original purpose, but as it stands in the open market-place and is destitute of a principal entrance, it is unsuitable for a palace. It forms a square, built of solid stone, with tympanum appropriately decorated. Above the roof rises a tower 66 ft. in height, containing a set of chimes, and terminating in a gilded ship. The ***View** hence embraces the city with its narrow streets, broad canals bordered with trees, innumerable houses with quaint furcated chimneys, a forest of masts, the Docks, Zuiderzee, the former Haarlemer Zee, and the environs covered with gardens and studded with numerous windmills and distant spires. To the W. the lofty roof of the church spire of Haarlem is visible, and the silvery thread of the canal, running parallel with the high road and the railway, may be traced from Amsterdam to Haarlem. To the E. and S. E. the towers of Utrecht and Amersfoort are visible; to the N., beyond the blue Y, an arm of the Zuiderzee, glitter the red roofs of Zaandam; still farther distant Alkmaar may also be distinguished.

Interior of the Palace. All the apartments are handsomely fitted up with white marble, and some of them are sumptuously decorated. The Council Chamber is a magnificent hall, 100 ft. in height, 120 ft. long, and 60 ft. broad. Over the principal entrance and opposite to it are flags and trophies taken from the Spaniards, Indians and other enemies. The flag in the throne-room, opposite to the throne, is that which was used by Gen. Chassé at the siege of Antwerp. The glass-cabinet near the throne contains remnants of old flags of the time of Alva and Philip II. The audience-chamber contains three good pictures: *F. Bol*, Fabricius in the camp of Pyrrhus; *G. Flink*, Marcus Curius Dentatus as a husbandman; * *Wappers* and *Eeckhout*, Self-sacrifice of Van Speyk (p. 136). Fee for a single visitor to the palace 50 c., and 50 c. more for the ascent of the tower; for a party 1 fl. or more in each case (entrance on the side opposite to the Dam).

[The original town-hall having been converted into a palace, the former Prinsenhof now serves as a **Stadhuis** (Pl. 62). It contains a library, a few antiquities, several good pictures, portraits of burgomasters and citizens of Amsterdam by *V. d. Helst*, *Hals*, *Flink* and other celebrated masters; also a *View of the Palace during its construction by *Lingelbach*; a View of the Palace after its completion, by *Van der Ulft*. Access to the interior before 10 a. m., or after 4 p. m., during the absence of the officials. Visitors ring at a door to the l. in the corner of the court, fee 50 c.]

Opposite to the Palace rises the **Exchange** (*Beurs*, Pl. 5), a handsome structure with a colonnade, resting on a foundation of 3469 piles, erected in 1845. The business-hour is 3. 15 to 4. 30 p. m. (admission at other times 25 c.), when the traveller should not omit to devote a few minutes to the animated scene. Almost all the principal merchants and brokers, as well as a number of sea-faring men, are always assembled here at that hour, and transact their business in eager, but subdued murmurs. During the first week of the Kermis (p. 210) the Exchange is converted into a playground for the younger members of the community, whose delight on these occasions is unbounded. This custom is said to have an historical origin. The tradition is, that boys playing here were once instrumental in discovering a conspiracy against the city of Amsterdam, and that this privilege was accorded to the children of the citizens in commemoration of the incident.

The square termed the *Dam* is adorned with a lofty **Fountain Monument**, known as *Het Metalen Kruis*, erected to commemorate the events of 1830 and 1831. — At the corner of the Dam and the Kalverstraat is situated the building in which the *Zeemans-hop Society* ('seaman's hope', Pl. 69) is established. It comprises upwards of 600 members, the majority of whom are sea-captains, who recognise each other's vessels at sea by the flag of the society. As every member's flag bears the number corresponding to his place in the lists of the society, the name and destination of the vessel, although beyond hailing distance, are easily ascertained, and a report of the meeting is then sent home. A fund for the widows and orphans of seamen is also connected with the society. Visitors may generally obtain access to the building by applying to the custodian in the forenoon (fee 50 c.).

In the vicinity of the curious old civic *Weighing-House* (Pl. 2) in the Botermarkt, dating from 1593, rises the ***Statue of Rembrandt**, in bronze, designed by *Royer* and erected in 1852.

Beyond the Leidsche Poort (Pl. D, 8) is a new *Park*, adorned with a modern statue of *Joost van den Vondel*, one of the most celebrated of Dutch dramatists. He was born at Cologne in 1587, but his parents, who were Dutch Baptists, shortly afterwards settled in Holland. Some of his tragedies with choruses are still occasionally performed.

An enumeration of the Churches affords the best evidence of the variety of religious sects at Amsterdam. The oldest and most interesting are the Reformed, 10 in number, and embellished with the tombs of celebrated Dutchmen. The following are also Protestant places of worship: 2 Walloon, 1 English Episcopalian, 1 English Presbyterian, 1 'Remonstrant' (a sect without definite creed, but which regards the Bible as its sole guide), 2 Evangelic Lutheran (a sect which professes to adhere to the spirit rather than to the letter of the Augsburg Confession), 1 're-established Lutheran' (differing slightly from the 'Reformed' church), 1 Baptist, 3 'Christian Seceding'. Then 16 Rom. Catholic churches, among which are 2 Jansenist, 1 Greek church. Finally 2 large (a German and a Portuguese), and 7 small synagogues. The Dutch are generally regular and devout church-goers, and

Sunday at Amsterdam is by no means entirely devoted to pleasure and dissipation as is the case in many European capitals.

The Church-Architecture of Amsterdam, as well as that of most Dutch towns, is generally extremely unattractive, recalling that of Switzerland and Scotland in the total absence of decoration, and what is familiarly known as the 'churchwarden' style in England in the egregiously bad taste frequently displayed. The churches here present a striking contrast to those of Belgium, the noble architecture and sumptuous decoration of which are unrivalled in any country of the same extent. The sole embellishment of the churches of Amsterdam consists of a few monuments of the admirals and other great men of the Republic, and a few stained-glass windows.

The **Nieuwe Kerk** (Pl. 28), adjoining the Palace, was erected in 1408, burned down in 1421, subsequently restored, in 1578 entirely gutted by the fanatical iconoclasts, and in 1645 again destroyed by fire. Notwithstanding these vicissitudes it is still one of the finest churches in Holland, although unfortunately disfigured by a modern addition. It is a cruciform structure, with a circular wooden ceiling. The remnants of some fine old stained glass represent the raising of the siege of Leyden (p. 243). The pulpit by *Vinkenberg*, executed in 1649, is beautifully carved. The screen between the nave and the choir is remarkably handsome. In the choir the monument of the celebrated Admiral *de Ruyter* occupies the place of the high altar. He died in 1676 of wounds received at the victorious Battle of Syracuse. On a pillar in the choir is the bust of Admiral *Bentinck*, who fell in the naval battle near the Doggersbank. Another monument is to the memory of Admiral *Johan van Galen*, who died in 1653 at Leghorn, of wounds received in the naval battle near that town. It bears the inscription:

'Hier leidt in 't graf van eer de dappere van Galen,
Die eerst ging buit op buit Castilien afhaalen,
En met een leeuwenhart nabij't Toskaaner strandt
De Britten heeft verjaagt, verovert en verbrand.'

Literally: 'Here lies in a tomb of honour the brave Van Galen, who formerly went to deprive Castille of booty upon booty, and with lion's heart, near the Tuscan strand, dispersed, conquered and burned the British'.

Another monument, that of Admiral *van Kinsbergen*, to the l. of the entrance to the church, is admirably sculptured, and merits inspection (erected in 1819). Opposite to it is the monument of the gallant *Van Speyk* (p. 136), who, as the inscription records 'maintained the honour of his country's flag at the cost of his life'. An inscription on a pillar in the S. aisle perpetuates the memory of *Joost van den Vondel* (d. 1679), the most celebrated of the earlier Dutch poets. (The sacristan lives on the S. E. side of the church; fee 25 c.)

The **Oude Kerk** (Pl. 33), in the Oudekerksplein, is a spacious edifice, erected about the year 1300, and supported by 42 slender detached pillars. The aisles are covered by separate roofs, which form gables over each window. The nave is of far greater height. The stained glass, dating from 1555, represents scenes from the history of the Virgin (Death, Adoration of the Magi, Visitation and Annunciation), by *Digman*. To the r. by the entrance is a window containing the armorial bearings of all the burgomasters of the city from 1578 to 1767; in the second window the recognition of the Netherlands by Philip IV. (p. 134). The monument of Admiral *van Heemskerk* bears an old Dutch inscription, alluding to the fact of his having twice endeavoured to discover a more direct route to the E. Indies by the Arctic Sea. He fell in 1607 at the victorious Battle of Gibraltar. The monument of Admiral *van der Hulst* (d. 1666) bears the inscription:

'Hier rust hij, die niet rusten kon, eer hij zijn vijant overwon.
Om hoogh leeft hij in vreughden, in marmer door zijn deughden'.

'Here rests he who never could rest until he had conquered his enemies. On high he lives in joy, in the marble he lives through his virtues.'

The church also contains several other monuments of admirals, generals, authors etc. — The **Westerkerk** (Pl. 38) possesses the loftiest tower in the city (280 ft.) and a fine set of chimes.

The Jews, who constitute one-tenth part of the population of Amsterdam, and live almost exclusively in one quarter of the city, possess nine **Synagogues**. The largest is that of the *Portuguese Jews* (Pl. 64) in the Muiderstraat, erected in 1670, and said to be an imitation of the Temple of Solomon. Brokers' shops and marine stores abound in these unwholesome purlieus, where the visitor will have frequent opportunities of observing begrimed visages and tawdry costumes of an Oriental type. After the expulsion of the Portuguese Jews from their native country towards the end of the 17th cent., they sought an asylum at Amsterdam, where the free exercise of their religious rites was accorded to them. Great numbers of German Jews also, in order to escape from the tyrannical treatment they received in their own country, flocked to Amsterdam, which they regarded almost as a second Jerusalem. *Spinoza*, the father of modern philosophy, born at Amsterdam in 1632, was the son of a Portuguese Jew. The wealth of the Jewish community still renders it one of the most influential in the city. In the numerous dissensions which formerly arose between the Republic and its stadtholders, the Jews invariably espoused the cause of the latter.

Amsterdam is celebrated for its numerous charitable institutions (upwards of 40), destined for the reception of sick, aged and indigent persons, lunatics, foundlings, widows etc., all of which are supported by voluntary contributions. The Blind Asylum (Pl. 6) in the Heerengracht, accessible to visitors on Wednesdays, 10—12 o'clock, enjoys a high reputation. Upwards of 20,000 poor persons are said to be maintained at the expense of the citizens, and the poor-houses resemble palaces rather than dwellings for the destitute. The Protestant asylum for the aged of both sexes (Pl. 50), on the Amstel, is one of the handsomest of these establishments. Many of the orphans educated at the different asylums wear picturesque costumes, which are seen to the best advantage on Sundays, especially in the Kalverstraat. The children themselves generally appear to enjoy excellent health and spirits.

The **Maatschappij tot Nut van 't Algemeen** (Pl. 49), i. e. the *Society for the Public Welfare*, is a very important body, whose sphere of action embraces the entire Kingdom of Holland. It was founded in 1784 by *Jan Nieuwenhuizen*, a Baptist preacher, and was at first established at Edam, but transferred to Amsterdam in 1787. Its object is the promotion of the education and moral culture of the lower classes. Members subscribe $5^1/_4$ fl. annually, and eight or more subscribers residing in a provincial town or district constitute a sub-committee, whose sphere of action is termed a department. There are upwards of 300 such departments, comprising 14,000 members. The principal board of control is at Amsterdam, where the general meeting of the society takes place annually on the second Tuesday in August. The society endeavours to attain its objects (1) by promoting the education of the young, even after they have left school; training teachers, publishing school-books and educational literature, founding libraries, Sunday-schools etc. — (2) by promoting the enlightenment and culture of adults: publishing popular and instructive literature, founding reading-rooms, instituting public lectures, establishing savings-banks for widows, orphans etc. — (3) by bestowing rewards and conferring public distinctions on those who have rendered themselves remarkable by their generous and philanthropic conduct.

Trades. The most remarkable is that of the *Diamond Polishers*, whose art was unknown in Europe before the 15th cent., and was long confined to the Jews of Antwerp and Amsterdam. Diamond mills are still numerous at Amsterdam, where they are chiefly in the possession of the Portuguese Jews, and situated in the vicinity of their Synagogue in the Jewish quarter of the city. The machinery of the mills is set in motion by horse or steam power, and the diamond to be polished is pressed by the workman against a rapidly revolving iron disc, moistened with a mixture of oil and diamond dust. The latter is indispensable, as it has been found that the impression cannot be made on diamonds by any other substance. In a similar manner the stones are cut or sawn through by means of wires covered with diamond dust. — *Refiners of Borax*, which is found in the mud of large lakes in Tibet, Persia, and S. America, and is employed by goldsmiths in the process of soldering, are numerous at Amsterdam. *Camphor* and *Smalt* are also among the staple commodities of the place. The latter, a glassy substance, used principally in porcelain-painting, is prepared by a peculiar process which is kept secret. It is prepared from cobalt, and may be obtained in many different colours.

A pleasant excursion recommended to lovers of the picturesque is to *Soestdijk* (21 M., p. 293), viâ *Muiden* at the influx of the Vecht into the Zuidersee, *Naarden*, a small fortified town, and *Laaren*; returning to Amsterdam by *Hilversum*, *s'Graveland* and *Weesp*. Carriage for the excursion 15 fl. The Amersfoort diligence, starting from Amsterdam at 8 a. m., also runs to Soestdijk ($2^1/_2$ fl.), whence another diligence returns at 6 p. m.

33. Broek.

Steamboats every $^1/_2$ hr. from the Nieuwe Stads-Herberg (p. 255) to the opposite bank of the Y, a trip of a few minutes only. From the landing-place to *Buiksloot*, the first village in N. Holland, $1^1/_2$ M., thence to Broek

4 M. more. Pedestrians cannot mistake the route from Buikslоot, the first half of which follows the Northern Canal. The latter is quitted at the second bridge, where the road and canal to Broek diverge to the r. The town is recognised in the distance by its pointed spire.

Canal Boats 5 times daily from the *Tolhuis* (opposite to Amsterdam, p. 275) to Broek in 3 hrs. The traveller may also avail himself of the steamer from Amsterdam to Purmerend (6 times daily) as far as the bridge above mentioned, whence Broek is 2 M. distant.

Carriages may be hired of Vuyk, at Buiksloot; one-horse for 1 pers. 3, 2—3 pers. 4 fl., two-horse 5 fl.; two-horse carr. to Purmerend 5, there and back 7 fl.; to the Nieuwe Diep by Alkmaar in 8 hrs., there and back 40 fl. — An excursion, occupying an entire day, may also be made to Broek, Monnikendam, Edam, Purmerend and Zaandam (carr. 15 fl.), but the country is monotonous, although perhaps interesting to farmers on account of the magnificent pastures and excellent drainage, and the towns are unattractive.

Opposite to Amsterdam, about $1^1/_2$ M. from *Buiksloot*, the *Willemsluis* forms the entrance to the **Great Northern Canal** (constructed in 1819—25 by *Blanken*, at a cost of about 18 million florins), which extends from Amsterdam to the Helder, a distance of 42 M., and is 130 ft. broad and 20 ft. deep. This magnificent canal, the largest in the world, is available for vessels of very large tonnage, which can pass each other without difficulty. The gates at the entrance, which rest on piles driven into the mud, are also of vast dimensions. The level of the canal at Buiksloot is 10 ft. below the average level of the sea at half-tide, whilst at high tide the difference is much greater. Vessels of the largest size can enter and quit the canal at any time, and thus avoid the perils of storms and the numerous sandbanks of the Zuiderzee. Vessels are generally towed from Amsterdam to the Nieuwe Diep in 18 hrs. by the canal, whilst formerly many days and even weeks were frequently consumed in accomplishing the same distance viâ the open Zuiderzee. About 5000 sea-going vessels, most of them of considerable tonnage, traverse the canal annually. In winter it is not unfrequently frozen over, and great expense is incurred in removing the ice. The canal has, however, recently been pronounced insufficient for the present requirements of navigation, and the government has accordingly, with consent of the Chambers (in 1862), resolved to construct a still broader and deeper channel through '*Holland op zyn Smalest*', viâ Zaandam and Velsen, to Wyk op Zee. The cost of the undertaking is estimated at 18 million florins.

Broek (pronounced 'Brook') (*Hotel* on the N. side; *Café* at the landing-place of the canal-boats), a village frequently visited by travellers, by whom it has in turn been ridiculed and extravagantly extolled, enjoys the reputation of being the cleanest in the world. Its 1200 inhabitants are almost exclusively occupied with the manufacture of the small, round 'Edam cheeses', sometimes termed *Zoetemelkskaas* (sweet-milk cheese), to distinguish them from the inferior qualities of Dutch cheese, which is prepared from sour milk. A few retired merchants and wealthy ship-owners formerly resided here, and their descendants still form a portion of the population.

The following notice (although no longer enforced) may be read at the entrance to the village:

'Niemand zal voor of na zonsondergang langs het dorp tabak mogen rooken, zijnde het alleen toegestaan op den dag, doch zal alsdan de pyp met eenen goeden dop daarop moeten vorzien zijn; alsmede wanneer iemand meet een paard door het dorp gaat, zal men daarop niet mogen zitten, maer moet hetzelve bij de kop houden en stapvoets geleiden'. ('No one may smoke tobacco in the village after sunset, that being allowed during the day only, and even then the pipe must be provided with a good cover. Likewise, whenever any one goes through the village with a horse, he may not ride upon it, but must hold it by the head and accompany it at a foot-pace').

Formerly no vehicle could enter the village, as the entire plain was intersected in every direction by innumerable ditches and cuttings, and was accessible by narrow footpaths only. Equestrians might therefore reasonably be objected to; and the difficulty of communication, which would render a conflagration far more dangerous than at the present day, doubtless gave rise to the prohibition against smoking after dark. The roads are now paved with 'klinkers', or bricks placed edgeways, and occasionally arranged in a kind of mosaic pattern. Most of the houses are constructed of wood, and are carefully painted in order to preserve them from the extreme dampness of the climate. The brightness of the colours and the variegated tiles of the roofs glittering in the sun impart a cheerful and picturesque appearance to the place. The dwellings of the poor are of one storey only; those of the wealthier classes are sometimes of considerable extent, and constructed in a quaint and often tasteless style. The gable-end is generally turned towards the street and contains the principal entrance to the house, two or three feet above the ground.

Most of the private houses are of course inaccessible to strangers unless provided with an introduction, but admission to one of the cottages of the cheese-manufacturers is easily obtained. The proprietor generally politely invites the visitor to scrape or wipe his boots before entering, whilst the inhabitants themselves leave their shoes or 'sabots' outside the door. The dwelling is entered through the cow-stable, which usually occupies three sides of the building, while the fourth is tenanted by the family. Everything is kept so scrupulously clean, that the stable often serves as a kind of reception-room. The floor is paved with 'klinkers', and the walls consist of carefully scrubbed, unpainted deal boards. — The process of cheese-making is also shown in the 'whey-chamber', where cheeses are seen in the press, or in the brine in which they are afterwards slightly salted.

34. Zaandam.

Steamboats in summer 8–10 times, in winter 4–6 times, from the *Nieuwe Stadsherberg* (p. 256) across the Y to Zaandam in 1 hr., returning almost immediately to Amsterdam. Fares 45 or 30 c. The traveller is recommended to start by the first boat from Amsterdam, and to breakfast at Zaandam, in order that the afternoon may be reserved for the sights of the city which are not accessible in the early mourning.

Hotels at Zaandam: Otter; Wapen van Zaandam, with a café; Wapen van Amsterdam. — De Beurs, a large café at the back of the Stadhuis.

Carriages may be hired of Klaarenbeck, near the landing-place at Zaandam: to Broek and the Tollhuis (p. 273) opposite to Amsterdam in 5 hrs., one-horse 6, two-horse 8 fl.; one-horse to Wormerveer 1½, to Crommenie 2¼, to Zaandijk 1¼, to Koog on the Zaan 1 fl. 10 c., to Westzaane 1 fl.; for the excursion to Broek, Monnikendam, Edam and Purmerend (comp. p. 284) 12 fl. — Unless the traveller contemplates a visit to the interior of some of the mills, a stay of 2 hrs. at Zaandam will enable him to see the principal points of interest; 4 hrs., therefore, will generally amply suffice for the whole excursion from Amsterdam thither and back.

Soon after quitting Amsterdam, the traveller perceives a long series of small houses to the l., built on piers projecting a considerable distance into the water. These form the summer-houses of the wealthier citizens, who here keep their yachts and pleasure-boats, and may be observed on fine afternoons cruising on the Y, or smoking their cigars and sipping their tea in the open air. Farther on is the *Swimming Bath* (p. 256).

The Y is so broad at several places that the coast almost

18*

disappears from the view of the steamboat-passenger. The horizon towards the W. is bounded by the Dunes, and the scene is enlivened by numerous sails, flocks of sea-gulls, buoys and signals, and in the distance a whole regiment of windmills.

Zaandam, sometimes erroneously called *Saardam*, a town with 11,968 inhab., several of whom are said to be millionaires, situated at the influx of the *Zaan* into the Y, consists of a long succession of windmills with the small buildings connected with them. These windmills, about 400 in number, extend along the bank of the Zaan as far as the neighbouring villages of *Zaandijk*, *Koog*, *Wormerveer* and *Crommenie*. The *Zaankanters* (i. e. dwellers on the banks of the Zaan) are in the habit of estimating their property according to the number of mills they possess, and one windmill or more generally forms the dowry of a bride in this district. A capital of several thousand florins is, however, necessary to enable the proprietor to work one of these establishments successfully. They are employed for many different purposes. Thus within a comparatively small space there are 111 oil, 100 saw, 57 corn, 29 colour, 28 paper, 15 snuff, 11 mustard and 4 smalt mills (p. 272), and 4 for beating hemp. Others work the pumps and apparatus by which the land is drained, and a few are used in preparing sand for domestic purposes from a kind of sandstone imported from Bremen. The most important perhaps of all the windmills are those employed in grinding 'trass', a volcanic product brought from the environs of Andernach on the Rhine. When reduced to powder, and mingled with lime and sand, the trass forms an admirable cement, possessing the rare property of hardening under water, and invaluable in a country the safety of which depends solely on the solidity of its subaqueous structures.

The **Hut of Peter the Great** is the principal curiosity at Zaandam. Immediately on landing, the traveller is assailed by a number of guides who offer to show the way to the hut. Their services are unnecessary, but the traveller may perhaps avoid loss of time and farther importunity by engaging one of them (10 c.). The way to the hut cannot be mistaken. The road leading W. from the landing-place of the steamer, and skirting the water, is followed as far as the '*Logement of the Czar Peter*', a small tavern; here a narrow street is entered to the r., a bridge crossed, and 120 paces farther a court-yard reached in which the hut is situated. It is a rude wooden structure consisting of two rooms, and now in a somewhat tottering condition, but protected by a roof supported by pillars of brick. A marble slab over the chimney-piece, bearing the inscription: *Petro Magno — Alexander*, was placed there by the Emp. Alexander on the occasion of his visit to Zaandam in 1814. Another tablet commemorates the visit of the present Emperor of Russia in 1839 (p. 265). A model of the hut, several portraits of Peter the Great and the Empress Catharine, a life-size portrait of the Czar in the costume of a Dutch artizan, visitors' books etc. are preserved here. The hut was occupied by the Czar Peter in 1697, whilst he worked as a ship-carpenter in the building yard of Mynheer *Kalf*, with a view to acquire a practical knowledge of the art, and to impart it to his countrymen. The popular story is that he arrived here in the dress of a common workman, under the name of *Peter Michaelof*, and long escaped recognition; but the truth is that Peter only remained here about a week, for he was unable long to preserve his incognito, and being incessantly annoyed by crowds of inquisitive idlers, he preferred to return to Amsterdam, where he could work unmolested in the building-yards of the E. India Company. The nautical phraseology of Russia still contains traces of a partially Dutch origin.

A short walk along the bank of the Zaan will enable the traveller to observe the peculiarities of this singular and picturesque town. It is intersected by narrow canals in every direction, and almost every house with its little garden is enclosed by a small canal of its own and connected with the mainland by means of bridges. The old church, $^1/_2$ M. to the N. of the Stadhuis, contains a picture representing a great inundation which took place here in 1825. The handsome modern church near the Stadhuis is of very recent origin. The *Reformatory* for youthful criminals at Zaandam is considered a model institution, and should be visited by those who are interested in such establishments.

35. From Amsterdam to the Helder. Northern Holland.

Railway by Haarlem to the Helder in 3 hrs. (four trains daily); fares 4 fl. 5, 3 fl. 25 c., 2 fl.

Steamboats to *Zaandam*, see p. 275. Screw-steamers from Amsterdam viâ Zaandam to *Alkmaar* at 4 p. m. daily (fares 1 fl. 20 c., or 80 c.), corresponding with the Alkmaar and Helder steamers. Screw-steamers of another company also ply twice daily between Amsterdam, Buikaloot and Purmerend.

This portion of Holland is most easily accessible by railway, but the traveller who has sufficient leisure and desires to become acquainted with the principal objects of interest in the country will prefer the following steamboat-route: By an early steamboat to Zaandam, visit Peter the Great's Hut, and walk through the town; in the evening (about 6 o'clock) by screw-steamer to Alkmaar; visit the weighing house, cheese-market and Stadhuis the following morning; about noon by steamboat or railway to the Nieuwe Diep, visit lighthouse, harbour etc., and return on the following day to Haarlem by railway.

This portion of Northern Holland, being somewhat removed from the ordinary track of tourists, is comparatively seldom visited. The inhabitants are consequently more primitive in their habits than those of Southern Holland, and still adhere more tenaciously to the picturesque costumes of their ancestors. The head-dress of the women is particularly remarkable. It consists of a broad band of gold in the shape of a horse-shoe across the forehead, serving to keep the hair back, and decorated at the sides with large oval rosettes of the same metal. Above this is worn a cap or veil of rich lace, with wings hanging down to the neck, while handsome earrings of gold and precious stones complete this elaborate and picturesque head-gear. These trinkets are always of gold, even among the humbler classes, and are handed down as heirlooms from one generation to another.

The province of N. Holland, 40 M. in length, and 20—25 in width, is a peninsula connected with the mainland by a very narrow isthmus, and almost entirely surrounded by the North Sea and the Zuiderzee. The land on the sea-coast consists of sand only, the soil of the interior is generally of a clayey consistency. Almost the entire district lies below the level of the sea, from which it is protected on the W. side by the Dunes, and on the E. by lofty embankments. The dykes in the vicinity of the Helder are the most extensive and massive in Holland, with the exception of those of West-Kappel in Zeeland. The province is traversed in almost its entire length by the great Northern Canal, the principal artery of the traffic of Amsterdam (p. 273). The cattle of this district are of a remarkably fine breed, and produce an abundant supply of milk of excellent quality. The mutton of N. Holland also enjoys a high reputation, and the wool of the sheep is highly prized.

By water from Amsterdam to Zaandam, see p. 275. At Zaandam the Amsterdam boat is quitted for the small steamer on the *Zaan*, about 3 min. walk distant. The voyage on this small canal-like river is interesting and picturesque as far as Wormerveer. The banks are sprinkled with a succession of remarkably neat and trim houses, most of them painted green, and peeping with their red roofs from among trees. Innumerable windmills are also passed. Stations *Koog*, *Zaandijk* and *Wormerveer*. About 1 hr. after quitting Zaandam the steamer enters the *Marker Vaart* (i. e. the 'Marken Canal'), stops near the village of *Marken*, traverses part of the *Alkmaarer Meer*, and then enters the *Northern Canal*. To the r. extends the *Schermer Polder* (p. 284). The traveller will observe that the canal here lies considerably higher than the surrounding country, which here consists almost entirely of moor and bog.

Railway to Haarlem, see p. 254. The line now turns to the N. The first stat. **Zandvoort**, or *Zandpoort*, a village 6 M. to the S. W. of Haarlem, situated on the extreme verge of the Dunes, has recently become a rival of Scheveningen as a sea-bathing place, and attracts a considerable number of visitors from Amsterdam. There is a good bath-house (*pension $3^3/_4$ fl. per day), with the usual adjuncts of a watering-place, but nothing to interest the passing traveller. (Bath 65 c., fee 15 c.) — To the r. of the railway extend luxuriant green pastures, where numerous herds of fine cattle graze.

Beverwijk *(Zon)* is a pattern of Dutch neatness and cleanliness in its carefully swept streets, its trim houses with their freshly painted jalousies and shutters, and its rows of trees pruned like hedges. The village of *Wijk aan Zee*, $1^1/_2$ M. to the W. of Beverwijk, is a sea-bathing place of much humbler pretension than Scheveningen or Zandvoort. The line now passes the *Wijker Meer*. Stat. *Uitgeest* and *Castricum*. English and Russian troops who had landed at the Helder in 1799 advanced thus far without opposition, but were defeated on Oct. 5th. by a numerous body of French troops under Gen. Brune.

Alkmaar *(Toelast; Hof van Holland; Burg)* derives its appellation (which signifies 'all sea') from the lake and morass which formerly surrounded it, but are now drained. The town, with 10,409 inhab., is another model of Dutch order and cleanness. The *Stadhuis* in the Langestraat, not far from the church, was erected in 1507. The small tower and gable shew traces of the Gothic style. The *Church of St. Laurence* is a magnificent example of Gothic architecture, with lofty vaulting of wood in the interior, and kept in admirable order. On the E. side is a painting in seven sections, by an unknown Dutch master (1504), representing the Seven Works of Mercy; the figure of the Saviour is introduced into each of the seven groups. The now empty choir contains a model of Admiral de Ruyter's ship suspended from the roof. The tomb of Florian V., Count of Holland (d. 1296), with the original tombstone and coat of arms, is also observed here. The tower of the church fell in the 15th cent. and has never been replaced. A view of the church and tower is to be seen on the wall of the choir.

Alkmaar carries on a very extensive cheese-trade. A market held here weekly is frequented by the peasantry of the entire province of N. Holland, and the cheese sold by them is exported to all parts of the world. Upwards of 4000 tons of cheese are annually weighed in the ·*Town Weighing House*, being about one-half of the produce of the province. The building with its handsome tower was erected in 1582 in the 'barock' style. The busy throng assembled here on market-days, and the huge piles of red and yellow cheeses heaped up in every direction present a curious and picturesque scene.

The *Bosch*, or park near Alkmaar, although inferior to those of Haarlem and the Hague, affords pleasant walks. *Trotting-matches (Harddraverij)* are occasionally held here, and the prize generally consists of a silver coffee-pot presented by the magistrates. One of these matches should if possible be witnessed by the traveller, who will not fail to admire the costumes of the peasantry and the unsophisticated pleasure of the spectators.

The *Cemetery* on the W. side of the Bosch, surrounded by a lofty wall, and resembling a park, contains few tombstones. The graves are all numbered and arranged in straight lines.

About 3 M. to the W. of Alkmaar are situated the scanty ruins of the castle and old abbey-church of **Egmond**, the ancestral seat of the illustrious family so often mentioned in the annals of the Netherlands. Many of the ancient Counts of Holland are interred here. The abbey at a very remote period was a zealous patron of science, and its chronicles formed the principal source of the early history of Holland. In 1572 the fanatical iconoclasts destroyed the venerable and once magnificent abbey. Three villages in the vicinity are named after the Egmont family, *Egmond Binnen*, *Egmond op den Hoef* and *Egmond aan Zee*. A lighthouse erected in 1833 near the latter is adorned with a colossal lion in honour of Van Speyk.

To the N. W. of Alkmaar lies *Bergen*, where the English army under the Duke of York was defeated by the French and Dutch under Brune in 1799.

Alkmaar lies on the W. side of the great *Northern Canal*. The landing-place of the steamboats is on the farther bank. Those from the Nieuwe Diep and from Amsterdam arrive about at the same time, and proceed on their respective voyages after a very short delay. Beyond the fields and pastures to the l. rise the extensive *Kamper-Dunes*, off which the English fleet gained a victory (known as that of 'Camperdown') over the French and Dutch.

The dunes derive their name from the village of *Kamp*, which lies on their N. slope. Between Kamp and *Petten*, a distance of $1^1/_2$ M., there is a gap in the chain of sand-hills, which is supposed once to have been one of the embouchures of the Rhine. This space, termed the *Hondbosschje*, is considered one of the most dangerous parts of the Dutch coast.

The Steamboat now traverses the *Zype*, an old polder, passes the station *'t Zand* ('the sand'), the name of which is suggestive of the character of the country, and stops at the great *Zyper Sluis*.

The *Anna-Paulowna-Polder*, a tract of several thousand acres, was reclaimed from the Zuiderzee after a labour of three years. The works were completed in 1850. The transverse embankment at the upper sluice-gate affords a view of the entire polder and the sea-dykes by which it is bounded. The canal which intersects the polder is connected with the N. Canal by means of a gate.

Towards the N. W. rises the slender lighthouse on the lofty *Kijk Duin*. The scenery between Alkmaar and the Nieuwe Diep is monotonous; extensive pastures with cattle and an occasional farm-house are its principal features. As the traveller approaches his destination, the masts and sails of the vessels in the harbour and roadstead of the Nieuwe Diep become visible. On the l. the green ramparts and casemates of the harbour-fortifications are observed. The steamboat stops near the great bridge, $^3/_4$ M. from the hotel.

The **Nieuwe Diep** (**Den Burg*, commanding a view of the roads; carriages at the landing-place of the steamers), or *Willemsoord* as it is sometimes termed with reference to the government dockyard here, the harbour of the Helder, has been constructed entirely by artificial means within the last 80 years. Its extensive piers and bulwarks are destined to afford protection to vessels entering or quitting the Northern Canal. A considerable number of Norwegian and English ships are always observed here. The flood-gates at the entrance to the basin are the broadest in Holland (about 68 ft.). The Dock Yard is shown (9 to 1.30 o'clock) to visitors who have obtained permission from the contre-admiral (*'schout bij nacht'*). The Arsenal contains a few historical pictures. (Fee 1 fl. for 1—3 pers., 2 fl. for a larger party.)

Part of the Dutch Fleet is generally stationed here, and the traveller may easily obtain permission from one of the captains to visit his vessel (fee to sailor 25—50 c.). The boatmen who row the visitor out to the roads demand several florins for the trip. An old frigate in the harbour serves as a barrack for naval cadets, and as a place of exercise for recruits. The band of the cadets plays in the Café Tivoli on Sundays (admission 25 c.). In front of the saloon in which the cadets play, the mast of Van Speyk's cannon-boat (p. 136) is planted as a memorial of his heroic conduct.

The Railway from Alkmaar to the Helder, passing *Hugowaard*, *N. Scharwoude*, *Schagen* and *Anna-Paulowna*, traverses a flat and uninteresting district.

The **Helder** (*Heerenlogement*) is connected with the Nieuwe Diep by the Helder Canal, $1^1/_2$ M. in length and bordered by an almost uninterrupted succession of small houses. Towards the close of the previous century the Helder was little more than a large fishing-village. In 1811 Napoleon caused extensive fortifications to be constructed here by Spanish prisoners of war, and the works were completed by the Dutch government in 1826. The Helder is now a prosperous and steadily increasing commercial town with 16,775 inhab., and at the same time a fortress of great importance, capable of accommodating 30,000 men, but tenable by one-fourth of that number. The fortifications extend from the North Sea to the Zuiderzee, strengthened by strong defences towards the sea on the N. and W., and by substantial works towards the land on the E. and S. sides, and farther protected by sluices for inundating the environs in case of a siege. The batteries command the strait of Marsdiep and the entrance to the harbour and the N. Canal. As this, the extreme promontory of N. Holland, is exposed more than any other part of the coast to the violence of the wind and the encroachments of the sea, it is protected on all sides by huge and massive dykes.

The great Helder Dyke, about 6 M. in length, and 12 ft. in width, is traversed by a good road from the Nieuwe Diep to the Helder. It descends into the sea to a distance of 200 ft., at an angle of 40°. The highest tide never reaches the summit, while the lowest still covers the foundations. Huge bulwarks projecting several hundred fathoms into the sea at certain intervals add to the solidity and safety of the structure. This remarkable artificial coast is entirely constructed of Norwegian granite.

The Helder is almost the only part of the Dutch coast where the sea is navigable in the immediate vicinity of the land. The force of the tide which runs through the strait between the Helder and the island of Texel prevents the accumulation of sand, and the channel is thus kept open.

The traveller is recommended to walk along the dyke as far as the *Fort Erfprins*, and thence by the coast and the sand-hills to the lighthouse and Fort Kijkduin, $3^1/_2$ M. from the Nieuwe Diep. Beyond the intrenchments of the first of these forts, the embankment is exposed to the full force of the North Sea. *Fort Kijkduin* rises on the highest point of the northern dyke. The lofty lighthouse, which may be visited by those who are unacquainted with such structures, commands a fine prospect. The neighbouring village of *Huisduinen* also belongs to the Helder.

A fierce and sanguinary naval battle took place off this Dune on Aug. 21st, 1673, between the combined English and French fleets and the Dutch under *De Ruyter* and *Tromp*, in which the latter were victorious. In September, 1799, an army of 10,000 English and 13,000 Russian troops, commanded by Admiral Abercrombie and the Duke of York, landed at this point. The Russians lost their way and were totally defeated by the French at *Bergen*

(p. 281), whilst the English were compelled, after a skirmish at Castricum, to yield to the superior forces of the French and to retreat, having failed in their endeavours to induce the Dutch to revolt against their new masters.

Opposite to the Helder, and separated from the mainland by the strait of *Marsdiep*, lies the island of **Texel**, to which a ferry-boat plies daily, starting at 9 a. m. from the Nieuwe Diep, and landing at *Oudeschild* about 2 hrs. later. *De Burg*, the capital of the island, is situated 3 M. inland. The island which is 70 sq. M. in extent, and has a population of 6200 souls, consists principally of pasture-land, and affords sustenance to about 34,000 sheep, yielding sometimes as much as 100 tons of fine wool annually. A highly esteemed quality of green cheese is prepared from the sheep's milk, and the mutton is also excellent. The northern extremity of the island is termed *Eierland* ('land of eggs'), on account of the myriads of sea-fowl which visit it, and are believed to come from Norway. The eggs are collected in great numbers and sent to Amsterdam, where they readily find purchasers.

Harlingen (p. 312) in Friesland may be reached by a sailing-boat with a favourable wind in 5—6 hrs., but there is no regular communication. A boat may be hired for the passage for 10—12 fl. The route is recommended in fine weather to travellers proceeding to Leeuwarden (p. 309), Groningen (p. 310) and Emden (p. 314).

Farmers should visit some of the Polders (p. 213) of Northern Holland (viz. *Anna Paulowna*, *Zype*, *Wieringerwaard*, *Hugowaard*, *Schermer*, *Beemster*), where they will have an opportunity of seeing many admirably organised dairy-farms. — A carriage from the Helder to Amsterdam, passing some of the most interesting of these farms, costs about 40 fl.: from the Helder to Hoorn in 6 hrs., thence to Purmerend in 4 hrs., to Buiksloot (p. 273) in 3 hrs. more. — Travellers who do not desire to inspect any of these farms, or become better acquainted with the people of the country, will prefer to return to Amsterdam by water or by railway, as the towns of N. Holland contain but few objects of interest.

Medemblik *(Valk)*, with 5258 inhab., was formerly the seat of an academy for the education of young seamen. **Enkhuizen** *(Valk)*, with 9390 inhab., once an important herring-fishing place, was the birthplace of the celebrated painter Paul Potter (d. 1654). **Hoorn** *(Doelen)*, with 9304 inhab., the ancient capital of N. Holland, was the birthplace of Willem Schouten, the first European who sailed round the southern extremity of S. America, and named it Cape Horn after his native place.

Purmerend *(Vergulde Roskam)* is situated on the N. Canal, at the S. extremity of the Beemster, between the three Polders of Beemster, Purmer and Wormer. **Edam** *(Heerenlogement)* is celebrated for its cheese. At **Monnikendam** *(Doelen)*, a great anchovy-market, the founder of the philanthropic *Society for the Public Welfare* (p. 271) is interred. Steamboats ply four times daily between Purmerend and Amsterdam (p. 273).

36. From Amsterdam or Rotterdam to Utrecht and Arnheim.

Railway from Amsterdam to Utrecht in $^{3}/_{4}$–$1^{1}/_{4}$ hr.; fares 1 fl. 70, 1 fl. 25, 85 c. — From Rotterdam to Utrecht in 1–$1^{1}/_{4}$ hr.; fares 2 fl. 70, 2 fl. 5, 1 fl. 35 c. — From Utrecht to Arnheim in $1^{1}/_{2}$–$1^{3}/_{4}$ hr.; fares 2 fl. 90, 2 fl. 40, 1 fl. 50 c.

Steamboat from Amsterdam by the Vecht to Utrecht 4 times weekly; also from Rotterdam by the Leck to Vreeswyk, and thence by another steamer on the canal to Utrecht.

Amsterdam to Utrecht. The immediate environs of Amsterdam consist almost exclusively of Polders (p. 213). The most remarkable of these, and one of the lowest in Holland, is the *Diemermeer* (18 ft. below the sea-level), the W. side of which the train skirts soon after quitting the station. Extensive nursery and kitchen gardens, intersected by numerous canals, are also passed. The old road, of which little is seen from the railway, is bordered by a succession of villas, summer-houses and gardens, most of them the property of wealthy merchants of Amsterdam, and extending the whole way to Utrecht. The prosperity and taste of the Dutch is nowhere more apparent than in this district, of which the traveller will enjoy a better survey from the steamboat.

Rotterdam to Utrecht. Canals and pastures constitute the principal features of the district traversed. Near stat. *Nieuwerkerk* the line skirts the E. side of the extensive *Zuidplas-Polder*. The traveller will occasionally find it difficult to determine whether land or water is the predominating element. Beyond stat. *Moordrecht* the *Kromme Gouw* is crossed.

Gouda, commonly termed *Ter-Gouw (Heerenlogement; Zalm)*, a town of some importance on the *Yssel* (which must not be confounded with the river of that name in Guelders, see p. 306), with 15,352 inhab., is encircled by fine old trees, and possesses several handsome churches. The *stained-glass windows, 31 in number, in the *Groote Kerk* (St. John), magnificently coloured and most elaborately executed by the brothers *Wouter* and *Dirk Krabeth* in the latter half of the 16th cent., enjoy an almost European reputation. The subjects depicted are scriptural and allegorical. In one of them is a portrait of Philip II., partially destroyed by lightning; in another that of the Duke of Alva. The stained glass was executed partly at the cost of different towns, partly by private subscription, on the occasion of the restoration of the church in 1560. One of the windows is of the 17th cent., and bears manifest indications of the decline of the art at that period. The original designs, coloured and drawn with the utmost accuracy, are preserved in the sacristy. — The *Stadhuis* with its Gothic façade is also worthy of inspection.

The staple commodities of Gouda are bricks (*'Klinkers'*) and clay-pipes (of which there are 54 manufactories). The material for the former is obtained from the muddy bed of the Yssel, the deposits of which are admirably adapted for the purpose. The clay of which the pipes are manufactured is brought partly from the environs of Coblenz on the Rhine, partly from Namur on the Meuse. The pipes are formed in moulds of brass, and bored with iron wire by hand, a process requiring great skill and attention. — The cheese named after this town and manufactured in the environs is of inferior quality.

Next stat. *Oudewater*, also on the Yssel, was the birthplace of the theologian Arminius (p. 305), the founder of the sect of 'Remonstrants'. A picture in the Stadhuis by Dirk Stoop commemorates the savage atrocities committed here by the Spaniards in 1575.

Woerden, with 4199 inhab., situated on the 'Old Rhine', formerly a fortress, was garrisoned by the Dutch in 1813, but was captured and plundered by the French under Gen. Molitor. The fortifications have recently been demolished, and their site converted into public promenades. The large building on the l. is a prison.

Woerden, Oudewater, and the picturesque and prosperous villages of *Zwammerdam* and *Bodegraven* on the road to Leyden were plundered and treated with great cruelty by the armies of Louis XIV. under Marshal Luxembourg in 1672, as Voltaire records.

Next stat. *Harmelen*, beyond which the canals become rarer, and the country more undulating and agricultural.

Utrecht, see R. 37. The town is pleasantly situated in the midst of gardens. (A tolerable *café* near the station.) The train now crosses the canal *(Rynvaart)* which connects Utrecht with the Leck (as the principal branch of the Rhine is termed, see p. 298). On the r. and l. are four well-preserved intrenchments *('lunettes')*, now disused.

Stat. *Zeist* (Driebergen), a picturesque and thriving village, not visible to the railway-passenger, is the seat of a Moravian colony (about 260 members), with which an excellent educational establishment is connected. The entire community resides in a pile of contiguous buildings, possessing many of their goods in common, and strictly observing the precepts of their peculiar sect. They somewhat resemble the Quakers of England, and are remarkable for the purity and simplicity of their lives. Married women, widows and young girls are distinguished by a difference of costume. The fertile environs are carefully cultivated. Gardens, orchards, plantations, corn-fields and pastures are passed in rapid succession. During the harvest the corn is stacked in a peculiar manner, and protected by roofs.

Next stat. *Maarsbergen*. Stat. *Veenendaal* is noted for its honey. A great part of the neighbouring district was inundated in March, 1855, in consequence of the bursting of an embankment, numerous farm-houses and cottages were half submerged, and railway-travellers were obliged to proceed for upwards of 2 M. in small boats. Stat. *Ede* is the station for *Wageningen* (p. 298), which lies $4\frac{1}{2}$ M. to the S. Near stat. *Wolfhezen* is an extensive plain stretching to the Zuiderzee, which has been frequently used as a military exercising-ground by Dutch and French armies. One of the latter, by command of Marshal Marmont in 1804, threw up a lofty mound, on the heights between Ede and Veenendaal, to commemorate the coronation of Napoleon I. As the train approaches Arnheim several picturesque glimpses are obtained of the Rhine and the *Betuwe* (p. 298) on the r., and of the *Hartjesberg* on the l.

Arnheim. *Zon, outside the town at the N. W. gate, the nearest to the station and the steamboat-pier of the Netherlands Co. (R. 1 fl., B. 60, L. and A. 60 c.); *Zwynshoofd ('Boar's Head', a common sign of Dutch inns), in the town (R. and B. $1\frac{1}{2}$ fl.); *Bellevue (R. and B. $1\frac{1}{2}$—2 fl., D. $1\frac{1}{2}$ fl.); *Pays-Bas, near the pier of the Cologne and Düsseldorf Co.; *De Paauw ('Peacock'), near the station, a small second-class inn.

Arnheim, the Roman *Arenacum*, with 28,872 inhab. (nearly $\frac{1}{2}$ Rom. Cath.), formerly the residence of the Dukes of Guelders, is still the capital of the Dutch province of that name, whose inhabitants are described by an old proverb as: '*Hoog van moed, klein van goed, een zwaard in de hand, is 't wapen van Gelderland*' ('Great in courage, poor in goods, sword in hand, such is the motto of Guelder-land'). The town is situated on the S. slopes of the Veluwe range of hills (p. 297), and was re-fortified by Gen. Coehoorn at the beginning of the 18th cent., after it had been taken by the French in 1672. The French camp which was pitched in the vicinity, as well as the town itself which was garrisoned by French troops, were taken on Nov. 13th, 1813, by Bülow's corps of the Prussian army, the same which distinguished itself at the Battle of Waterloo. The French Gen. Charpentier fell on this occasion.

Arnheim presents the usual features of a clean and prosperous Dutch town, which are especially striking to the traveller descending from the poorer district of the Upper Rhine. The choir of the *Groote Kerk* contains the monument of Charles of Egmont, Duke of Guelders (1513), a recumbent mail-clad figure in white marble, on a sarcophagus of black and white marble, adorned with statues of the Apostles etc. Above, on the N. wall of the choir, is the kneeling figure of the Duke beneath a wooden canopy, covered with the suit of armour, worn by him during his life-time. (The sacristan lives on the N. side of the church, fee 15—20 c.) Near the Groote Kerk is the *Stadhuis*, erected by Maarten van Rossum, general of Duke Charles of Guelders, the indefatigable opponent of the Emp. Charles V. It is locally termed the *Duivelshuis* ('Devil's House'), owing to its grotesque decorations, and contains the public library. — The *Rom. Catholic Church*, near the old church, contains a lofty modern altar of carved wood and a handsome pulpit in the Gothic style.

The district around Arnheim is the most picturesque in Holland. The finest point in the environs is the estate of the **Hartjesberg* ('Hart's Mount') or *Sonsbeek*, the property of a wealthy Dutch family. The entrance is near the railway station, about $1/_2$ M. to the N. of the town. The park and grounds are open to the public (visitors ring the 'Bel voor deen Portier'). The custodian of the grounds, who also shows the Belvedere Tower, lives at the entrance (fee for 1 pers. $1/_2$ fl., for a party 1—2 fl.). The park contains fine groups of trees, fish-ponds, waterfalls, grottoes,

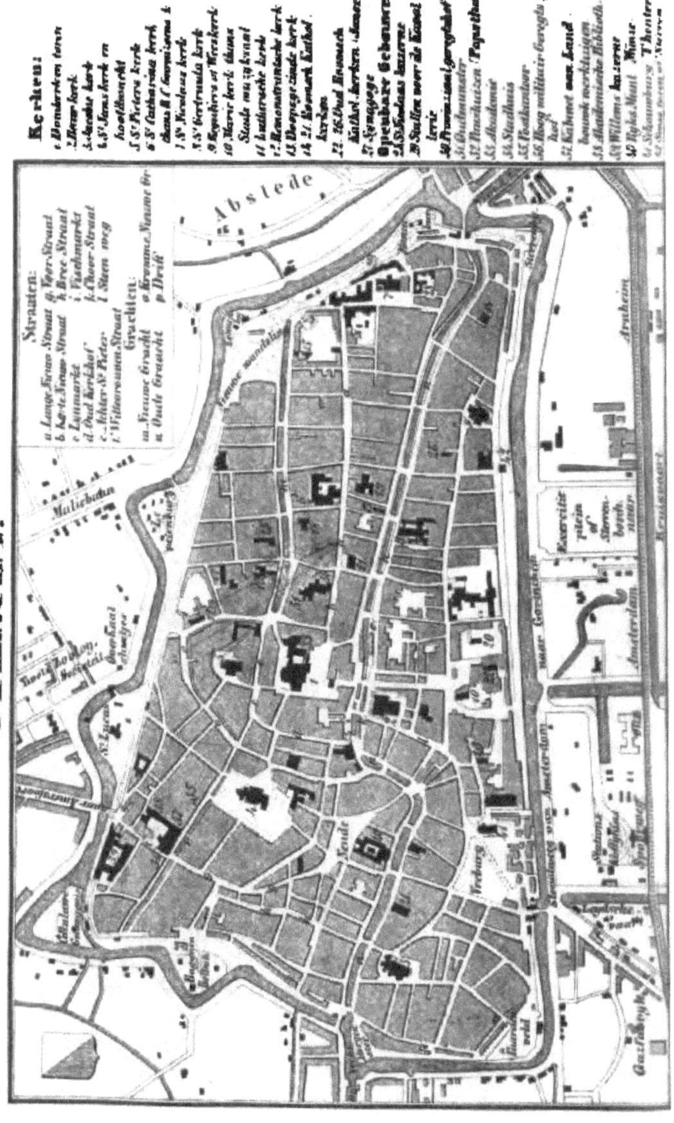
UTRECHT.
Kerken:
Straaten:
Grachten:
Abstede
Maliebaan
Openbare Gebouwen:

a deer-park, a riding-course etc. The stud is also worthy of inspection. The Belvedere commands a beautiful view of the park and the fertile Betuwe as far as the Eltener Berg and the distant heights of Cleve. The whole visit, which occupies about 2 hrs., will amply reward the traveller in fine weather.

Immediately below the town rises the *Rehberg*, a slight eminence with pleasure-grounds. Higher up is the country-residence of *Heidenoord*, adjoining which there are beautiful walks through the woods in all directions provided with benches at intervals. — Near the thriving village of *Velp*, about 3 M. to the E. of Arnheim, rises a range of heights on which several beautiful parks and pleasure-grounds are situated, all of them open to the public.

37. Utrecht.

Hotels. *Pays-Bas, in the Junkershof; *Kasteel van Antwerpen, on the Oude Gracht, R. 1 fl., L. 60, B. 70 c.; Hôtel de l'Europe and Bellevue on the Vreeburg; *Hôtel de la Station, with restaurant and café.

Cafés. Restaurant Suisse, near the cathedral; Nieuwe Bak, in the Lijnstraat; Café de la Station.

Bookseller. Kemink & Son, by the cathedral.

Utrecht (57,339 inhab., 19,090 Rom. Cath.), the *Trajectum ad Rhenum* of the Romans (derived from '*Oude Trecht*', 'the old ford'), subsequently called *Ultra Trajectum*, and *Wiltaburg* or *Wilttrecht*, is one of the most ancient towns in the Netherlands. Dagobert, the first king of the E. Franks, founded the first church at Utrecht, which was then occupied by Frisians, whose bishop was St. Willebrordus. St. Boniface, a monk from Scotland, who afterwards became Pope, once taught here. The archbishops of Utrecht were among the most powerful of mediæval prelates, and the town was celebrated at an early period for the beauty of its churches. It first appertained to Lorraine, then to the German Empire, and was frequently the residence of the emperors. The Emp. Conrad II. died here in 1039, and the Emp. Henry V., the last of the powerful Salic line, in 1125, and were both interred in the cathedral of Spires. The Emp. Charles V. erected the *Vreeburg* here in order to keep the citizens in check, but it was destroyed in 1577 on the outbreak of the War of Liberation. The site of the castle, which was never rebuilt, immediately at the entrance to the town from the station, still retains the name. *Adrian Florisoon Boeyens D'Edel*, the tutor of Charles V., one of the most pious and learned men of his age, who afterwards became Pope as Adrian VI., was a native of Utrecht. The '*Paushuisen*' ('pope's house') is still pointed out as the house in which he was born. It is situated on the Oude Gracht, near the Weesbrug, and contains a few pictures referring to the history of Adrian. In 1579 the Union of the seven provinces of Holland, Zeeland, Utrecht, Guelders, Over-Yssel, Friesland and Groningen, by which Prince William I. of Orange was appointed stadtholder, and the independence of the Netherlands established, was concluded in the Hall of the Academy of Utrecht. The States General were in the habit of assembling here from that date down to 1593, when the seat of government was transferred to the Hague. In 1672 Louis XIV. levied a heavy contribution from the citizens. The celebrated Peace of Utrecht, which terminated the Spanish War of Succession, was concluded here on April 11th, 1713.

At Utrecht the Rhine divides into two branches, one of which, termed the '*Old Rhine*', falls into the N. Sea near Katwijk (p. 247), while the other, termed the *Vecht*, empties itself into the Zuiderzee near Muiden. The town itself is intersected by two canals, the Oude and Nieuwe Gracht. Before the great inundation of 839, in consequence of which the greater volume of the water of the Rhine was carried off by the Leck, the principal branch of the river flowed past Utrecht.

The ***Cathedral**, dedicated to St. Martin, was founded and consecrated by St. Willebrordus, Bishop of Utrecht, about the year 720, and enlarged by Bishop Adelbold in 1015. After having been repeatedly injured by storms and conflagrations, the sacred edifice was entirely remodelled by Bishop Henry of Vianden (1251—67). On Aug. 1st, 1674, during a fearful hurricane, the aisle connecting the choir with the tower fell, and as it was never re-erected, its site is still vacant. At an earlier period the church had suffered severely from the ravages of the puritans. The choir, which is 100ft. in height, and 30ft. in width, has been comparatively recently disfigured by pews, so that the impression produced by this venerable Gothic relic and the slender pillars is almost entirely destroyed. The only monument worthy of note is that of Admiral *Van Gent*, who fell in 1672 at the naval battle of Soulsbai. It was executed in black and white marble by *Verhulst* in 1676. A canopy of painted stone with armorial bearings, adjacent to the latter, is the monument of Bishop *George of Egmont* (1549). The extensive vaults beneath the church contain the hearts of the German Emperors Conrad II. and Henry V. who died at Utrecht. An old monument which is sometimes alleged to be that of St. Willebrord, is that of *Schenk van Thoutenberg* (d. 1580), the last Bishop of Utrecht. The fine Gothic *Cloisters* now partially belong to the University. The church, which is externally supported by piers and flying buttresses, has recently been restored. (Sacristan's fee 50 c., more for a party.)

The **Cathedral Tower**, formerly 354 ft., now 321 ft. only in height, erected in 1321—82, rests upon a handsome vaulted passage 36 ft. in height. It forms a simple square, with a double superstructure, of which the upper is octagonal and of open work. A figure of St. Martin on horseback serves as a weather-cock. The chimes consist of 42 bells. A flight of 120 steps ascends to the dwelling of the sacristan, 200 more to the gallery, and 133 thence to the platform. The view embraces the greater part of Holland; a part of Guelders and N. Brabant. The sacristan (fee 25 c. for each pers.) accompanies visitors with a telescope, with the aid of which Hertogenbosch, Rotterdam, Oudewater, Montfort, Amsterdam, the Zuiderzee, Amersfoort, Wageningen, Rhenen and the Leck are distinctly visible in clear weather. — The church of *St. John*, situated a short distance to the N. of the cathedral, with a Gothic choir, contains a few monuments of little interest.

The **University**, founded in 1636 (22 professors and upwards of 400 students), has lost nothing of its ancient reputation. The collections connected with it, with the exception of the library, will bear no comparison with the treasures which belong to the university of Leyden. The university-building adjoins the cathedral.

The *Kweekschool voor militaire Geneeskundigen* ('School for Military Physicians'), where all the medical men in the Dutch army receive their education, should be visited by professional men.

The **Stadhuis**, erected in 1830, contains a collection of pictures and other objects of art, open to the public on Wedn. 12—2$^1/_2$ o'clock, at other times by payment of a fee (25 c.).

19*

Most of the pictures are from the suppressed monasteries of Utrecht, and are interesting links in the history of art. (Catalogue for the use of the public.)

1st and 2nd Rooms: Mediæval sculptures. — 3rd R.: Architectural drawings; model of the statue of Prince William at the Hague (p. 229). — 4th R. (large saloon): Chair and table of carved ebony, on which the Peace of Utrecht was signed (Apr. 11th, 1713). Most of the drawings on the wall represent the outrages committed in the cathedral by the iconoclasts. — 5th R.: No. 21. Portrait of D. de Goyer, Burgomaster of Utrecht; *19. *Jan Schoreel*, Madonna with the donors; 23. Portrait of the Emp. Charles V.; *5. *Schoreel* (1495–1547), Portraits of five donors, in the centre the painter himself; 14. *Schoreel*, Pope Adrian VI.; 1–4. *Schoreel*, Busts of donors. In the centre a model of the cathedral and models of locks. — 6th R.: A glass-cabinet here contains various coins, keys of the town, heralds' batons, Venetian glasses etc.; 11. *Bloemart*, Peter praying; 33. *Huchtenburgh*, Battle. Several old weapons and standards. — 7th R.: Plans. — Council Chamber: *Pienemann*, Homage done by the town of Utrecht on the accession of William III.

The *Agricultural Collection* contains a few objects which may interest farmers (e. g. a series of ploughs of various primitive forms). Those who have leisure may also visit the *Natural History Collection*. The *Veterinary School* at Utrecht is the only establishment of the kind in Holland. The *Chemical Laboratory* enjoys a high reputation. An *Observatory*, provided with good instruments was erected a few years ago on the old town-wall.

The **Mint** *('s Ryks Munt)*, where all the money current in Holland and its E. Indian colonies is coined, is situated in the Promenade, near the Tivoli. It is connected by a railway with the town-moat, where vessels are in waiting to receive their precious freight.

On the E. side of the town is the celebrated *Maliebaan*, a quadruple avenue of lime-trees, more than ½ M. in length. which were spared by the express command of Louis XIV. at a period when no respect was paid by his armies to public or private property. The former *Ramparts* have been converted into pleasant promenades, bounded on all sides by flowing water. The latter and the springs which Utrecht possesses constitute an advantage enjoyed by few other Dutch towns. Amsterdam derives a portion of its drinking water from Utrecht.

The district for many miles around Utrecht is attractive, being adorned with numerous country-seats, parks and gardens. The finest of these estates is the château of **Soestdijk**, about 12 M. to the N. of Utrecht, which was presented by the States General to the Prince of Orange (afterwards King William II., d. 1849), in recognition of his bravery at the Battle of Waterloo, which is commemorated by a handsome monument in the avenue. It is now the residence of the Queen Dowager. Another pleasant excursion may be taken to *Zeist* (p. 287), *Driebergen* and *Doorn* (carriages may be hired of Meijer, in the Marienplaats, 15 fl. for the day).

Utrecht is the principal seat of the Jansenists, a sect of Rom. Catholics who call themselves the Church of Utrecht, and who now exist in Holland only. The founder of the sect was Bishop Jansenius of Ypern (p. 28), whose five theses on the necessity of divine grace in accordance with the tenets of St. Augustine (published by him in a book termed '*Augustinus*') was condemned by a bull of Alexander VII. in 1665 at the instance of the Jesuits, as heretical. The adherents of the bishop refused to recognise this bull, thus *de facto* separating themselves from the Romisch Church. The sect was formerly not uncommon in France and Brabant, but was suppressed in the former country by a bull of Clement XI. in 1713, termed '*Unigenitus*', to which the French government gave effect. The Dutch branch of the sect, however, continued to adhere to their peculiar doctrines. After various disputes with the court of Rome, a provincial synod was held at Utrecht in 1763.

According to the resolutions of that assembly the 'Old Rom. Catholics', as the Jansenists style themselves, do not desire to renounce their allegiance to the Pope and the Church of Rome. But (1) they reject the constitution of Alexander VII. of 1656, on the ground that the five theses which it condemns are not truly to be found in the writings of Jansenius as alleged. They recognise the infallibility of the pope, which however they deny to be capable of extension to historical matters. (2) They repudiate the bull '*Unigenitus*', and appeal from it to a general Council, and they adhere to the Augustine doctrine and its strict code of morality. (3) They deny the right of chapters of cathedrals to elect their own bishops.

In all other respects the Jansenists differ but slightly from the Rom. Catholics. The tendency to great simplicity of form is exhibited in some of their rites and ecclesiastical vestments, and the vernacular is more frequently used than the Latin language, but in all essential points the service and doctrine are those of the church of Rome. Their church-discipline is more severe than that of other Rom. Catholics. Thus they profess to abstain from animal food during the whole season of Lent, not on Fridays only, but throughout the entire week.

The *Archiepiscopal See of Utrecht* comprises three parishes at Utrecht, and sixteen in other towns and villages of Holland. To the *Episcopal Diocese of Haarlem* belong two parishes at Amsterdam, and six in other parts of Holland. A Jansenist community also exists at Nordstrand in Denmark. At *Amersfoort*, the second town (with 12,000 inhab.) in the province, there is a seminary connected with this church, the adherents of which (now about 5000) are gradually diminishing in number.

From Utrecht to Zwolle by railway in 2 hrs. The prolongation of this line to Leeuwarden and Groningen connects the provinces of Utrecht and Friesland, but is of no great importance to the ordinary traveller. The most important station on the line is **Harderwijk** *(Hôtel de la Paix; Het Wapen van Zutphen)*, a small fortress on the coast of the Zuiderzée, where recruits for the Indian service are assembled and trained. *Zwolle*, see p. 308, thence to Leeuwarden and Groningen p. 309.

38. From Arnheim to Cologne.

1. Viâ Emmerich and Düsseldorf.

Railway in $4^{1}/_{2}$—6 hrs., distance 93 M.; Prussian frontier at Elten. — Steamboat daily in summer, in 13 hrs.; Prussian frontier at Emmerich. — Travellers entering Prussia are reminded that all new articles, or objects not intended for personal use, are liable to duty, but the examination is generally lenient.

Stat. *Zevenaar* is the last in Holland, *Elten* the first station in Prussia.

Stat. **Emmerich** *(Holländischer Hof)* is a clean, Dutch-looking town. At the upper extremity rises the Gothic tower of the church of *St. Aldegund* (1283), at the lower is the *Münster*, a church showing the transition from the style of the 11th to that of the 12th cent. — The next place of importance is **Wesel** *(*Dornbusch)*, a strongly fortified town with 17,429 inhab. (5000 Rom. Cath.), situated at the confluence of the *Lippe* and the Rhine. The Gothic *Rathhaus*, or Town Hall, and the lofty gabled houses are picturesque.

Stat. **Oberhausen** *(*Rail. Restaurant)*, on the *Ruhr*, is the junction for Ruhrort, an important commercial place situated at the mouth of that river. This is one of the most important coal-districts in Prussia, whence the entire Rhenish province principally derives its supplies. — Stat. *Duisburg* (18,000 inhab., 5000 Rom. Cath.), a town of very ancient origin, is said once to have been fortified by Charlemagne. *Calcum* is the stat. for *Kaiserswerth*, a venerable town situated on the Rhine, $1^{1}/_{2}$ M. to the W. (p. 296).

Stat. **Düsseldorf** (*Prinz von Preussen; Breidenbacher Hof*, etc.), with 41,292 inhab. (8600 Protest.), formerly the capital of the -chy of Berg, is celebrated as the seat of a *School of Painting*, founded in 1767 by the Elector Palatine Charles Theodore, and revived in 1822. This institution, one of the great cradles of German art, is established in the Palace, which was partially destroyed by the French in 1794, but restored in 1846. One of the annual exhibitions of modern pictures should if possible be visited. The market-place is adorned with an *Equestrian Statue* of the Elector John William (d. 1716).

Cologne, see *Baedeker's Rhine and N. Germany.*

Steamboat Route. On the traveller's right, soon after Arnheim has been quitted, lies *Huissen*, a short distance below which the Yssel (pronounced *ice'l*), one of the most important branches of the Rhine, diverges to the l., descending to the Zuiderzee.

l. *Huis Loo*, or *Candia*, an old château of brick, with three towers.

l. *Pannerden*, a village with a pointed spire, a windmill and well built houses.

Near *Millingen* the most important of the numerous branches of the Rhine diverges to the W., and from this point down to its junction with the Maas takes the name of *Waal*.

l. *Lobith* is the last Dutch village, where the luggage of travellers descending the river is examined. — On the opposite bank of the river, and at some distance from it, is the *Schenkenschanz*, situated on another branch of the river. It was formerly a strong fortress, and lay at the bifurcation of the Waal and Lower Rhine, the situation of which has gradually changed, and is now at Millingen. The stunted church-tower of the village of Schenkenschanz now rises from the ruins. The Rhine was crossed near this point on June 12th, 1672, by Louis XIV. with Prince Condé, who was wounded here, and a large army, with a view to conquer Holland. The boldness of this 'Passage of the Rhine' is greatly extolled by Boileau in his elaborate lines written on the occasion, but owing to an unusual drought the river was nearly dried up, and the undertaking was probably attended with no real difficulty.

The first indication of the traveller's approach to the mountainous and picturesque scenery of the Rhine is the range of wooded heights on the r., which form the watershed between the Rhine and Meuse, and on which *Cleve* (see below) is pleasantly situated, about 3 M. from the river. The first eminence on the bank of the river itself is the *Eltener Berg* with its ancient abbey (now suppressed), which rises on the l. as Emmerich is approached. The traveller is, however, still nearly a hundred miles distant from the far-famed Seven Mountains, which rise at the commencement of the most picturesque portion of the river.

l. **Emmerich,** see above.

r. *Grieth.*

l. *Rees*, once strongly fortified. At the upper end of the town rises the trunk of an old windmill. The Rom. Cath. church, with its two square towers, was erected at the commencement of the present century.

r. *Xanten*, situated 2 M. from the Rhine, is a town of very ancient origin, with a handsome Gothic church, the spires of which are conspicuous.

l. **Wesel** (p. 294). On the same bank, higher up, rises the old castle of *Haus Wohnung*.

r. *Orsoy*.

l. **Ruhrort** lies at the mouth of the *Ruhr*, which here forms an important harbour. The coal-traffic renders the town a busy commercial place. Coal-trains are transported hence to Homberg, the terminus of the Aix-la-Chapelle railway, by means of a powerful steam-ferry.

r. *Homberg*, whence Aix-la-Chapelle may be reached in 3—4 hrs.

l. *Duisburg* (p. 294), situated $1^1/_2$ M. from the river.

r. *Uerdingen*, a busy manufacturing place.

l. *Kaiserswerth* ('emperor's island') was formerly an island, which derived its name from the Emp. Frederick I. The brick walls and archways of the ancient castle of the Franks, which was considerably enlarged by that monarch, are still extant. In 1062 the Archbishop of Cologne carried off the young German king Henry IV. from this castle. The parish-church, dating from the 13th cent., contains the relics of St. Suitbertus, who first preached the Gospel in this district.

l. **Düsseldorf** (p. 294). Farther on, the tower of the beautiful church of St. Quirinus at *Neuss*, erected in 1209, comes in view on the r., at some distance from the river.

r. *Grimlinghausen*.

r. *Worringen*, a small town, near which, on June 4th, 1288, John Duke of Brabant and Adolph Count of Berg defeated and took prisoner the Archbishop Siegfried of Cologne (p. 80), a victory which added the fertile Duchy of Limburg to the dominions of Brabant.

l. *Mülheim*, a manufacturing place, at the lower extremity of which rises *Stammheim*, a château of Count Fürstenberg, with a Gothic chapel. The numerous towers of Cologne and its dense mass of houses now become visible.

Cologne, see *Baedeker's Rhine and N. Germany*.

2. Viâ Cleve and Crefeld.

Railway in 4–5 hrs., distance 96 M. — Scenery uninteresting.

Zevenaar, the frontier-station of Holland, and *Elten*, that of Prussia, have been mentioned in the previous part of this Route. The line here diverges from that already described, and crosses the Rhine by means of a floating bridge propelled by steam.

Cleve (**Maiwald*; **Robbers*; **Styrum*), once the capital of a Duchy of that name, is charmingly situated on three hills. On an abrupt and picturesque eminence in the middle of the town rises the old palace, with its *Schwanenthurm* ('swan's tower'), 180 ft. in height, erected by Duke Adolph I. in 1493. A branch-line to Nymegen diverges here.

Near stat. *Goch* the low range of sand-hills which form the watershed between the Rhine and the Meuse is quitted, and the train now traverses a flat agricultural district. Stat. *Kevelaer* is a favourite resort of pilgrims. Stat. *Geldern* was once the capital of the Duchy of Guelders. Stat. *Kempen* was the birthplace of Thomas-a-Kempis. **Crefeld** is a wealthy commercial town, one of the most important in Prussia. The silk and velvet manufactured at Crefeld are said to be worth $1^1/_2$ million pounds sterling per annum. — Stat. *Osterath*, then

Neuss (*Drei Könige*; **Rheinischer Hof*), where the line is crossed by that from Aix-la-Chapelle to Düsseldorf. This is one of the most ancient towns in Germany, having been founded by the Ubii, B. C. 35, and frequently mentioned by Tacitus as *Novesium*, a Roman stronghold. It was unsuccessfully besieged during 48 weeks by Charles the Bold, Duke of Burgundy, in 1474, and in 1536 was captured by Alexander Farnese, by whom the inhabitants were treated with great cruelty. It once lay on the bank of the Rhine; but the river, having gradually altered its course, is now $1^1/_2$ M. distant from the town. The spacious *Church of St. Quirinus*, founded in 1209, is in the transition-style from the Romanesque to the Gothic.

Stat. *Horrem* is the station for *Dormagen*, the *Durnomagus* of the Romans. On the Rhine is situated *Sons*, the Roman *Sontium*, with numerous towers. Stat. *Worringen*, the Rom. *Buruncum*, is celebrated in the annals of the Netherlands for the victory mentioned in the previous part of this Route.

Cologne, see *Bædeker's Rhine and N. Germany*.

39. From Arnheim to Rotterdam. The Rhine and Leck.

Railway viâ Utrecht, see p. 285. — *Steamboat daily in summer in $5^1/_2$–6 hrs., returning in 9–10 hrs. — Diligence to Nymegen 3 times daily in $1^3/_4$ hr.

The range of wooded hills on the r. bank of the Rhine below Arnheim is studded with numerous country-residences ('*Buitens*'). On the l. rises the tower of the village of *Elst*. At the base of the hills on the r. lies *Oosterbeek*, a village with a number of villas, where the Emp. Henry III. was born in 1017. Farther on the house *Duno*, now an inn, then the château of *Doorenwaard*. The r. bank of the river is the *Veluwe* (i. e. 'barren, or unfruitful island'), the l. bank is the *Betuwe* ('good island'), both of which are districts separated from the mainland by different ramifications of the Rhine. The hills here are almost the only heights in Holland, and farther down the river the traveller sees nothing but a perfectly level country, the monotony of which is nowhere relieved except by the Dunes or sand-hills on the coast of the N. Sea.

l. The villages of *Heteren* and *Renkum*.

r. *Wageningen* (5362 inhab.), an ancient town of some importance, is connected with the Rhine by means of a short canal. *Ede* (p. 287), $4^1/_2$ M. to the N., is the nearest railway-station.

l. *Opheusden*, a village with a flying bridge.

On the bank of the river, about half way between Wageningen and Rhenen, rises the *Heimenberg* (*Ridder's Inn), an eminence commanding an extensive view over the Veluwe. A bench at the summit, termed the '*Koningstafel*', derives its name from the Elector Palatine Frederick, King of Bohemia, who, having been banished from his dominions after the Battle of the White Mount, near Prague, in 1620, sought an asylum with his uncle Prince Maurice of Orange, and lived in retirement at Rhenen. Some of the events in his romantic career are well described by James in his novel entitled 'Heidelberg'.

r. *Rhenen* (Koning van Boheme) possesses a Gothic church and elegant tower, erected in 1492—1531, the finest structure of the kind in Holland. The town is insignificant.

r. *Elst*, an extensive village; farther on, the tower of *Amerongen*. The channel of the river becomes narrower, and at

r. *Wyk by Duurstede* it divides into two branches. The narrow arm diverging to the r. retains the name of 'Rhine' ('*Kromme Rijn*', or 'crooked Rhine'), whilst that to the l. is termed *Leck* and here describes a wide curve. Wyk by Duurstede, the *Batavodurum* of the Romans, was an important commercial place at the time of Charlemagne. A fine breed of cattle may be seen grazing in the rich pastures on both banks of the river.

l. *Culenborg*, once the seat of the counts of that name, and frequently mentioned in the history of the War of Liberation in the Netherlands, peeps forth with its stunted tower from the midst of a plantation. A railway bridge across the Leck is in course of construction here. Below Culenborg lies *Fort Willem II.*, recently constructed to command the river. It consists of two strong block-houses, one on each bank. Between Culenborg and

l. *Vianen* (Brederode's Inn), which is supposed to be the *Fanum Dianae* of Ptolemy, are sluice-gates by means of which the surrounding district can be laid under water in case of a hostile invasion. On the opposite bank, connected with Vianen by a bridge of boats, is situated

r. *Vreeswyk*, sometimes termed *De Vaart*, whence diligences and steamboats run several times daily to Utrecht. The ebb and flow of the tide is perceptible as far as Vreeswyk.

r. *Jaarsveld*; then l. *Ameyde*, where the narrow *Zederik* canal diverges, intersecting the Betuwe (p. 298), and uniting with the Waal at Gorcum (p. 303).

l. *Nieuwpoort*, and nearly opposite to it the town of *Schoonhoven* (Heerenlogement), formerly well-known for its salmon-fishery, now for its traffic in precious stones.

Between this point and Gouda, in June, 1787, the consort of William V. of Orange, stadtholder of the Netherlands, and sister of Frederick William II. of Prussia, was intercepted on her way to the Hague by the 'patriotic' party and compelled to return to Nymegen. This was the immediate cause of the invasion of Holland by the Prussians, who in a bloodless campaign of one month totally defeated the rebels and reinstated the stadtholder in his office.

r. *Streefkerk* possesses a picturesque church-tower, surrounded with flying buttresses.

r. *Lekkerkerk* is protected by means of long walls and dykes from the inundations of the Leck. The anxious care bestowed on these important structures is here apparent.

l. *Kinderdijk* consists of a long row of small and well-built houses on and near an embankment, with numerous windmills. The name ('children's dyke') owes its origin to a tradition that during an inundation two children in a cradle were landed here in safety, and that the embankment was constructed to commemorate the almost miraculous event. At the extremity of the Kinderdijk are extensive iron-foundries, the proprietor of which (d. 1867), originally a journeyman carpenter, is said to have been a millionaire at the time of his death.

r. *Krimpen*, with its pointed spire, is situated near the confluence of the Leck and Meuse.

l. *'t Huis ten Donk* is a handsome country-house surrounded by lofty trees which extend to the water's edge.

l. *Ysselmonde* lies opposite the influx of the 'Dutch *Yssel*' (as distinguished from that of Guelders) into the Maas. The château with its four towers in the vicinity was erected by a wealthy burgomaster of Rotterdam.

r. *Kralingen* possesses extensive salmon-fishing apparatus. The embankments are here constructed with the utmost care.

l. *Fijenoord* is a busy manufacturing place, with an extensive machine-factory and dockyard belonging to the Netherlands Steamboat Co. (proprietors of the 'Batavier' and 'Fijenoord'), with a staff of 700 workmen. Permission to visit this establishment must be obtained from M. van Oord, the director of the Co., who resides at Rotterdam. Ferry between Rotterdam and Fijenoord every 1/4 hr., 5 c.

Immediately after the steamboat has passed Fijenoord, the '*Guard Ship*', a small vessel of war, comes in sight and announces the proximity of the great commercial city of Rotterdam. An extensive amphitheatre of houses now becomes visible, stretching along the bank of the river, which is here upwards of 1 M. in width. The steamer lands its passengers on the *Boompjes* (p. 222), or wharf.

Rotterdam, see p. 220.

40. From Nymegen to Rotterdam. The Waal and Maas.

Steamboat several times daily in 6 1/2 hrs., returning in 10 hrs.

Nymegen is reached by railway from Cleve in 1/2 hr. (stations *Cranenburg* and *Groesbeek*), or by diligence from Arnheim. Steamboats of the Netherlands Co. also descend daily from the Upper Rhine to Nymegen and Rotterdam.

Nymegen *(Stadt Frankfurt; Place Royale; Salm; Rotterdamer Wagen)*, sometimes called *Nimwegen*, with 22,274 inhab., the *Castellum Noviomagum* of Cæsar, stands upon seven hills on the l. bank of the *Waal*. In the middle ages it was frequently the residence of the emperors, especially of Charlemagne, who presided over a court of justice in the ancient Frank palace of the *Valkenhof*. Eginhard, his son-in-law and biographer, assigns to this edifice an equal rank with the celebrated palace at Ingelheim on the Upper Rhine; but it was unfortunately destroyed by the French bombardment in 1794. The scanty ruins are situated outside the town, on an eminence planted with trees and laid out in pleasure-grounds. Of the church connected with the palace a fragment of the choir only is extant. A most interesting and well-preserved relic is the sixteen-sided *Baptistery*, which is said to have existed before the Christian era, and to have been consecrated as a Christian place of worship by Pope Leo III. at the request of Charlemagne. The pointed windows and the groined vaulting of the interior, as well as other characteristics of the present structure, appear rather to indicate the 12th or 13th cent. as the date of its erection.

At the E. extremity of the town, near the Valkenhof, rises the **Belvedere*, a lofty building resembling a tower (now a café, 20 cents charged for the ascent). An old tower, said to have been erected by the Duke of Alva, formerly occupied this site, and the present building stands on the same foundations. The platform commands an extensive and pleasing prospect, embracing Cleve, Arnheim, the heights of Elten, the fertile fields and rich pastures of the Betuwe, the greater part of Guelders, and the Waal, Rhine, Maas and Yssel. A number of picturesque sails on the rivers and distant canals will be observed in clear weather.

The **Raadhuis* ('Town Hall'), erected in the Renaissance style in 1554, and judiciously restored, is adorned with the statues of those kings and emperors who have been the patrons of the town. It contains a few pictures and a collection of Roman antiquities. The sword with which Counts Egmont and Horn were beheaded at Brussels (1568) is also shown (p. 77). The vestibule contains raised seats adorned with carving, and formerly occupied by the magistrates on certain judicial occasions. A wooden statue of Charlemagne is also shown. The curious mechanism of a clock is worthy of notice. The custodian points out a picture bearing an inscription to the effect that it is the 'Riddle of Nymegen'. It represents a complicated relationship, a problem which the visitor will probably not attempt to solve. On the night of Aug. 10th,

1678, the celebrated Peace of Nymegen between Louis XIV. of France, Charles II. of Spain, and the States General was signed in this building. The portraits of the ambassadors are still shown. The Town Hall was the scene of a barbarous outrage at the beginning of the 18th cent. The building was stormed by the democratic party, who had rebelled against the stadtholder, and the venerable and worthy burgomaster beheaded. The insurgents then proceeded to hang five of his adherents from the window-sills.

The *St. Stevenskerk*, a fine Gothic structure in the form of a Greek cross, was begun in 1272. Contrary to the rules of the Gothic style, the vaulting of the nave is circular instead of pointed, and is supported by 35 slender pillars. The choir contains the *Monument of Catharine of Bourbon* (d. 1469), wife of Adolph Duke of Guelders; the 'brass' which the marble encloses is destitute of artistic merit. At the sides below are represented the 12 Apostles and 16 coats of arms of the House of Bourbon. The organ is a fine instrument. The tower which was burned down in 1566 has been replaced by the present unsightly structure.

Nymegen, rising amphitheatrically from the river, presents an imposing appearance when viewed from the opposite bank of the Waal, with which a 'flying bridge' communicates. The town is strongly fortified on the land side. The opposite bank was also formerly fortified by an intrenchment which has long since disappeared. *Lent* is the village on the r. bank. Martin Schenk of Nijdek, who is still gratefully remembered by the townspeople, was drowned in the river here in 1589, during an unsuccessful attempt to deliver the town from the Spaniards. His body having been found by his enemies was quartered and suspended in chains from the principal gates of the town. One of these chains is still preserved at the Raadhuis. The mutilated remains were afterwards buried in the principal church.

A diligence runs daily from Nymegen viâ *Grave*, a fortress on the Maas, to

Hertogenbosch, or simply *s' Bosch* (i. e. 'the duke's wood', or 'the wood'), French *Bois le Duc (Lion d'Or, Maison Verte)*, is the strongly fortified capital of the province of N. Brabant, with 24,000 inhab., and derives its name from Duke Godfrey of Brabant, who conferred on it the privileges of a town in 1184. The church of St. Jan, a fine Gothic structure with double aisles, was erected in 1280, and restored at the close of the

5th cent. The *Stadhuis* boasts of a picture-gallery and a collection of weapons. In the *Nat. Hist. Museum* a meteoric stone which fell in 1840 is shown. The town also contains several fine squares, with well-built houses.

r. **Tiel** *(Bellevue)*, with 6991 inhab., received its municipal liberties as early as 972, under Otho I., and was at that period an important commercial place. In 1582 it was unsuccessfully besieged by the Spaniards, but was captured by Turenne in 1672. Gen. Chassé (p. 111) was born here.

l. **Bommel**, or *Zaltbommel (Hof van Gelderland)*, formerly a strongly fortified place, was besieged in 1599 by the Spaniards, whose utmost efforts however proved fruitless. In 1672 it was taken by Turenne after a gallant defence by the small garrison. The ebb and flow of the tide affect the river as far as this point. The railway now in course of construction between Utrecht and Hertogenbosch will cross the Waal near Bommel.

The *Bommeler Waard*, or Island of Bommel, formed by the Waal and the Maas, was strongly fortified by the French in 1813, but was taken by a skilful manœuvre of the Prussian Gen. v. Bülow (p. 96). The French finding themselves completely shut in on three sides, availed themselves of the only passage left to them and retreated to Crèvecœur. The island is defended on the E. side by the *Andreas* intrenchment, constructed by the Spaniards at the end of the 16th cent., in order that they might thence carry on their operations against the town of Bommel. On the W. side of the island rises the

l. *Castle of Loevenstein*, at the base of which the waters of the Maas and Waal unite. The river below the point of confluence is called the *Merwe*, or *Merwede*, but as it approaches Rotterdam it is usually again termed the Maas. In 1619 *Hogerbeets*, president of the senate, and *Grotius*, the learned pensionary or chief senator of Rotterdam, were condemned to incarceration in this castle for life (comp. p. 230). The latter, however, effected his escape in a book-chest, with the aid of his wife.

l. **Woudrichem**, or *Worcum*, another fortified place, commands the mouth of the Maas.

r. **Gorinchem**, or *Gorcum (Doelen; Hooiwagen)*, a fortified town with 9000 inhab., is situated at the mouth of the *Linge*, a small river which intersects the entire Betuwe. It was one of the first towns which the 'Water Gueux', or those of the insurgents who aided their compatriots by sea, took from the Spaniards in 1572. At the beginning of the present century Gorcum was taken by the French, and occupied by them till Feb., 1814, when it was surrendered to the Prussians with its valuable military stores. The garrison of 3500 men were taken prisoners. The town was also captured by the Prussians in 1787, when Fred. William II. marched into Holland to assist his brother-in-law against the insurgent 'patriots'.

A vast district, termed the *Biesbosch* (literally 'reed-forest'), consisting of upwards of 100 islands, and upwards of 40 sq. M. in area, now extends before the traveller, and is intersected by the broad artificial channel of the *Nieuwe Merwede*. This '*verdronken land*' (comp. p. 314), once a smiling agricultural tract, was totally swallowed up by an inundation on Nov. 18th, 1421; no fewer than 72 wealthy market towns and villages were destroyed, and 100,000 persons perished. The ruin of the *Huis Merwede*, a solitary and venerable tower, is now the only relic of a human habitation in this desolate scene. The inhabitants of the long, straggling village on the slope of the embankment on the r., over which the road to Gorcum passes, obtain a livelihood by collecting the produce of these islands, consisting of hay, willows, reeds for thatching, and rushes for the manufacture of mats.

1. **Dordrecht** (*Bellevue*, at the steamboat-pier; *Lion d'Or*), usually called *Dordt* by the natives, with 23,840 inhab., one of the oldest towns in Holland, was a powerful and opulent commercial city in the middle ages, and was separated from the mainland by the calamitous inundation already mentioned. Its situation still renders it an important mercantile place. The harbour formed by the river in front of the city admits sea-going vessels of heavy tonnage. The extensive rafts floated down the Rhine from the forests of Germany are generally broken up here, and the wood is then sawn by the windmills. Timber forms the staple commodity of Dordrecht.

The principal *Church*, a Gothic structure supported by 56 pillars, with a lofty and conspicuous tower, was consecrated in 1339, and contains a handsome marble pulpit executed in 1756. The fine old carved choir-stalls are unfortunately falling to decay. A well executed screen of brass separates the choir from the nave. A simple monument here is sacred to the memory of Schotel

(d. 1838), a celebrated painter of sea-pieces. The church is in a good state of preservation, and its chaste simplicity is impressive. Some valuable ecclesiastical vessels are preserved here.

The *Stadhuis*, a modern building, contains six pictures of no great artistic merit: Last Supper, by *Blockland* (d. 1583); Burning of the new church, with good portraits, painted in 1568 by *Doudyn;* Samson and Delilah, by *Honthorst* (d. 1662); the Synod of Dordrecht, by *Hoogstraeten*, a picture of historical value only; Siege of Dordrecht by John Duke of Brabant in 1418, and siege of Dordrecht by the French in 1813, by *Schouman* and *Schotel*.

Dordrecht occupies an important page in the history of Holland, and especially in that of the Protestant faith. In 1572 the first assembly of the independent states of Holland was held here, and resulted in the foundation of the Republic of the United Dutch Provinces. A century later William III., Prince of Orange, was appointed stadtholder, commander-in-chief and admiral of Holland for life by the States at Dordrecht. In 1618 and 1619 the Dutch Protestant theologians assembled at a great Synod at Dordrecht, with a view to reconcile the adherents of the austere tenets of Calvin ('*Gomarists*') with those of the milder doctrines of Zwingli ('*Arminians*'). In 1610 the latter had addressed a 'Remonstrance' to the States General (whence their name 'Remonstrants', which is still employed), of which the following were the principal propositions: "God has ordained that all believers shall be saved; man requires divine grace, but it does not operate irresistibly; it is impossible to fall away from grace". Although these doctrines were now to be discussed, the Calvinists who formed the great majority of the assembly refused to give the Remonstrants a hearing and unanimously condemned them. Deputies from England and Scotland, Germany and Switzerland had been invited by the Calvinists to assist at the meeting, which lasted seven months in all, and is said to have cost the States a million florins. The resolutions of the synod were long regarded as the law of the Dutch Reformed Church.

The hall in which the assembly met has recently been demolished. The house, termed *Kloveniers Doelen* (House of the Arquebusiers), is situated in one of the narrow old streets. An apartment on the ground-floor contains a chimney-piece with fine sculpturing.

The old *Gate*, on the great dyke, erected in 1618, bears the inscription: '*Pax civium et concordia tutissime urbem muniunt*'.

The eminent painter Ary Scheffer, to whom a monument was erected here in 1862, was a native of Dordrecht. The statue was designed by Mezzera, who declined to accept any remuneration for this tribute to the memory of his friend. The right hand of the master grasps his brush, while the left with the palette rests on a design of the bust of his mother. The inscription records the dates of his birth (1795) and death (at Argenteuil in France, 1858).

At Dordrecht the steamer quits the broad channel of the Maas and enters a narrow arm termed the *Merwede* (p. 303). A railway to Rotterdam, crossing the Maas and Leck, is in course construction.

r. *Alblasserdam*, with a new octagonal church, possesses considerable ship-building yards, the property of the Brothers Smit, the wealthiest shipbuilders in Holland.

r. *Kinderdijk*, where the Merwede unites with the *Leck* and again takes the name of *Maas*. From this point to Rotterdam see p. 299.

41. From Arnheim to Zwolle and Groningen.

Railway from Arnheim to *Zwolle* in 3 1/4 hrs.; fares 3 fl. 80, 3 fl. 5, 1 fl. 90 c. — From Zwolle to *Groningen* viâ *Leeuwarden* in 5 hrs. — Or the traveller may prefer to proceed by train from Zwolle to *Meppel* only (3/4 hr.), and thence by canal to Groningen.

The railway from Arnheim to Zütphen traverses an uninteresting district and passes several unimportant stations. It runs nearly parallel with the Yssel, which it reaches near Zütphen.

The *New Yssel* (pron. *ice'l*) is that ramification of the Rhine which diverges towards the N., about 3 M. above Arnheim. This channel was constructed 1800 years ago by the Roman general Drusus *(Fossa Drusiana)*, stepson of the Emp. Augustus, extending as far as Doesborgh, where it unites with the 'Old Yssel' *(Nabalia)*. A direct mode of communication between the Rhine and the Zuiderzee was thus afforded. The inhabitants of the banks of the Old Yssel, which rises among the moors of Münster, and falls into the Zuiderzee at Kampen, were Salic Franks, the bitterest and most inveterate enemies of the Romans. They made frequent and successful incursions into the dominions of the Romans and their allies, and afterwards took possession of the island of the Batavi, the Betuwe of the present day (p. 298). They subsequently became so powerful that they undertook piratical expeditions as far as the Mediterranean, where they pillaged Syracuse and many other wealthy places.

Doesborgh *(Hof Geldria)*, an ancient fortified town at the union of the Old and New Yssel, was the birthplace of Admiral van Kinsbergen (p. 269). In 1585 it was captured and pillaged by the Spaniards. In 1813 it was taken from the French by the Prussians under Gen. v. Oppen.

Zütphen *(Keizerskroon; Hollandsche Tuin; Zwaan)*, situated at the confluence of the *Berkel* and the Yssel, is a strongly fortified town with 15,315 inhab., which was taken by the Prussians in 1813, on the day after the capture of Doesborgh. The most important edifice is the *Church of St. Walburgis*, dating from the 12th cent. It contains a venerable brazen font, a Gothic candelabrum of gilded iron, half-relief sculptures on the pulpit, old monuments of the Counts of Zütphen, and a handsome modern monument of the Van Heeckeren family, all of which are worthy of inspection. The tower dates from 1600, its predecessors having been destroyed by lightning. The Wijnhuis Tower, with its two galleries, contains a good set of chimes. The timber which is floated in rafts from the Black Forest down the Rhine and Yssel forms the chief article of commerce at Zütphen.

About $2^{1}/_{2}$ M. to the N. of Zütphen is situated the agricultural colony of **Nederlandsch Mettray**, a Protest. establishment founded in 1851 for the education of poor boys and foundlings. It was first instituted by a M. Schutter, who presented 16,000 fl. for the purpose, and has since been liberally supported and extended by private contributions. The estate of *Ryssell*, about 50 acres in area, has been purchased by the society, and upwards of 150 boys are educated here (about 12 in each house). Those who wish to become acquainted with the interesting arrangements of the establishment will find good accommodation at the '*Laatste Stuiver*' Inn.

A railway diverging from Zütphen to *Salzbergen* (p. 316), a station on the Emden-Hamm line, affords the most direct communication between N. Germany and the cities of Amsterdam and Rotterdam. To *Rheine* and *Emden*, see R. 43.

Beyond Zütphen the train crosses the Yssel.

Deventer (*Engel; Moriaan*), situated on the frontier of Guelders and Over-Yssel (i. e. 'beyond the Yssel'), is a clean and prosperous fortified town with 17,521 inhab., the birthplace of the celebrated philologist Jacob Gronovius. The handsome old church of *St. Lebuinus* is surmounted by a remarkably fine Gothic tower. The crypt beneath the church is very ancient. The *Stadhuis* contains a good picture by Terburg. An old cauldron is shown in the public weighing-house, in which a coiner is said to have been boiled alive in 1434. The town possesses several flourishing iron-foundries and carpet-manufactories. The chief commodity for which Deventer enjoys a Dutch, if not an European celebrity, is its honey-cakes, a species of gingerbread, of which tons are annually sent to many different parts of Holland.

The royal château of Loo, the favourite residence of William I. and of the present king also, is situated near *Apeldoorn*, a large and wealthy village

20*

with 11,302 inhab. — A treaty between Prussia and Holland was concluded here after the brief campaign of 1788 (p. 217).

Stat. *Diepenveen* lies $1^1/_2$ M. from the station. *Olst*, with 4000 inhab., is situated on the Yssel.

Zwolle (*Keizerskroon; Heerenlogement*), the capital of the province of Over-Yssel, with 20,331 inhab., is situated on the *Zwarte Water*, a small river which falls into the Zuiderzee. The Gothic church of St. Michael contains a fine carved pulpit. The organ is one of the best in Holland. *Thomas a Kempis*, the pious author of the 'Imitation of Christ', which has been translated into almost every known language, lived for 64 years in a monastery on the *Agnetenberg*, where he died in 1471, in his 92nd year. This eminence, 3 M. from Zwolle, is still the burial-place of the wealthier inhabitants of Zwolle. The ground in the immediate vicinity of the town is so saturated with moisture, that a grave cannot be dug without immediately being filled with water. A broken tombstone here is said to be that of Thomas a Kempis, who was born at Kempen, a town on the Lower Rhine, whence he derived his name.

Gerard Terburg, the greatest of the Dutch genre-painters, was born at Zwolle in 1608, and died in 1681 at Deventer, where he filled the office of burgomaster. He was a great traveller, and practised his art in Germany, Italy and Spain. Most of the actors in the scenes he depicts belong to the upper ranks, and he rarely descends to the low subjects which delighted Jan Steen and Ostade. His finest works are conversation-peaces, in which a lady with a dress of white satin is frequently introduced. His colouring is clear, harmonious and silvery.

Meppel (*Heerenlogement*), an uninteresting town with 6900 inhab. Stat. *Steenwijk*.

The Pauper Colonies of **Frederiksoord**, **Wilhelminoord** and **Willemsoord** lie to the N. E. of *Steenwijk*. The society was founded during the famine of 1816 and 1817, when the paupers in Holland had become an extremely numerous class. No fewer than 20,000 members speedily subscribed their names, each of them paying 2 fl. 60 c. annually, and the first experiments were made in 1818. The number of paupers now supported here amounts to nearly 3000. Each adult, if able-bodied and willing to work, is provided with a small cottage, two acres of land, a cow, a pig, and occasionally 6—10 sheep. There are also other excellent arrangements, by means of which the majority of the colonists are rendered entirely self-supporting after the first outlay has been made. Those who prove idle or dishonest are sent to the penal colony of *Ommerschans* (see below). The houses are visited almost daily by the superintending officials, and the strictest discipline is everywhere observed.

The road from Frederiksoord to the orphan and mendicant establishments at Veenhuizen leads past the Agricultural School of Wateren, founded by the same society, situated 6 M. from Frederiksoord, and 9 M. from Veenhuizen. The object of this institution is to provide a superior kind of education for the best conducted and most able of the colonists' children, with a view to qualify them for official posts in the colony. About 72 pupils are here instructed in botany, chemistry, mathematics, modern languages etc., in addition to the more elementary branches of education. Each pupil receives an allotment of land, which he is permitted to cultivate according to his own taste. On attaining their 21st year the pupils are either appointed as overseers in the colony, or permitted to seek their fortunes elsewhere.

The Colonies at Veenhuizen, 9 M. from Wateren, and the same distance from *Assen* (p. 311), consist of three extensive buildings, about 1/2 M. apart, one of which is destined for the reception of orphans, the other two for mendicants. Another similar colony is that of Ommerschans, 9 M. to the S. E. of *Meppel*, in the province of Over-Yssel. The latter is partly employed as a penal settlement for the idle and the disorderly, partly as a reformatory for beggars. *Ommerschans*, a ruined fortress situated on a fertile spot in the midst of a barren moor, was fitted up for the purpose in 1821. Weavers, smiths, carpenters, tailors and other artisans ply their trades here, under the strict supervision of their overseers and custodians. In order to prevent the escape of the inmates, the entire establishment is surrounded by a broad canal, and is also encircled by a staff of 25 watchmen or sentinels posted at intervals of 1/4 M. from each other. The number of mendicants here is 2290. The population of all the colonies of the society amounts to nearly 11,000. The average cost of their maintenance is 75 fl. per annum for each person. The number of subscribers has greatly fallen off within the last few years, and the colonies are now partially supported by government.

Stat. **Heerenveen**, a small and thriving town, is the next station of importance.

Leeuwarden (** Nieuwe Doelen; Beugelaer*), the ancient capital of the Frisians, with 24,866 inhab., possesses a fine old town-hall and a handsome modern court-house. The museum of Frisian antiquities is also worthy of mention. The old palace of the governors of Friesland, members of the Nassau-Diez family and ancestors of the royal family of Holland, is an insignificant edifice. Leeuwarden is one of the most important corn and cattle marts in Holland. The Frisian women, especially those of this town, enjoy a great reputation for personal beauty. Costume, see p. 278.

The Frisians are the only Germanic tribe which has preserved its name unaltered since the time of Tacitus. They are remarkable for their physical strength, their bravery and love of independence. Charlemagne entered into a treaty with this remarkable race, by which they agreed to submit to the rulers he should place over them, on condition that they should govern in accordance with Frisian laws. That monarch caused a collection of these laws to be made, and they still exist in the *Asegabuch* in the old Frisian language, as well as in Latin. — Their language differs considerably from that of the rest of Holland, most of the roots being from the Anglo-Saxon, and often closely resembling English.

Several unimportant stations are passed beyond Leeuwarden.

Groningen (**Doelen; *Nieuwe Munster; Café Forman*, at the back of the S. wing of the Stadhuis), the capital of the province of the same name, with 32,299 inhab. (6000 Rom. Cath.), lies at the junction of the *Drenthe'sche Aa*, or *Drentsche Diep*, and the *Hunse*. The latter is termed *Reiddiep* from this point to its mouth, and being converted into a canal, is navigable for large sea-going vessels. Rape-seed and grain are the great staple commodities of the place, and many of the merchants of the town and the farmers of the neighbourhood are very wealthy.

The *Breede Markt*, or market-place, is one of the most spacious in Holland. The *Church of St. Martin* situated here is a fine Gothic structure with a lofty tower (432 ft.), erected after a fire in 1627. Opposite to it is the *Stadhuis*, erected in 1810. The (Rom. Cath.) *Broederkerk* contains two tolerable altar-pieces by *De Koen*.

The *University* (290 stud.), founded in 1614, possesses an admirable natural history museum, which is established in the handsome academy buildings with their fine cloisters, opposite to the Rom. Cath. church. A collection of Germanic antiquities is in course of formation. The *Deaf and Dumb Asylum*, supported chiefly by voluntary contributions, educates 150 pupils. Public examinations on Wednesdays, 11—12 o'clock. In the ox-market, in front of the building, a statue to the founder *Guyot* has been erected.

The *Fortifications*, constructed by the celebrated engineer Gen. Coehoorn in 1698, are still carefully maintained. The gateways are handsome and substantial structures. — The *Harbour* generally presents a busy scene. Extensive magazines have recently been erected on the W. side. — The projecting corner of a street in the vicinity, termed the *'oude kijk in't gat straat'* (i. e. 'the old peep into the open street'), is adorned with the head of a bearded man, with the inscription *'Ick kijk noch in't'* (I still peep into it'). It commemorates a siege in 1672, when the besiegers were compelled to retreat, as they were unable to prevent supplies 'ng brought into the town by the Reiddiep. The inscription signifies, that as long as the channel is clear and unobstructed, no real danger from besiegers need be apprehended.

Assen, the most important place on the canal between Groningen and Meppel (p. 309), a small town with 5000 inhab., is the capital of the Province of Drenthe. The tumuli or "giants' graves" in this neighbourhood are objects of great interest to the antiquarian. The huge stones which mark these spots recal those of Stonehenge. *Tacitus (Germ. 37)* mentions them as the monuments of a great and powerful people. Similar monuments found in most Celtic-Cimbrian countries have probably all the same origin. Most of these tumuli, which were originally covered with a pavement of flint, have lost their original form. Excavations have brought to light cinerary urns, battle-axes and hatchets of flint etc. A model of the tumuli, as well as many of the relics themselves, may be inspected in the Museum of Antiquities at Leyden (p. 245). — Assen lies 15 M. to the S. of Groningen, and 27 M. to the N. E. of Meppel. The pauper and mendicant colonies (p. 308), which should if possible be visited, are most easily reached from the canal or diligence route between Groningen and Meppel.

42. From Amsterdam to Harlingen and Groningen.

Steamboat from Amsterdam (Nieuwe Stads-Herberg, p. 255) twice daily to *Harlingen* in $6^1/_2$ hrs.; restaurant on board. **Railway** thence to *Groningen* viâ *Franeker* and *Leeuwarden* in $2^3/_4$ hrs.

The steamboat steers to the E. for the first half-hour, then at the lighthouse on the S. E. extremity of N. Holland turns to the N., and passes the island of *Marken*, on which another lighthouse stands. The towers of *Monnikendam*, *Edam* and *Hoorn* (p. 284) rise in the distance towards the W. In 2 hrs. the steamer reaches

Enkhuizen *(Valk)*, once a flourishing town with 40,000 inhab., who at the beginning of the 17th cent. possessed a fleet of upwards of 400 herring-fishing vessels. The population is now 5449 only, and the number of fishing smacks has dwindled down to seven. The Stadhuis, erected in 1588, and the Westerkerk are handsome buildings, recalling the former prosperity of the place. Externally the town with its harbour, church-towers, and handsome gateway half hidden by trees has an important appearance.

Paul Potter, one of the greatest Dutch painters of animals, was born at Enkhuizen in 1625 (d. at Amsterdam in 1654). He went at an early age to the Hague, where he was patronised by the Prince of Orange, and afterwards settled at Amsterdam. His career was brief, but most laborious and successful. In his extraordinary fidelity to nature he stands preeminent. His cattle often appear to stand forth in living reality.

The steamer after quitting Enkhuizen proceeds to the N. E. The lighthouse of **Staveren**, rising on the extreme W. promontory of Friesland, soon becomes conspicuous. The ancient Stavoren, the city of the heathen god *Stavo*, the Thor of the Frisians, is now an insignificant place with 570 inhab. only. It was once the residence of the Frisian monarchs, and at a subsequent period a wealthy and populous commercial free city, the third in the celebrated Hanseatic League. Its vessels are said to have been the first which passed through the Sound, and its naval enterprises prospered as early as the 12th cent. Old chroniclers relate that the citizens of this favoured spot were in the habit of employing pure gold for many purposes to which the baser metals are usually applied. Thus the bolts on the doors of their houses, the rivets and fastenings of their yachts and pleasure-boats, and the weather-cocks on their churches are said frequently to have been made of that precious metal. The town is now a very poor place, not even possessing the means of rescuing its handsome church-tower from the ruin which threatens it. The decay of the place is attributed almost exclusively to the fact that the harbour is gradually becoming filled with sand and thus rendered useless. The *Vrouwensand*, a broad grass-grown sandbank in front of the harbour, derives its name from the tradition that the wife of a wealthy merchant once desired one of her husband's captains to bring her from abroad 'the most precious thing in the world'. The worthy Dutch mariner, in conscientious fulfilment of the request, accordingly brought back a cargo of wheat from Danzig! The lady, indignant at what she regarded as the captain's stupidity, ordered the valuable freight to be thrown overboard at the mouth of the harbour. This act of wanton waste ultimately caused the ruin of the proud and luxurious city. The grain is said to have taken root, and to have formed the foundation of the sandbank, which is daily increasing in extent and constitutes an insuperable barrier to the entrance of the once excellent haven.

The steamer now skirts the W. coast of Friesland. The lofty tower of the small town of *Hindeloopen* is a conspicuous object in the landscape. Farther N. lies the town of *Workum*.

Harlingen *(Heerenlogement)*, where the traveller now disembarks, an important harbour of the Zuiderzee, with 9913 inhab., occupies the site of a city which was entirely swallowed up by an inundation in 1134. In 1566 the surrounding district was again devastated and depopulated by another encroachment of the sea, in consequence of which the Spanish governor *Robles de Billy* caused the entire province to be surrounded by lofty dykes. The grateful inhabitants, in commemoration of this important service, erected a statue to the governor, termed the *Stenen Man*, which is still to be seen on the sea-wall near the town. — Steamers affording tolerable passenger accommodation ply regularly from Harlingen to London, Hull, Leith etc.

The Railway journey hence to Leeuwarden is monotonous, presenting the usual Dutch characteristics — extensive pastures intersected by canals, a high road paved with 'klinkers' and bordered by rows of trees, neat country-houses, substantial farm-buildings, and fields and gardens bounded by ditches instead of walls or hedges. The jawbones of whales erected in the meadows are for the benefit of the cattle, which may occasionally be seen rubbing themselves against them. The first important station is

Franeker (**Heerenlogement*), the seat of a university founded in 1585, but suppressed by Napoleon in 1811. The savants *Vitringa*, *Heineccius*, *Schultens*, *Hemsterhuis*, *Valkenaer* etc. once taught here. The traveller should on no account omit to see the greatest curiosity of the place, an astronomical model which shows all the motions of the planets, the sun and the moon, with the utmost scientific accuracy. It was constructed by *Eise Eisinga*, a simple burgher of Franeker, in 1774—81.

Leeuwarden, and thence to Groningen, see p. 309.

43. From Groningen to Emden and Rheine.

Railway to meet the Emden-Rheine line completed as far as Nieuwe Schans; the remaining portion will also shortly be opened.

Steamboat and Barge daily about 8 a. m. by canal from Groningen to *Delfzyl*, both performing the journey in 3—3½ hrs. (fares 1 fl. or 60 c.). The former is preferable in fine, the latter in rainy weather. Touters for the barge or '*schuit*' generally lie in wait for travellers at the Steentilpoort.

Steamboat from Delfzyl to *Emden* once daily in 1¼ hr. (fare 20 Sgr., i. e. 1 fl. 17 c., or 2 *s.*). Steamboat from Emden to *Norderney* (an island much frequented as a sea-bathing place, see *Baedeker's N. Germany*) in 6 hrs., fares 1⅔ or 1 Thlr.; to Borkum in 4 hrs. — Railway from Emden to Rheine in 5 hrs.

The *Damsterdiep*, the winding canal traversed by the steamboat and barge, intersects a long succession of uninteresting pastures and gardens, diversified with an occasional farm-house or windmill. The stations at which the boats touch are *Halfweg* and *Appingadam*, the latter a small ship-building place. Near Delfzyl are several large manufactories of bricks and draining-tiles.

Delfzyl (*De Beurs*, also the steamboat-office, at the E. gate, tolerable), a small fortified harbour near the influx of the Ems into the N. Sea, is an unattractive place, where however the traveller will probably be detained for an hour or more before the steamer starts for Emden. A walk on the ramparts is recommended.

The Dollart, a bay 6 M. in breadth at the mouth of the Ems, was formed by a calamitous inundation in 1277, occasioned by the waters of the river having been confined for a considerable period by ice, and suddenly bursting their barrier on the approach of spring. Thirty-three populous villages were submerged by this appalling catastrophe, and most of the inhabitants perished in the icy flood. During the two following centuries the encroachment of the sea steadily increased, but new embankments have since been constructed, and a considerable extent of valuable land is gradually being reclaimed. As the vessel crosses the bay several villages are conspicuous on the E. Frisian coast.

Emden (**Börse*, by the Rathhaus-bridge, R. and B. $22^1/_2$, A. 5 Sgr.; **Weisses Haus*, opp. the Rathhaus; **Prinz von Preussen*. — 5 Silbergroschen = 6 pence) is in the Prussian dominions, and passengers' luggage is examined here. The town, with 12,490 inhab., was a free city of the Empire from 1595 to 1744; it belonged to Prussia till 1804, then to Holland, and since 1866 to Prussia again. It was formerly situated on the Ems, which is now $1^1/_2$ M. distant, but it is connected with the river and the sea by a canal, admitting vessels of considerable tonnage. The town, which possesses about 150 vessels, and was formerly the most important harbour of the Kingdom of Hanover (now annexed to Prussia), still carries on a considerable traffic in oats, butter and cheese.

The **Rathhaus*, erected in 1576, is a rich example of the architecture of the Renaissance, somewhat resembling the imposing town-halls of Belgium. The tower, like that of the Hôtel de Ville at Brussels, from some unexplained cause does not rise from the centre of the structure. The Rathhaus contains a very interesting *Arsenal, with a collection of curious and valuable old fire-arms, said to have been captured by the inhabitants of Emden together with the vessel in which they were being conveyed to England by order of Count Mansfeld (d. 1628), the celebrated general in the Thirty Years' War, who had taken them from his enemies and was about to send them to a place of safety. Three automata, a drummer, two knights engaged in a duel, and a watchman are shown by the guide. The council-chamber on the ground-floor contains portraits of George IV. of England, and of several Kings of Prussia. The tower affords a good survey of the environs (fee 5 Sgr.).

The *Grosse Kirche* contains a monument in marble and alabaster to the memory of Count Enno II. of E. Friesland. The *Nat. Hist. Museum*, tickets of admission to which are obtained at the Rathhaus (5 Sgr.), comprises a valuable collection of specimens of amber.

During the bathing-season numerous travellers, many of whom belong to the highest classes, pass through Emden on their way to Norderney, a favourite watering-place which was formerly frequently visited by the King of Hanover.

From Emden by railway to Münster in $6^1/_2$ hrs., to Hanover in 11 hrs. The district traversed is far from attractive, consisting of vast tracts of marsh and moor, with an occasional village or farm on a green oasis of better soil. The underwood on these moors is generally set on fire in spring, in order to obtain the ashes as manure for buckwheat, which is extensively cultivated here. The suffocating smell of the smoke is sometimes perceived on these occasions in very distant parts of Germany (Heidelberg, Berlin, Vienna etc.). The railway runs on the E. bank of the tortuous Ems, which is seldom visible. The first important station is **Leer** *(Prinz von Oranien; Voigt's Hôtel)*, a thriving commercial town with 7000 inhab., situated in the most fertile district of E. Friesland, at the confluence of the *Leda* and the Ems. The excellent wharf enables vessels to discharge their cargoes at the very doors of the magazines.

Papenburg, the next important station, with 5000 inhab., is the largest of the 'Veen Colonies', and possesses several hundred vessels of considerable size which communicate with the sea by means of the Ems. Several small places, then *Meppen* (Bünger's Inn), the capital of the former Duchy of Meppen. *Lingen* (Langschmidt) was formerly the chief town of the County of that name. The Ems is crossed here. *Salzbergen* (p. 307), then **Rheine** (* *Rail. Restaurant;* * *Hôtel Schulze*, in the town).

From Rheine to *Cologne* and the *Rhine*, to *Hanover* and *Berlin*, to *Bremen*, *Hamburg* etc., see *Baedeker's Rhine and N. Germany*.

INDEX.

Leipzig: Printed by Breitkopf & Härtel.

Zeitfracht Medien GmbH
Ferdinand-Jühlke-Straße 7
99095 Erfurt, Deutschland
produktsicherheit@kolibri360.de